New Perspectives on the Seventeenth-Century English Religious Lyric

❖ ❖ ❖

New Perspectives on the Seventeenth-Century English Religious Lyric

Edited by

JOHN R. ROBERTS

❊ ❊ ❊

University of Missouri Press / Columbia and London

Copyright © 1994 by
The Curators of the University of Missouri
University of Missouri Press, Columbia, Missouri 65201
Printed and bound in the United States of America
All rights reserved
5 4 3 2 1   98 97 96 95 94

Library of Congress Cataloging-in-Publication Data

New perspectives on the seventeenth-century English religious lyric / edited by John R. Roberts.
    p. cm.
Includes bibliographical references and index.
ISBN 0-8262-0909-2 (alk. paper)
    1. English poetry—Early modern, 1500–1700—History and criticism. 2. Religious poetry, English—History and criticism. 3. Christian poetry, English—History and criticism. I. Roberts, John Richard.
PR545.R4N48 1993
821'.0409382—dc20   93-30212
                                                                                                           CIP

∞ This paper meets the requirements of the
American National Standard for Permanence of Paper
for Printed Library Materials, Z39.48, 1984.

Designer: Kristie Lee
Typesetter: Connell-Zeko Type & Graphics
Printer and Binder: Thomson-Shore, Inc.
Typefaces: Palatino and Medici Script

FOR MY CHILDREN

Stephanie Ann

Mary Therese

Claire Elizabeth

Milissa Jane

Lisa Ellen

John Richard, Jr.

CONTENTS

ACKNOWLEDGMENTS ix

INTRODUCTION 1

"CURIOUS FRAME": THE SEVENTEENTH-CENTURY
RELIGIOUS LYRIC AS GENRE 9
   Helen Wilcox

ENLARGING THE LIMITS OF THE "RELIGIOUS LYRIC":
THE CASE OF HERRICK'S *HESPERIDES* 28
   Achsah Guibbory

HERRICK, VAUGHAN, AND THE POETRY OF ANGLICAN
SURVIVALISM 46
   Claude J. Summers

THE POETRY OF SUPPLICATION: TOWARD A CULTURAL
POETICS OF THE RELIGIOUS LYRIC 75
   Michael C. Schoenfeldt

LITURGY, WORSHIP, AND THE SONS OF LIGHT 105
   P. G. Stanwood

"ALL THINGS ARE BIGGE WITH JEST": WIT AS A MEANS
OF GRACE 124
   Judith Dundas

CHRIST AND APOLLO IN THE SEVENTEENTH-CENTURY
RELIGIOUS LYRIC   143
  Stella P. Revard

DONNE, HERBERT, AND THE POSTMODERN MUSE   168
  R. V. Young, Jr.

THE POETRY OF MEDITATION: SEARCHING THE MEMORY   188
  Louis L. Martz

JOHN DONNE: "THE HOLY GHOST IS AMOROUS IN HIS
METAPHORS"   201
  Anthony Low

"SHOWING HOLY": HERBERT AND THE RHETORIC OF
SANCTITY   222
  Christopher Hodgkins

OPENING THE RELIGIOUS LYRIC: CRASHAW'S RITUAL,
LIMINAL, AND VISUAL WOUNDS   237
  Eugene R. Cunnar

THE SEVENTEENTH-CENTURY ENGLISH RELIGIOUS
LYRIC: A SELECTIVE BIBLIOGRAPHY OF MODERN
CRITICISM, 1952–1990   269
  John R. Roberts

NOTES ON THE CONTRIBUTORS   323

INDEX   329

ACKNOWLEDGMENTS

I wish to thank my wife, Lorraine, whose critical judgment and impeccable scholarship I relied on heavily as I was editing the essays that appear in this collection. I also wish to thank my research assistant, Willy Wood, who checked to ascertain that all quotations in the essays are accurate and who kindly assisted me in numerous ways, and Sean McDowell, who shared with me his computer knowledge and skills.

My primary debt, of course, is to the authors of the essays, who generously allowed me to publish their studies and thus gave me the great privilege of sharing the results of their research and critical intelligence with others.

My hope is that these essays will serve as yet another impetus to further reevaluations of the English religious lyric of the seventeenth century.

New Perspectives on the Seventeenth-Century English Religious Lyric

INTRODUCTION

For the past forty years, the English religious lyric of the late sixteenth and seventeenth centuries has very actively engaged the attention of a wide range of literary critics and scholars, some of whose studies have resulted in seminal works that have thrown light not only on these devotional poets and their poems but also have contributed immensely to our understanding of literary works in general. Nor is the critical interest in the religious lyric of this period waning. Even a cursory glance at the annual Modern Language Association bibliography shows that, as we approach the twenty-first century, these poets continue to attract some of the best minds currently engaged in literary study.

It can be convincingly argued that no other period of English literature is richer in devotional poetry of such a very high order. Looking backward in time from the 1590s, one must reach the fourteenth century before encountering any religious lyrics that bear comparison with those of the seventeenth century. Looking forward, one must pass over most of the eighteenth century and the early nineteenth century to such poets as Christina Rossetti and Gerard Manley Hopkins, for instance, to find a later period that is rich in devotional lyricism. Although poets of the fifteenth and most of the sixteenth centuries wrote moral, ethical, philosophical, and even theological verse; these centuries do not stand out as major periods of religious lyricism; nor do the evangelical hymns and pious verse of the eighteenth century qualify as a serious challenge to the artistic superiority of the seventeenth-century religious lyric.

The more we think we know about this extraordinary and varied period of devotional poetry, the more there seems to explain and to discover. The twelve original essays that make up this volume are part of the ongoing exploration of the meaning and significance of the religious lyric in literary and cultural history. These are not, however, simply a random collection of loosely related opinions about the poets and poetry of this period; rather the contributors were asked to address one of several important and basic questions that inform the purpose and focus of this book: First of all, is the religious lyric truly a distinct genre or is it simply a lyric poem on a religious subject or theme? Secondly, what do we mean by "religious" in this context? Is our understanding of "religious" too narrow and restricted? And thirdly, to what extent did the religious lyric participate in, and how was it shaped by, the political, social, theological, and cultural contexts in which it was written? In other words, were these poets simply expressing their own private religious convictions and emotions on devotional matters, or were they, at the same time, commenting on the world in which they lived and figuring forth its concerns and interests?

In the first essay, "'Curious Frame': The Seventeenth-Century Religious Lyric as Genre," Helen Wilcox explores the first question of whether or not we mean anything more by the phrase "seventeenth-century religious lyric" than simply the devotional poems of a "loose compendium of poets, inclusion among whom is simply an accident of history." She maintains that, although these poets did not all share the same theology or religious doctrines, they all did agree that the English language had the potential "to express, as much as any human system of expression could, the experience of the divine." In particular, Wilcox explains how these religious poets had in common an "intensely *verbal* sense of God and the redemptive process"; or, in other words, how they regarded "verbal activity to be a central and vital part of understanding the divine." For these poets, she argues, the verbal was much more than simply a vehicle for the poet; it was rather seen as "an issue vital to the understanding of a God who compressed his essence in the riddle of the incarnate word." Another major unifying feature of the religious poets of the period, she argues, is their concern with poetic structures by which they tested "the multiple dimensions of the lyric as well as giving form to an ideal of expressiveness." Equally important, Wilcox suggests, is their view that the natural world about them functioned as an "oversized emblem book" that could be interpreted by the poet. All three of these features, she remarks, are attempts to gain transcendence; they are "devices of human wit to discover spiritual perspectives, often through a startling reworking of the familiar." In their poems, typically "the individual voice and text are themselves transcended in their effort to achieve a spiritual transcendence." Wilcox further maintains that to seventeenth-century devotional poets religious art was "not so much a making as a finding" and that "the wit that mattered was not that of the poet but of God's love." She also comments on how these poets were consciously trying to reshape and convert secular poetry to sacred ends. She concludes that the religious lyric is, in fact, a genre "not so much by birth (for it was undoubtedly not newly created by these poets) but by *baptism;* the lyric was converted and born again, as it were, through the offices of this group of poets." Wilcox reminds us, however, that these poets showed "a continuing ambivalence toward their lyrics, delighting in the possibilities of the newly revitalized genre but always aware of its transitoriness": they were "in the genre but not of it."

In response to the question of what we mean by "religious" in the phrase *religious lyric,* Achsah Guibbory in "Enlarging the Limits of the 'Religious' Lyric: The Case of Herrick's *Hesperides,*" argues that, for the most part, critics have defined religious poetry too narrowly and that through a study of Herrick's collection of seemingly "pagan" or "secular" poems, we can expand our sense of what is "religious" and, consequently, our understanding of what "religious poetry" is. She readily acknowledges, of course, that not all of the poems in *Hesperides* are religious, but she insists that the cumulative effect of Herrick's poetry is. She maintains that the hallmark of Herrick's poetry, in fact, is "an eclecticism that derives from his passion for enlarging the boundaries of the sacred" and resulted, in part at least, from his repudiation of Puritanism, which "sought to draw the boundaries of the true church in ways that Herrick and others found immensely disturbing." Herrick's poetry, Guibbory maintains, in opposition to Puritan sensibility, resolutely mingles the Christian and the pagan, the sacred and the profane, and the world of the flesh and of the spirit in such a way that often it is almost impossible to separate them, and it often deals with practices of the Church of England that Puritans rejected as "pagan," such as the use of candles, holy water, and incense as well as the uses of ritual and ceremony. Guibbory discusses in some detail how Herrick's poetry is "far from innocent of controversial religiopolitical significance" but was influenced and shaped by his response to the conflicted culture in which he lived.

Claude J. Summers in "Herrick, Vaughan, and the Poetry of Anglican Survivalism," expanding on Guibbory's point, argues very persuasively that the seventeenth-century religious lyric fully participates in "the mystification of politics and poetry that is characteristic of the discursive practices of late Renaissance culture generally." In other words, Summers holds that the religious lyric—although highly successful in expressing a "heightened spirituality"—"is never completely divorced from the pressures of worldly concerns" and that "it is inevitably (and sometimes triumphantly) rooted in the sociopolitical contexts of its time." In particular, the religious lyric reflects, he maintains, the religiopolitical debates that flourished in England during the first two-thirds of the seventeenth century. Summers focuses his critical remarks primarily on Robert Herrick's *Noble Numbers* and Henry Vaughan's *Silex Scintillans* to show that, although the two poets are not usually associated with one another, they did share, in fact, "a similar political perspective and embraced like responses to what they discerned as the experience of persecution" for their Anglican faith. For both poets, Summers argues, "the transformation of the Established Church by the victorious Parliamentarians was a public and personal disaster, one that necessarily and profoundly affected their art."

Employing the techniques of the "New Historicism," Michael C. Schoenfeldt in "The Poetry of Supplication: Toward a Cultural Poetics of the Religious Lyric" also argues convincingly that the religious lyric too often has been interpreted "in deliberate isolation from the social and cultural forces" that form the contexts for these poems. He illustrates in his essay "the genesis of the very assumptions that still hinder our full comprehension of the seventeenth-century religious lyric by attending to the social resonances of religious poems by Donne and Herbert" and by showing that "something significantly different is going on in the religious poems of Vaughan, Herrick, and Traherne." Schoenfeldt also maintains that "the tools made available by current theoretical work in a range of fields are particularly appropriate to the project of excavating the unmistakable riches that the early seventeenth-century conflation of social and devotional languages produced." He insists that "the social circumstances of Renaissance England conspired with Donne's own dependent status and his verbal prowess to create an enormously rich language of devotion—a language that Herbert would use with even greater precision, but that would be progressively dulled in the course of the turbulent century."

In particular, Schoenfeldt shows how the religious lyric "absorbed and then rejected social conversation as a model for discourse with the divine."

In "Liturgy, Worship, and the Sons of Light," P. G. Stanwood argues that, no matter what other influences may have shaped it, "liturgy defines religious lyric poetry, whether the poet's designs are obvious or implicit in the resulting work." He maintains that liturgy, taken in its broadest sense, suggests "shape, form, repetition, order, [and] the regulation of private feelings into normalized, public expression." Stanwood surveys briefly devotional poetry that explicitly manages form in a liturgical setting (for example, the canonical hours) as well as that which contains an implicit form, in which the poet "does not deliberately set out to write in a liturgical environment or in obedience to any liturgical form, yet in avoiding the form comes inevitably to have it."

In "'All Things are Bigge with Jest': Wit as a Means of Grace," Judith Dundas explains that "the identification of wit with levity" led some critics and poets of the late sixteenth and seventeenth centuries to conclude that wit was "not only a breech of decorum" but also was "a sign of lack of faith." However, imaginative religious poets, she argues, such as Donne, Herbert, and Marvell, "knew the value of wit for the expression of their faith and did not hesitate to use it." In fact, they recognized that wit has "a particular role to play in the conversion of sinners and may be decorous according to the principles of both art and religion." Dundas argues that Donne, Herbert, and Marvell articulated, in fact, "a new decorum for religious poetry" and that, for them, wit became "a net in which to catch sinners, making the poets fishers of men."

In "Christ and Apollo in the Seventeenth-Century Religious Lyric," Stella P. Revard discusses how the English religious poets of the seventeenth century, well versed in both classical poetry and Continental neo-Latin verse, allow their literary heritage to inform their sacred poems. She focuses her comments specifically on how these religious poets treat the figure of Apollo that was handed down to them by Neoplatonic and Christian humanist poets of the fifteenth and sixteenth centuries. Revard maintains that, when Apollo "appears in seventeenth-century poetry as god of poetry or as the wooer of the reluctant laurel," most of the religious poets "respond with enthusiasm or with wit"; but "when as sun-god he casts over them the burning rays of his great axle-tree, they respond quite differently." Revard maintains that in the poetry of Milton and Crashaw we can see "the extremes of that response." As a Catholic, Crashaw finds syncretism natural; and, in fact, it becomes even more pronounced in his later poetry. However, Milton, the Protestant, exorcises Apollo as a divine presence in his Nativity Ode since he should have regarded such syncretism as evocative of the Rome of the Renaissance popes, who had fostered a cult of Apollo. Revard points out that Milton's later poetry, however, shows that he was unable to exorcise Apollo permanently.

Robert V. Young, Jr., in "Donne, Herbert, and the Postmodern Muse" gives the reader a new perspective on the religious lyric by arguing that the devotional poetry of Donne and Herbert (as well as their successors, Crashaw and Vaughan) continues to fascinate modern critics precisely because "it addresses essentially the same issue that holds a central place among the deliberations of contemporary literary theory: the capacity of the speaking self to define its identity in meaningful utterance and the relationship between the words of its discourse and an absolute source of significance." Young maintains that essentially the devotional poet and the deconstructionist are alike "in deploring the secular humanist's illusion of self-sufficiency" and thus "the confrontation between seventeenth-century devotional poetry and contemporary literary theory is, then, an academic version of the conflict between faith and unbelief; and for this reason its outcome has more than academic interest."

Probably no other single book in the twentieth century has shaped discussion of seventeenth-century religious poetry more than Louis L. Martz's *The Poetry of Meditation: A Study in English Religious Literature of the Seventeenth Century,* first published in 1954. In his essay "The Poetry of Meditation: Searching the Memory," Martz recounts various steps in the creation of his immensely influential study as well as the genesis of *The Paradise Within: Studies in Vaughan, Traherne, and Milton* (1964). He defends "New Criticism" against contemporary critics who mistake its intentions and methods, and he shows how his historical studies of meditational modes were grounded in "New Criticism." Martz claims, in fact, that his study of the importance of discursive meditation on the religious writers of the late sixteenth and seventeenth centuries might be called a work of "Critical Historicism." He also shows how his study has some affinities with the "New Historicism," and he reiterates his point that the term *poetry of meditation* should be applied to religious poetry only and that it should not replace the term *metaphysical poetry*. Martz insists that the religious poetry of the 1590s and of the seventeenth century was influenced by many factors, not just meditation; and he points out that his study does not neglect "other sources of poetic inspiration cultivated by English Protestants," in particular, the literary forms found in the Bible. Also Martz locates with careful distinctions how his book relates to more recent studies of "Protestant poetics" and Reformation theology. Martz acknowledges ways in which his studies of both Catholic and Protestant meditation could be improved. He concludes, however, that the basic argument of *The Poetry of Meditation* remains valid, but that "it needs, and has been subjected to, constant modification and supplementation," by others as well as by himself.

In the last three essays of this collection, Anthony Low, Christopher Hodgkins, and Eugene R. Cunnar discuss from new perspectives the sacred poetry of three of the most important religious lyricists of the period—John Donne, George Herbert, and Richard Crashaw. Low in "John Donne: 'The Holy Ghost is Amorous in His Metaphors'" explores anew the relation between Donne's secular love poems and his sacred love poems, in particular his use of human sexual love and marriage in his religious lyrics. Far from being simply "pious exercises in the established conventions about love," Low maintains that "the focus of Donne's inner psychological or spiritual tensions is on the speaker's sexual identity—on his confusion between what amount to conflicting roles." In other words, according to Low, in his religious lyrics Donne is "both an insistently masculine seeker after mistresses or truths and the necessarily feminine and passive recipient of God's love." Low shows how, for Donne, it was not easy to surrender "to the imperatives of this metaphorical role reversal" and that, for him, "the relinquishment of his usually dominant and aggressively masculine stance is never anything but uncomfortable." Low points out, however, that it is from this "devotional stance that is troubled and conflicted" that Donne "characteristically makes great poetry."

In "'Showing Holy': Herbert and the Rhetoric of Sanctity," Christopher Hodgkins examines from a fresh point of view Herbert's uses of rhetoric and language, taking as his point of departure the chapter on preaching in *The Countrey Parson,* in which Herbert catalogues the gestures, rhetorical strategies, and language appropriate for the preacher to employ in order to effect change in his audience. Hodgkins rejects the view that the Herbert one glimpses in his preachers' manual is an elitist and an aggressive, authoritarian manipulator who orchestrates "his motions, expressions, voice, and words like so many players." Rather, Hodgkins argues, Herbert is "more compelling as man and poet for having known such temptations intimately." Hodgkins illustrates how in poem after poem in *The Temple* Herbert shows his awareness of the seductive power of language and rhetoric and how often in his poems he consciously "subverts the language of conventional piety," often leaving "their zealously religious speakers either sputtering or wordless." In other words, Hodgkins argues that the lyrics of *The Temple* "treat in abundant and diverse ways the humiliation of eloquence, and of language itself, in the presence of the divine Word." From this essay, a portrait of Herbert emerges in which we see not clerical duplicity or arrogance, as some critics have suggested, but a dedicated priest, fully aware of these dangers from personal experience, humbly urging novice clerics how to avoid these pitfalls, and a poet who in his religious lyrics demonstrates the limitations of rhetoric and language.

Eugene R. Cunnar in "Opening the Religious Lyric: Crashaw's Ritual, Liminal, and Visual Wounds," concludes the collection by examining and contextualizing the often misunderstood and ridiculed imagery of Richard Crashaw's religious lyrics, especially his imagery of Christ's wounds, in terms of ritual liminality, theology, and the visual arts in order to show how Crashaw opened up the religious lyric to new social, psychological, and theological dimensions.

These twelve essays, of course, are not meant to offer a definitive account of the religious lyric of the seventeenth century. When they are read together, however, they throw considerable new light on individual poets and poems of the late Renaissance and also contribute significantly to a fuller understanding and greater appreciation of this elusive and fascinating genre.

"CURIOUS FRAME"
The Seventeenth-Century Religious Lyric as Genre

❊ ❊ ❊ *Helen Wilcox* ❊ ❊ ❊

When for the thorns with which I long, too long,
   With many a piercing wound,
   My Saviour's head have crowned,
I seek with garlands to redress that wrong:
   Through every garden, every mead,
I gather flowers (my fruits are only flowers),
   Dismantling all the fragrant towers
That once adorned my shepherdess's head.
And now when I have summed up all my store,
   Thinking (so I myself deceive)
   So rich a chaplet thence to weave
As never yet the King of Glory wore:
   Alas, I find the Serpent old
   That, twining in his speckled breast,
   About the flowers disguised does fold,
   With wreaths of fame and interest.
Ah, foolish man, that would'st debase with them,
And mortal glory, heaven's diadem!
But thou who only could'st the Serpent tame,
Either his slipp'ry knots at once untie,
And disentangle all his winding snare;
Or shatter too with him my curious frame,

> And let these wither, so that he may die,
> Though set with skill and chosen out with care.
> That they, while Thou on both their spoils dost tread,
> May crown thy feet, that could not crown thy head.[1]

Marvell's "The Coronet" is often cited, quite aptly, as a classic example of the "seventeenth-century religious lyric" in English; and many of us who employ this phrase no doubt have the impression that it conveys some useful information about the poem and its contemporaries to other readers, students, and critics. The purpose of this paper, which functions in a predominantly interrogative mode, is to enquire whether anything more can indeed be meant by the "seventeenth-century religious lyric" than the assembled devotional poems of John Donne, Thomas Campion, George Herbert, Henry Vaughan, Richard Crashaw, Andrew Marvell, Robert Herrick, and Thomas Traherne—plus perhaps the work of less familiar poets such as An Collins, Thomas Washbourne, Patrick Cary, Elisabeth Major, Henry Colman, and Cardell Goodman. Does this generic phrase imply anything further than a loose compendium of poets, inclusion among whom is simply an accident of history? Might it suggest, for example, a common theological or stylistic foundation upon which the individual authors constructed their own "fragrant towers" and wove their particular verbal "garlands"? Could it convey an idea of some common principles by which the writers "set with skill" and "care" the words chosen not to adorn "shepherdesses" but the "King of Glory"? If so, what is it that unites these texts? What possible "frame" could adequately contain and display the shared properties of the poems that are themselves such fine and "curious frames"?

It may seem all too obvious to begin with a consideration of the common ground of chronology and subject matter—although we might pause for a moment to observe some special qualities in both these fundamental elements of the seventeenth-century religious lyric. The poems in question were, after all, written by the first generation of English poets who had grown up alongside, or within, the post-Reformation English church. It would be quite inaccurate to suggest that this historical positioning gave the writers any kind of uniform theology or

---

1. Andrew Marvell, "The Coronet," in *Selected Poetry and Prose*, ed. Robert Wilcher (London: Methuen, 1986), 24–25.

undisturbed doctrine (we have only to think of the shifting allegiances of Donne or Crashaw), but these poets lived, worshipped, and wrote at a significant and crucial stage after the introduction of Protestantism into English religious life. They took very seriously, for instance, the potential of the English language to express, as much as any human system of expression could, their experience of the divine; the Book of Common Prayer and the arguments of Sir Philip Sidney combined to release possibilities in the vernacular at just this moment of English history.[2] The subject matter about which they wrote—God and themselves—was also in a profound state of flux, making possible and desirable the literary exploration of the self and its spiritual or material creators. The nature of God and the workings of Providence were being debated and defined anew; the nature of the individual and a sense of selfhood—the new "dialogue of one"—were being articulated for the first time in a psychological and internalized language.[3] Protestant theology, coinciding with developments in science, language, and culture, thus made the early seventeenth century a particularly auspicious moment for the growth of devotional writing in England.

It was therefore no accident that these poets should have written so fruitfully against the self-evident common background of historical period and poetic material. However, these shared elements are in themselves insufficient to support the case that there was a genuine coherence within this group of writers. So let us look more closely at what the poets actually produced. This strategy is initially not particularly helpful, for we find that devotional poets from Donne to Traherne wrote in a bewildering variety of poetic forms and traditions, including Ignatian meditations, love sonnets and lyrics, hymns, dialogue-poems, and pastoral elegies. If we are to discern some framework that unites these works, then, it is clear that it will be neither simply historical nor strictly formal, but rather a range of stylistic and

---

2. Sir Philip Sidney, *An Apology for Poetry: or The Defence of Poesy*, ed. Geoffrey Shepherd (Manchester: Manchester University Press, 1973). The English language was equal to "any other tongue in the world" for "uttering sweetly and properly the conceits of the mind, which is the end of speech" (140).

3. John Donne, "The Ecstacy," l. 74, in *John Donne: The Complete English Poems*, ed. A. J. Smith (Harmondsworth: Penguin, 1971), 56. Donne's phrase alerts us to the explorations of the self taking place in sixteenth- and seventeenth-century English poetry; see, for example, Anne Ferry, *The "Inward" Language: Sonnets of Wyatt, Sidney, Shakespeare, Donne* (Chicago: University of Chicago Press, 1983).

ideological features, which may be found to form the basis of a common devotional poetics.[4]

First among these defining characteristics, in my view, is the intensely *verbal* sense of God and the redemptive process that these poets had in common. Donne, for example, held that "the soul of man is incorporate in his words," that the "best" of human qualities are our "Reason" and our "Discourse," and the process of imitating Christ is not just a "reading" but a "writing over" the exemplum of the saviour.[5] The seventeenth-century religious poets took verbal activity to be a central and vital part of understanding the divine. Words were perceived as a kind of incarnation of the spiritual in the physical realm and the means by which one might, paradoxically, give expression to that which is beyond expression. The poets we are considering were believers for whom, as Herbert wrote in "The Flower," "Thy word is all, if we could spell."[6] Their hesitant yet probing texts, from the opaque in a writer like Donne to the transparent words of Vaughan and Traherne, were a means of approaching the ultimate Word, the divine "Logos," which contains and perfects human language.[7] The process enacted by their lyrics is one of learning to "spell": that is, breaking down words and experiences into their constituent parts as well as putting letters and words together into coherence. The poems deconstruct as well as construct texts; their business is, often quite self-consciously, to read, interpret, and rewrite the books of the Bible, Nature, and the individual soul.

This first unifying, underlying principle—the poets' active perception of the spiritual through the verbal—reveals itself in a variety of ways within the poetic texts themselves. One particularly notable in-

---

4. This essay is not intended as a dispute with earlier studies, such as those by Louis Martz and Barbara Lewalski, on specific aspects of seventeenth-century religious lyrics but is an enquiry into the possibility of a looser generic union between these very varied poets, which might enable one descriptive category to contain, for example, their denominational and formal differences.

5. *The Sermons of John Donne*, ed. George R. Potter and Evelyn M. Simpson (Berkeley and Los Angeles: University of California Press, 1962), 10:46, 196.

6. *The English Poems of George Herbert*, ed. C. A. Patrides (London: Dent, 1974), 172.

7. Among the many discussions of the implications of the opening lines of St. John's Gospel for religious writers of this period, see P. G. Stanwood and Heather Ross Asals, eds., *John Donne and the Theology of Language* (Columbia: University of Missouri Press, 1986).

stance is Donne's "Hymn to God the Father," with its wittily serious implication that in the changing of one letter could lie the difference between damnation and salvation:

> Wilt thou forgive that sin where I begun,
>   Which was my sin, though it were done before?
> Wilt thou forgive that sin through which I run,
>   And do run still: though still I do deplore?
>   When thou hast done, thou hast not done,
>   For, I have more.
>
> Wilt thou forgive that sin which I have won
>   Others to sin? and, made my sin their door?
> Wilt thou forgive that sin which I did shun
>   A year, or two: but wallowed in, a score?
>   When thou hast done, thou hast not done,
>   For I have more.
>
> I have a sin of fear, that when I have spun
>   My last thread, I shall perish on the shore;
> But swear by thy self, that at my death thy son
>   Shall shine as he shines now, and heretofore;
>   And, having done that, thou hast done,
>   I fear no more.[8]

The lyric resonates with the sound and meaning of the repeated word *sin,* used eight times and defined in at least five different ways from original sin to personal deathbed doubts. What transforms the mood of the poem, and its conclusion, is the tiny change from that repeated word *sin* to the single word *son*—a minuscule adjustment in spelling and pronunciation, but symbolic of the most enormous alteration from the judgment of multiple "sins" to redemption by the single act of Christ, the glorious "son/sun." The poem hinges on this awareness of the depths of potential in words, as well as the closeness of words of opposing meanings; through this precise linguistic sensitivity, the majestic simplicity of the redemption is conveyed.

This emphasis on the Word in words may also be seen in other characteristic features of the poets' output, such as their sense of the efficacy of individual words, especially names. In Herbert's "Jesu," for

---

8. Donne, *English Poems,* 348–49.

example, the name Jesu is broken and respelt for the distressed Christian as "I ease you," thus releasing the message felt by the poet to be compressed within the four letters.[9] This attitude also seems to me to lie behind the persistent delight in paradoxes, found in the poems of Donne—for whom paradoxes were "alarums to truth"—and in Crashaw's "Flaming fountain" and other "kind contrarieties," teasing out an idea from within the apparent contradictions of language.[10] Further, it may be seen to link closely with the epigrammatic tendency found in these seventeenth-century religious lyrics, from Campion to Crashaw. As Campion commented, the epigram demonstrates as much "artifice" and contains as much "difficultie" as a longer poem;[11] it represents an attempt to contain in concise and riddling words a religious truth or mystery. Once again, the verbal is more than a medium for the poet; it is perceived as an issue vital to the understanding of a God who compressed his essence in the riddle of the incarnate Word.

All of these features remind us of the central activity of the religious lyricist: the struggle to articulate the relationship between the human and the divine. This struggle reveals itself in a second major feature of the seventeenth-century religious lyric: the preoccupation with poetic *structures*. Words in their isolatedly semantic role were not sufficient for these poets, who were as a group great experimenters with the possibilities of expression through form. Herbert is the individual writer who probably springs to mind most immediately in this connection, with his shaped poems, pruned rhymes, and interwoven biblical texts, employed for the purpose of "catching" both the reader and the divine sense by every possible means and dimension.[12] But Herbert was by

---

9. Herbert, *English Poems*, 125.

10. Donne, from a letter written c. 1600, cited in John Donne, *Paradoxes and Problems*, ed. Helen Peters (Oxford: Clarendon Press, 1980), xxvi; Richard Crashaw, "Saint Mary Magdalene or The Weeper," in *George Herbert and the Seventeenth-Century Religious Poets*, ed. Mario A. Di Cesare (New York: W. W. Norton, 1978), 80, 83.

11. *Ayres & Observations: Selected Poems of Thomas Campion*, ed. Joan Hart (Cheadle Hulme: Carcanet Press, 1976), 34.

12. See "The Altar," "Easter-wings," "Paradise," and "Coloss. 3.3," in Herbert, *English Poems*, 47, 63, 143, 100. The danger inherent in this attention to expressive poetic structures is made clear in the contradictions underpinning Herbert's own aesthetics. He referred to poems as a "bait of pleasure" to catch the reader who

no means alone in this attention to the formal potential of the lyric, nor in the adventurous use of it. Herrick, Goodman, and Patrick Cary all experimented with deliberately patterned and strikingly shaped poems, and Elisabeth Major, among others, took advantage of the acrostic to explore the relationship between her maker and her self:

> E ternal God, open my blinded eyes,
> L ighten my sadded heart that in me lies:
> I ncrease thy grace in me, indear my heart,
> S avior to thee, by faith to have a part
> A bove with thee in glory, there to shine,
> B eloved with that lasting love of thine;
> E vil is my life, I walk in earthen ways,
> T each me thy path, in it to spend my days;
> H ear me in him on whom my hopes Anchor stays.
>
> M ercy, O Saviour, teach me to ask aright,
> A nd then for comfort, 'tis thy chief delight:
> I beg and faint, I fear and hope again,
> O Lord, I see all self, and earth is vain,
> R enouncing all, on thee Lord, I remain.[13]

As in the case of Herbert's "Jesu," Major's poem unleashes the hidden possibilities of a name—here, the author's own, used not only to trigger a prayer but also to give structure to the verse. The splendid irony in this struggle between the self and her saviour is encapsulated in the last two lines, where the statement that renounces the "vain" world and "all self" simultaneously completes the inscription of her own name. The mold for this poem, literally and symbolically, is the author's own being, highlighted and set in focus by the acrostic device. Such attentiveness to poetic structure was, for Major and her contemporaries, an expression of a sense of proportion and an interest in what Marvell termed the proper or "sober frame."[14] The frame was, then, both the actual poetic form and its larger significance; the poets were testing the multiple dimensions of the lyric as well as giving form to an

---

would otherwise "fly" religious teaching, but he also wrote of the problem of complex verse in which the reader is disconcertingly "catching the sense at two removes" (33, 75).

13. *Honey on the Rod* (London: Thomas Maxey, 1656), 212.
14. From the opening of "Upon Appleton House," *Selected Poetry*, 66.

ideal of expressiveness. Like Donne's God, these poetic structures were both "literall" and "figurative."[15]

This serious game-playing, as we might term it, with the poem as "speaking picture,"[16] could only have flourished at a time when the world, as well as the word, was felt to be charged with significance. As Donne's "The Cross" vividly indicates, the poet's task was not only to deal in "images," particularly familiar religious signs such as the cross, but also to "spy out" instances of these images in the everyday world. Thus Donne recorded seeing crosses in the shape of a bird flying above him, or in "meridians crossing parallels," in addition to finding plenty of grammatical functions for the word *cross* itself.[17] The poets' sensitivity to the signifying capacity of the world about them led to what may perhaps be described as an *emblematic* tendency in their work. Most of them wrote verse that did not in any straightforward sense explicate a visual emblem, but they tended to assume that the visible and sensory world was by nature emblematic, "telling a tale" of higher matters. This interpretative aesthetic may clearly be seen in Patrick Cary's poem that took as its epigraph the words of Romans 1:20, "The invisible things of him from the Creation of the World are cleerely seene; being Understood by the things that are made":

> Whilst I beheld the necke o'th' *Dove*,
> I spy'de and read these words.
> *This pritty Dye*
> *Which takes your Eye,*
> *Is not att all, the Bird's.*
> *The dusky* Raven *might*
> *Have with these colours pleas'd your sight,*
> *Had God but chose soe to ordayne above.*
> This Labell wore the *Dove.*
>
> Whilst I admir'd the *Nightingale,*
> These notes She warbled o're.
> *Noe melody*
> *Indeed have I,*

---

15. "Expostulation 19," *Devotions upon Emergent Occasions,* ed. Anthony Raspa (Montreal and London: McGill-Queen's University Press, 1975), 99.

16. Sidney, *Apology,* 101: poetry, according to Sidney's definition, was a "figuring forth" as well as the more classically familiar "speaking picture."

17. Donne, *English Poems,* 326.

Admire me then noe more:
God has itt in his choice
To give the Owle *or* Mee *this voyce;*
'Tis Hee, 'tis Hee that makes mee tell my Tale.
Thus sang the *Nightingale*.

I smelt and prays'd the fragrant *Rose*;
Blushing, thus answer'd She.
The Prayse You gave,
The Sent I have,
Doe not belong to mee;
This harmelesse Odour, None
But onely God indeed does owne;
To bee his Keepers, my poore Leaves Hee chose.
And thus reply'de the *Rose*.

I tooke the Honny from the *Bee*;
On th'Bagge these Words were seene.
More sweet then this
Perchance Nought is,
Yet Gall *itt might have beene:*
If God itt should soe please,
He could still make itt such with ease;
And well Gall *to* Honny *change can Hee.*
This learn't I of the *Bee*.

I touch'd, and lik'd the *Downe* o'th' *Swanne*;
But felt these words there writt.
Bristles, Thornes, here
I soone should beare,
Did God ordayne but itt:
If my Downe *to thy Touch*
Seeme soft, and smoth, God made itt such;
Give more, or take all this away, Hee can.
This was I taught by th' *Swan*.[18]

All five human senses are shown here to have access to holy truths residing in archetypal sensory objects; the natural world functions as some oversized emblem book to be interpreted by the poet. Part of that

18. *The Poems of Patrick Cary,* ed. Sister Veronica Delany (Oxford: Clarendon Press, 1978), 46–47.

interpretative process involves the human vulnerability of the poet. He expects the beauty of the nightingale's song or the sweetness of honey to be fixed pleasures, but he is taught that these worldly emblems are arbitrary and transient; the swan's smooth down may tomorrow be as sharp as thorns. Thus the world speaks and teaches, but the only consistency of the lesson lies in the overarching power of the creator. The world itself may have been merely a "shadow,"[19] or a passing distraction, in the view of these poets, but that shadow could also be a sign of encouragement, a brief hint or pale reflection of heavenly truths. As Vaughan put it,

> When on some *gilded cloud,* or *flower*
> My gazing soul would dwell an hour,
> And in those weaker glories spy
> Some shadows of eternity.[20]

The seventeenth-century religious lyricists rendered personal the mediating forces that they took to speak to them of God: the "types" of Christ found in the Old Testament, the emblems of a spiritual dimension read in the earthly environment, and, in the case of Crashaw, truths discovered in the example and physical ecstacy of the saints. Thus the devotional poems from this period were emblematic in a double sense, discerning and interpreting emblems present around them and becoming in their own right new emblems of spiritual life for their readers. As Traherne put it in "Shadows In The Water," the sensory world gives

> A *Seeming* somewhat more than *View*;
> That doth instruct the mind
> In things that lie behind.[21]

The three fundamental features of the seventeenth-century religious lyric highlighted so far—a strongly linguistic theology, an active interest in expressive poetic structures, and a commitment to the emblematic function of devotional verse—may all be seen as ways of dealing

---

19. Campion, *Selected Poems*, 37.
20. "The Retreat," in *The Oxford Authors: George Herbert and Henry Vaughan*, ed. Louis L. Martz (Oxford: Oxford University Press, 1986), 274.
21. *Religious Poets*, 195.

with, and gaining, *transcendence*. Language, form, and image in the poems are devices of human wit to discover spiritual perspectives, often through a startling reworking of the familiar. These lyrics consequently have in common one further defining characteristic: a sort of divine "times trans-shifting,"[22] a creative disrupting and transcending of the normal patterns of time and space. The passing of time, for instance, so newly a regular and measurable phenomenon in the seventeenth century thanks to contemporary scientific invention, is measured in the poems not in the steadiness of "moments, months, and years" but by the falling of tears or the capacity to skip the "trailing" weekdays in favor of Sundays, emblems of the Resurrection.[23] In fact, as Herbert defiantly insists in "Easter," all earthly time is absorbed into the eternal day established on the first Easter Sunday:

> Can there be any day but this,
> Though many sunnes to shine endeavour?
> We count three hundred, but we misse:
> There is but one, and that one ever.[24]

The poets make a common effort in their texts to transcend the pedestrian "counting" of time and to find instead ways of discerning and expressing the impact of the divine intrusion into the ordinary, or what Crashaw summed up as "eternity shut in a span."[25] So it is that in Vaughan's poems, to progress is to go "by backward steps," a triumphant reversal of the norm that is to "love" a "forward motion." By this dislocation of accepted human processes, Vaughan could approach the longed-for state in which he might feel "through all this fleshly dress / Bright *shoots* of everlastingness."[26]

The desire to anticipate heavenly values and experiences while on earth is a common Christian wish; what distinguishes these lyricists is their vivid depiction of the quality of surprise in the difference that

---

22. Robert Herrick, "The Argument of His Book," in *Cavalier Poets: Selected Poems*, ed. Thomas Clayton (Oxford: Oxford University Press, 1978), 3.
23. Crashaw, "The Weeper," *Religious Poets*, 83; Herbert, "Sunday," *English Poems*, 93.
24. Herbert, "Easter," *English Poems*, 62.
25. "In the Holy Nativity of Our Lord God," *Religious Poets*, 80.
26. "The Retreat," *Oxford Authors*, 274.

such transcendence can bring. An Collins suggested this startling sense of otherness in her poem "The Soul's Home":

> Such is the force of each created thing
> That it no solid happiness can bring,
> Which to our minds can give contentment sound;
> For, like as Noah's dove no succour found,
> Till she return'd to him that sent her out,
> Just so, the soul in vain may seek about
> For rest or satisfaction any where,
> Save in his presence who hath sent her here;
> Yea though all earthly glories should unite
> Their pomp and splendour to give such delight,
> Yet could they no more sound contentment bring
> Than star-light can make grass or flowers spring.[27]

The last lines here raise an unexpected idea, forcing us to rethink the differences between the borrowed light that merely illuminates and the genuine light that nourishes. The stars, traditionally emblems of distant beauty and guidance for travelers, are jolted into inferiority; their light is shown to be cold, disconnected, not life-giving. In such a way, we are to conclude, must conventional human values be seen when transcended by the divine; a sharp vision of the "soul's home" cuts through the earthly language of these lyrics.

The seventeenth-century English religious lyric not only deals in transcendence, but also, it would seem, attempts in its own textuality to transcend certain kinds of limitations inherent in the short poem. We speak of the poetic form as the "lyric," conventionally brief as well as musical, but, in fact, most of these poems are experienced by readers in the larger context of a written sequence or collection, so that the overall effect transcends the specificity of the individual text or performance. The best known of these collections is Herbert's *The Temple*, in which a number of short poems combine to construct an architectural impression and a composite picture of the human soul, the "temple of the Holy Spirit."[28] In Herbert's own metaphor, each verse is a "star,"

---

27. *Divine Songs and Meditations* (London: R. Bishop, 1653), cited from the modernized text in *The World Split Open: Four Centuries of Women Poets in England and America, 1552–1950*, ed. Louise Bernikow (London: Women's Press, 1979), 66.

28. I Corinthians 3.16.

but all the verses put together create the effect of a "constellation."[29] Herbert's contemporaries also conceived or published their lyrics in collections: *Steps to the Temple, The Synagogue, Beawty in Raggs, Silex Scintillans, Honey on the Rod,* and so on. As the titles suggest, particular lyrics were given a generality, associated with a holy place, attitude, or text, by their gathered context. The poet's own name and personality, as well as the singularity of each lyric, was "transsshifted," to use Herrick's term again; the individual voice and text are themselves transcended in their effort to achieve a spiritual transcendence.

It may therefore be suggested that the seventeenth-century religious lyricists shared certain fundamental features in their particular concerns with language, form, emblematic representation, and transcendence. But does this common poetic practice actually make their devotional poems as a group into a *genre*? This is, of course, a hotly debated term, meaning to some readers and critics simply a distinct literary form but to others a myth or metaphor for a vision of truth or, perhaps even more grandly, a poetics of culture.[30] Is there any possible sense in describing the seventeenth-century religious lyric as a genre? And if so, what is meant by the term in this instance, and is *lyric* the appropriate label for it?

Rosalie Colie usefully defined a genre as a "body of almost unexpressed assumptions," and if we investigate the seventeenth-century religious poets' assumptions about their own work, then it becomes clear that they shared a "body" of ideas about the kind of writing they were engaged upon, and about the sources of their poetic mode.[31] Although not all the poems produced by these writers are "lyrical" in the conventional sense (it is hard to think of acrostics, or parable narratives, as obviously associated with music), their purposes are invariably identified with those assigned by Sidney to the lyric: to praise, or to persuade.[32] The terminology of the lyric mode dominates the poets'

---

29. "The H. Scriptures (II)," *English Poems,* 77.
30. See, for example, Alastair Fowler, *Kinds of Literature: An Introduction to the Theory of Genres and Modes* (Cambridge: Harvard University Press, 1982); Rosalie L. Colie, *The Resources of Kind: Genre-Theory in the Renaissance* (Berkeley and Los Angeles: University of California Press, 1973); Stephen Greenblatt, ed., *The Power of Forms in the English Renaissance* (Norman, Oklahoma: Pilgrim Books, 1982).
31. Colie, *Resources,* 115.
32. *Apology,* 118, 137–38.

own accounts of their writing, from Herrick's generalized intention to "write of hell" but "sing" of "heaven" to Dudley North's categorization of all religious verse in the 1640s as "hymns."[33] An Collins was typical of her contemporaries in calling her 1653 collection of miscellaneous religious poems *Divine Songs and Meditations,* while admirers of George Herbert gave him the accolade of "sweet singer" of the new "Temple."[34]

As the Old Testament symbolism of a phrase like "sweet singer of our Temple" suggests, the major sources of tradition and convention for the religious lyric, vital to its status as a genre, were the "Psalms, hymns, and spiritual songs" of the Bible.[35] With such a pedigree, both literary and spiritual, it is no wonder that the poets were intimidated as well as justified by this sense of the standing of their poetic mode. An Collins spoke for many when she asserted that "tis not want of skill/That's more blameworthy than want of good will"; from Campion onwards, there was a clear assumption that "Devotion needes not Art" since "God's power" will "sweeten" the poets' words.[36] Thus truth and plainness were given priority over fiction and artifice; as the title of Cardell Goodman's lyric collection hinted, the "Beawty" of God's love for humankind might be found in the "Raggs" of lowly verse.[37] The poets held in common the attitude expressed by Herbert that real "beauty" lies not in the poet's imagination but in the "discovery" of God's own creativity and love.[38] Religious art to the seventeenth-century lyricists was not so much a making as a finding, and

---

33. Herrick, *Cavalier Poets,* 3; Dudley, Lord North, *A Forest of Varieties* (Kirtling: Private printing, 1645), 5, 197.

34. For example, Barnabas Oley, "A Prefatory View of the Life and Vertues of the Authour," *Herbert's Remains* (London: Timothy Garthwait, 1652), a11v.

35. Colossians 3.16. Among many detailed discussions of the inheritance from the Psalms, the following deserve mention: Coburn Freer, *Music for a King: George Herbert's Style and the Metrical Psalms* (Baltimore: Johns Hopkins University Press, 1972); Barbara Kiefer Lewalski, *Protestant Poetics and the Seventeenth-Century Religious Lyric* (Princeton: Princeton University Press, 1979); Gijsbert J. Siertsema, *A Great Pasport of Poetrie* (Amsterdam: Free University, 1991).

36. "The Discourse," *Divine Songs* (1653), modernized text from *Her Own Life: autobiographical writings by seventeenth-century Englishwomen,* ed. Elspeth Graham, Hilary Hinds, Elaine Hobby, and Helen Wilcox (London: Routledge, 1989), 57; Campion, *Selected Poems,* 37.

37. *Beawty in Raggs Or Divine Phancies putt into Broken Verse,* ed. R. J. Roberts (Reading: University of Reading, 1958).

38. "Sonnet II," from Walton's *Life, English Poems,* 206.

the wit that mattered was not that of the poet but of God's love. This sense of the givenness of their art and its truths was essential to what Colie termed the "body of almost unexpressed assumptions" that bound the poets' work together as a genre.[39]

The religious lyric has two further important sources beyond the biblical—the classical hymn and the secular love lyric. This fact reminds us that the seventeenth-century devotional lyricists not only "discovered" their poetic resources but also, in many cases, transformed them. The work of these poets may be characterized as writing from an oppositional perspective. They were antipastoralists, sacred parodists, converters of what they regarded as fair but false traditions; they took what existed in other poetic and ideological systems and seriously "parodied" it, writing new words (literally and metaphorically) to old tunes.[40] As Robert Southwell wrote at the end of the sixteenth century, "The best course to let them [secular love poets] see the errour of their workes, is to weave a new webbe in their owne loome."[41] The sense of conversion and renewal in the seventeenth-century religious lyric is most powerfully expressed in the third stanza of Herbert's "The Forerunners," in which the poet addresses his "sweet phrases, lovely metaphors":

> when ye before
> Of stews and brothels onely knew the doores,
> Then did I wash you with my tears, and more,
> Brought you to Church well drest and clad:
> My God must have my best, ev'n all I had.[42]

Tarnished poetic language is here likened to a fallen woman rescued by the poet, bathed in the tears of his own remorse, and presented in modesty and renewed beauty at the church door. Though the gendering of this metaphor may be less than ideal for women poets (and modern readers), the baptismal idea implicit in it may be helpful in our consideration of the religious lyric of the period. To employ appropriately theological language, we may say that the religious lyric was

---

39. *Resources*, 115.
40. The term *sacred parody* was glossed most fully by Rosemond Tuve in "Sacred 'Parody' of Love Poetry, and Herbert," *Studies in the Renaissance* 8 (1961): 249–90.
41. "The Author to his loving Cosen," in *The Poems of Robert Southwell, S. J.*, ed. James H. McDonald and Nancy Pollard Brown (Oxford: Clarendon Press, 1967), 1.
42. Herbert, *English Poems*, 181.

then a genre not so much by birth (for it was undoubtedly not newly created by these poets) but by *baptism;* the lyric was converted and born again, as it were, through the offices of this group of poets. It was the Jordan, river of baptismal renewal, rather than the fountain of the classical muses to which these poets turned for refreshment. The "sweet phrases" of Herbert's poem were quite deliberately washed—baptized in a poetic Jordan—and re-"dressed" for religious purposes, and in this freshness of inspiration the lyric itself was seen to begin to "redress" the balance of sin and love, error and redemption. The double sense of redress indicates that the poems were a reworking of an existing genre on both poetic and didactic principles. As Marvell wrote in "The Coronet," he gathered up all the poetic "store" from which he had once "adorned" his "shepherdess's head," and sought instead to use his verbal "garlands" to "redress" the repeated "wrong" done to Christ.[43] The poets' self-consciousness as new lyricists, then, was constructed on a specifically baptismal as well as a literary basis, and their works may, I suggest, only be perceived as a distinct genre in this "born again" context.

The seventeenth-century religious lyric was given new definition as a poetic genre by a strong sense of purpose on the part of the authors.[44] In the words of Joseph Hall's discussion of religious meditation, these poets brought to the lyric a "bending of the mind upon some spiritual object."[45] In the lyrics this "object" was two-fold: the religious matters on which a poem focused, and the "objective" of honoring God and benefiting the writer/reader. Herbert's "A true Hymne" unequivocally linked the two by asserting that "the finenesse which a hymne or psalme affords, / Is, when the soul unto the lines accords."[46] There is an impression here, common to all seventeenth-century religious lyrics, that the value of the work lies in the interrelation of "lines" and "soul"; writer, text, reader, and God together write

---

43. "The Coronet," *Selected Poetry*, 25.

44. There is, of course, the potential for a sort of generic "intentional fallacy" here. However, the religious lyric would not be alone in relying upon definition through purpose; it would have at least comedy and satire for companions.

45. *The Art of Divine Meditation*, rpt. in Frank L. Huntley, *Bishop Joseph Hall and Protestant Meditation in Seventeenth-Century England* (Binghamton, N.Y.: Center for Medieval and Early Renaissance Studies, 1981), 72.

46. Herbert, "A true Hymne," *English Poems*, 174.

the "true hymn." This sense of authorial cooperation again gives a sharpened spiritual edge to our sense of a genre; if we consider Heather Dubrow's definition of a literary genre as a "code of behavior" between author and reader, then assuredly we must allow a third, divine party into the literary etiquette of this particular genre.[47]

Let us return to the words of Marvell's with which this enquiry began: "curious frame." It is not entirely fanciful to use the phrase as a shorthand for the genre we have been considering. Kenneth Burke's terms for a genre are fix or "frame";[48] this discussion of the lyric has, in turn, enumerated some defining characteristics and assumptions that supplied a "frame" for the religious poetry of the period. What, then, is this "curious frame"? Marvell's words are typically tightly packed with meaning. "Curious" conveys, in its truly seventeenth-century implication, the idea of a well-wrought work of art, attentive to language and form (as we have found to be true of the lyrics) but also potentially dangerous and entrapping, recalling Campion's advice to "strive not yet for curious wayes" for fear of temptations to arrogant wit.[49] Marvell himself in "The Coronet" implied the parallel between the "curious" intricate ways of his text and the "wreaths of fame and interest" and "winding snare" of the serpent.[50] The second word in Marvell's phrase, "frame," has multiple significances. First, it is the poet's self, which, like that of all the lyricists, is central to the spiritual and aesthetic impact of the poem and is, typically, emblematic in its function. A frame is also an ordering device, a means of setting everything in its proper proportion, as in Herbert's confident assertion that if he should stray, the God of Love would "bring my minde in frame."[51] In the immediate setting of Marvell's lyric, the "frame" is, of course, also the poem itself, the containing framework of language, pattern, and tradition. Like the genre as a whole, the individual poem is, as Marvell wrote in "On a Drop of Dew," an attempt to "frame as it

---

47. *Genre* (London: Methuen, 1982), 2.
48. Cited by Dubrow, *Genre*, 32.
49. *Selected Poems*, 38.
50. Marvell's sense that "winding," whether in lines or souls, is threatening to religious equilibrium may be linked with Herbert's dislike of the "winding stair" of verse in "Jordan (I)," *Selected Poetry*, 75.
51. "The 23rd Psalme," *English Poems*, 178.

can its native element," to contain within its "little globe's extent" a breath of heaven.[52]

"Curious frame," though a richly expressive phrase, may not seem too auspicious as the epitome of the genre, the seventeenth-century religious lyric—for the poem from which it derives ends with a request to "shatter" itself:

> Or shatter too with him [the serpent] my curious frame,
> And let these wither, so that he may die,
> Though set with skill and chosen out with care.
> That they, while Thou on both their spoils dost tread,
> May crown thy feet, that could not crown thy head.

However, these closing lines are an essential reminder of one final element in this genre: its imperfection. The poets are marked out by their dread of complacency in religious verse, and their texts show an acute consciousness of their weakness and the consequent need to be broken in order to succeed. Like a baptized body, the lyric was cleansed and renewed, "chosen out with care," but it had in each case eventually to be "shattered," left behind, transcended. The poets demonstrated a continuing ambivalence toward their lyrics, delighting in the possibilities of the newly revitalized genre but always aware of its transitoriness. They were, we might say, "in" the genre but not "of" it. Once again, the seventeenth-century religious context implies something very important about a genre: it is an imperfect means, not an end. As in Marvell's "The Coronet," the "frame" must be broken in order for the soul to gain liberation from the unwanted restrictions of human systems, such as words, forms, and emblems, some of the central focuses of the seventeenth-century religious lyric. Although the lyrics in themselves surprise the reader and transcend some of the normal limitations of the familiar, they can only ever, as Marvell concludes, achieve their spiritual goal—to "crown" the "feet" of Christ—by being trampled upon. Real transcendence, the implication is, comes through sacrifice. Marvell manages to end the poem with the ultimate aim of the religious lyric: to "crown" the "head" of Christ. But within the text it has to remain a hope—a prayer, even—which, if fulfilled, will eventually transcend the poem, time, and all other human "frames."

52. "On a Drop of Dew," *Selected Poetry*, 18.

So the "curious frame" gets curiouser and curiouser: first linking poets in a general devotional poetics while their work can seem to be so various; and then identifying as a genre a mode of writing defined by spiritual as well as literary factors, containing strong features of self-denial and self-destruction even in its wit and beauty. But, odd though this outcome may be, it has at the very least pointed out that there is a great deal more to connect these poets than contemporaneity to one another and to the turmoil of post-Reformation Britain. They have been shown to share distinctive attitudes to words and the Word, poetic structures, emblematic modes, transcendence, and the baptismal humility of their own calling. There was indeed a generic frame within which these poets, however uneasily, were working. Much remains to be done on this subject, but in the meantime, we may proceed to discuss this fascinating group of poets with greater confidence in the idea of the English seventeenth-century religious lyric as a generic entity.

ENLARGING THE LIMITS OF THE "RELIGIOUS LYRIC"
The Case of Herrick's *Hesperides*

❈ ❈ ❈ *Achsah Guibbory* ❈ ❈ ❈

Robert Herrick's poetry constitutes a gentle but powerful argument for the need to enlarge the genre of the "religious lyric." We usually think of the seventeenth-century religious lyric as devotional poetry addressed to God, introspective meditations on the state of one's soul or on biblical events and persons, and as poetry that is overtly, specifically Christian. The poetry of Donne and Herbert fits comfortably into this category. But what of the work of that other Anglican priest, Robert Herrick, who referred to his volume *Hesperides* as a *"Temple,"* with, perhaps, a self-conscious glance at Herbert's earlier volume? Herrick, with his playful tone, his secular subjects, such as celebrating May or drinking sack, his dedication to pleasure rather than suffering, his imitation of Greek and Roman poets, tends to be thought of as "pagan" in spirit, too interested in the physical pleasures of this world to be a real Christian. Certainly, he is not thought of as a "religious" poet, despite his *Noble Numbers,* a collection of rather dull poems on conventionally Christian devotional topics. We need, however, to reconsider the genre "religious poetry" and to look again at *Hesperides.* With its persistent criticism of those who define religion too narrowly, Herrick's volume attempts to enlarge our sense of what is "religious" and, consequently, of "religious poetry." Not *every* poem in *Hesperides* is religious, but the cumulative effect of his verse is.

Enlarging the Limits of the "Religious Lyric" • 29

In certain ways, Herrick admittedly makes it difficult for readers to see his poetry as religious. Though he calls *Hesperides* a "Poetick Liturgie," a "*Psalter,*" and a "*Temple*" where he is the priest,[1] some poems seem difficult to reconcile with this dignified, religious setting—the poems on Julia's various body parts (nipples, breasts, legs), or the obscene epigrams on farting, adultery, or physically repulsive characters like the laundress who cleans her clothes in "pisse" (H-237). Moreover, if "The Argument of his Book" suggests an easy continuity between the secular pleasures of this world (catalogued as the topics of his poems) and the heavenly rewards of the next, which he "hope[s] to have . . . after all" (H-1), the concluding poem of *Hesperides* (H-1130) implies a discontinuity between the hedonism of his verse and the religious life of the priest:

> To his Book's end this last line he'd have plac't,
> *Jocond his Muse was; but his Life was chast.*

Although Herrick seems to delight in throwing obstacles in the way of the reader's thinking of *Hesperides* as "religious poetry," the opening poems of *Hesperides* carefully suggest a religious aspect to his poetry. As they imagine how readers might react to his book, they insist, paradoxically, that Herrick be taken both lightly and seriously. The "Virgin shie" may blush "while *Brutus* standeth by," but not when he is gone (H-4). Only a censorious, puritanical presence—not anything in the poetry itself—would cause even a chaste, innocent reader discomfort. Herrick curses hostile readers who hate the book (H-6) or use it to "wipe . . . The place, where swelling *Piles* do breed" (H-5). The reader who thus defiles Herrick's poetry will be punished much as a person who desecrates a holy place or thing: "May every Ill, that bites, or smarts, / Perplexe him in his hinder-parts" (H-5). In "*When he would have his verses read*" (H-8), Herrick speaks of his verse as "holy incantation," as if there is something both magically powerful and sacred about it, though it should be read only in the evening when "men have

---

1. "*To his Kinswoman, Mistresse* Penelope Wheeler" (H-510), "*His Prayer to* Ben. Johnson" (H-604), and "*To his Honoured Kinsman, Sir* Richard Stone" (H-496), in *The Complete Poetry of Robert Herrick,* ed. J. Max Patrick (New York: W. W. Norton, 1968). All quotations of Herrick's poetry are from this edition. Hereafter, references to *Hesperides* are cited as H and poem number, with references to *Noble Numbers* cited as N and poem number.

30 • Achsah Guibbory

both well drunke, and fed." If "rigid *Cato*" reads Herrick in the right spirit, even he will lose the inflexibility that enforces rigid distinctions between what is acceptable and not. Herrick's reference to the Roman censor in a poem addressed to his contemporaries implies that in seventeenth-century England, as in classical Rome, there are rigid, intolerant people, and that Herrick wants to make them more accepting. The reader is asked, in so many ways, to rethink what is "holy," to reconsider the categories of sacred and profane.

As a way of questioning those categories, Herrick persistently mingles the sacred and the secular throughout *Hesperides*. Some intermixture of sacred and secular is, of course, common in seventeenth-century religious poetry. Herbert draws on images and analogies from the secular world to describe his relation with God. Crashaw uses shockingly sensual images and analogies to talk about divine subjects. In Donne's devotional poetry, the language of sexual, passionate love expresses his desire for an intimate relation with God. But none of these poets are like Herrick: we never wonder whether their devotional poetry is really religious; it is always regularly included in discussions and anthologies of the seventeenth-century "religious lyric."

Herrick's celebration of the joys of this world has long seemed "pagan" to readers who expect that a truly Christian perspective would emphasize the spirit rather than the body, the joys to be had in the afterlife rather than the pleasures of this one. But Herrick's poetry defies such dualistic, dichotomous assumptions. The volume of poetry, with its classical name and its frontispiece depicting the hill of Parnassus, the spring of Helicon, Pegasus, and the poet about to be crowned with wreaths, flaunts its "pagan" appearance and includes many carpe diem poems; but it also includes, within the physical compass of the bound book, the decidedly Christian, sacred *Noble Numbers*. Within the "secular" part of *Hesperides*, there are hymns and vows to pagan gods, such as Bacchus and Cupid, linked to the natural world and sensual pleasures, but there are also poems on *"Mattens, or morning Prayer"* and *"Evensong"* (H-320, H-321), parts of the Church of England's liturgy. Near the end of *Hesperides*, Herrick anticipates receiving the "incorruptible" crown promised in the New Testament (I Cor. 9:25) to those faithful to Christ:

> AFter thy labour take thine ease,
> Here with the sweet *Pierides*.

> But if so be that men will not
> Give thee the Laurell Crowne for lot;
> Be yet assur'd, thou shalt have one
> Not subject to corruption.
>   (H-1123)

Identifying heaven with Parnassus, he envisions God crowning him in part as a reward for his poetic achievement. His Christian God will not punish him for including the seemingly "pagan" and "secular" within his "temple" of poetry.

The hallmark of Herrick's poetry, in fact, is an eclecticism that derives from his passion for enlarging the boundaries of the sacred. Not only does the volume of *Hesperides* bring together rituals from various pagan, folk, and Christian practices, but individual poems themselves effect such a mixture. Herrick plays with mixtures of things that a supposedly "purer" sensibility might cringe at. "Corinna's *going a Maying*" (H-178) is the obvious, most famous example. Corinna is invited to participate in a May ritual that is an unabashedly sensual celebration of spring but also a sacred act of "Devotion" (l. 32) embracing all nature, seen as instinctively alive with devotional impulses: "Each Flower has wept, and bow'd toward the East"; "all the Birds have Mattens seyd, / And sung their thankfull Hymnes" (ll. 7, 10–11). Customary divisions beween humans and nature, and between secular and sacred, are blurred as Corinna is invited to "put on [her] Foliage" (l. 15) and join these acts of ceremonial devotion.[2] The poem itself enacts an intermingling, as it assimilates the rituals and language of folk and pagan traditions, classical mythology, the Old Testament, and Christianity. The point and effect of "Corinna's *going a Maying*," and of *Hesperides* more generally, is that we cannot neatly divide the pagan and the Christian, the secular and the sacred.

A number of years ago, Virginia R. Mollenkott eloquently argued for an appreciation of Herrick's "holistic concept of religion," in which pleasure is sacramental and God is seen in everything, and she con-

---

2. Leah S. Marcus reads "Corinna's *going a Maying*" as supporting the Royalist position in the controversy over the Book of Sports. See her "Herrick's *Hesperides* and the 'Proclamation made for May,'" *SP* 76 (1979): 49–74; and *The Politics of Mirth: Jonson, Herrick, Milton, Marvell and the Defense of Old Holiday Pastimes* (Chicago: University of Chicago Press, 1986), chap. 5.

cluded that "Herrick expands religion beyond the walls of the church and into every aspect of life."[3] I want to argue here that Herrick's holistic sense of religion must be understood not only, as Mollenkott suggests, as a transhistorical phenomenon, possibly finding its counterpart in Eastern philosophies or in Blake, or as a matter of his personal sensibility, but also as tied to his particular historical moment—the period of the Civil War and the years immediately preceding it. This period was marked by serious conflicts over, among other things, the nature and boundaries of Christian religion. Herrick's intermingling of the "pagan" and Christian and his intertwining of spiritual and physical, sacred and secular, challenge the increasingly powerful influence of Puritanism, which sought to draw the boundaries of the true church in ways that Herrick and others found immensely disturbing.

Hesperides frequently criticizes "precisians" and "zealots," conventional terms of abuse against Puritans.

> IS *Zelot* pure? he is: ye see he weares
> The signe of *Cirumcision* in his eares.
> (H-666)

Herrick may well be referring to the Star-Chamber's notorious punishment of William Prynne, an outspoken critic of the changes in the Church of England under Archbishop William Laud, whereby Prynne's ears were twice chopped off (in 1634 and 1637) and, on the second occasion, his cheeks branded. As the 666th poem in *Hesperides*, "Upon Zelot" shares the number traditionally assigned to the beast described in Revelations. Herrick cleverly turns against the Puritans their habit of identifying the Church of Rome and the Pope with the Beast or Antichrist, and he implies that the proliferation of Puritans is a sign that the apocalyptic end is near.[4] Puritans are probably the butt

---

3. "Herrick and the Cleansing of Perception," in *"Trust to Good Verses": Herrick Tercentenary Essays*, ed. Roger B. Rollin and J. Max Patrick (Pittsburgh: University of Pittsburgh Press, 1978), 197–209; quotations from 198, 208.

4. Cf. *"Upon* Peason. *Epigram"* (H-843), which mocks "our Zelot *Peason"* who weares long hair to hide "That Stubble [that] stands, where once large eares have been." On Herrick's Royalism and his anti-Puritanism, see Robert H. Deming, *Ceremony and Art: Robert Herrick's Poetry* (The Hague: Mouton, 1974), 141–57; Marcus, "Herrick's *Hesperides"* and *The Politics of Mirth;* Claude J. Summers, "Herrick's

of many of Herrick's nastiest epigrams on the supposedly uncivilized lower classes (e.g., "*Upon* Lungs. *Epigram*," H-637, "*Upon* Skoles. *Epigram*," H-650, or "*Upon* Dundrige," H-533). But Herrick's resistance to Puritanism goes deeper than the occasional, epigrammatic insult, for he saw Puritanism in his own day as a divisive rather than a communal force, and as dangerously constricting religion and limiting our ideas of what is "religious."

Puritans, critical of the Church of England under Laud and Charles I, thought that the institution of the English Church had become too carnal and ceremonial, retaining in its worship pagan, Jewish, and Roman Catholic elements and practices.[5] In their increasingly sharp criticisms of the directions in which the Church and English court culture seemed to be moving, Puritans insisted on the necessity of separating the Christian from the pagan, the holy from the profane, saints from sinners, the spirit from the carnal intrusions of the "flesh." Perhaps the best known contemporary attack on the pagan character of English culture is William Prynne's *Histriomastix*, which condemned many customs of supposedly pagan origin that were still current in England. The practice of these customs was, for Prynne, of a piece with the Laudian emphasis on ceremonies in religious worship: both were remnants of pagan religion. Such "pagan" customs were "carnal," concerned with the body and its pleasures, and thus not fitting for godly Christians, who should be of the spirit, not the flesh.[6]

Political Counterplots," *Studies in English Literature, 1500–1900* 25 (1985): 165–82; and Ann Baynes Coiro, *Robert Herrick's "Hesperides" and the Epigram Book Tradition* (Baltimore: Johns Hopkins University Press, 1988), esp. 136–37, 172, 174–206, though Coiro emphasizes the tensions in his Royalism that move *Hesperides* far beyond idealizing praise.

5. On religious conflict and differences between "Puritan" and "Anglican," see Nicholas Tyacke, *Anti-Calvinists: The Rise of English Arminianism c. 1590–1640*, Oxford Historical Monographs (Oxford: Clarendon Press, 1987); J. Sears McGee, *The Godly Man in Stuart England: Anglicans, Puritans, and the Two Tables, 1620–1670*, Yale Historical Publications Miscellany, 110 (New Haven: Yale University Press, 1976); John F. H. New, *Anglican and Puritan: The Basis of Their Opposition, 1558–1640* (Stanford: Stanford University Press, 1964); P. G. Lake, "Calvinism and the English Church 1570–1635," *Past and Present*, no. 114 (Feb. 1987): 32–76. On Charles I's court culture and its connections with religion, see R. Malcolm Smuts, *Court Culture and the Origins of a Royalist Tradition in Early Stuart England* (Philadelphia: University of Pennsylvania Press, 1987), esp. chap. 8.

6. *Histriomastix* (London, 1633), 17–20, 48, 294. See also Prynne's *Healthes: Sick-*

Milton struck a similar stance in the anti-prelatical tracts of the 1640s, with their sense of necessary distinctions between fleshly and spiritual, pagan and Christian. *Of Reformation* attacks the Church of England for having at once backslid "into the Jewish beggery, of old cast rudiments" and for having stumbled forward "into the new-vomited Paganisme of sensuall Idolatry," Roman Catholicism. The prelates, incapable of making themselves *"Spirituall,"* have made the church service "earthly, and fleshly." In order to establish "the *pure worship* of God," Milton insists we must reform religion, purging our worship of the pagan, the fleshly, the sensual, having nothing to do with paganism or the idolatry of popery.[7] Despite the complexity of Milton's later poetic treatment of classical culture and the monistic assumptions underpinning *Paradise Lost* and *Christian Doctrine*, in the anti-prelatical prose he shares Prynne's conviction that it is both possible and necessary to divide the Christian from the pagan, spiritual from carnal. As Prynne writes, quoting key passages from Corinthians: *"What fellowship hath Righteousnesse, with Vnrighteousnesse? What communion hath Light with Darkeness? What concord hath Christ with Belial? what part hath hee that Beleeveth with an Infidell? or what agreement hath the Temple of God with Idoles?* God, and the Devill, Christ, and Belial, are contrary, are inconsistent: therefore the service, and ceremonies of the one, are altogether incompatible with the other."[8] Note the insistence on purity and the resistance to communion and concord as dangerously polluting. The same biblical passages were cited by Henry Burton, another critic of the prelatical church, to prove the "vnreconcileable opposition betweene the Apostolicke Church of *Christ*" and the Church of Rome, "the Apostate Synagogue of *Antichrist*," whose worship has infected the English Church. There are, as Burton puts it, firm "bounders" [sic; boundaries] "disterminating" [sic] true religion from false.[9]

For all the differences in the extent to which they wished to reform or separate from the established Church of England, Prynne, Milton,

---

nesse. Or, A Compendious and briefe Discourse; proving the Drinking, and Pledging of Healthes, to be Sinfull, and utterly Vnlawfull unto Christians (London, 1628).

7. *Of Reformation*, ed. Don M. Wolfe, in *Complete Prose Works of John Milton*, ed. Don M. Wolfe, et al. (New Haven: Yale University Press, 1953), 1:520, 79.

8. *Histriomastix*, 33.

9. *Truth's Triumph over Trent* (London, 1629), subtitle and "The Preface to the Reader."

and Burton shared a "Puritan" ideology marked by a sense of absolute, categorical distinctions.[10] Convinced that the profane and carnal elements in their society and in the Church must be cast out, they wield a powerful discourse of division and opposition. Puritan polemical writings of the late 1620s through the 1640s assume that the sanctified saint can readily distinguish between the Christian and non-Christian, between the spiritual and the carnal (identified as pagan-Jewish-popish), and that religious worship, indeed, one's experience of the "religious life," must be purged of contaminating carnal and non-Christian elements. And throughout Puritan discourse, the "carnal" and "pagan" are condemned as placing an inappropriate emphasis on pleasure. In a passage that expresses precisely the point of view that *Hesperides,* in its celebration of mirth, seems written against, Prynne warns: "*This is no place, no time, no world for Christians to laugh or to be merry in: but to bewaile their owne and others sinnes, that so they may escape the eternall torments of them at the last.*"[11] All who pursue pleasure on earth will be rewarded with "torments" in the afterlife. The godly life (as opposed to the Cavalier "good life") turns out to be sober, sad, and miserable—an ideology with special appeal to those lacking material comforts.

How different this Puritan sensibility is from the spirit of Herrick's poetry. Whereas Puritans insisted on the oppositions between Christian and pagan, holy and profane, the fleshly body and the inner world of the spirit, Herrick's poetry resolutely mingles these things so that it is often virtually impossible to separate them.

Herrick's poems blur clear distinctions between the domains of body and spirit. In part, they do so by stressing the intimate relation between the human and natural world, giving funeral rites to the rose (H-686), remarking Julia's "Sister-hood" with flowers (H-9), finding in blossoms or daffodils significant lessons for human beings (H-467, H-316). Herrick's insistence on placing humans firmly within the physical world of nature contrasts sharply with the Puritan attention to the

---

10. While recognizing the limitations of the term *Puritan,* I follow those historians who argue for the usefulness and necessity of distinguishing between "Anglicans" and "Puritans" in England. See McGee, *The Godly Man,* 9–10; New, *Anglican and Puritan;* and Peter Lake, *Anglicans and Puritans?: Presbyterianism and English Conformist Thought from Whitgift to Hooker* (London: Unwin Hyman, 1988), esp. Introduction.

11. *Histriomastix,* 293–94.

divisions between nature and grace. Moreover, his poems repeatedly and variously show how the spiritual invests the physical. In "Corinna's *going a Maying*" (H-178), flowers bow to the east toward the rising sun, and birds sing morning hymns. Herrick takes these "natural," commonly observable, sensibly perceptible phenomena and represents them as instinctive acts of spiritual worship. His many ceremony poems are all founded on the belief that divinity can be approached through participation in physical, bodily acts of devotion—exactly the assumption of the ceremonial religious worship encouraged by Laud.[12] The rites of May or Christmas participate in, indeed perhaps insure, the cyclical renewal of life that is seen as the expression and blessing of divinity. Ritualized acts of devotion both recognize and effect the connection between the material and spiritual, between the natural world and God:

> FIrst offer Incense, then thy field and meads
> Shall smile and smell the better by thy beads.
> The spangling Dew dreg'd o're the grasse shall be
> Turn'd all to Mell, and Manna there for thee.
> Butter of *Amber, Cream,* and *Wine,* and *Oile*
> Shall run, as rivers, all throughout thy soyl.
> Wod'st thou to sincere-silver turn thy mold?
> Pray once, twice pray; and turn thy ground to gold.
> (H-370)

This sense of an intimate connection between the physical and spiritual pervades *Hesperides*, even Herrick's poems on his mistresses. Julia's physical body seems "Cloth'd all with incorrupted light" (H-819), suggesting that while on earth she manifests something of the glory of heaven. Even her clothes possess movement and vitality (H-779), her petticoat "erring" and "wandring," panting and sighing as if it had a life of its own (H-175). The physical, sensual world Herrick celebrates is alive with spirit.

It is, significantly, the body devoid of spirit and grace that forms the subject of his satirical, nasty epigrams:

---

12. On Laud's concern with ceremony, see esp. J. Sears McGee, "William Laud and the Outward Face of Religion," in *Leaders of the Reformation,* ed. Richard L. DeMolen (London: Associated University Presses, 1984), 318–44.

> *SKinns* he din'd well to day; how do you think?
> His Nails they were his meat, his Reume the drink.
> (H-409)
>
> *DUndridge* his Issue hath; but is not styl'd
> For all his Issue, Father of one Child.
> (H-533)
>
> *JOne* wo'd go tel her haires; and well she might,
> Having but seven in all; three black, foure white.
> (H-531)

The state of spiritless, graceless materiality is for Herrick both the consequence and the appropriate punishment for those (Puritans) who would presume to draw neat lines between the holy and the profane, the spirit and the flesh.[13] What they end up with is the unredeemed body, which contrasts so sharply with the transfigured body of one of Herrick's mistresses, Julia, whose very sweat is the "oyle of Blossomes" and whose breath is "rich spices" (H-719).

> *JOne* is a wench that's painted;
> *Jone* is a Girle that's tainted;
>   Yet *Jone* she goes
>   Like one of those
> Whom purity had Sainted.
>
> *Jane* is a Girle that's prittie;
> *Jane* is a wench that's wittie;
>   Yet, who wo'd think,
>   Her breath do's stinke,
> As so it doth? that's pittie.
> (H-659)

Just as Herrick's poetry celebrates the interconnection of body and spirit, so he mingles pagan and Christian. The religion of the "Temple" of

---

13. One of only a few critics to give serious attention to the mocking epigrams, Coiro, in her excellent book (*Robert Herrick's Hesperides*, chap. 8), has argued that these poems are "self-parody" (168), reflecting Herrick's own "self-doubts" (169) and "bring[ing] into question the ontological status of beauty itself" (160). I see these poems quite differently, however, not as self-questioning but as self-affirming, even self-justifying, in their anti-Puritanism.

Hesperides is, like that of "Oberons *Chappell*," a "mixt Religion" (H-223).[14] It includes prayers and vows to "pagan" deities as well as spells to "affright . . . the evill Sp'rite" (H-769), folk charms to protect stables (e.g., H-891), and *"The old Wives Prayer"* to the *"Holy-Rood"* to "guard us" (H-473). Herrick asks readers to "pray" for the "soule of *Lucia*" to "free" her from *"Purgatory"* (H-814), recalling the Roman Catholic doctrine rejected by Protestant churches, including the Church of England. He also incorporates practices of the Church of England that Puritans had rejected as "pagan." In Herrick's temple of poetry, tapers burn (H-604), holy water and incense abound (H-320, H-898, H-957, H-974, H-1069), and ceremonies are performed.

Attempting to purify worship from all traces of paganism, Parliament outlawed the Church of England's ceremonies along with the Book of Common Prayer in January 1645. Herrick's 1648 volume of poetry includes prohibited ceremonies such as the "churching" of women after childbirth (H-898).[15] Whereas the *Directory for the Public Worship of God* (London, 1645), which replaced the Book of Common Prayer, rejected burial ceremonies as excessively concerned with the body, Herrick's many funeral rite poems stress the importance of having a proper burial and of paying careful attention to the body as a sign of reverence for the spirit of the deceased person. In a poem addressed to his father, Herrick worries that for many years he never came "to doe the *Rites* to thy Religious Tombe" (H-82). Concerned with what will happen to himself at death, he instructs his mistresses—Perilla, Anthea, Perenna (H-14, H-22, H-976), and Julia—to perform all the "Rites that doe belong to me" (H-627). As they affirm the importance of rituals banned by Parliament and incorporate ancient Roman customs, these poems celebrate the very connection between ancient pagan rites and contemporary Anglican ones that made the church's rites abhorrent to Puritans.

---

14. On *"The Faerie Temple: or, Oberons Chappell,"* with its "mixed" religion as a defense of the Laudian position, see Marcus, "Herrick's *Hesperides*," 49–74, and her *The Politics of Mirth*, chap. 5.

15. John Rushworth, *Historical Collections* (London, 1721): 5:785. On Herrick's inclusion of the ceremonies criticized by Puritans, see my essay "The Temple of *Hesperides* and Anglican-Puritan Controversy," in *"The Muses Common-Weale": Poetry and Politics in the Seventeenth Century*, ed. Claude J. Summers and Ted-Larry Pebworth (Columbia: University of Missouri Press, 1988), 135–47.

Enlarging the Limits of the "Religious Lyric" • 39

Hesperides includes not only ceremonial rites that had been banned from religious worship but also popular traditions and customs that Puritans condemned as pagan.[16] Herrick's volume offers a virtual catalogue of Prynne's forbidden delights. Where Prynne in *Histriomastix* found it "unlawfull" for Christians *"to deck up their Houses with Lawrell, Yvie, and greene boughs,* (as we use to do in the Christmas season)," Herrick encourages the tradition in poems like *"Ceremonies for Candlemasse Eve"* (H-892). Puritans rejected "Grand Christmasses" as pagan celebrations, but Herrick recorded many folk customs connected with Christmas (H-784–87, H-892, H-980), seeking to preserve them in his poetry at a time when these traditions, indeed the whole culture of which they were a part, seemed threatened with extinction. If Christmas seemed suspiciously pagan to Puritans, so did the traditional celebration of New Year's Day, with its custom of exchanging gifts. Herrick, however, sends poems as "New-yeares gift[s]" (H-319), and reminds readers in *Noble Numbers* that January first is also the festival of Christ's circumcision (N-97, N-98). Yet another contemporary "pagan" practice that Prynne condemned was "the wearing of a Laurell Crowne, or flowrie Garland."[17] But garlands and laurel crowns abound in *Hesperides*. Herrick announces that his business as a poet is to make "garlands" for others to wear (H-224), and he himself frequently appears crowned with wreaths (H-111, H-197, H-224, H-1062). Even Herrick's language intertwines the classical and the Christian, as he calls each poetic garland he offers his friends "a crowne of life" (H-224), echoing Revelations 2:10.

Herrick's celebration of tradition is far from innocent of controversial religiopolitical significance, for the traditions he includes are precisely those then under attack by Puritans as heathen customs and sacrilegious contaminations of worship, which they believed should be grounded solely in Scripture, the Word of God. Underlying Herrick's eclectic collection of traditions and ceremonies is his deep sense of the harmony among customs and rites from various religions and cultures. Whether Christian or "pagan," all these rituals share a sense of the cyclical order of the natural world, an order that they affirm and

---

16. On the ideological conflict surrounding old holiday pastimes and festivity, see Marcus, *The Politics of Mirth*.
17. *Histriomastix*, 20.

seek to perpetuate. What, for Herrick, unites Jewish, pagan, folk, and Christian customs is the shared recognition that renewal, protection, and prosperity depend upon God, who can be called on through rites, invocations, and charms. Folk charms to protect horses, a potion to keep off the evil spirit, a vow to Neptune, a prayer to release a soul from purgatory—from either a skeptically secular or a firmly Protestant/Puritan perspective, all of these seem foolish superstitions, but from another noncensorious perspective they all work on the assumption that ceremony has a real, magical efficacy, that humans, through prayers, charms, and rites, can connect with the divine power that controls life. As he enlarges the bounds of religion to include traditions and ceremonies from various cultures and societies, Herrick recaptures a sense that religion is not separate from magic, an experience of religion that was fundamentally challenged and altered by the Protestant Reformation, which sought to remove the magical elements from religion.[18] But both the sense of nostalgia and the discrepancy between the naive, childlike tone of his charms and spells and the sophistication of so much of his poetry register Herrick's recognition that this older sense of religion was probably irretrievably past, out of place in the early modern world of mid-seventeenth-century England.

Herrick's eclectic mingling of customs, his emphasis on the harmony between classical and Christian, and, above all, his insistence on drawing the boundaries of religion to include the Roman Catholic and the pre-Christian are all anti-Puritan features that clearly associate the poet with an ideological perspective within the Church of England identified with Laud and his supporters but not limited to them. Whereas Puritans, wanting a "purer" worship, a religion of the "spirit," attacked the "mixed" character of the Church of England's worship and liturgy, apologists of the Church, such as Archbishop Laud, Peter Heylyn, and John Cosin, defended that mixture as evidence of a valued continuity. Puritans, seeking to purge all corrupt, human traditions, insisted on the need for a decisive break with the Jewish-pagan-popish past, and saw continuity with these traditions as the very mark of error and corruption. But the apologists for the established Church

---

18. Keith Thomas, *Religion and the Decline of Magic: Studies in Popular Beliefs in Sixteenth and Seventeenth Century England* (New York: Weidenfeld and Nicolson, 1971), chaps. 2–3.

of England valued just that continuity, defending the church's practices on the basis of their antiquity and their conformity with and preservation of earlier devotional practices.

Bishop Cosin defended aspects of the English service criticized by Puritans, such as the singing of prayers or the specific practices surrounding Holy Communion, on the basis that they were old customs. Their very antiquity legitimized them. Peter Heylyn similarly invoked the arguments of antiquity and continuity in defending the sacredness of altars, sacrifices, priests, and temples. He pointed out the continuity among the practices of Jews, "*Gentiles*," and Christians, who, in their respective societies, all at first worshipped God "in the open aire" but then built temples once their religion was established.[19] Like Herrick, Heylyn stressed harmony between pagan and Christian, past and present. Heylyn used the consonance between the practices of the pagans and "Gods owne people" to argue for the legitimacy of Laud's program for repairing and beautifying England's places of worship.[20] But how could the Anglican argument of harmony or consonance ever persuade Puritans, when Puritan ideology, with its insistence on necessary divisions and distinctions, implicitly rejected those Anglican values?

Conservative Anglicans valued the historical continuity of the Church, diminishing—sometimes virtually erasing—the divisive features of the Protestant Reformation. They saw the Church of England as preserving "the old religion." Cosin, defending the English Church's retention of some Roman Catholic ceremonies, argued that "we have continued the old religion."[21] At his trial, Laud was accused of being a papist by Prynne, who brought as evidence Laud's book of private devotions, which included Roman Catholic prayers; but Laud insisted there was nothing wrong with such eclecticism: "I would have them remember, that we live in a Church *Reformed*; not in one made *New*. Now all *Reformation*, that is good and orderly, takes away nothing from the old, but that which is Faulty and Erroneous. If any thing be good, it leaves that standing. . . . Nay, the less alteration is made in the Publick

---

19. John Cosin, *Notes and Collections on the Book of Common Prayer*, in *The Works of . . . John Cosin* (Oxford: John Henry and James Parker, 1855): 5:58–59, 111, 131; Peter Heylyn, *Antidotum Lincolniense* (London, 1637), Section II, 70–71.
20. *Antidotum*, 70.
21. *Notes*, 13.

Ancient *Service* of the Church, the better it is."[22] Where Puritans attacked this continuity as a mark of the established English Church's pagan carnality, Anglican defenders of the Church saw continuity with earlier practices as a sign that England's Church was a true Church *because* it was "catholic" and universal, not divisive and sectarian.

Indeed, during the very time that Herrick was writing his poetry, some priests in the Church of England were voicing an ideal of a "catholic" or universal church that seems remarkably close to the assumptions about religion underlying *Hesperides*. In *Apello Caesarem*, which was repressed in response to Puritan outrage, Richard Montagu criticized the divisiveness of those "Purer *Brethren*" who identified themselves narrowly as members of a Protestant sect: "I am not, nor would be accounted willingly *Arminian, Calvinist,* or *Lutheran*, (names of Division) but a *Christian*. . . . A *Christian* I am, and so glory to be; only denominated of *Christ Iesus* my Lord and Master." Montagu's ideal of unity, his desire for a "catholic" (in the sense of universal) Church of England, led him to emphasize the "Essentials and Fundamentals" English and Roman Catholic Churches share rather than the differences that divide them.[23] Laud took the same position in his *Relation of the Conference Betweene . . . Laud . . . and Mr. Fisher the Jesuite*, when he insisted that salvation cannot be restricted to one particular Church. He declared that his aim was "to lay open those *wider-Gates* of the *Catholike Church*, confined to no *Age, Time,* or *Place*; Nor knowing any *Bounds, but that Faith, which was once* (and but once for all) *deliver'd to the Saints*."[24] Though Puritans insisted that the notion of a "catholic" church was only a mask for "papist" leanings, Laud saw his efforts to enlarge the boundaries of the Church as an attempt to realize the ideal Church, which is timeless and universal.

Ironically, Laud's generous rhetoric was at odds with his repression of dissent and his rigorous enforcement of his policies. As Puritans bitterly noted, Laud was eager to make overtures of friendship to the

---

22. William Laud, *The History of the Troubles and Tryall of . . . William Laud*, ed. Henry Wharton (London, 1695), 113. See William Prynne's description of Laud's book of devotions in *Canterburies Doome* (London, 1646), 67.

23. *Apello Caesarem* (London, 1625), 6, 10, 112–13.

24. *Relation of the Conference Betweene William Laud . . . and Mr. Fisher the Jesuite . . .* (London, 1639), "Dedicatory Epistle to King Charles." See Tyacke, *Anti-Calvinists*, on the Arminian movement within the Church.

Roman Catholic Church but was intolerant of Puritan consciences at home. But the concern to establish a more tolerant relation with Rome was also voiced by moderate members of the Church of England who did not necessarily endorse Laud's repressive activities against Puritans. John Hales encouraged "communion and Christian fellowship" with the Church of Rome, emphasizing the many "*Prayers,* and *holy ceremonies,* which are common to them and us." "*It is the unity of the Spirit in the bond of peace,* and not *Identitie of conceit,* which the Holy Ghost requires at the hands of Christians." Sir Thomas Browne said he would have no trouble worshipping in a Roman Catholic church, complaining that "those who doe confine the Church of God, either to particular Nations, Churches, or Families, have made it far narrower than our Saviour ever meant it."[25] Like Browne, who insisted on the importance of exercising "charitie" in religion, Hales suggested that English Protestants should be "Universally compassionate"[26] to Roman Catholics, and he drew an analogy between Protestants' relation to Catholics, and Christians' to Jews and pagans that is particularly relevant to understanding the religious spirit of Herrick's poetry:

> As therefore our religion is, so must our compassion be, catholick. To tye it either to persons or to place, is but a kinde of *morale Judaisme.* . . . In some things we agree, as we are men, and thus far the very heathen themselves are to be received. . . . St. *Paul* loved the *Jews* because they were *his brethren according to the Flesh.* We that are of the *heathen* by the same analogy ought to be as tenderly affected to the rest of our brethren, who though they be not as we are *now,* yet now are that which we sometimes were.[27]

Our human bonds are perhaps more important than our differences. I would like to think that Herrick is closer in temperament to Hales or Browne than to Laud.

But we would do well to remember that even the moderate Anglican emphasis on a unity that charitably includes differences of belief could be a way of containing and suppressing dissent rather than a sign of

---

25. John Hales, *Golden Remains of the ever Memorable John Hales* (London, 1659), 57–58, 54; Sir Thomas Browne, *Religio Medici* (pt. I, sec. 55), in *Selected Writings,* ed. Geoffrey Keynes (Chicago: University of Chicago Press, 1968), 62.
26. *Golden Remains,* 36.
27. Ibid., 34–35.

tolerance for diversity. It would be wrong to misread a seventeenth-century vocabulary of inclusion as expressing late twentieth-century ideas of tolerance, pluralism, or diversity. Herrick himself is hardly universally charitable in *Hesperides,* as his satirical and obscene epigrams suggest. He separates those he promises to immortalize in his poetry from the "bastard Slips" that will die (H-859). But his intolerance is usually aimed at those who would draw the lines of division between sacred and secular too sharply. Herrick's unregenerate are the Puritans, whom he condemns for their oppositional, divisive stance, for drawing the circle of salvation so narrowly that they themselves, in retribution, will be excluded.

Herrick was clearly not alone in his reaction against those who would narrowly define God's Church or in his effort to enlarge the bounds of religion. But Herrick's poetry pushes the issue further than Anglican apologists, persistently testing the bounds of religion. For he virtually implies that the "Faith" necessary for one to be included in his temple is not strictly the New Testament faith in Christ, delivered as Laud said to the "saints," but rather a generic faith in God, available even to pagans.

Indeed, Herrick seems peculiarly interested in the uncertain, tricky place at the very boundaries or limits of religion. Particularly revealing is the poem *"To* Anthea" (H-55), in which he asks to be buried at the oak tree that marks the parish boundary:

> NOw is the time, when all the lights wax dim;
> And thou *(Anthea)* must withdraw from him
> Who was thy servant. Dearest, bury me
> Under that *Holy-oke,* or *Gospel-tree:*
> Where (though thou see'st not) thou may'st think upon
> Me, when thou yeerly go'st Procession:
> Or for mine honour, lay me in that Tombe
> In which thy sacred Reliques shall have roome:
> For my Embalming (Sweetest) there will be
> No Spices wanting, when I'm laid by thee.

He envisions himself here at the very limits of the religious circle, being visited and remembered when every year Anthea participates in the ritual procession along the parish boundaries during Rogation Days. As Keith Thomas observes, the procession was, in part, "intended to make sure that the parish boundaries had not been encroached upon during the course of the year."[28] Traditionally, this ritual was meant to confirm the boundaries of sacred space, but Herrick positions himself at the edge. This desire to be at the boundary of the parish, at the place where the holy, consecrated ground meets the unconsecrated, captures the unique quality of Herrick's "religious" poetry. It also suggests his recognition that he is taking risks: he is almost beyond the pale, perhaps might even be thought so by some (I doubt Milton would have considered Herrick's poetry religious)—which is exactly what has been the fate of his poetry, absent from discussions of the religious lyric.

I wonder, finally, whether twentieth-century criticism in not even considering Herrick a religious poet has not proved to be the inheritor of Puritanism, with its insistence on clear distinctions between religious and secular, pagan and Christian. Have we not drawn the boundaries of what is "religious" too narrowly? If one truly accepts that religion (and the religious impulse) is universal, that it embraces pagan, Catholic, Jewish, and "Protestant" practices, then much of Herrick's poetry must count as "religious." What is especially appealing is Herrick's emphasis on harmony and inclusiveness at a time when so many of his contemporaries felt driven to draw the boundaries of religion precisely, authoritatively, in ways that excluded those who did not share either their doctrines or their practices.

28. See J. Max Patrick's note on the poem in his edition (31); see also Thomas, *Religion and the Decline of Magic,* 63.

HERRICK, VAUGHAN, AND THE POETRY OF ANGLICAN SURVIVALISM

❊ ❊ ❊ *Claude J. Summers* ❊ ❊ ❊

The seventeenth-century religious lyric participates in the mystification of politics and poetry that is characteristic of the discursive practices of late Renaissance culture generally. As an exercise of private devotion, as a colloquy between man and God, and as an expression of spiritual transcendence, the religious lyric may seem to exist on a plane apart from the mundane and the temporal. But such an appearance is misleading, for the religious lyric—however successful it may be in achieving a heightened spirituality—is never completely divorced from the pressures of worldly concerns, and it is inevitably (and sometimes triumphantly) rooted in the sociopolitical contexts of its time. In seventeenth-century England those contexts included numerous and vociferous ecclesiastical and theological disputes and religious persecutions of various kinds and degrees. While the major religious poets of the seventeenth century were not, in their poetry at any rate, merely polemicists or propagandists, they could neither escape nor evade the particulars of the contentious religious and political climate in which they lived. On the contrary, their artistic imaginations were frequently stirred by the controversies and conflicts of their age, especially the intermingled religious and political differences that eventually led to civil war, differences that were less doctrinal and theological than ecclesiastical and liturgical. The tensions between the temporal and the spiritual, the political and the transcendent, and the public and the private were not only expressed in their religious lyrics but were also themselves sometimes the source of art. The political dimension of the seventeenth-century religious lyric is a crucial if insufficiently recognized aspect of its achievement.

The political dimension of the religious lyric is especially apparent in poems that feature representations of the visible Church, itself the focus of so much controversy in the seventeenth century. Several major poets, including John Donne, George Herbert, Robert Herrick, and Henry Vaughan, wrote poems that confront directly the question of how to recognize true religion at a time of schism, when the seamless garment of Christian faith seemed to have been rent by the competing claims of rival institutions to be the earthly manifestation of the Bride of the Apocalypse, the spouse of Christ. These poets all, in fact, wrote lyrics that personify the historical and mystical embodiment of the Church in ways that both express the individual sensibility of each author and strikingly reflect the evolution of the religiopolitical debate in England in the seventeenth century. More than that, the personifications of the Church in these poems are themselves necessarily and profoundly political representations.

In the Holy Sonnet "Show me deare Christ," for instance, Donne, who was reared a Catholic and had carefully studied the claims and counterclaims of the competing religious sects of his day before entering the Anglican priesthood, expresses a vision that is at once skeptical of the rival temporal institutions and also tolerant of them, juxtaposing their questionable historical records against a transcendent image of unity and love jarringly difficult to equate with his unbridelike personifications of Roman Catholicism and Protestantism. He finds true religion expressed exclusively in the love song between his "amorous soule" and Christ's "mild Dove," a union that may be consummated only in a realm beyond the visible world. In "The British Church," Herbert, on the other hand, discovers in his maternal personification of Anglicanism both the only truly pleasing historical institution and the Bride of the Apocalypse. Writing in the midst of the rancorous ecclesiastical debate that was eventually to divide the Established Church, he delineates the opposing claimants for the mantle of the Bride as not merely Protestantism and Roman Catholicism (as in Donne's poem), but instead the Roman, Genevan, and British Churches, the last of which he depicts in its "perfect lineaments and hue" as a divinely favored compromise between alleged Roman excess and Genevan nakedness.[1]

Herbert's conception of a triple rivalry speaks eloquently of the way in which the religiopolitical debate in England had evolved by the late 1620s and the early 1630s. By the 1640s and the 1650s, however, that debate had evolved further still. Indeed, it took on an entirely new dimension as the Civil War erupted, in the aftermath of which the Established Church was radically dismantled and transformed by the triumphant Parliamentarians.[2] This is the historical moment at which Herrick published *Noble Numbers* (1647/8), including "The Widdowes teares: or, Dirge of Dorcas" (N-123), his lamentation that personifies Anglicanism as a dead widow; and in which Vaughan wrote the two parts of *Silex Scintillans* (1650, 1655), including "The Brittish Church," in which Anglicanism is depicted as a ravished bride who urges the Bridegroom to flee lest he be recrucified by their ascendant enemies.[3] Although the representations of the Church in Herrick's "The Widdowes teares" and Vaughan's "The Brittish Church" are startlingly different from that in Herbert's "The British Church," both later poems are significantly influenced by the earlier one; their authors specifically evoke Herbert's poem in order to rewrite it for radically changed

---

1. On Donne's "Show me deare Christ" and Herbert's "The British Church," see my essay, "The Bride of the Apocalypse and the Quest for True Religion: Donne, Herbert, and Spenser," in *"Bright Shootes of Everlastingnesse": The Seventeenth-Century Religious Lyric,* ed. Claude J. Summers and Ted-Larry Pebworth (Columbia: University of Missouri Press, 1987), 72–95. Quotations from Donne are from *The Complete Poetry of John Donne,* ed. John T. Shawcross, The Anchor Seventeenth-Century Series (Garden City, N.Y.: Doubleday, 1967); those from Herbert are from *The Works of George Herbert,* ed. F. E. Hutchinson (1941; corr. rpt. Oxford: Clarendon Press, 1945).

2. For an account of the step-by-step dismantlement of the Established Church by Parliament between 1641 and 1646, see John Morrill, "The Church in England, 1642–9," in *Reactions to the English Civil War 1642–1649,* ed. John Morrill (New York: St. Martin's Press, 1982), 89–114.

3. On "The Widdowes teares" as a thinly disguised lamentation for the demise of the British Church as Herrick had known it, see my essay "Tears for Herrick's Church," *George Herbert Journal* 14 (Fall 1990/Spring 1991): 51–71, part of which is incorporated into the present article; for a discussion of Vaughan's "The Brittish Church," see Claude J. Summers and Ted-Larry Pebworth, "Herbert, Vaughan, and Public Concerns in Private Modes," *George Herbert Journal* 3 (Fall 1979/Spring 1980): 1–21.

circumstances. Indeed, those altered political circumstances—the defeat of King Charles in the Civil War and the subsequent transformation of the Established Church—provide the most significant public context for understanding the religious lyrics of Herrick and Vaughan, and for revealing some crucial similarities between these otherwise dissimilar poets.

I

The religious lyrics of Herrick and Vaughan are important contributions to the poetry of Anglican survivalism. Written in the midst of the Parliamentarian triumph, this poetry mourns the desecration of the Established Church, which is a conspicuously absent (or disguised) presence in both *Noble Numbers* and *Silex Scintillans*. Both collections of lyrics exhibit the distinctive marks of Renaissance Anglicanism, which John N. Wall identifies as the creation of a vernacular discipline of common prayer as the appropriate context for biblical reading, an emphasis on a renewed sense of divine intervention in human—especially English—history, and a retreat from individualized devotional practices in favor of corporate rites designed to further an outward love for neighbor and corporate growth in the Spirit.[4] In addition, however, they also emphasize and are significantly shaped by a felt experience of marginalization and persecution. As might be expected, the poetry of Anglican survivalism is indignantly and defiantly anti-Puritan, expressing disdain for Puritan "innovations" in the Established Church; and it embraces Anglican liturgical practices, particularly those found objectionable by the Puritans and especially those associated with the Eucharist. Predictably, this Anglican poetry tends to focus on communal worship, either by inducing participation in the ceremonies of the (recently disestablished) Church or by mourning the loss of community in the reality of the Parliamentarian victory. Perhaps more surprisingly, the poetry of Anglican survivalism is also apocalyptic, though in a specific and limited way. Actually, however, it ought not to be surprising that Anglican poets embraced apocalypticism during the period of the Established Church's captivity by the

4. *Transformations of the Word: Spenser, Herbert, Vaughan* (Athens: University of Georgia Press, 1988), 16.

Puritans, for, as T. F. Glasson notes, "Apocalypses were usually written at a time of crisis and danger. One of their purposes was to strengthen the believer at a time of persecution and to encourage him to stand firm.... Although apocalypses spring from profound faith and burning conviction, the writers generally despair of the present and pin all their hopes on the future."[5] Like St. John of Patmos, Herrick and Vaughan believed that the truly wicked had gained control of their world and were persecuting those who were faithful to God.

Still, apocalypticism is usually associated with Puritanism rather than with Anglicanism. Indeed, as Bernard Capp has observed, the Arminian party of the Established Church mocked the Puritans' obsession with apocalyptic thought and even questioned the hoary Protestant identification of the papacy with the Antichrist.[6] In the early 1620s, for example, Richard Corbett, the Arminian Dean of Christ Church, Oxford, and later Bishop of Oxford and then of Norwich, satirized "The Distracted Puritan" for having been driven mad by "the Light of Revelation," specifically targeting the Puritans' promiscuous applications of the prophetic symbols and figures of the Apocalypse to contemporaneous events.[7] In the 1630s, Laudian hostility both to Puritans and to apocalyptic speculation coalesced, with the effect of driving the two even closer together. In response, some Puritans came to identify King Charles and the Laudian Church with the Antichrist. During the revolutionary era, the association of apocalypticism with Puritanism intensified even more, and many Puritans came to view the war as a crusade to construct the New Jerusalem on earth and to usher in the millennium. Anticipating, in the words of Thomas Goodwin, "a glorious visible Kingdom which Christ sets up on Earth and peaceably possesseth together with his saints,"[8] the millenarians emerged

---

5. *The Revelation of John*, The Cambridge Bible Commentary (Cambridge: Cambridge University Press, 1965), 2.

6. See Bernard Capp, "The Political Dimension of Apocalyptic Thought," in *The Apocalypse in English Renaissance Thought and Literature: Patterns, Antecedents and Repercussions*, ed. C. A. Patrides and Joseph Wittreich (Ithaca: Cornell University Press, 1984), 93–124. See also Capp's *The Fifth Monarchy Men: A Study in Seventeenth-Century English Millenarianism* (London: Faber and Faber, 1972), especially 23–49.

7. See *The Poems of Richard Corbett*, ed. J. A. W. Bennett and H. R. Trevor-Roper (Oxford: Clarendon Press, 1955), 56–59.

8. *An Exposition of the Revelation* (1639), as quoted in Capp, "The Political Dimension," 107.

as a potent force during the 1640s and the 1650s. But the project of establishing an imminent kingdom of the saints in England was ultimately rejected by Cromwell, to the bitter disappointment of the Fifth Monarchists and other millenarians.

The apocalypticism of Anglican survivalism is of a different order altogether, avoiding much (though by no means all) of the violent language of apocalyptic discourse and eschewing the specific application of apocalyptic prophecies to particular contemporaneous events. Nonmillenarian in emphasis, it concentrates neither on the promise of the Second Coming—which for Herrick in "Christs twofold coming" (N-257) is merely an opportunity to "heale my Earths infirmitie" (l. 4)[9]—nor on the opportunities for establishing Christ's reign on earth. Rather, the apocalypticism of Anglican survivalism focuses on the mystical marriage of the Lamb of God and on the Last Judgment. Indeed, many Anglican interpreters of the Apocalypse denied the imminence of the millennium entirely. Bishop Joseph Hall, in his commentary on Revelation (1650), discounted the millennium on the grounds that the world was about to end, a view echoed by Bishop Brian Duppa, who observed in the following year that "the world was now drawn low, and in the dreggs."[10] For Herrick and Vaughan, apocalypticism is fundamentally an attempt to escape history by means of an

---

9. All quotations from Herrick's poetry follow *The Complete Poetry of Robert Herrick*, ed. J. Max Patrick (New York: New York University Press, 1963) and are cited by poem and line number in my text. In addition, *Hesperides* is abbreviated H; *Noble Numbers* is abbreviated N.

10. *The Revelation Unrevealed* (1650), 224–27; *The Correspondence of Bishop Brian Duppa and Sir Justinian Isham*, ed. Sir Gyles Isham (Northants. Record Soc., xvii, 1955), 37–38; as cited by Capp, *The Fifth Monarchy Men*, 41. Helen Wilcox, "Exploring the Language of Devotion in the English Revolution," in *Literature and the English Civil War*, ed. Thomas Healy and Jonathan Sawday (Cambridge: Cambridge University Press, 1990), 75–88, rightly observes that devotional poetry in the revolutionary period was obsessed with "last things," and that this focus crossed political and religious divides. Unknowingly, however, the examples she gives to illustrate her point that the focus on "last things" was common to all political persuasions actually reveals the important distinction that I am stressing between Puritan and Anglican apocalypticism. In her selection from the Puritan Vavasor Powell, he pleads, "Come quickly, come Lord Jesus Christ, / Thy Saints do wait and stay / To see thy kingdom on earth / And to behold thine eyes"; while in her quotation from the Anglican Thomas Washbourne, he beseeches, "Come, O come Lord Jesus, / Quickly come and ease us" (quoted on 81). Both poets appeal to apocalypticism, but Powell's plea is millenarian, while Washbourne's is not.

appeal to a vision of eternity and an expression of faith in God's eventual intervention in human affairs. Their embrace of apocalypticism is a strategy for coping with defeat and persecution by placing the suffering of dispossessed Anglicans in the larger context of God's mysterious will and by discovering in the dark conceits of St. John of Patmos prophetic reassurance. The apocalypticism that pervades the poetry of Anglican survivalism provides an eschatological perspective through which to view a present reality of loss and diminishment. This perspective facilitates an acceptance of the current afflictions as trials to be endured and as injustices to be redressed in the fullness of God's time.

II

The persecution of the Church is a reiterated concern in Herrick's *Noble Numbers,* pervasively informing the collection as a whole and contributing to its pronounced sense of apprehensiveness and defeat and to its barely muffled cry of despair. Notably, however, the Church itself is largely absent from the collection, present more as a painful reminder of loss and of how—in the words of the very first line of *Noble Numbers*—"our foule Dayes do exceed our faire" (N-1, l. 1). The Church is explicitly evoked in only a very few poems, such as the tellingly entitled, sardonic indictment of Puritantism "Persecutions purifie" (N-31) and the disarmingly disingenuous "Graces for Children" (N-93), which adopts a child's voice to transform a conventional prayer for the Church and the monarch into a plea fraught with topicality: "He His Church save, and the King, / And our Peace here, like a Spring, / Make it ever flourishing" (ll. 7–9). In conflating the fate of the Church with that of the King in the prospect—and, by the time the poem was published,[11] the retrospect—of a war that was to have disastrous consequences for both, this homely prayer not only announces its ardent devotion to the Established Church, but also mourns

11. The title page of *Noble Numbers* is dated 1647 (which, if the year is given Old Style, could indicate a printing date as late as March 1648), while the title page of *Hesperides* is dated 1648, when the volume containing both parts was actually published. It is not possible to date most of Herrick's poems with much precision, but from internal evidence it is clear that many of them were written very near to the time they were published.

the loss of the pastoral springtime of peace nostalgically associated with the Stuart monarchy. Read in the context of the King's defeat and the Church's desecration by his enemies, this deceptively simple lyric is a surprisingly moving anticipatory tally of the consequences of the Civil War for Church and nation alike. The Church is figured forth most prominently in *Noble Numbers* in the collection's longest and most elaborately orchestrated work, "The Widdowes teares" (N-123). Significantly, however, in this major poem, which brilliantly combines the highly symbolic and the narrowly topical, Herrick's beleaguered Church is personified—and disguised—as Dorcas, the biblical widow who was restored to life by St. Peter. But in "The Widdowes teares" the Church is pointedly and poignantly *not* resurrected. She remains asleep in death, awaiting the restoration of the King—"The Caroll of our gladnesse" (l. 57)—whose return, it is implied, will usher in a new springtime of mirth and the rebirth of the Church and her hierarchy.

Given the transformation of the Established Church by the Parliamentarians, it is not surprising that the Church is so seldom referred to explicitly in *Noble Numbers*. Yet Herrick's Anglicanism is made apparent in the collection in a number of less obvious but unmistakable ways. The poet's frequent adoption of a childish persona affirms, as Leah Marcus has observed, "his commitment to the conservative Anglican ideal of the English as submissive children of their mother the church."[12] Moreover, *Noble Numbers* includes numerous catechetical recitations of Anglican and Arminian doctrinal positions, such as the forthright statement of "His Creed" (N-78) and the series of epigrams, beginning with N-215 and ending with N-220, that rejects predestination and emphasizes man's free will and God's freely offered grace, as well as the personalized adaptation of the English Litany from the Book of Common Prayer, "His Letanie, to the Holy Spirit" (N-41). In addition, the lovingly detailed account of the liturgical ornaments and trappings of the celebration of the Eucharist in "The Paraseve, or Preparation" (N-65) is defiantly Anglican in tone and emphasis:

---

12. *Childhood and Cultural Despair: A Theme and Variations in Seventeenth-Century Literature* (Pittsburgh: University of Pittsburgh Press, 1978), 129. On the didacticism of *Noble Numbers,* see also David W. Landrum, "'To Seek of God': Enthusiasm and the Anglican Response in Robert Herrick's *Noble Numbers,*" *Studies in Philology* 89 (1992): 244–55.

> To a Love-Feast we both invited are:
> The figur'd Damask, or pure Diaper,
> Over the golden Altar now is spread,
> With Bread, and Wine, and Vessells furnished;
> The *sacred Towell*, and the *holy Eure*
> Are ready by, to make the Guests all pure:
> Let's go (my *Alma*) yet e're we receive,
> Fit, fit it is, we have our *Parasceve*.
> Who to that *sweet Bread* unprepar'd doth come
> Better he starv'd, then but to tast one crumme.

Disputes concerning the Eucharist were among the most bitterly contested theological and liturgical issues between Puritans and conservative adherents to the Established Church, and for many Anglicans the de-emphasis of the centrality of the Eucharist was one of the most serious consequences of the Puritan transformation of the Church.[13] Read in the late 1640s, when the Anglican celebration of the Eucharist was forbidden by law, "The Parasceve" is a touching reminder of what has been lost, for the invitation it proffers is one that can no longer be accepted. Indeed, Herrick's choice to write about the preparation for the Eucharist rather than the sacrament itself undoubtedly reflects the fact that the Anglican Eucharist was no longer available to the faithful, having been relegated by the Parliamentarians to an allegedly erroneous past. Significantly, however, the poem is anticipatory rather than reflective; it uses the continuous present tense and describes the

---

13. On the debate over sacraments and services, see Charles H. George and Katherine George, *The Protestant Mind of the English Reformation 1570–1640* (Princeton: Princeton University Press, 1961), 348–63; Nicholas Tyacke, "Puritanism, Arminianism and Counter-Revolution," in *The Origins of the English Civil War*, ed. Conrad Russell (London: Macmillan, 1973), 119–43, and *Anti-Calvinists: The Rise of English Arminianism, c. 1590–1640* (Oxford: Clarendon Press, 1987); and Andrew Foster, "Church Policies of the 1630s," in *Conflict in Early Stuart England: Studies in Religion and Politics 1603–42*, ed. Richard Cust and Ann Hughes (London: Longman, 1989), 193–223. Parliamentary ordinances banned the celebration of Holy Communion on feast days and attempted to permit access to the communion table only to those judged morally and spiritually prepared. For a discussion of the restriction of the celebration of Holy Communion during the period of Parliamentary control, see Morrill, "The Church in England," 105–8. See also the section "Of the Celebration of the Communion, or Sacrament of the Lords Supper" in the *Directory for Public Worship* (January 4, 1644/5) in *Acts and Ordinances of the Interregnum, 1642–1660*, ed. C. H. Firth and R. S. Rait (London: His Majesty's Stationery Office, 1911), 1:596–98.

"Love Feast" as something to come rather than merely something that has been tragically lost. It, thus, looks forward either to the restoration of Anglicanism in England or, perhaps more likely, to the heavenly wedding feast that the Anglican Eucharist foreshadows. Herrick's poem not only rebelliously proclaims a reverence for the liturgical articles of Anglicanism, which he enumerates in carefully measured couplets and with a characteristically sensual vividness, but it also reveals his habitual proclivity toward ceremonialism and communal worship, a proclivity not to be satisfied in the transformed Church of the Parliamentarians. Although "The Parasceve" is addressed to Herrick's soul (*Alma*) and to that extent at least anticipates a private spiritual experience and perhaps even the soul's reception into heaven, nevertheless the conception of the Eucharist as a "Love-Feast," the almost exclusive concern with the external and ceremonial aspects of the celebration, the direct address of the opening lines, and the echo of the Book of Common Prayer's admonition against receiving the Eucharist unworthily are all consonant with the general pattern in *Noble Numbers* of redefining "religious experience away from the idea of inner, individual struggle and toward shared communal observance."[14]

This pattern, which is of course Laudian rather than Puritan, is also apparent in most of the other more elaborate "pious pieces" of *Noble Numbers*. "The Widdowes teares," for example, begins with a kind of *improperia* beseeching "ye Passers by" (l. 3) to share in the grief for the deceased widow who is the British Church: "Come pitie us; and bring your eares, / And eyes, to pitie Widdowes teares" (ll. 5–6), the speaker implores. Moreover, the poem concludes with the enactment of an obsequy, a ceremony performed over the body of the deceased in defiance of the Parliamentarian *Directory for Public Worship*, which specifically prohibited the performance of any rite in the burial of the dead.[15] The anthems and carols composed for presentation in the Chapel Royal at White Hall (N-17, N-96, N-97, N-98, and N-102) are also clearly intended for communal occasions; they not only specifically celebrate Christmas and other holy days repugnant to Puritans (and forbidden in England after 1645), but observe them in ceremonies rife with Anglican liturgical flourishes, featuring incense, holy water, and

14. Marcus, *Childhood and Cultural Despair*, 131.
15. See *Acts and Ordinances of the Interregnum*, 1:604.

raised altars. These poems—especially when read in the context of their publication in *Noble Numbers* in 1647/8, when such celebrations and ceremonies had been prohibited—serve as forceful reminders of the religious and political losses that Herrick and his co-religionists had suffered and as living memorials that bravely defy the prohibitions. They also—subtly but unmistakably—participate in the royalist typological practice of representing the King and his heirs as shadows of Christ,[16] as when in "A Christmas *Caroll*, sung to the King, in the Presence at *White-Hall*" (N-96) there is studied ambiguity in the chorus's honoring the Christ-child as "our King, / And Lord of all this Revelling" (ll. 30–31) and when "Another New-yeeres Gift, or Song for the Circumcision" (N-98) concludes with a joint blessing for the Babe and the King. "The Star-Song: A Caroll to the King; sung at White-Hall" (N-102) celebrates not only the Epiphany of Christ but also the birth of Prince Charles, who, like the Christ-child, is also "*A King, before conception crown'd*" (l. 18). The most daring of Herrick's communal poems that depict the King as a shadow of Christ is "Good Friday: *Rex Tragicus*, or Christ going to His Crosse" (N-263), which not only represents Christ's death as a king's tragedy but also simultaneously imagines the feared execution of Charles I as a reenactment of the Crucifixion. This extraordinary meditation on the Passion also inaugurates a royalist rhetorical tactic that ultimately prevailed even against the polemics of so worthy an opponent as John Milton: the rhetoric of martyrolatry.[17]

If the presence of the Church in *Noble Numbers* is felt largely as a painful absence and conveyed mostly through the loving evocation of its rituals and doctrines, the book's references to persecution and affliction are both direct and numerous. As Anthony Low observed some time ago, "An inordinate number of poems [in *Noble Numbers*] are concerned with the twin themes of affliction and chastisement."[18] Low explains Herrick's preoccupation with affliction as a corollary of his epicureanism, but it seems to me that it is also (or rather) an

---

16. On seventeenth-century royalist typology, see, e.g., Stephen N. Zwicker, *Dryden's Political Poetry: The Typology of King and Nation* (Providence: Brown University Press, 1972), especially 39–55.

17. See my essay, "Herrick's Political Counterplots," *Studies in English Literature* 25 (Winter 1985): 165–82.

18. *Love's Architecture: Devotional Modes in Seventeenth-Century English Poetry* (New York: New York University Press, 1978), 212.

immediate consequence of his own experience of "the times most bad." In coping with his sense of persecution, Herrick develops a hermeneutics of suffering and incorporates the experience of persecution into his salvational history. He clings to a faith that the pain that he and other dispossessed Anglicans must undergo in their season of adversity will serve as a kind of medicine to strengthen them and heal the nation. In "Persecutions purifie," for example, he interprets the purging of the Church by the Puritans as part of God's plan to purify him in the crucible of suffering; while in *"Mora Sponsi,* the stay of the Bridegroome" (N-153), Herrick finds in Christ's apparent abandonment of his Church an opportunity for her to prepare herself for the mystical marriage: "The time the Bridegroom stayes from hence, / Is but the time of penitence," he writes, alluding to Christ's injunction to "repent: for the kingdom of Heaven is at hand" (Matt. 4:17). In "All things run well for the Righteous" (N-44), the poet takes comfort in the fact that "Adverse and prosperous Fortunes both work on / Here, for the righteous mans salvation" (ll. 1–2). And in "Patience, or Comforts in Crosses" (N-57), he declares that the numerous plagues that he has lately suffered do not make him sad, for "the sense / Of suffring gives me patience" (ll. 3–4). In "To God, in time of plundering" (N-124), which immediately follows "The Widdowes teares," he asks for the strength to accept rapine with gratitude: "Let me say grace when there's no more" (l. 6), he prays. The topicality of this poem is indicated by the key word in the title, *plundering,* which alludes to the Committee of Plundered Ministers, the agency empowered by Parliament to eject royalist and Laudian priests from their parishes. Hence, the epigram, obviously written before Herrick's actual expulsion from his pulpit, both anticipates that expulsion from his beloved Church and also takes a gibe at those who were to expel him, labeling them as the plunderers, much as in "Persecutions purifie" he inverts the Puritans' purifying zeal and therapeutic purges and turns them on their heads. Even as they document the pain and suffering of the faithful, these poems struggle to view affliction itself as a manifestation of God's continuing, caring presence in the world.

The burden of Herrick's poems on affliction is to define persecution as a means God uses to test the faithful and to shape them for his own mysterious ends. By placing persecution in the larger context of God's will and interpreting his suffering as an opportunity for growth, Herrick is able to find comfort even in the presence of sacrilege, plundering, and "Crosses" of all kinds. But the apparent equanimity with which he accepts persecution stems primarily from his intensely held conviction that the injustices of this life will be redressed at the Last Judgment. Herrick's appeal to the Last Judgment is a component of the Stoicism and pessimism that color all of his work, even those poems of *Hesperides* that most delight in the pleasures of this life; but it must also be seen as part of a strategy of Anglican survivalism, an attempt to cope with defeat in the Civil War by trusting that God's stones will be "hurl'd / Against the wicked, in another world" ("To God," N-74, ll. 3–4). This strategy is enunciated most clearly in another poem addressed "To God" (N-25), a beautifully accented, concrete yet evocative lyric in which Herrick compares himself with St. John of Patmos and explicitly evokes the Apocalypse, from which the poem derives all of its imagery:

> Do with me, God! as Thou didst deal with *John*,
> (Who writ that heavenly *Revelation*)
> Let me (like him) first cracks of thunder heare;
> Then let the Harps inchantments strike mine eare;
> Here give me thornes; there, in thy Kingdome, set
> Upon my head the golden coronet;
> There give me day; but here my dreadfull night:
> My sackcloth here; but there my *Stole* of white.

This lyric, striking in its balanced contrasts and resonant plainness of style, encapsulates Herrick's apocalypticism and clarifies its relationship to his hermeneutics of suffering. The apocalypticism here is quite specifically nonmillenarian; the insistent contrasts of heaven and earth focus the poem not on the possible creation of a New Jerusalem on earth but on Herrick's prospective enjoyment of bliss in heaven as recompense for having endured tribulations on earth for Christ's sake. Faith in the ultimate rewards of the Apocalypse and its redressing of earthly injustice consoles Herrick in his oppressive present. The dreadful night of the Anglican defeat is made bearable by the sweet prospect of apocalyptic victory.

The apocalyptic strategy of Anglican survivalism is implicit as well in "Teares" (N-90), which declares that "Our present Teares here . . . / Are but the handsells of our joyes hereafter." More pointedly, in "Doomes-Day" (N-126), the Apocalypse is envisioned as a time when the faithful will have an opportunity to judge their enemies: "Let not that Day

Gods Friends and Servants scare: / The Bench is then their place; and not the Barre." The anticipation of ultimately judging and punishing those who desecrate the Church helps sustain the faithful as they taste the bitter ashes of defeat. They find comfort in the anticipation of apocalyptic justice: "He that ascended in a cloud, shall come / In clouds, descending to the publike *Doome*" ("Clouds," N-162), Herrick writes, alluding to the prophecy of Revelation 1:7, "Behold he cometh with clouds; and every eye shall see him, and they also which pierced him: and all kindreds of the earth shall wail because of him" (see also Rev. 20:11–15). The topicality of this sentiment is clear in "Comforts in contentions" (N-163), a succinct warning to the victorious Parliamentarians: "The same, who crownes the Conquerour, will be / A coadjutor in the Agonie." This tart couplet economically anticipates the regicide, equates the prospective death of Charles I with the Passion of Christ, and prophesies a horrible judgment on those who would destroy the Stuart monarchy by crowning a conquering Parliamentarian. Most revealing, however, is its title, which identifies the prospective punishment as a source of comfort in a time of contention. By placing human history in the context of apocalyptic history, Herrick is able to evade the reality of the royalist defeat even as he bemoans the anticipated regicide that is the most spectacular fruit of that elided reality. Moreover, his steadfast faith in apocalyptic justice buttresses his resolute commitment to the royalist cause, as in the tellingly titled "Neutrality loathsome" (N-54), which echoes Revelation 3:15–16, implicitly applying the biblical injunction to the contemporaneous religiopolitical disputes: "Either be hot, or cold: God doth despise, / Abhorre, and spew out all Neutralities" (ll. 3–4).

Herrick scatters poems on the Apocalypse throughout *Noble Numbers* (in addition to those already cited, see, e.g., N-74, N-142, N-149, N-162, N-198, N-224, and N-234) and frequently incorporates apocalyptic imagery in others, thereby establishing the eschatological perspective as a necessary context that informs both the book as a whole and its individual components. In "To God" (N-232), for example, he opposes the apocalyptic anger of the God of power to the transcendent mercy of the God of love:

> Come to me God; but do not come
> To me, as to the gen'rall Doome,

> In power; or come Thou in that state,
> When Thou Thy Lawes didst promulgate,
> When as the Mountaine quak'd for dread,
> And sullen clouds bound up his head.
> No, lay thy stately terrours by,
> To talke with me familiarly;
> For if Thy thunder-claps I heare,
> I shall less swoone, then die for feare.
> Speake thou of love and I'le reply
> By way of *Epithalamie,*
> Or sing of *mercy*, and I'le suit
> To it my Violl and my Lute:
> Thus let Thy lips but love distill,
> Then come my God, and hap what will.

In this poem, which effectively juxtaposes the contradictory moods of John's Revelation, Herrick envisions himself among the harpers in heaven (Rev. 14:2), who are redeemed by virtue of God's overwhelming love. The success of this beautiful lyric lies in the disarming simplicity and concreteness of its petition to a tender and gently loving God, to whom Herrick responds with a characteristic immediacy and sharp vividness, pledging eagerly to use his poetic powers to celebrate in a nuptial song the mystical marriage of the Lamb. But this limpid and pleasingly intimate vision depends in large part on its stark contrast with the equally vividly sketched God of power and the fearsomeness of the "gen'rall Doome" in which God's enemies will be punished. Significantly, the God of power is "stately" while the God of love is familiar, crystallizing a public/private dichotomy in which Herrick both contemplates the destruction of the world as a wrathful act of public policy and at the same time anticipates—and touchingly imagines—a tenderly intimate relationship with a merciful God. Hence, even this affectingly personal vision of a heavenly afterlife spent worshiping a God of love is inseparably linked to Herrick's fervent expectation of an apocalyptic redressing of public grievances by a God of wrath. The contrast of a God of power and a God of love is, of course, commonplace in Christian thought and poetry, developed most memorably among seventeenth-century religious lyrics by Herbert in "The Flower"; but Herrick's distinct association of the God of power with public issues and the God of love with personal ones strikingly differentiates his perspective from Herbert's more intensely private application of the familiar paradigm, and it underlines the primacy of the political context for a reading of Herrick's religious lyrics.

The apocalyptic imagery Herrick uses in two other visionary poems similarly reveals the political dimension of even those religious lyrics most apparently removed from mundane concerns. In "On Heaven" (N-106), for example, Herrick also envisions the Throne of God, that "happy place!" (l. 3) where the faithful will be rewarded and will perpetually hymn the praises of the triune God. The description of the saints, each adorned "In long white stole, / And Palmes in hand" (ll. 8–9), like Herrick's anticipation of a *"Stole* of white" (l. 8) in "To God" (N-25), alludes to the description in Revelation 7:9 of the multitude who stood before the Lamb "clothed with white robes, and palms in their hands." These, an angel exegete explains, "are they which came out of great tribulation, and have washed their robes, and made them white in the blood of the Lamb" (Rev. 7:14). Similarly, "The white Island: or place of the Blest" (N-128) also uses the apocalyptic appellation *white* to define heaven in opposition to a world of persecution and suffering. This world, the *"Isle of Dreames"* (l. 1), is one where "we sit by sorrowes streames" reciting "Teares and terrors" (ll. 2–3), a description that recalls Psalm 137, a song of exile that looks forward to the defeat of enemies and the restoration of the faithful: "By the rivers of Babylon, there we sat down, yea, we wept, when we remembered Zion" (v. 1), the psalmist laments. In contrast, Herrick depicts that *"whiter Island"* (l. 9) of eternity as a place of respite from adversity and sorrow. "There in calm and cooling sleep / We our eyes shall never steep; / But eternall watch shall keep, / Attending" (ll. 17–20), Herrick writes, alluding to Revelation 7:15–17, which describes the ultimate bliss of those who have endured great tribulations in the service of God. Roger Rollin has somewhat slightingly dismissed Herrick's conception of heaven in "The white Island" as simply a "minimization of pain and maximization of pleasure" in accord with his epicureanism,[19] but such a view ignores the fact that the imagined afterlife of this poem is specifically apocalyptic, reflecting the promise of Revelation 21:3–4

---

19. *Robert Herrick* (New York: Twayne, 1966), 162. Similar judgments are offered by John Press, *Robert Herrick,* Writers and Their Work, no. 132 (London: Longmans, Green, 1961), 31–32, and by Low, *Love's Architecture,* 214.

that in the New Jerusalem the blessed will dwell with God, and "God shall wipe away all tears from their eyes; and there shall be no more death, neither sorrow, nor crying, neither shall there be any more pain: for the former things are passed away." Herrick's most intense eschatological visions are not exercises in indulgence or expressions of epicureanism; rather, they are rooted in his experience of persecution. His anticipation of glory is indelibly informed by his consciousness of having suffered for faith's sake.

Noble Numbers concludes with a beautiful but extremely curious sequence of Holy Week poems, beginning with the Crucifixion in "Good Friday: *Rex Tragicus*" and ending with three poems set in Christ's empty sepulcher (N-269, N-270, N-271). What is startling about this series is that it does not culminate, as one would expect, in an Easter celebration. As Leah Marcus has observed, "it is a descent not followed by ascent—a crucifixion and burial without an Easter resurrection."[20] *Noble Numbers* thus ends on a note of sorrow, with the poet "Ravisht" and "Confus'd" in the achingly empty tomb of the vanished Christ ("To his Saviours Sepulcher: his Devotion," N-269, ll. 20, 21). Herrick deliberately withholds the happy ending that would translate the tragedy of Good Friday into the triumphant Christian comedy of Easter, and he does so it seems to me in order to make a fundamentally political statement. Yet another instance of the Stoic pessimism that recurs in both *Hesperides* and *Noble Numbers,* the failure of ascent is a pregnant comment on what Herrick perceived as the dolorous state of affairs in England in the late 1640s. In the final poem of the sequence, "His coming to the Sepulcher" (N-271), Herrick plaintively questions the "white Angell" (l. 3) who attends the tomb as to where Christ has gone. The angel does not reply, but in effect the answer is given in the couplet that concludes *Noble Numbers,* the untitled gnomic utterance that quotes the apocalyptic definition of Christ as the beginning and the end, the alpha and the omega (N-272; the phrase is repeated several times in Revelation). This answer is not so much evasive as a mysterious yet pointed prophecy of apocalyptic justice. The eschatological expectations on which *Noble Numbers* ends constitute a grim warning to those responsible for the troublesome times; but also implicit in the prophecy is a message of comfort to the faithful, those who

---

20. *Childhood and Cultural Despair,* 137.

have not abandoned their imprisoned King and besieged Church. The withholding of the anticipated Resurrection at the end of *Noble Numbers* is at once a measure of despair and an act of faith. This conclusion expresses profound sorrow at the contemporaneous religiopolitical situation in England, but it also pledges its author's endurance—his continuing commitment to the vanished Christ and the wounded Church—even in "the times most bad."

III

Like Herrick, Vaughan was deeply affected by the religious and political events of his era. The title of his collection *Silex Scintillans* was suggested by a passage in John Nieremberg's *De Arte Voluntatis*. Vaughan's translation of the work, entitled *Of Temperance and Patience*, renders that passage as follows: "Certaine Divine Raies breake out of the Soul in adversity, like sparks of fire out of the afflicted *flint*."[21] Undoubtedly the most significant and distressing of the adversities that afflicted Vaughan and helped give rise to his poetry was the Parliamentarian despoliation of his beloved Church. In *The Mount of Olives: or, Solitary Devotions*, he addresses God as "O Thou, that art every where" and laments that the church buildings are now "vilified and shut up" (*W*, 147). He enjoins his readers, the Anglican faithful, to exercise their religion privately "in these times of persecution and triall" (*W*, 149). In the same work, he offers "A Prayer in time of persecution and Heresie," indignantly and sorrowfully rehearsing the disfigurement of the Church by the Parliamentarians:

> Consider, O Lord, the teares of thy Spouse which are daily upon her cheeks, whose adversaries are grown mighty, and her enemies prosper. The wayes of *Zion* do mourne, our beautiful gates are shut up, and the Comforter that should relieve our souls is gone far from us. Thy Service and thy Sabbaths, thy own sacred institutions and the pledges of thy love are denied unto us; Thy Ministers are trodden down, and the basest of the people are set up in thy holy place. (*W*, 166)

---

21. All quotations from Vaughan follow the text of *The Works of Henry Vaughan*, ed. L. C. Martin, 2d ed. (Oxford: Clarendon Press, 1957); the prose works are cited by the abbreviation *W* and page numbers and the poetry by line numbers.

Vaughan's painful awareness of loss and persecution are everywhere reflected and expressed in *Silex Scintillans,* manifested especially in the pervasive tone of gloom and pessimism and the sense of decline in this shadowy, "late and dusky" ("Abels blood," l. 51), "last and lewdest age" ("White Sunday," l. 39); in the recurrent, bitter attacks on Puritans, who are mocked as impudent, stiff-necked, self-styled saints and hypocritical "black Parasites" ("The Proffer," l. 1), capable of even greater cruelties than the soldiers who tormented Christ; and in the repeated—and repeatedly frustrated—longing for deliverance from civil and religious bondage, so that Englishmen might learn obedience, order, peace, and love, and thereby "Become an humble, holy nation" ("The Constellation," l. 56). Although sometimes regarded as the work of a withdrawn contemplative, Vaughan's poetry is actually thoroughly immersed in the concerns of his contemporary world, expressing hatred, bitterness, and despair, as well as transcendence.[22] A profoundly political account of the spiritual life during the Puritans' "sad captivity" ("L'Envoy," l. 62) of the Church, *Silex Scintillans* is the masterwork of the poetry of Anglican survivalism.

As in *Noble Numbers,* the Church in *Silex Scintillans* is conspicuous by virtue of its absence. Driven underground by the Parliamentarians, the Church is most often present as a powerful and haunting memory, a symbol of loss and abandonment. However, in "Regeneration," the first poem of *Silex Scintillans,* the poet-pilgrim discovers in a garden encircled by trees the architecture of Anglicanism, and he learns not only that the House of God can be anywhere but also that the garden is a temple more rewarding and more intimate than that edifice now so "destituted" and rent by the Puritans.[23] Vaughan's representation of

---

22. On this point, see James D. Simmonds, *Masques of God: Form and Theme in the Poetry of Henry Vaughan* (Pittsburgh: University of Pittsburgh Press, 1972), 20.

23. See Claude J. Summers and Ted-Larry Pebworth, "Vaughan's Temple in Nature and the Context of 'Regeneration,'" *Journal of English and Germanic Philology* 74 (1975): 351–60; rpt. in *Essential Articles for the Study of Henry Vaughan,* ed. Alan Rudrum (Hamden, Conn.: Archon, 1987), 215–25. Other recent studies that stress Vaughan's response to contemporaneous social and political conditions include E. L. Marilla, "The Mysticism of Henry Vaughan: Some Observations," *Review of English Studies* n.s. 18 (1967): 164–66; Simmonds, *Masques of God;* Marcus, *Childhood and Cultural Despair;* Jonathan F. S. Post, *Henry Vaughan: The Unfolding Vision* (Princeton: Princeton University Press, 1982); Robert Wilcher, "'Then keep the ancient way!': A Study of Henry Vaughan's *Silex Scintillans,*" *Durham University Journal* n.s.

the Church as a garden is inspired by the Song of Songs, which is traditionally interpreted as a love song between Christ and his Church, and which describes the Bride as an enclosed garden, as in the verses that Vaughan uses as an epigraph to "Regeneration" (4:12–15). Thus, although the Church has been desecrated and forced to flee from its (now desanctified) buildings, it has not been utterly destroyed. In *Silex Scintillans*, it is figured forth variously as, in addition to the enclosed garden, a ravished bride forcibly separated from her bridegroom ("The Brittish Church"); as a spouse whose "perfect, and pure dress" has been rent by Puritan "zeale," "noise," and "black self-wil" in this time of disobedience and false prophets ("The Constellation," ll. 57, 40, 44, 37); as an oppressed and bowed tree watered by the tears of the faithful ("The Palm-tree"); and as a spring that—as the result of the Parliamentarian transformation—has become polluted, even poisoned, "And 'stead of Phisick, a disease" ("Religion," l. 44). In the conclusion of "Religion," Vaughan invokes the precedent of the miracles at Bethesda and Cana (John 5:1–15; 2:1–12) to plead for divine intervention, imploring Christ to heal the diseased Church and to restore the fellowship of Holy Communion:

> Heale then these waters, Lord; or bring thy flock,
> Since these are troubled, to the springing rock,
> Looke downe great Master of the feast: O shine,
> And turn once more our *Water* into *Wine*!
> (ll. 49–52)

Here the poet contrasts the polluted waters of the transfigured Church and the "springing rock" of the enduring Church. The "springing rock" alludes to Exodus 17:6, in which God instructs Moses to smite the rock of Horeb, whereupon "there shall come water out of it, that the people may drinke." The poem's epigraph—"*My sister, my spouse is a garden inclosed, as a Spring shut up, and a fountain sealed up*" (Song 4:12)— clearly locates that springing rock in the enclosed garden of the allegorized Song of Songs, a temple in nature to which the Established Church has fled in a time of persecution. The intervention of Christ, the "great Master of the feast," can restore the Church and its sacraments and

---

15 (1983): 11–24; Noel Kennedy Thomas, *Henry Vaughan: Poet of Revelation* (Worthing, West Sussex: Churchman, 1986); and Wall, *Transformations of the Word*.

thereby heal the nation. Vaughan knows, however, that even in the absence of that intervention, during the dark days of civil and religious oppression, the spirit of God continues to reside in the human heart, "that dread place, that awful Cell, / That secret Ark, where the milde Dove doth dwell / When the proud waters rage: when Heathens rule / By Gods permission, and man turns a Mule" ("Jacobs Pillow, and Pillar," ll. 27–30).

Louis Martz has observed that Vaughan's poems typically develop in terms of the Bible, nature, and the self, pointedly remarking that "it is as though the earthly church had vanished, and man were left to work alone with God."[24] The banishment of the earthly church is indeed one of the principal realities with which Vaughan must cope in *Silex Scintillans*, and may, in fact, account for Vaughan's repeated quests for direct encounters with God and for his recurrent laments that God and the angels no longer frequent the earth; yet Martz's statement is misleading insofar as it implies that the Church is irrelevant or inconsequential to Vaughan's work. On the contrary, in the preface to the expanded, second edition of *Silex Scintillans*, the poet specifically dedicates "this my poor *Talent* to the *Church*, under the *protection* and *conduct* of her *glorious Head:* who (if he will vouchsafe to *own* it and *go along* with it) can make it as useful now in the *publick*, as it hath been to me in *private*" (*W*, 392). The ambiguity as to whether the Church's "*glorious Head*" refers to Christ or to the exiled heir of the martyred King Charles I is probably deliberate. In any case, Vaughan's insistence on a public role for *Silex Scintillans* is a crucial aspect of the large and ambitious project that the collection attempts. That project is, in the words of John N. Wall, no less than "to find ways of giving us the experience of Anglicanism apart from Anglicanism, or to make possible the continued experience of being a part of the Body of Christ in Anglican terms in the absence of the ways in which those terms had their meaning prior to the 1640s."[25] As Wall has demonstrated, Vaughan

---

24. *The Paradise Within: Studies in Vaughan, Traherne and Milton* (New Haven: Yale University Press, 1964), 12.

25. *Transformations of the Word*, 303. Wall's discussion of Vaughan provides a full and convincing account of how the absence of the Established Church affected *Silex Scintillans*. Wall anticipates my own concerns, but I am less interested in offering a comprehensive study of *Silex Scintillans* than in emphasizing the strategies of Anglican survivalism that it shares with *Noble Numbers*.

uses a variety of strategies—evocation of Herbert as an Anglican poet-priest, typological language, echoes of the Book of Common Prayer, incorporation of the Anglican liturgical calendar, celebration of Anglican rituals, biblical analogies, eschatological perspectives and expectations, etc.—to sustain Anglicanism in the dangerous and difficult days of its official banishment. Vaughan claims the period of isolation and persecution as an opportunity to nurture the community of believers, to chronicle their sufferings, and to exemplify means of keeping the faith in a land grown dark and inhospitable. Always conscious of the adversity that surrounds him, Vaughan nevertheless repeatedly expresses his faith in the continuity and eventual vindication of the beleaguered Church in heaven if not on earth.

Like Herrick, Vaughan also turns to the Apocalypse for comfort and sustenance. Indeed, St. John's Revelation is one of Vaughan's key texts in *Silex Scintillans*,[26] the source or inspiration for many of Vaughan's most breathtakingly beautiful visionary passages, including, for example, the stunning opening trope of "The World": "I saw Eternity the other night / Like a great *Ring* of pure and endless light, / All calm, as it was bright" (ll. 1–3). The great ring is finally revealed to be the wedding ring of Christ and his Church: *"This Ring the Bride-groome did for none provide / But for his bride"* (ll. 59–60), an unidentified but obviously divine or angelic exegete whispers in explanation. Insistently contrasting darkness and light, the timebound and the eternal, the world of the here and now and the New Jerusalem to come, "The World" condemns the pride and lust of the doting lover, darksome statesman, fearful miser, and downright epicure, all of whom "prefer dark night / Before true light" (ll. 49–50); but it celebrates the comparative few who follow the will of God and suffer for his sake—who "all

---

26. The fullest study of Vaughan's use of Revelation is Thomas, *Henry Vaughan: Poet of Revelation*, especially 134–96. See also Barbara K. Lewalski, *Protestant Poetics and the Seventeenth-Century Religious Lyric* (Princeton: Princeton University Press, 1979), 324–26; and Post, *Henry Vaughan: The Unfolding Vision*, 186–211, for discussions of Vaughan's apocalypticism. Wall, in *Transformations of the Word*, also expresses awareness of Vaughan's reliance on Revelation but prefers to speak of Vaughan's eschatological perspectives and expectations rather than of his apocalypticism; he criticizes Post's argument that *Silex Scintillans II* is an apocalyptic work (Wall, 417). But Wall is simply wrong in his contention that Vaughan never resorts to apocalyptic imagery (335), and his distinction between apocalyptic and eschatological discourse is fuzzy.

this while did weep and sing" (l. 46). Because of their patience and faithfulness, the latter—and only they—are permitted to soar "into the *Ring*" (l. 47) and participate in the mystical marriage of the Church to Christ. A key metaphor in the poem's conclusion is flight. The faithful few "soar'd up," while the benighted many "would use no wing" (ll. 47, 48). The figure of the wing is probably meant to allude to Herbert's "Easter Wings," in which the speaker begs of Christ, "With thee / Let me combine / And feel this day thy victorie: / For, if I imp my wing on thine, / Affliction shall advance the flight in me" (ll. 16–20). Hence, the apocalyptic resonance of "The World" is intimately bound up with the experience of affliction. The suffering of the Anglican faithful will be rewarded in the mystical marriage, while those who persecuted or abandoned the Church will be excluded from glory.

As in *Noble Numbers*, the apocalyptic perspective in Vaughan's collection most frequently serves to develop a hermeneutics of suffering and to remind the poet and his readers of God's promises to the faithful. "Buriall," for example, concludes with a desperate and heartfelt plea that Christ fulfill the promise repeated at the end of Revelation to return speedily (see Rev. 22:7, 12, and 20): "Lord haste, Lord come, / O come Lord *Jesus* quickly" (ll. 39–40), Vaughan beseeches. But in the first poem entitled "Day of Judgement," he sketches a vivid picture of the Last Judgment, then realizes that he is not yet ready for it to occur. He requests—in lines probably inspired by Herrick's epigrams, such as "Persecutions purifie" and "Patients, or Comforts in Crosses"—that God first prepare him for the prophesied day through suffering:

> Give me, O give me Crosses here,
>   Still more afflictions lend,
> That pill, though bitter, is most deare
>   That brings health in the end.
>   (ll. 33–36)

The efficacy of suffering is also expressed in "Chearfulness," which declares in words that echo the sentiments of Herrick's epigrams (and quote the last line of N-232), "Affliction thus, meere pleasure is, / And hap what will, / If [Christ] be in't, 'tis welcome still" (ll. 9–11); and in "Providence," which, like so many of Herrick's poems, prescribes faith as a means of enduring persecution. The adversity of "Providence" specifically includes that visited upon the Church by the Puritans, as the code words *plundered* and *sequester* make clear:

> I will not fear what man
> With all his plots and power can;
> Bags that wax old may plundered be,
> But none can sequester or let
> A state that with the Sun doth set
> And comes next morning fresh as he.
> (ll. 19–24)

As in many of Herrick's poems, suffering is embraced as a necessary prelude to glory in "Palm-Sunday," in which Vaughan exults, "If I lose all, and must endure / The proverb'd griefs of holy *Job,* / I care not, so I may secure / But one *green Branch* and a *white robe*" (ll. 43–46); while in "The Dawning," the apocalyptic anticipation—"Ah! What time wilt thou come? when shalt that crie / The *Bridegroome's Comming!* fill the sky?" (ll. 1–2)—culminates in the resolution to work in the service of Christ "all my busie age" (l. 37) and to remain alert and prepared, watching for "the Break of thy great day" (l. 48).

In other poems, such as "The Feast," "The Throne," "The Wreath," and "Tears" (a poem that may have been inspired by Herrick's epigrams of the same title, N-90, N-139, and N-145), Vaughan, much like Herrick in "The white Island," contemplates life with God in heaven, envisioning it in images derived from the Apocalypse. In "The Wreath," Vaughan plans to bring Christ "a twin'd wreath of *grief* and *praise,* / Praise soil'd with tears, and tears again / Shining with joy" (ll. 9–11), when he arrives at "that glad place, / Where cloudless Quires sing without tears, / Sing thy just praise, and see thy face" (ll. 17–19). One of many poems in *Silex Scintillans* expressing reverence for the Eucharist (see, e.g., "The Dressing" and "The Law, and the Gospel"), "The Feast" is especially interesting for its imagining the marriage supper of the Lamb in terms of the Anglican Eucharist, or, perhaps more accurately, discerning in the Eucharist a foretaste of heaven. Like Herrick's "The Paraseve," "The Feast" is anticipatory, and its emphasis is similarly on the preparation necessary for receiving the Eucharist. "Come while my heart is clean & steddy!" Vaughan implores, "While Faith and Grace / Adorn the place, / Making dust and ashes ready" (ll. 3–6).

The Bread and Wine of the Eucharist sustain Vaughan in the present world, even when the Anglican celebration is forbidden ("Under veyls here / Thou art my chear, / Present and sure without my seeing" [ll. 40–42]), by their lessons of Christ's past suffering and their promise of the forthcoming Heavenly banquet, as emphasized in the epigraph, *"Blessed are they, which are called unto the marriage Supper of the Lamb!"* (Rev. 19:9).

In still other poems, however, Vaughan invokes the terrors of the Apocalypse as a warning to his own depraved age, as in the dramatic conclusion to "Corruption":

> Sin triumphs still, and man is sunk below
>   The Center, and his shrowd;
> All's in deep sleep, and night; Thick darknes lyes
>   And hatcheth o'r thy people;
> But hark! what trumpets that? what Angel cries
>   *Arise! Thrust in thy sickle.*
>
>   (ll. 35–40)

The angelic shriek echoes Revelation 14:14–20, and prophesies that, like Babylon, the corrupt English commonwealth of Vaughan's day will also fall, be harvested by angels bearing scythes, and finally be "cast into the great winepress of the wrath of God" (v. 19). That prospect is similarly at the heart of "The Seed growing secretly," a poem infused with apocalyptic imagery. It concludes with an injunction to the Anglican faithful to "Keep clean, bear fruit, earn life and watch / Till the white winged Reapers come!" (ll. 47–48). In "Abels blood," those royalists and Anglicans who have suffered death at the hands of the Parliamentarians and Puritans are specifically identified with the souls under the altar of Revelation 6:9–10: "And when he had opened the fifth seal, I saw under the altar the souls of them that were slain for the word of God, and for the testimony which they held; And they cried with a loud voice, saying How long, O Lord, holy and true, dost thou not judge and avenge our blood on them that dwell on the earth?" Vaughan's poem, his most explicit poetic indictment of the Civil War's bloodshed, finally disavows any desire for earthly vengeance, but the souls' "incessant cry / . . . *How long?*" (ll. 21–22) nevertheless implacably prophesies the vengeance of God on behalf of those who suffered and died in his cause.

In the second poem entitled "The day of Judgement," the Silurist combines the contrasting moods of Revelation much as Herrick does in "To God" (N-232), but in Vaughan's work the emphasis falls decidedly on the punishment to be meted out to God's enemies rather than on the intimate pleasures of heaven. "The day of Judgement" opens with a confident plea for the "Dearly lov'd day!" to arrive (l. 12). "I / With earnest groans for freedom cry, / My fellow-creatures too say, *Come!*" (ll. 13–15), Vaughan writes, happily anticipating release and glory. But he then turns to the abuses of the time, particularly those committed by the Puritans in their hostility to the Church and especially their distortions and misinterpretations of the Bible:

> Dear Lord! make haste,
> Sin every day commits more waste,
> And thy old enemy, which knows
> His time is short, more raging grows.
> Nor moan I onely (though profuse)
> Thy Creatures bondage and abuse;
> But what is highest sin and shame,
> The vile despight done to thy name;
> The forgeries, which impious wit
> And power force on Holy Writ,
> With all detestable designs
> That may dishonor those pure lines.
> (ll. 27–38)

The poem concludes by boldly suggesting that mercy, the greatest attribute of God, ought to be denied to the enemies of the Church, who respond to him with "meer disdain" (l. 43). In lines that combine bitter denunciation and fervent expectation, Vaughan begs for the swift execution of God's justice:

> let not man say
> *Thy arm doth sleep;* but write this day
> Thy judging one: Descend, descend!
> Make all things new! and without end!
> (ll. 43–46)

The allusion is, of course, to Christ's promise in Revelation 21 of "a new heaven and a new earth" (v. 1), a pledge that contains within it both rewards for the true and faithful (vv. 3–7) and ghastly punishments for others, who "shall have their part in the lake which burneth with fire and brimstone" (v. 8). "The day of Judgement" leaves no doubt that Vaughan would cheerfully consign the Puritan captors of his Church to the blazing lake.

For all Vaughan's bitterness against those whom he sees as despoilers of his Church, however, he is capable of embracing a somewhat more moderate stance than the uncharitable one of "The day of Judgement." In "White Sunday," for example, he condemns Puritan pretensions, but he pleads for the "Prophetic fire" (l. 8) of the Pentecost (as opposed to the Apocalypse) to "refine us" (l. 61). And in "The Men of War," he is fortified by the prophecy of Revelation 13:10 that "He that leadeth into captivity shall go into captivity," which is versified in the poem's first eight lines, and by the example of Christ's gentle response to persecution. Although he is aware that Christ has armies in heaven "which fight, / And follow thee all cloath'd in white" (ll. 21–22), he is even more conscious that the savior willingly chose martyrdom on earth. The poet rejoices in the fact that the true saints (as opposed to the self-styled Puritan ones) are not conquerors—a term also used by Herrick as a code word for the Parliamentarians—but long-suffering, meek, and defeated. (Cf. the description of "the patience of the Saints" in "The Palm Tree," ll. 17–24, and l. 72 of "St. Mary Magdalen": "Who Saint themselves, they are no *Saints*.") The pacificism of Vaughan's apocalypticism—also apparent in "Abels blood"—is in distinct contrast to that of the Puritan millenarians, who interpreted the military imagery of Daniel and Revelation as authorizing literal warfare.[27] In "The Men of War," Vaughan disavows violence, vengeance, and the persecution of others; he prays for humility, peace, and the patience of the true saints, so that he can be "to my greatest haters kinde" (l. 44). Finally, he hopes that when he and the conquerors are brought before the judgment throne,

>I may be found (preserv'd by thee)
>Amongst that chosen company,
>Who by no blood (here) overcame
>But the blood of the *blessed Lamb*.
>   (ll. 49–52)

---

27. See Capp, *The Fifth Monarchy Men*, 36.

The apocalyptic perspective of "The Men of War" implies punishment for the Parliamentarian conquerors, but what is most interesting about the poem is its recognition of the need for patience and forbearance. This need may itself be in direct proportion to the rage that the persecution of the Church roused in Vaughan, but his forswearing of bloodshed and his adoption of an eschatological perspective that trusts in the efficacy of Christ's blood to right all earthly injustice are themselves deliberate strategies for coping with oppression and a catastrophic history. They are, in fact, the very strategies that Herrick embraced and recommended in *Noble Numbers.*

In the final poem of *Silex Scintillans*, "L'Envoy," Vaughan once again invokes God's apocalyptic judgment on the enemies of the Church, the haters who "brag / Thy seamless coat is grown a rag" and who "vex thy spouse, / And take the glory of thy house / To deck their own" (ll. 29–30, 33–35). He pleads that Christ will "Dry up their arms" and "Frustrate those cancerous, close arts / Which cause solution in all parts, / And strike them dumb, who for meer words / Wound thy beloved, more then swords" (ll. 33, 39–42). But he then counters this invocation of wrath with a positive vision of an England cleansed and united by the returned Christ and his transforming grace:

> Dear Lord, do this! and then let grace
> Descend, and hallow all the place.
> Incline each hard heart to do good,
> And cement us with thy sons blood,
> That like true sheep, all in one fold
> We may be fed, and one minde hold.
> (ll. 43–48)

In this healed and renewed England, mercy will reign "and blessings flow / As fast, as persecutions now" (ll. 57–58). Although Vaughan indubitably sees judgment as a necessary prerequisite to the recovery of order and unanimity within the Anglican Establishment, the final vision of *Silex Scintillans* is of the joyous restoration of the Church through the direct intervention of the returned Christ. If this is a millenarian dream, it is quite different from the kingdom of the saints imagined by the Puritans. A vision of the future that comments disparagingly on an oppressive present, it at once signifies both Vaughan's desperate desire to be released from "our sad captivity" and the stubborn tenacity of Anglican survivalism.

Herrick and Vaughan are not often considered in the same breath. As poets, each is distinct and in many ways quite different from the other. Yet they shared a similar political perspective and embraced like responses to what they discerned as the experience of persecution. In fact, it is quite probable that Herrick's undervalued *Noble Numbers* exerted considerable influence on Vaughan's more widely celebrated *Silex Scintillans*. For both men, the transformation of the Established Church by the victorious Parliamentarians was a public and personal disaster, one that necessarily and profoundly affected their art. The Puritan triumph is indeed the public context that most frequently and fully impinges on both *Noble Numbers* and *Silex Scintillans*. In reaction to the religiopolitical upheavals of their day, Herrick and Vaughan attempted both to mourn the desecration of the Church and to infuse the spirit and distinctive practices of Anglicanism into their poetry. They coped with their sense of alienation and persecution by cultivating patience and faith, passive resistance and active anticipation. They adopted a hermeneutics of suffering and an eschatological perspective that assured them of recompense for their tribulations in the better world to come. In the process, they practiced the poetry of Anglican survivalism, a poetry that concretely and movingly illustrates the intermingling of the spiritual and the political in the seventeenth-century religious lyric.

THE POETRY OF SUPPLICATION
Toward a Cultural Poetics of the Religious Lyric

❋ ❋ ❋   *Michael C. Schoenfeldt*   ❋ ❋ ❋

It is ironic that readers have tended to interpret the seventeenth-century religious lyric in deliberate isolation from social and cultural forces, since the early seventeenth-century practitioners of the devotional lyric—primarily Donne and Herbert—were themselves so profoundly aware of the social dimensions of their work. Yet it is also historically explicable, since the curve of devotional utterance in that turbulent century traces a progressive withdrawal from the social—a withdrawal that our culture still endorses. In this essay I hope to illustrate the genesis of the very assumptions that still hinder our full comprehension of the seventeenth-century religious lyric by attending to the social resonances of religious poems by Donne and Herbert, and by indicating that something significantly different is going on in the religious poems of Vaughan, Herrick, and Traherne. I hope, furthermore, to show how the tools made available by current theoretical work in a range of fields are particularly appropriate to the project of excavating the unmistakable riches that the early seventeenth-century conflation of social and devotional languages produced.

The constricting parameters of critical discourse about the religious lyric were set by Samuel Johnson, and they are worth analyzing in some depth in order to distend them. In his discussion of why Edmund

Waller's "Sacred Poems do not please like some of his other works," Johnson takes the opportunity to explain why, in his opinion, "poetical devotion [in general] cannot often please" in comparison to other subjects. "The essence of poetry is invention," observes Johnson, "such invention as, by producing something unexpected, surprises and delights. . . . [But] the topics of devotion are few . . . [and] can receive no grace from novelty of sentiment, and very little from novelty of expression." The divine subject of religious devotion, moreover, leaves little room for the creative expansion that poetry entails: "Omnipotence cannot be exalted; Infinity cannot be amplified; Perfection cannot be improved."[1] Johnson divides the "employments of pious meditation" into four categories—"faith, thanksgiving, repentance, and supplication"—in order to demonstrate the suffocating narrowness that in his estimation awaits the devotional poet:

> Faith, invariably uniform, cannot be invested by fancy with decorations. Thanksgiving, the most joyful of all holy effusions, yet addressed to a Being without passions, is confined to a few modes, and is to be felt rather than expressed. Repentance, trembling in the presence of the judge, is not at leisure for cadences and epithets. Supplication of man to man may diffuse itself through many topics of persuasion; but supplication to God can only cry for mercy.[2]

For Johnson, finally, the very conventions that generate the interest of poetry make it an inadequate vehicle for devotional utterance. What is necessary to the definition of poetry is supererogatory to the performance of devotion.

It is significant that neither Donne nor Herbert is featured prominently in Johnson's *Lives of the English Poets,* for a close reading of the early seventeenth-century devotional lyric produced by these two figures would have shown Johnson a series of brilliant poetic solutions to the severe generic constrictions he astutely describes. In Donne's case, the solution involves a particularly acute self-consciousness about the tensions and continuities that link his social and religious experience. For Herbert, this self-consciousness is nourished into a profound interrogation of the tactical maneuvers implicit in the most sincere prayer.

---

1. *Lives of the English Poets,* 2 vols. (London: Dent, 1925), 1:173, 174.
2. Ibid., 174.

Both practice a poetry of supplication, which uses the strategies of social supplication to complicate and enrich the act of petitioning God far beyond the inarticulate cry for mercy posited by Dr. Johnson. In emphasizing the social lineage of the religious lyric, I do not mean to deny the force exerted upon it by the meditative or liturgical traditions, or by a Protestant poetics, or by any particular theology. But alongside the meditative and biblical resources appropriately studied by scholars of the religious lyric runs the language of everyday hierarchical interaction as a dynamic resource of ways for talking to and about God.[3] Over the course of the century, though, social petition becomes a far less vibrant mode for approaching God, as writers such as Herrick, Vaughan, and Traherne deliberately disengage both themselves and their religious poetry from the social drama that Donne and Herbert exploit. It is not that the poetry becomes apolitical—indeed, some of Vaughan's and Herrick's poems are explicitly political, as Claude J. Summers demonstrates in the preceding essay—but rather that it loses its social plangency. To explore the precise historical conditions that produced the separation and ultimate opposition between social and devotional territory is certainly beyond the scope of this essay. But that should not preclude our acknowledging the significant differences between the deployment of supplicatory modes modeled on the social in Donne and Herbert and the recoil from such language in Vaughan, Herrick, and Traherne. Perhaps the violent politicization of religious language that the Civil War precipitated forced devotion to

---

3. I am thinking here particularly of Rosemond Tuve, *A Reading of George Herbert* (Chicago: University of Chicago Press, 1952); Louis L. Martz, *The Poetry of Meditation: A Study in English Religious Literature of the Seventeenth Century* (New Haven: Yale University Press, rev. ed. 1962); Barbara Kiefer Lewalski, *Protestant Poetics and the Seventeenth-Century Religious Lyric* (Princeton: Princeton University Press, 1979); Richard Strier, *Love Known: Theology and Experience in George Herbert's Poetry* (Chicago: University of Chicago Press 1983); Chana Bloch, *Spelling the Word: George Herbert and the Bible* (Berkeley and Los Angeles: University of California Press, 1985); and the essay by Paul Stanwood in this collection. Indeed, in the appendix to his anthology of *English Seventeenth-Century Verse*, vol. 1 (New York: Norton, 1973), Martz provides a text of "The Practical Methode of Meditation" (1614) by the Jesuit Edward Dawson, which identifies the end of meditation as "some affectionate speach or Colloquium to God" in which "wee may talke with God as a servant with his Maister, as a sonne with his Father, as one friend with another, as a spouse with her beloved bridgrome, or as a guilty prisoner with his Judge" (508). Social conversation, then, is a fulfillment of, rather than an alternative to, the meditative model.

retreat from the social world that threatened it, and rendered the separation of social and devotional experience a strategy for psychological as well as political survival.[4] Whatever the cause, by the time we get to Vaughan and Traherne, the social and the devotional seem for the most part immiscible, like oil and water, rather than the unstable and potentially explosive blend they presented to Donne and Herbert. In looking to resources beyond the social, Vaughan, Herrick, and Traherne initiate the delimitation of devotional poetry that Johnson describes.

Criticism is currently well poised to begin to shake off the assumptions articulated by Johnson, and so to appreciate anew the religious lyric as the social artifact that its early seventeenth-century practitioners imagined it to be. The recontextualizations of Renaissance literature often termed "the New Historicism" have taught us to attend to correspondences between discourses normally kept discrete. A proper deployment of New Historicist techniques should amplify the assonances of religious and devotional language that our own inherited biases about the necessary separation of social and religious issues would silence. The New Historicism, moreover, has given us a vocabulary for analyzing the practices of power and submission that supply so much of the matter of the devotional lyric.[5] Rather than just being fashionable impositions of contemporary theoretical concerns on texts

---

[4]. For an account of the effect of the war on the language of devotion, see Helen Wilcox, "Exploring the Language of Devotion in the English Revolution," in *Literature and the English Civil War*, ed. Thomas Healy and Jonathan Sawday (Cambridge: Cambridge University Press, 1990), 75–88, and Claude J. Summers, "Herrick, Vaughan, and the Poetry of Anglican Survivalism," in this collection.

[5]. The phrase *poetics of culture* was first used by Stephen Greenblatt in *Renaissance Self-Fashioning: From More to Shakespeare* (Chicago: University of Chicago Press, 1980), 4–5, the inaugural text of the critical movement that Greenblatt later termed "New Historicism" in his introduction to *The Forms of Power and the Power of Forms in the Renaissance*, a special issue of *Genre* 15 (1982): 3–6. Despite the fact that the first three chapters of *Renaissance Self-Fashioning* offer a brilliant meditation on the interrelations of cultural and religious forces in More, Tyndale, and Wyatt, the New Historicism has been notoriously slow to explore the religious lyric as a subject in its own right. Leah Sinanoglou Marcus, *Childhood and Cultural Despair: A Theme and Variations in Seventeenth-Century Literature* (Pittsburgh: University of Pittsburgh Press, 1978), provides a notable antecedent and exception, which I shall discuss throughout this essay. Likewise, Debora Kuller Shuger's recent *Habits of Thought in the English Renaissance: Religion, Politics, and the Dominant Culture* (Berkeley and Los Angeles: University of California Press, 1990) explores the links between theological concepts of God and notions of social and political order.

from a distant past, such techniques offer us the opportunity to recover elements that the historically contingent assumptions articulated by Johnson would efface. By exploring the different social and religious resources available to and used by seventeenth-century poets in their attempts to map and master the unruly territory of the self, this essay can only begin to suggest the rich insights that current critical methodologies might offer to a new understanding of the religious lyric as a cultural artifact.

I

In a very early sermon, preached four months after the death of his wife, Donne explored with great self-consciousness what he perceived as the inevitable links between one's social experience and one's imagination of God:

> The Prophets, and the other Secretaries of the holy Ghost in penning the books of Scriptures, do for the most part retain, and express in their writings some impressions, and some air of the former professions: those that had been bred in Courts and Cities, those that had been Shepheards and Heardsmen, those that had been Fishers, and so of the rest; ever inserting into their writings some phrases, some metaphors, some allusions, taken from that profession which they had exercised before.[6]

Where Johnson argues that God's omnipotence automatically segregates religious utterance from any possible link to social conversation, Donne explicitly locates one's sense of the divine amid the vocabulary of one's social and professional experience. The very description of the prophets as "Secretaries of the holy Ghost" bestows upon them a title analogous to that which Donne himself had held in the service of Sir Thomas Egerton. Donne, moreover, proceeds to discover the epitome of social companionship in a mortal's relations with God: "Let no man be afraid to seek or find [God] for fear of the loss of good company; Religion is no sullen thing, it is not a melancholly [thing], there is not so sociable a

---

6. *The Sermons of John Donne*, ed. George R. Potter and Evelyn M. Simpson, 10 vols. (Berkeley and Los Angeles: University of California Press, 1953–1962), 1:236. Hereafter, references are cited as *Sermons*.

thing as the love of Christ Jesus" (*Sermons*, 1:246). What many of Donne's best religious poems do is explore the profound sociability that links humans and God by addressing God in the deferential language that Donne had come to know so well in his own professional experience.

In his brilliant study of Donne's erotic anthropomorphism, William Kerrigan has demonstrated Donne's willingness to push his poetry beyond mere metaphor, into the kinds of discursive behavior that such metaphor entails.[7] This willingness offers a continual source of energy and complexity to the Holy Sonnets. Far more than just anthropomorphic depictions of God, the poems explore the corollary decorums of devotional and social conduct. "Through contrasts as well as analogies between the monarchical and the divine, the courtly and the heavenly," argues Arthur Marotti in the most sustained account of the social function and location of Donne's poetry, "Donne reinforced the connection between the political and the religious in his sacred poetry."[8] I want to extend this point even further by arguing that the social circumstances of Renaissance England conspired with Donne's own dependent status and his verbal prowess to create an enormously rich language of devotion—a language that Herbert would use with even greater precision, but that would be progressively dulled in the course of the turbulent century.

The capacity to address God as a social superior was precipitated by Donne's deployment in his secular writings of the analogy between sacred and secular supplication. In the letters to Sir George More and Sir Thomas Egerton in which Donne attempted to repair the breach caused by his marriage to Ann More, for example, Donne continually conflated the power and displeasure of his mortal superiors with that of God. His own utterances thus become, as Donne describes his first letter to More, "prayer[s] to yow." In a subsequent letter, Donne compares his petition to the prayer of a religious penitent: "Since we have no meanes to move God, when he wyll not hear our prayers, to heare them, but by prayeng, I humbly beseech yow to allow by his gracious

---

7. "The Fearful Accommodations of John Donne," *English Literary Renaissance* 4 (1974): 340. "What has disturbed critics of 'Batter my heart,'" remarks Kerrigan, "is Donne's eagerness to display the most anthropomorphic consequences of anthropomorphism."
8. *John Donne, Coterie Poet* (Madison: University of Wisconsin Press, 1986), 248. See also Shuger, "Absolutist Theology: The Sermons of John Donne," in *Habits of Thought*.

example, my penitence so good entertainment, as yt may have a beeliefe and a pittie." He concludes with a plea for "mercy, which I beg of him, my Lord, and yow," merging his three powerful and implacable autocrats—another letter refers to "God and my Lord and yow"—in a series of nearly interchangeable titles. In a later letter to Egerton, Donne assures his angry patron that he dare approach him only because of the precedent of divine petition; since God "gives me now audience by prayer, yt emboldneth me also to address my humble request to your Lordship." He reminds Egerton that "redemtion was no lesse worke than creation."[9] Donne mines religious language in his social interactions not only to produce potentially ingratiating praise but also to urge upon his angry patrons a pattern of conduct that tempers wrath with mercy. What is playful in the verse letters to the countess of Bedford—addressing her, for example, as a "divinity" whose "friends" are her "elect[ed]" "saints"—is in these letters to More and Egerton a mark of terror at the apparent willfulness of secular and sacred power.

The Holy Sonnets offer an unsettled and unsettling compound of playfulness and terror, as Donne explores the processes by which the approach to God mirrors and diffracts the experience of social supplication. God, Donne confides to his friend Sir Henry Goodyer, is in many ways more accessible than a mortal patron: "That advantage of nearer familiarity with God, which the act of incarnation gave us, is grounded upon God's assuming us, not our going to Him. And our accesses to His presence are but His descents into us."[10] Yet this deep awareness of divine familiarity and condescension does not preclude Donne's sense that God is also far more distant than even the most exalted monarch. In "Oh, to vex me," for example, Donne measures his own perpetual "inconstancy" by the differing degrees of confidence with which he addresses his God:

> I durst not view heaven yesterday; and to day
> In prayers, and flattering speaches I court God:
> To morrow I quake with true feare of his rod.
> (ll. 9–11)

---

9. The letters to More and Egerton are cited from *John Donne: Selected Prose*, chosen by Evelyn Simpson, ed. Helen Gardner and Timothy Healy (Oxford: Clarendon Press, 1967), 113–15, 120.

10. Edmund Gosse, *Life and Letters of John Donne*, 2 vols. (London, 1899), 1:228.

Here the courting of God with the kind of "flattering speaches" Donne directed toward his mortal superiors is registered as an expression of misplaced confidence in comparison with those moments when the speaker experiences the authentic terror of God's punitive power. The adjective *true* indicates that not only the courting but also the fear to which it is contrasted can become strategic. Only in the poem's unsettling close does Donne explicitly hierarchize the differences between courting and true fear: "Those are my best dayes, when I shake with feare."[11] An aggressive act of courtly submission is supplanted by a superficially similar but intrinsically different acknowledgment of God's terrifying power.

Other Holy Sonnets frequently perform the rhythmic oscillation between confident courtship and authentic fear that "Oh, to vex me" describes. "If poysonous mineralls" begins with a brazen interrogation of divine justice:

> If poysonous minerals, and if that tree,
> Whose fruit threw death on else immortall us
> If lecherous goats, if serpents envious
> Cannot be damn'd; Alas; why should I bee?
>
> (ll. 1–4)

But such threatening questions only produce an interrogation of the speaker's own identity and status in discourse with God: "But who am I, that dare dispute with thee?" (l. 9). The poem concludes, moreover, by tracing a recoil from boldly questioning God's justice to equivocally praising God's mercy: "That thou remember them, some claime as debt, / I thinke it mercy, if thou wilt forget" (ll. 13–14). Although the object of *them* is ostensibly the "sinnes" of the previous line, it also may include the subsequent "some." If so, it curiously praises as an act of divine mercy what George Herbert, in the conclusion of "Affliction (I)," depicts as the ultimate psychological terror: being forgotten by God.

"Spit in my face you Jewes" offers a rigorous exploration of the consonances and contrasts between secular and social conduct that "Oh, to vex me" generates. Whereas mortal monarchs merely suspend

---

11. *The Complete English Poems of John Donne*, ed. C. A. Patrides (London: Dent, 1985). All subsequent citations of Donne's poetry are from this edition.

sentence, the speaker's heavenly monarch actually condescended to suffer the punishment his subject deserves: "Kings pardon, but he bore our punishment" (l. 10). Analogously, mortal submission to God is revealed to be a kind of disguised aggression in comparison to Christ's submission to the flesh:

> And *Jacob* came cloth'd in vile harsh attire
> But to supplant, and with gainfull intent:
> God cloth'd himselfe in vile mans flesh, that so
> Hee might be weake enough to suffer woe.
> (ll. 11–14)

Jacob's covering himself with the skin of a goat in order to receive the blessing meant for his hirsute elder brother Esau is represented as a mode of strategic submission, akin to the courting of God with flattering speeches censured in "Oh, to vex me." In retrospect, one can see how even the apparently devout petition to be made to suffer as Christ suffered is an act of grandiose self-abasement rather than authentic humility; it springs, as John Carey remarks, from "envy of the Crucified Jesus, rather than pity for him."[12] The poem shows how its own initial gestures of imitative devotion and Jacob's calculated submission are, in fact, cognate methods of courting divine favor. In contrast to Jacob's tactical adoption of a posture of humiliation in the cause of self-exaltation, Christ's disguising himself in "vile mans flesh" in order to become the sacrificial lamb that enables mortals to rise to heaven is the epitome of a selfless submission. Christ descends the hierarchy not to receive an unwarranted blessing but to earn an unmerited blessing for his inferiors.

In "Thou hast made me" and "As due by many titles," Donne approaches his God through strategies that are strikingly similar to those he employed toward his mortal patrons. In a letter to James Hay, viscount Doncaster and, later, earl of Carlisle, Donne cleverly presents himself as the "work" of Hay in order to interest Hay in the project of "preferring him still." "I am therefore in much confidence," writes Donne, "that your Lordship . . . will at least allow your work in me, And as you have laid a foundation, so you will by preferring me still, in your good opinion, build me up to such a capacity and worthiness,

---

12. *John Donne: Life, Mind and Art* (New York: Oxford University Press, 1980), 48.

as may be fit for your Lordship to dwell in." The opening gambit of "Thou hast made me, And shall thy worke decay?" is to attempt precisely the same tactic, reminding his divine maker that he stands to lose something in which he has already invested much creative energy if he does not quickly intervene. In a letter to Robert Carr, viscount Rochester, Donne uses a related tack, cataloguing the transactions by which he has become the property of his superior: "After I was grown to be your Lordships, by all the titles that I could thinke upon, it hath pleased your Lordship to make another title to me, by buying me. You may have many better bargains in your purchases, but never a better title than to me, nor anything which you may call yours more absolutely and entirely than me."[13] "As due by many titles" shows how useful this tactic could be in a devotional context, bending conspicuously similar language toward its divine audience in the attempt to encourage God's continued care for his creature:

> As due by many titles I resigne
> My selfe to thee, O God, first I was made
> By thee, and for thee, and when I was decay'd
> Thy blood bought that, the which before was thine,
> I am thy sonne, made with thy selfe to shine,
> Thy servant, whose paines thou hast still repaid,
> Thy sheepe, thine Image, and till I betray'd
> My selfe, a temple of thy Spirit divine.
> (ll. 1–8)

Like Rochester, God has a double title to the speaker, granted by the dual prerogative of creation and redemption. Yet where Donne leaves as an unstated but logical conclusion the need for Rochester's continued benevolence, in the Holy Sonnet Donne appeals directly to the self-interest of his divine lord: "Except thou rise and for thine owne work fight, / Oh I shall soone despaire" (ll. 11–12). "Instead of a prayer for unmerited mercy," remarks Richard Strier, the speaker "produces something like a threat." There is, moreover, an unresolved tension between the preexisting obligation the lines record and the agency

---

13. Gosse, *Life and Letters*, 1:202, 2:22.

involved in the process of signing the self over to God.[14] By invoking a series of subordinate relationships that include the social, Donne not only emphasizes his willing submission but also demands divine aid.

In a celebrated letter to Sir Henry Goodyer, Donne offers a terrifying vision of the self entirely outside of the relations that "As due by many titles" catalogues: "To be part of no body, is to be nothing. . . . At most, the greatest persons, are but great wens and excrescenses . . . except they be so incorporated into the body of the world, that they contribute something to the sustenation of the whole."[15] In contrast to the religious poets with whom this essay will conclude, who locate the value of the self in opposition to social forms, Donne invests the self with a value directly proportional to its relationship to the "body of the world." This intensely social sense of self, akin to Herbert's frequently expressed horror of uselessness, continually forces Donne to turn to social relationships as a vehicle for representing his relationship with the divine. Indeed, as John Stachniewski observes, Donne's social experience may have colluded with contemporaneous theology to produce the peculiar blend of social and sacred supplication that marks many of the Holy Sonnets: "It is not strange, in view of his social predicament, that Donne accepted as cosmic reality the orthodox ideology of his day when that ideology seemed such an accurate projection from his own experience. Donne felt his dependence on God to resemble his dependence on secular patronage with its attendant frustration, humiliation and despair."[16] The spiritual hypochondria of these poems offers a mirror image of Donne's social precariousness. The religious poems are so powerful, I want to argue, in part because

---

14. Richard Strier, "John Donne Awry and Squint: The 'Holy Sonnets,' 1608–1610," *Modern Philology* 86 (1989): 370. On the tension I describe, see M. Thomas Hester, "Re-Signing the Text of the Self: Donne's 'As due by many titles,'" in *"Bright Shootes of Everlastingnesse": The Seventeenth-Century Religious Lyric*, ed. Claude J. Summers and Ted-Larry Pebworth (Columbia: University of Missouri Press, 1987), 59–71.

15. Simpson, *Selected Prose*, 129.

16. "John Donne: The Despair of the 'Holy Sonnets,'" *ELH* 48 (1981): 702–3, rpt. in expanded form in *The Persecutory Imagination: English Puritanism and the Literature of Religious Despair* (Oxford: Clarendon Press, 1991), 254–90. See, though, Strier, "John Donne Awry and Squint," who argues that the Holy Sonnets are the work not of a "convinced Calvinist" but rather "of a person who would like to be a convinced Calvinist but who is both unable to be so and unable to admit that he is unable to be so" (361).

of their delicate but deliberate use of what Donne in "The Will" somewhat scoffingly terms "my best civility / And Courtship." Enriched by its social implications and honed by frequent practice with mortal superiors, this devotional language provided Donne with a vocabulary of supplication, which he brilliantly exploited. Through having to cringe before his superiors, Donne developed a rhetoric of supplication that could record at once the sincere desire for submission and the lingering ambitions of the self; he learned how the acknowledgment of creatureliness and indebtedness could place claims on one's benefactor; and he discovered the ingratiating force of fervent submission. In this arena, as in many others, Doctor Donne learned much from the experiences of Jack Donne, the antecedent self whose secular practices he purportedly abjured.

George Herbert, in turn, learned much from Donne's exploration of the lyric potential of social language and from his own social experience.[17] Far from being the inferior version of Donne that nineteenth- and early twentieth-century criticism describes, Herbert is, if anything, Donne's superior as a religious poet; his work attains at once an authenticity and an artfulness that Donne's poems only gesture toward. The vast disparity in size and location between Herbert's Bemerton and Donne's St. Paul's—the final sites of religious practice for both—should not blind us to the striking similarities in their devotional performances. As a gifted and ambitious younger brother from an aristocratic family, and particularly as University Orator at Cambridge, Herbert developed a supplicatory art at least the equal of that possessed by the Dean of St. Paul's. The devotional lyrics capitalize upon the surprising poetic riches implicit in this art.

Unlike Donne's sacred poems, whose provenance is at once complex and scattered, *The Temple* is a book, a deliberately ordered collection of poems. While the structure of *The Temple* has proved to be a genuine critical conundrum, it can be comprehended, at least in part, by attending to Herbert's wish to situate his devotional lyrics amid the discourses of social practice and historical pattern. Indeed, Herbert's intention to implicate his devotional discourse in the strategies of so-

---

17. The subsequent discussion of Herbert draws upon my *Prayer and Power: George Herbert and Renaissance Courtship* (Chicago: University of Chicago Press, 1991).

cial supplication is announced in the first poem a reader encounters upon entering *The Temple*: "The Dedication." As I have shown elsewhere, Herbert deliberately constructs this short poem from the conventions of secular patronage: "*Lord, my first fruits present themselves to thee; / Yet not mine neither: for from thee they came, / And must return.*"[18] In "The Printers to the Reader," Nicholas Ferrar's brief prefatory remarks to *The Temple*, Ferrar demonstrates that he clearly understands the force of Herbert's address to God as his patron: "The dedication of this work having been made by the Authour to the *Divine Majestie* onely, how should we now presume to interest any mortall man in the patronage of it?" The poem that follows "The Dedication," "The Church-porch," explicitly links social to sacred behavior, as its "precepts" prepare the reader to "approach, and taste / The churches mysticall repast" ("Superliminare," ll. 3–4). The fact that Herbert imagines social rules to offer a necessary threshold of comportment for admission to a realm of lyric interiority indicates the force with which the social impinges on the devotional in Herbert's imagination.

The most-often-quoted part of *The Temple* in the seventeenth century, "The Church-porch" has been little appreciated in our own.[19] Most readers who have looked at "The Church-porch" have emphasized the differences rather than the similarities between it and "The Church." Richard Strier, for example, argues that "The Church-porch" is marked by a "spiritual commercialism" as well as a "disingenuousness with regard to wealth and worldly position" that "Herbert came to transcend." Debora Shuger notes a similar disjunction, but instead of locating it in a biographical framework Shuger argues that the disjunction between "The Church-porch" and "The Church" represents wider discontinuities in Renaissance notions of self. Where "'The Church Porch' assumes and teaches a self capable of and perfected by moral activity," she asserts, "'The Church' generally conceives of the self as passive,

---

18. In "Submission and Assertion: The 'Double Motion' of Herbert's 'Dedication,'" *John Donne Journal* 2, no. 2 (1983): 39–49, and in "'Respective Boldnesse': Herbert and the Art of Submission," in *"A Fine Tuning": Studies in the Religious Poetry of Herbert and Milton*, ed. Mary Maleski (Binghamton, N.Y.: Medieval and Renaissance Texts and Studies, 1989), 77–94. All citations of Herbert are from *The Works of George Herbert*, ed. F. E. Hutchinson (Oxford: Clarendon Press, 1941).

19. See Robert H. Ray, *The Herbert Allusion Book: Allusions to George Herbert in the Seventeenth Century*, Studies in Philology 83, no. 4 (1986): v.

incapable of self-control, and threatened by social norms."[20] I would argue, however, that the discontinuities Shuger and Strier alertly locate are present not just in the structure of *The Temple* but also in most of the lyrics of "The Church." As Robert B. Hinman has observed, "Herbert's 'Church' encompasses his 'Church-porch' and his 'Church-porch' pervades his 'Church.'"[21] Just as "The Church-porch" concludes its lessons on social behavior with a discussion of conduct in church, "The Church" welcomes the tactics of social negotiation into the space of devotional worship. What is so interesting about the structure of *The Temple* is the way it forces its reader to perceive continuities as well as contrasts between social and devotional practices. The relation between the shrewd maxims of "The Church-porch" and the devotional utterances of "The Church" is contingent rather than transcendent; to borrow the title of a contemporaneous work, *The Temple* as a whole offers "A Dialogue between Pollicy and Piety."[22]

The prophetic, historical, and diffuse poem that concludes the tripartite *Temple*—"The Church-Militant"—is so different from anything in the first two sections that many readers have argued it is not properly a part of *The Temple*.[23] I think, however, that "The Church-Militant" is the product of an aesthetically unsuccessful attempt on Herbert's part to link the social conduct of "The Church-porch" and the devotional interiority of "The Church" with a larger historical pattern. "A poem concerned," in Stanley Stewart's apt description, "not with the struggle of the soul in time, but with the movement of the Church

---

20. Richard Strier, "Sanctifying the Aristocracy: 'Devout Humanism' in Francois de Sales, John Donne, and George Herbert," *Journal of Religion* 69 (1989): 57; Shuger, *Habits of Thought*, 93. A related tension between Renaissance humanism and Reformation theology in Herbert is explored by Richard Strier in "Ironic Humanism in *The Temple*," in *"Too Rich to Clothe the Sunne": Essays on George Herbert*, ed. Claude J. Summers and Ted-Larry Pebworth (Pittsburgh: University of Pittsburgh Press, 1980), 33–52.

21. "The 'Verser' at *The Temple Door:* Herbert's 'The Church-porch,'" in *Too Rich to Clothe the Sunne*, 67.

22. See *"A Dialogue between Pollicy and Piety,* by Robert Davenport," ed. Albert H. Tricomi, *English Literary Renaissance* 21 (1991): 190–216.

23. Readers who emphasize the disjunction between "The Church-Militant" and the rest of *The Temple* include Annabel M. Endicott [Patterson], "The Structure of George Herbert's *Temple:* A Reconsideration," *University of Toronto Quarterly* 34 (1965): 226–37; and Stanley Fish, *The Living Temple: George Herbert and Catechizing* (Berkeley and Los Angeles: University of California Press, 1978).

throughout all time," "The Church Militant" offers a conclusion to *The Temple* whose anomalies are more illusory than actual.[24] As the contemporaneous social conventions advised in "The Church-porch" are absorbed into the lyrics of "The Church," so does the historical narrative of "The Church-Militant" signal the processes by which the trajectory of historical change impinges on the very possibility of a religious self. Both are marked by a sense of restless change without apparent progress; religion, according to "The Church-Militant," is "like a pilgrime, westward bent, / Knocking at all doores, ever as she went" (ll. 29–30). Both the religious soul and institutional religion are dogged in their unending pilgrimage by sin. As Shuger argues, "There is no progress, meaning, or fulfillment within the temporal order in either 'The Church Militant' or (often) 'The Church.'"[25] The westward migration of the Church that the poem traces is a macrocosmic and historical version of the "repining restlessness" that Herbert in "The Pulley" mythologizes as God's determination of the fate of the individual soul on earth. As Donne would write one of his finest religious poems on the personal occasion of "Good Friday 1613. Riding Westward," so does Herbert discover in the historical narrative of religion a movement from east to west that indicates that true religion will ultimately flee England for America: "Yet as the church shall thither westward flie, / So Sinne shall trace and dog her instantly" (ll. 259–60). In Herbert's imagination, history stalks religion as relentlessly as sin stalks the Church.

The structure of *The Temple*, then, reveals the devotional self not as withdrawn from the world but rather as situated between social practice and historical force. Although critics from M. M. Ross through Marion Singleton have argued that "in *The Temple* Herbert retreated from the unsettling ferment of contemporary England into a private realm removed from time," the collection itself is deliberately punctuated by the temporality that Ross and Singleton would expel.[26] "The

---

24. "Time and *The Temple*," *Studies in English Literature, 1500–1900* 6 (1966): 105.
25. *Habits of Thought*, 114
26. See Malcolm Mackenzie Ross, *Poetry and Dogma: The Transfiguration of Eucharistic Symbols in Seventeenth-Century English Poetry* (New Brunswick: Rutgers University Press, 1954); Richard Strier, "George Herbert and the World," *Journal of Medieval and Renaissance Studies* 11 (1981): 211–36; and Marion White Singleton, *God's Courtier: Configuring a Different Grace in George Herbert's Temple* (Cambridge: Cam-

Church-porch" does advise solitude as the occasion for an introspection unavailable when one is engaged in the social world: "By all means use sometimes to be alone. / Salute thy self: see what thy soul doth wear. / Dare to look in thy chest" (ll. 145–47). When attending church, moreover, one is to "seal up both thine eies, / And send them to thine heart . . . Christ purg'd his temple; so must thou thy heart" (ll. 415–23). But such internal activities are part of a continuum of social conduct rather than an escape from it. They prepare one to enter the social world rather than providing an alternative to it.

The Temple is marked by its culture, then, and not just in what Ivan Earle Taylor identifies as the badges of "cavalier sophistication" in Herbert's poetry—an interest in "wine, game, women, sophisticated conversation, dress, and the like."[27] Rather, throughout *The Temple*, the world of the spirit is articulated in profoundly worldly terms. "To all Angels and Saints," for example, offers a portrait of heaven modeled on the terrestrial court that Herbert had known and served. The poem offers an uneasy apology to figures he would like to petition, but whom his monarch does not allow him to address: "I would addresse / My vows to thee most gladly . . . But now, alas, I dare not; for our King . . . Bids no such thing" (ll. 8–18). The referent of "our King," as Louis Martz proposes, is at once God and James.[28] Paralleling such confusion about the referent of "our King" is a portrait of heaven that is at once egalitarian—"Where ev'ry one is king" (l. 4)—and absolutist, the domain of a single, jealous monarch who will allow no one but himself to be petitioned. Offering a brilliant if roiled conflation of secular and sacred power, the poem gains its resonance not just from the theological turbulence of early seventeenth-century England but also from the political tensions between the theory of absolute monarchy and the necessity of the bureaucratic dispersal of power that marked the Jaco-

---

bridge University Press, 1987). The quotation is from Marcus, *Childhood and Cultural Despair*, 132; her account of Herbert's escapism was revised in "George Herbert and the Anglican Plain Style," in *Too Rich to Clothe the Sunne*, 179–93.

27. "Cavalier Sophistication in the Poetry of George Herbert," *Anglican Theological Review* 39 (1957): 229–43.

28. *Poetry of Meditation*, 98. Richard Strier, "'To all Angels and Saints': Herbert's Puritan Poem," *Modern Philology* 77 (1979): 135, offers a powerful account of the poem's two political systems, but comprehends the "King" the poem fears exclusively as the absolutist God of Puritan theology, and so dampens the tone of deep regret that suffuses Herbert's apology.

bean court. Indeed, as Linda Levy Peck argues, the theological model of heaven was often invoked to explain the structures of court patronage: "The favorite served as a mediator between subjects and king, a theological vision of brokerage implied by the contemporary advice to William Trumbull to direct himself to the 'right saint.' 'The whole Kingdom hath cast their eye upon you as the new rising Star, and no man thinks his business can prosper at Court unless he hath you for his good Angel.'"[29] Like the culture that in part produced it, "To all Angels and Saints" is powerfully divided between bureaucratic and absolutist models of the dispersal of power and grace.

"The Starre," too, depicts spiritual favor in terms derived from the mediation of power at terrestrial courts. The speaker asks a "Bright spark," a falling star, first to purge him of folly and lust, then to take him "Unto the place where thou / Before didst bow," and to "Get me a standing there" (ll. 19–21). The star is imagined as a courtly favorite who can both tutor the speaker in proper courtly conduct and attain employment for him. This correspondence among a theological heaven, the astronomical heavens, and a terrestrial but exalted court in turn glosses some otherwise enigmatic lines present in the Williams manuscript version of "Charms and Knots": "A falling starr has lost his place: / The Courtier gets itt, that has grace" (ll. 19–20). Punning on heavenly and social conceptions of grace—a conceptual pun that runs throughout *The Temple*—Herbert aligns social and religious distributions of favor.

This parallel between the courts of heaven and earth culminates in a deployment of the language of secular supplication appropriate to terrestrial courts in the act of petitioning God. Praying is, Herbert indicates in "The Church-porch," the highest activity available to the devout soul: "Resort to sermons, but to prayers most: / Praying's the end of preaching" (ll. 409–10). At its most effective, homiletic occasions supplication. Whereas in "Oh, to vex me" Donne contrasts the disingenuous spirituality of "court[ing] God" to the authentic quaking of

---

29. *Court Patronage and Corruption in Early Stuart England* (Boston: Unwin Hyman, 1990), 50, citing Roger Lockyer, *Buckingham: The Life and Political Career of George Villiers, First Duke of Buckingham, 1592–1628* (London: Longman, 1981), 13. For a parallel in Tudor England, see Frank Whigham, *Ambition and Privilege: The Social Tropes of Elizabethan Courtesy Theory* (Berkeley and Los Angeles: University of California Press, 1984), 12.

"true fear," Herbert explores throughout *The Temple* the explosive interaction of courtly supplication and religious fear. "Prayer (II)" opens with an implicit comparison between the availability of God and the distance of mortal monarchs:

> Of what an easie quick accesse,
> My blessed Lord, art thou! how suddenly
>   May our requests thine eare invade!
> To shew that state dislikes not easinesse,
> If I but lift mine eyes, my suit is made:
> Thou canst no more not heare, then thou canst die.
>   (ll. 1–6)

As George Ryley remarks on these lines: "It is a peculiar felicity to the subjects when the king is so; God the king of heaven, and the object of prayer and all religious worship is so."[30] "Affliction (I)" explosively blends a courtly lament against an unrewarding sovereign with the devout Christian's special privilege of complaint. Both "The Thanksgiving" and "Gratefulnesse" explore the processes by which the offering of thanks can become a mode of negotiation; in both cases, the speaker urges the sincere utterance of gratitude and hopes this utterance will make God's "gifts occasion more" ("Gratefulnesse"). Even the tendering of divine praise—a practice licensed by liturgical practice as well as devotional forms—is infiltrated by strategic concerns; as Arnold Stein observes, "the art of praise may employ prayer in a rhetoric of bargaining which God is expected to condone, or allow, or perhaps encourage."[31] The speakers of "Employment (I and II)," "The Temper (I and II)," "Dulnesse," "Praise (I)," and "Submission" offer the essential strategy of courtly negotiation, proposing to increase the quality and quantity of praise they offer their divine sovereign if he will only "mend [their] estate." In "Dialogue" and most cogently in "Love (III)," the final lyric of "The Church," Herbert uses the "quick Wit and Conversation" he partially repudiates in "The Quip" to mediate the relation between reluctant humanity and gracious divinity.

---

30. *Mr. Herbert's Temple and Church Militant Explained and Improved* (Bodleian MS Rawl. D. 199), ed. Maureen C. Boyd and Cedric C. Brown (New York: Garland, 1987), 136. Strier, *Love Known*, 57–58, 177–88, analyzes Herbert's violations of decorum.
31. *George Herbert's Lyrics* (Baltimore: Johns Hopkins University Press, 1968), 107.

Herbert's poetry attains social resonance, moreover, in the explicit link he draws between the lyric record of his own subjective devotional experience and the effect he hopes it will have on the conduct of the reading public. His poetry, in other words, makes the recording of private experience a public action. It mediates between public and private concerns not just in the "subtle rhetoric of political allusion" used in poems such as "Divinitie," "The British Church," and "Church-rents and schismes"; rather, Herbert imagines a social function for even his most seemingly private utterances.[32] Herbert makes clear the designs he has on his reader in "The Dedication"—"*Turn their eyes hither, who shall make a gain*" (1. 5)—and in the opening stanza of "The Church-porch":

> Thou, whose sweet youth and early hopes inhance
> Thy rate and price, and mark thee for a treasure;
> Hearken unto a Verser, who may chance
> Ryme thee to good, and make a bait of pleasure.
>   A verse may finde him, who a sermon flies,
>   And turn delight into a sacrifice.
>
>   (ll. 1–6)

Herbert, then, reveals a social function for devotional verse unremarked upon by the Dean of St. Paul's—its conversionary power. "Praise (III)" wishes "O that I might some other hearts convert, / And so take up at use good store: / That to thy chest there might be coming in / Both all my praise, and more!" (ll. 39–42). Likewise, at the end of "Obedience," a poem about signing the self over to God, Herbert expresses the hope that "some kinde man" will thrust his heart into the lines of Herbert's submission (l. 42). For Herbert, finally, the devotional lyric escapes the dangers of solipsism by inviting its reader to merge with the intense subjectivity revealed and so to engage in an analogous act of praise and submission.

---

32. I borrow the phrase from Claude J. Summers and Ted-Larry Pebworth, "Herbert, Vaughan, and Public Concerns in Private Modes," *George Herbert Journal* 3, nos. 1 and 2 (1979/1980): 9. On public and private in Herbert, see also Summers and Pebworth, "The Politics of *The Temple*: 'The British Church' and 'The Familie,'" *George Herbert Journal* 8, no. 1 (1984): 1–15, and Sidney Gottlieb, "Herbert's Case of 'Conscience': Public or Private Poem?" *Studies in English Literature, 1500–1900* 25 (1985): 109–26.

Many seventeenth-century writers accepted the invitation; so many, in fact, that Stanley Stewart has proposed we reconceive the canon of seventeenth-century religious poetry as "The School of Herbert" rather than "The School of Donne" imagined by traditional criticism.[33] Christopher Harvey produced a volume entitled *The Synagogue, Or, The Shadow of The Temple: Sacred Poems and Private Ejaculations: In Imitation of Mr. George Herbert* (1640), and which was frequently bound with *The Temple*. Richard Crashaw named his collection of sacred verse *Steps to the Temple* (1646); the anonymous author of "The Preface to the Reader" describes Crashaw as "Herbert's second, but equall." Ralph Knevet designated his unpublished collection of sacred poems *A Gallery to the Temple* (1641–1652?). The subtitle of the second part of Henry Vaughan's *Silex Scintillans* (1655) is *Sacred Poems and Private Ejaculations*, in imitation of the subtitle of Herbert's *Temple*. The author's preface, moreover, refers to "the blessed man, Mr. *George Herbert*, whose holy *life* and *verse* gained many pious *Converts*, (of whom I am the least)." In "The Match," Vaughan explicitly accepts the invitation Herbert issues at the end of "Obedience," telling his "Dear friend" that "Here I joyn hands, and thrust my stubborn heart / Into thy *Deed*" (ll. 7–8). Throughout *Silex*, Vaughan thrusts his heart and brain so completely into Herbert's poetic deeds that, as F. E. Hutchinson remarks, "there is no example in English literature of one poet adopting another poet's words so extensively."[34]

Yet even so total and deliberate an assimilation as that performed by Vaughan reveals striking differences in the prospects for devotional poetry over the course of the century. As Jonathan Post remarks, "In modeling his poetry after Herbert's, Vaughan transformed both the look and the feel, the outer edge and the inner life, of the earlier verse to create the substance of *Silex*."[35] An essential element of this transformation, I want to argue, is the muffling of the social resonances of devotional performance. While Vaughan can respond to Herbert as a "Dear Friend," turning, as Post argues, "a Cavalier ideal of 'friendship' into an extended conversation with his 'dear friend,'" Vaughan nevertheless produced "a very different mode of verse" from that of either

33. "The School of George Herbert," in *George Herbert* (Boston: G. K. Hall, 1986).
34. *The Complete Poetry of Henry Vaughan*, ed. French Fogle (New York: Norton, 1964), 260; *The Works of George Herbert*, xlii.
35. *Henry Vaughan: The Unfolding Vision* (Princeton: Princeton University Press, 1982), 80.

his friend or the Cavaliers: "The humanized poetics associated with the Tribe of Ben are carried on in solitude." Rather than resonant social interaction, Vaughan offers a dialogue with the dead. Summers and Pebworth argue that "the Puritan desecration of the Established Church, including the abolition of the Book of Common Prayer, had robbed [Vaughan] of the public sources of inspiration and imagery so vital to Herbert."[36] Perhaps this theft also entailed the loss of the sense of community on which the opportunity for social interaction depended.

Vaughan's "Rules and Lessons," written in deliberate imitation of Herbert's "Church-porch," demonstrates the social narrowing that marks Vaughan's solitary poetic. Whereas Herbert offers detailed advice for dining and discoursing with others of all social levels ("Church-porch," ll. 126–38, 289–365), Vaughan seems only to partake of solitary suppers with his God: "To *meales* when thou doest come, give him the praise / Whose *Arm* supply'd thee . . . O admire his ways / Who fils the worlds unempty'd granaries!" (ll. 97–98). Whereas Herbert's "Church-porch" addresses all aspects of social life, "Vaughan's rules and lessons," as Martz remarks, "lay down certain ways of individual communion with God in every hour of the day." His "rule" of conduct is solipsistic rather than social and culminates in the observation that "a sweet *self-privacy* in a right soul / Out-runs the Earth" (ll. 53–54). As Robert Ellrodt argues, *Silex Scintillans* is "a record of private experience: secretive self-communings"; Vaughan "only meets himself in solitude, not in dialogue with a Mistress or his Master."[37] The Preface to *Silex Scintillans,* Part 2, does gesture toward a social function for religious poetry in its hope that "the *Church*" will "make [my poor *Talent*] as useful now in the *publick,* as it hath been to me in *private.*" But this equivocal endorsement of religious didacticism is buried amid Vaughan's castigation of secular poetry, and lacks the categorical force of Herbert's conviction that his verse will "ryme thee to good."

36. Ibid., xxi. Claude J. Summers and Ted-Larry Pebworth, "Vaughan's Temple in Nature and the Context of 'Regeneration,'" *Journal of English and Germanic Philology* 74 (1975): 352. See also Chris Fitter, "Henry Vaughan's Landscapes of Military Occupation," *Essays in Criticism* 42 (1992): 123–47.

37. Louis L. Martz, *The Paradise Within: Studies in Vaughan, Traherne, and Milton* (New Haven: Yale University Press, 1964), 13; Robert Ellrodt, "George Herbert and the Religious Lyric," in *English Poetry and Prose 1540–1674,* ed. Christopher Ricks (London: Sphere Books, 1970), 193.

What we find in Vaughan, then, is a hermeticism cultivated in deliberate opposition to the social. Frank Kermode has characterized Vaughan's poetry as "a cheque drawn on the bank of Hermes Trismegistus." The poems do, as many critics have demonstrated, continue to refer to contemporary political events, particularly the situation of the Anglican Church amid the triumph of Parliamentary forces. "Abels Blood," for example, directly and powerfully bemoans the horrors of civil war from the perspective of defeat. But as Christopher Hill argues, "the fierce despair of the political poems" is linked to "the escapism of many of [Vaughan's] religious poems"; references to a sinful and despoiled political world at once occasion and justify the poet's withdrawal into the temple of nature.[38] "The Constellation" likewise contrasts the patricide of the Puritan revolutionaries ("But here Commission'd by a black self-wil / The sons the father kil," ll. 37–38) with the "exact obedience" practiced by the stars. But the celestial imagery that Herbert used in "The Starre" to represent terrestrial courts Vaughan keeps at a galactic distance from the chaotic political world he inhabits. As in "The World," whose spectacular opening image ("I Saw Eternity the other night / Like a great *Ring* of pure and endless light") offers an explicit contrast to "the darksome States-man hung with weights and woe" (1. 16), the realm of politics remains opposed rather than reconciled to the ideals of religion. Granted, a poem like "Regeneration" opens with a blend of social and spiritual servitude worthy of Herbert: "A ward, and still in bonds." But where Herbert would sustain the metaphor if only to explore the vast differences between earth and heaven (witness "Redemption"), Vaughan simply drops the metaphor in favor of immersion in a splendid, if isolating, nature. Relatedly, Vaughan frequently adopts the persona of a child. But his deployment of this persona is not so much the engagement of a model of social relations as it is a disengagement from all social relations. He nostalgizes childhood as an idyllic state to which he longs to return rather than as a familial status with a variety of bonds and duties incumbent upon it; he hopes "by meer playing [to] go to Heaven" ("Childe-hood," l. 8). His attitude encompasses a retreat from social responsibility rather than an adoption of it.

38. Frank Kermode, "The Private Imagery of Henry Vaughan," *Review of English Studies* ns. 1 (1950): 210; Christopher Hill, "Henry Vaughan," in *Writing and Revolution in Seventeenth-Century England*, vol. 1 of *Collected Essays* (Sussex: Harvester, 1985), 211.

Writing, like Vaughan, as civil war devastated the country and publishing his volume of sacred verse just two years before the first part of *Silex Scintillans*, Robert Herrick also turns to childhood as a refuge from social pressure. But for Herrick, the image is not just a retreat but is itself a political gesture; as Marcus argues, "*Noble Numbers* plays royalism in a religious key, affirming its author's commitment to the conservative Anglican ideal of the English as submissive children of their mother the church."[39] Likewise, his repeated use of imagery of correction may tacitly indulge a vision of God as a punishing father. Nevertheless, Herrick's poetic childhood, like Vaughan's, remains much narrower than the multivalent childhood explored by Herbert. Whereas in "The Collar," Herbert achieves a complex and unsentimental comprehension of childhood as representing at once a status of total dependence, a time of absolute willfulness, and a firm bond with God the Father, Vaughan and Herrick both imagine childhood as a state of spiritual transcendence that rests comfortably beyond social parameters. They mute rather than amplify the social resonance available in poetic recourse to childhood. Herrick in particular offers, in Starkman's terms, "an adult assumption of a *ingenu* role" (8–9). The role attracts him because it represents a purity and simplicity unavailable to inhabitants of a violent and defiling social world.

Although Robert Herrick does not parade Herbert as a model as explicitly as Vaughan does, his poetry is in some ways closer to the tone of civility that marks so much of Herbert's talk with God. A poem from *Hesperides*, "His Prayer to Ben. Johnson," wittily shows Herrick's awareness of the potential for crossing secular and sacred supplication: "WHen I a Verse shall make, / Know I have praid thee, / For old *Religions* sake, / Saint *Ben* to aide me" (H-604, ll. 1–4). As with Vaughan, though, the similarities only throw into relief the marked differences. Like Herbert's *Temple*, Herrick's *Noble Numbers* (1648) looks closely at the gratitude mortals owe to God. But whereas in "Gratefulnesse," Herbert at once practices and exposes the coercions of proffering

---

39. *Childhood*, 129. See also Miriam K. Starkman, "*Noble Numbers* and the Poetry of Devotion," in *Reason and the Imagination: Studies in the History of Ideas 1600–1800*, ed. J. A. Mazzeo (New York: Columbia University Press, 1962), 1–27. Citations of Herrick are from *The Complete Poetry of Robert Herrick*, ed. J. Max Patrick (New York: Norton, 1968). References to *Hesperides* are cited as H and poem number, with references to *Noble Numbers* cited as N and poem number.

gratitude, Herrick's *"Thanksgiving"* (N-42) flattens such insights into epigrammatic platitude: "THanksgiving for a former, doth invite / God to bestow a second benefit" (ll. 1–2). Likewise, *"A Thanksgiving to God, for his House"* (N-47) is one of Herrick's most delightful poems, and may involve, as Starkman argues, "the most ingenuous questioning of the ways of God to man," but its charm wears thin beside Herbert's relentless investigation of the aggression that can linger in expressions of sincere gratitude in his *"Thanksgiving."* Herrick's *"To his Saviour. The New Yeeres gift"* (N-125) imagines a gift-exchange with God. But this poem carries none of the tortured recognition we see in Herbert of the impossibly beneficent economy of the Christian dispensation; for Herrick, this exchange is merely that of his "bleeding Heart" for "THat little prettie bleeding part / Of Foreskin" (ll. 1–3).

Herrick, like Herbert, links royal and heavenly monarchies in a range of poems. "*A Christmas* Caroll, *sung to the King in the Presence at* White-Hall" (N-96), "Another New-yeeres Gift, or Song for the Circumcision" (N-98) and "The Star-Song: A Caroll to the King; sung at White-Hall" (N-102) cannily make their praise of Christ also serve for King Charles: "Let's blesse the Babe: And, as we sing / His praise; so let us blesse the King" (ll. 25–26). *"To God"* (N-262) in turn beseeches his divine monarch to make him "Thy *Poet*, and Thy *Prophet Lawreat*," cleverly aligning earthly and heavenly positions of honor. But the poetic effect—economical compliment of his two monarchs in a single utterance—is somewhat lackluster compared to the dazzling conflation of divine and regal power that Herbert exploits throughout *The Temple*.[40] "*Good Friday:* Rex Tragicus, *or Christ going to His Crosse*" parallels the past suffering of Herrick's heavenly king with the present persecution of his earthly monarch. Likewise, in *"The Widdowes teares: or, Dirge of Dorcas,"* as Claude J. Summers argues in the preceding essay, Herrick laments the fate of the Anglican Church, an institution whose comfort and stability Herbert had praised in maternal terms in "The British Church," but from which Parliamentary forces had ejected Herrick in

---

40. It is, though, strategically similar to the gratitude Herbert frequently directed to the powerful as university orator; see my *Prayer and Power,* chap. 1, "'Subject to Ev'ry Mounters Bended Knee': Herbert and Authority," and chap. 2, "'My God, My King': Socializing God."

1647 as part of its program of reform.[41] Herrick's politically referential poetry differs profoundly from Herbert's socially resonant poetry in that the former's poems record the violence of the political world upon the purportedly private space of devotion, while the latter's lyrics absorb the violence of the social world into the confessedly public act of devotion. Herrick, in other words, forges a religious poetic that produces political allegories rather than acts of social intercourse.

Unlike Herbert and Donne, who continually imagine God in social terms, Herrick's imagination of God is informed ultimately by a kind of *via negativa* that delimits religious poetry in just the way that Dr. Johnson prescribed. Herrick's poem *"To finde God"* (N-3) uses the impossibility theme to mock those who would purport to be able to "shew me Him / That rides the glorious *Cherubim*" (ll. 15–16), while the subsequent poem, *"What God is"* (N-4), epigrammatically remarks: "GOD is above the sphere of our esteem, / And is the best known, not defining Him" (ll. 1–2). Such an attitude about the ineffability of God is perhaps good theology, but it does not necessarily make for good poetry, since it automatically impoverishes the experiential resources that poetry demands.

The apogee of this attitude to God is attained in the mystical and solipsistic meditations of Thomas Traherne. In his poetry, we can see how the *via negativa* produces a devotional attitude that isolates both the devotee and his image of God from the social world. "The word 'infinity' might well be selected as the key to Traherne's total devotion," observes Rosalie Colie. Traherne's devotional infinity is explicitly opposed to the deep immersion in history that we see in the poetry of both Donne and Herbert, or even the nostalgic lament for a lost historical moment offered in the work of Herrick and Vaughan. Joan Webber aptly describes Traherne as "a seventeenth-century inhabitant of eternity." Like Vaughan and Herrick, Traherne finds in childhood a space of social retreat and spiritual privilege rather than the occasion for a social relation with God the Father. Indeed, for Traherne, it is not so much childhood as "Sweet infancy" ("The Rapture"), a state prior to

---

41. See also Claude J. Summers, "Herrick's Political Counterplots," *Studies in English Literature, 1500–1900* 25 (1985): 165–82, as well as his "Tears for Herrick's Church," in *Robert Herrick*, ed. Ann Baynes Coiro, special issue, *George Herbert Journal* 14, nos. 1 and 2 (1990/1991): 51–71.

speech, that offers the temporal site of the paradisal existence he struggles to regain. Traherne's God is, in turn, modeled not on earthly superiors but "on the sun—an inexhaustible orb radiating light and energy throughout the universe."[42] Traherne's celestial deity is light-years away from the constellations of courtly power represented in Herbert's "The Starre" as well as from the affable divinity envisaged in Donne's remark that "there is not so sociable a thing as the love of Christ Jesus." The lingering sociability that occasionally traverses Traherne's lyrics takes the form of a child's imaginary play-friends ("Shadows in the Water") rather than any true social relationship. For Traherne, God's power and love are comprehended through the mysteries of geometry and infinity rather than those of state or society.

Significantly, Traherne's poetry was completely unknown until 1896, nearly absent from the history he abdicated, and offering in its publication history (or lack thereof) an equivalent to the near-fetish its author made of privacy.[43] His was a very different sense of poetry's place in the world from Herbert's anxious concern for the effect of his writings on potential readers, and even from Donne's coterie performances. Nevertheless, in "The Author to the Critical Peruser," a poem in the collection *Poems of Felicity*, which Traherne's brother Philip apparently prepared for the press (although it was never published), Thomas Traherne does imagine that his poetry will show a reader "the naked Truth" so that "thy Soul might see / With open Eys thy Great *Felicity*" (ll. 1–8). He pledges to practice a poetry free of "curling Metaphors that gild the Sence," offering instead "real Crowns and Thrones and Diadems" (ll. 11–14). He promises to "Ransack all Nature's Rooms, and add the things / Which *Persian* Courts enrich; to make Us Kings: / To make us Kings indeed! Not verbal Ones, / But reall Kings, exalted unto

---

42. Rosalie L. Colie, *Paradoxia Epidemica: The Renaissance Tradition of Paradox* (Princeton: Princeton University Press, 1966), 146; Joan Webber, *The Eloquent "I": Style and Self in Seventeenth-Century Prose* (Madison: University of Wisconsin Press, 1968), 219; Marcus, *Childhood*, 181. See, though, the recent article by Julia J. Smith, "Thomas Traherne and the Restoration," *Seventeenth Century* 3, no. 2 (1988): 203–22, which argues that Traherne's "imagination was deeply involved with the Restoration monarchy" (219).

43. Traherne did publish in the year before his death an anti-Catholic polemic entitled *Roman Forgeries* (1673); the *Christian Ethics* (1675) appeared two years later. Traherne's poems are cited from *Thomas Traherne: Centuries, Poems, and Thanksgivings*, ed. H. M. Margoliouth, 2 vols. (Oxford: Clarendon Press, 1958).

Thrones" (ll. 31–34). Yet because few poets have written of crowns and thrones that were less "real" in any material sense, one must invest "reality" with a tenuous Platonic idealism in order to comprehend such assertions at all. Paradoxically, Traherne's turn from the material and historical world into an idealized realm of infant perception allows him to imagine that he can communicate by means of things rather than signs. Traherne continually portrays a devotional subjectivity that absorbs in order to obliterate the outside world; the speaker of "An Hymne upon St. Bartholomews Day" remarks "All Kingdoms I Descrie / In Me," while the speaker of "Solitude" describes a removal from the world so total that he felt "As if no Kings / On Earth there were, or living Things" (ll. 13–14).

In a recent book on Traherne, A. Leigh DeNeef observes rightly that "the old historicism has constructed a Traherne that is blatantly unhistorical" and suggests that this unhistorical construction has "also kept [Traherne] conveniently alien to modern readers."[44] DeNeef proposes to break down this alienation by developing a series of parallels between Traherne's thought and the work of three deeply influential twentieth-century thinkers—Heidegger, Lacan, and Derrida. Amid the admittedly striking connections DeNeef draws, however, the seventeenth-century poet becomes even more isolated from his own time, yet remains somewhat insulated from our own. Perhaps the old historicism was right. Traherne's poetry, I would argue, is less engaging for the twentieth-century reader than that of Donne or Herbert precisely because of its deliberate distance from any sense of social or historical engagement.[45] Reading Traherne's frequently hyperventilating catalogues and perpetually solipsistic monologues—poems that Dr. Johnson could not have known—I respond with greater sympathy to Dr. Johnson's sense of the enervating limitations imposed on the religious poet. By exhausting asocial modes of approaching God, the poetry of Traherne throws into relief the social and poetic accomplishment of the religious lyrics of Donne and Herbert.

---

44. *Traherne in Dialogue: Heidegger, Lacan, and Derrida* (Durham: Duke University Press, 1988), 6. Marcus, *Childhood*, comments that "in many ways Traherne seems much more modern than the other poets we have studied" (198).

45. See, though, the interesting argument about Traherne's use of "politically subversive language to describe a spiritual state" advanced by Julia Smith in "Thomas Traherne and the Restoration."

II

Whatever canon we construct of seventeenth-century devotional poetry will reinforce the very criteria we use to order it and to assess its parts. Indeed, it is instructive to remember amid current battles about the canon that *The Temple*, the collection of religious verse that offers, I think, the finest synthesis of social and devotional languages available in English, was not published between 1709 and 1799.[46] The narrative by which I try to locate a pattern in the seventeenth-century religious lyric resembles—in its broad outlines—some of the most compelling and influential narratives used to order the religious poetry of the century: T. S. Eliot's dissociation of sensibility, M. M. Ross's theologizing of Eliot, Louis Martz's art of meditation, and Barbara Lewalski's Protestant poetics.[47] In attempting to tell the story of an art of devotional supplication, then, I intend to supplement rather than supplant standard accounts of the century's religious poetry. I have tried to show how the genre of the religious lyric absorbed and then rejected social conversation as a model for discourse with the divine. Prayer became a largely private action, and writers turned from social discourse to natural or hermetic or geometrical imagery to convey their apprehension of divine power and love. Produced by Donne, developed by Herbert, and progressively, if unevenly, diminished in the poetry of Vaughan, Herrick, and Traherne, the art of devotional supplication offered for a brief time a resource exploited brilliantly by some of the best religious poets of any age.

I will be the first to admit that the story I tell is influenced by my own moment in the history of literary criticism—a moment when the discovery of ideological strategies and social motives has attained the kind of privilege that previous moments accorded to the revelation of organic form or the discovery of intellectual precedent. I will also be the first to acknowledge the partiality (in both senses) of the story I tell. Much scholarly and theoretical work remains to be done before we really have something like a cultural poetics of the religious lyric. The task—at once archival, historical, and sociological—of mapping the

46. See *Works of George Herbert*, xlv-xlvii.
47. T. S. Eliot, "The Metaphysical Poets" [1921], in *Selected Essays* (New York: Harcourt, Brace and World, 1960), 241–50; Ross, *Poetry and Dogma;* Martz, *Poetry of Meditation;* Lewalski, *Protestant Poetics*.

ways that the violently changing political circumstances of the seventeenth century disturbed the conventions of social conversation is a prerequisite to tracking the corollary disturbances exhibited in sacred conversation. Feminist work on the ways in which cultures construct gender-specific categories and how those categories impinge on the construction of subjectivity and the direction of desire offers much of value to a study of the seventeenth-century devotional lyric. Likewise, criticism should continue to explore the ways that homoerotic sentiments infiltrate the expression of a male poet's love for a God traditionally imagined as male.[48] Relatedly, the attention that cultural historians have recently devoted to the historical presence of physical bodies may have much to teach us about the processes by which religious writers deny or redirect the somatic experience of pleasure or pain in the act of religious devotion.[49]

Nevertheless, scholars seeking to develop a cultural poetics of the religious lyric might well begin, as I have tried to do, with an appreciation of the social forces that shape and distort the artful presentation of devotional subjectivity to an audience composed at once of an omnipotent deity and a mortal readership. The language of social supplica-

---

48. On the role of gender in the construction of devotional subjectivity, see Wilcox, "Exploring the Language of Devotion in the English Revolution"; Maureen Sabine, *Feminine Engendered Faith: The Poetry of John Donne and Richard Crashaw* (London: Macmillan, 1992); and the essay by Anthony Low in this collection. On homoeroticism, see Marotti, *John Donne,* 259–60; my *Prayer and Power,* 249–51, 264–70; Leonard Barkan, *Transuming Passion: Ganymede and the Erotics of Humanism* (Stanford: Stanford University Press, 1991); Gregory W. Bredbeck, *Sodomy and Interpretation* (Ithaca: Cornell University Press, 1991); Jonathan Goldberg, *Sodometries: Renaissance Texts, Modern Sexualities,* (Stanford: Stanford University Press, 1992); and Claude J. Summers, "The (Homo)sexual Temptation of *Paradise Regained,*" forthcoming. Sustained study of such motives might help us better understand not only a poem like Herbert's "Love (III)" but also one like Traherne's "Love," in which the speaker's God first visits him in the form of a shower of golden rain (as Jove impregnated Danae), then makes him "His Ganimede! His Life! His Joy! . . . That I might be his boy, / And fill, and taste, and give, and drink the cup."

49. See, for example, Peter Brown, *The Body and Society: Men, Women, and Sexual Renunciation in Early Christianity* (New York: Columbia University Press, 1988); Thomas Laqueur, *Making Sex: Body and Gender from the Greeks to Freud* (Cambridge: Harvard University Press, 1990); and Caroline Walker Bynum, *Fragmentation and Redemption: Essays on Gender and the Human Body in Medieval Religion* (New York: Zone Books, 1991). A fascinating line can be drawn from Herbert's and Donne's nervous engagements with the body through Traherne's unequivocal celebrations of it in his "Thanksgivings for the Body."

tion provides these poets with a discourse that dodges the generic restrictions identified by Dr. Johnson. It also allows them to avoid the dangers of self-congratulatory piety and masochistic self-indulgence, which stalk religious utterance in any age. Donne and Herbert attain in their lyrics a voice that feels authentic, immediate, even contemporary, precisely because it is so fully grounded in history. This paradox, that the apparent timelessness of an utterance is proportional to the degree to which it is timebound, is matched by a related one: that the most authentic expression of inwardness is attained by recourse to the language of social intercourse. Both paradoxes, though, are more apparent than real; it should not surprise us that devotional interiority is produced from the extrinsic materials supplied by social history. The final stanza of "The Church-porch" advises, "In brief, acquit thee bravely; play the man" (1. 457), engaging at once a model of masculine self-control and a theatricalized self-presentation, which at least partly undercuts the authenticity this model values. For Herbert, finally, the self can only be imagined in terms of a socially defined role that one consciously assumes.[50] Over the course of the seventeenth century, though, one can trace a shift in the concept of subjectivity, from one that is responsive and vulnerable to social forces to one that is in retreat from and opposed to them. Because this opposition still structures our current analytical organization of ourselves and of those we study, it is important that we understand its deeply contingent nature. The devotional lyric offers one compelling site for attaining just such an understanding and for assessing the aesthetic and social costs of sustaining an easy opposition between public and private selves.

---

50. As John Mulder astutely remarks, "Although Herbert may seem to wear his heart on his sleeve, he only plays different parts to suit different stages or occasions. His persona is a foil by which Herbert himself retains aristocratic reticence" ("*The Temple* as Picture," in *Too Rich to Clothe the Sunne*, 12). On the important difference between Renaissance and modern conceptions of privacy, see Anne Ferry, *The "Inward" Language: Sonnets of Wyatt, Sidney, Shakespeare, Donne* (Chicago: University of Chicago Press, 1983), particularly 53–55.

LITURGY, WORSHIP, AND THE SONS OF LIGHT

❖ ❖ ❖ *P. G. Stanwood* ❖ ❖ ❖

The earlier seventeenth century is justly celebrated for the profusion of its lyric verse, a kind of poetry that I understand generally to refer to almost any brief metrical composition intended to suit a variety of occasions and audiences. Thus we may think at once of John Donne's *Songs and Sonets* and his many occasional poems on religious themes, including his Holy Sonnets; and we will certainly think especially of George Herbert's *The Temple,* in which we find well illustrated most of the lyric forms cultivated in his age, with others that Herbert himself invented. But lyrics appear also embedded within longer and more "formal" works so that even *Paradise Lost* yields passages that may be properly called "lyric," about which I will have something to say later.

My present concern is with *religious* lyric poetry, although the distinction between it and secular verse is sometimes difficult to make, especially in poetry written during the first half of the seventeenth century. But I wish to urge one distinguishing feature of religious lyric poetry by centering on verse that has a devotional purpose, that means to offer some kind of praise or worship or thanksgiving to God. Such religious poetry is always broadly liturgical, my fundamental point being that liturgy defines religious poetry, whether the poet's designs are obvious or implicit in the resulting work.

Liturgy, of course, applies generally to all the public and written offices of the Church and particularly to the Eucharistic rite. This ecclesiastical sense defines the form and often the setting of much early religious poetry, such as hymns or psalms or verse that accompanies public worship. Without forgetting this sense, I should wish to apply the term in a further way; for *liturgy* should inevitably suggest shape, form, repetition, order, the regulation of private feelings into normalized, public expression. The notion, commonly put forward in the earlier seventeenth century (and still a current belief), that "spontaneous" prayer is valid while "set" prayer is not, cannot, in my view, be possible; for each kind of prayer contains the other. When applied to religious—or particularly devotional—poetry, I argue that form contains freedom and that spontaneity demands perfection. On this seeming paradox depends my thesis, and in demonstrating it, my plan is to move from the explicit management of form in a liturgical setting (as with the canonical hours) to the implicit form, in which the poet does not deliberately set out to write in a liturgical environment or in obedience to any liturgical form, yet in avoiding the form comes inevitably to have it. Thus, we may move between the external desire that accepts pattern and ritual to the internal, perhaps unacknowledged, desire that generates structure.

A helpful starting place is a traditional liturgical work, John Cosin's *A Collection of Private Devotions,* first published in 1627, but, as the full title says, based on "the practise of the ancient church, called The Houres of Prayer. As they were after this maner published by Authoritie of Q. Eliz[abeth]. . . . Taken Out of the Holy Scriptures, the Ancient Fathers, and the divine Service of our own Church." In compiling the *Devotions,* Cosin freely adapted the formularies of the Elizabethan primers, the Sarum liturgical texts, and borrowed from a variety of materials, including a little recusant book of prayers, *A Manual of Prayers newly gathered out of many . . . authours . . .* (1583), and the Book of Common Prayer itself. Since Cosin was providing a Book of Hours for the Caroline Church,[1] he felt the pull of party affection and missed

---

1. John Cosin (1595–1672), who was early associated with "Laud's faction" and the Arminian party, and at the Restoration became bishop of Durham, compiled his *Devotions* in response to the desire of advisers to the court of Charles I. They wished to provide a Book of Hours for the Protestant ladies at court in order to help sustain

no chance to slight his presumed antagonists, urging, as Richard Hooker had done before him, the authority of "prayer and doctrine."[2] His first reason for setting out this office book, he writes, "is to continue & preserve the authority of the ancient *Lawes,* and old godly *Canons* of the Church . . . that men before they set themselves to pray, might know what to say, & avoid, as neer as might be, all extemporall effusions of irksome & indigested Prayers, which they use to make, that herein are subject to no good order or forme of words, but pray both what, & how, & when they list."[3] Nor must we pray differently in private than in public, lest we "lose our selves with confusion in any sudden, abrupt, or rude dictates, which are framed by Private Spirits, and Ghosts of our owne."

Cosin's insistence on orderly devotion certainly relies on a familiar and traditional framework; yet, one must admit that a distinctive ethos marks the *Devotions:* Cosin provides many of his own translations of familiar office hymns, such as his pleasing version of *Veni Creator,* "Come Holy Ghost; our soules inspire"; he composes many new prayers appropriate for a variety of special occasions or daily circumstances, as "At the washing of our hands" or "For the health of our Bodies";[4] and he encourages an unburdened devotional life while providing for

---

them in their loyalty to the English Church in the face of the influence of the Catholic Queen and her entourage. See the "Introduction" to my edition of Cosin's *Devotions* (Oxford: Clarendon Press, 1967), repr. in P. G. Stanwood, *The Sempiternal Season: Studies in Seventeenth-Century Writing* (New York: Peter Lang, 1992), 97–123.

2. See Richard Hooker, *Of the Laws of Ecclesiastical Polity,* ed. W. Speed Hill, Folger Library Edition of the Works of Richard Hooker (Cambridge: Belknap Press, Harvard University Press, 1977), 2:110: "Betwene the throne of God in heaven and his Church upon earth here militant if it be so that Angels have theire continuall intercorse, where should we finde the same more verified then in these two ghostlie exercises, the one *'Doctrine',* the other *'Prayer'*?" (book V, chap. 23).

3. See Cosin, *Devotions,* 11–12, and cf. Hooker, V, 25–27, to whom Cosin is generally indebted.

4. See Cosin, *Devotions,* 66, 261: "*At the washing of our hands:* Cleanse me, O God, by the bright fountaine of thy mercy, and water me with the dew of thine abundant grace, that being purified from my sinnes, I may grow up in good workes, truly serving thee in holines and righteousnes all the dayes of my life. *For the health of our Bodies:* O God the Father of Lights, from whom commeth downe every good and perfect gift, mercifully looke upon our frailtie and infirmitie, and grant us such health of Body, as thou knowest to be needfull for us: that both in our Bodies and Soules we may evermore serve thee with all our strength and might, through Jesus Christ our Lord."

its orderliness and practicality. In spite of the obvious formal demands of the genre in which he is working, Cosin, nevertheless, manages to invest his work with liveliness and vigor. If not quite spontaneous, Cosin is yet creative, making something new out of the old shapes. Above all, he enriches his book with that same ethos that we may observe in his contemporaries, such as Lancelot Andrewes, John Donne, and George Herbert. All of these persons celebrated and interpreted liturgy generously in their lives and also in their devotional writing.

Lancelot Andrewes (1555–1626) may be most remembered for his sermons, especially those—seventeen in all—on the Incarnation, and of these undoubtedly that one of 1622 made famous by T. S. Eliot's quotation in the "Journey of the Magi": "A cold coming we had of it, / Just the worst time of the year." Andrewes's compressed style is precise, with every phrase counting, as Eliot might have said, for its own epitaph. Conspicuous about this style is also its logic and careful structure: no word is used out of place nor misses its mark—the exposition of the text in order to meet the spiritual needs and longings both of the poet and of his auditors. This style is represented in his *Preces Privatae*, or *Private Devotions*, which Andrewes compiled out of many sources in the fashion of Cosin, arranging the various parts into regular patterns, though he seems to have intended these *Devotions* for his sole use. He first gives a preparatory section of daily prayers, appropriate for morning and evening, then gives a course of prayers for each day of the week, each day having an introduction, confession, prayer for grace, profession of faith, intercession, and expression of praise. He concludes with "Deprecations," a litany of the Trinity, and forms of intercession, with meditations on the Last Judgment, on human frailty, and finally on receiving the Holy Communion.

Nothing about Andrewes's compilation is original, yet everything about it is strikingly individual and fresh. In his essay "For Lancelot Andrewes," Eliot quotes from F. E. Brightman's introduction to his edition of the *Private Devotions,* and this passage helps to clarify what I see also in Andrewes's creative use of form:

> The structure is not merely an external scheme or framework: the internal structure is as close as the external. Andrewes develops an idea he has in his mind: every line tells and adds something. He does not expatiate, but moves forward: if he repeats, it is because the repeti-

tion has a real force of expression; if he accumulates, each new word or phrase represents a new development, a substantive addition to what he is saying. He assimilates his material and advances by means of it. His quotation is not decoration or irrelevance, but the matter in which he expresses what he wants to say. His single thoughts are no doubt often suggested by the words he borrows, but the thoughts are made his own, and the constructive force, the fire that fuses them, is his own. And this internal, progressive, often poetic structure is marked outwardly. . . . The prayers are arranged, not merely in paragraphs, but in lines advanced and recessed, so as in a measure to mark the inner structure and the steps and stages of the movement. Both in form and in matter Andrewes's prayers may often be described rather as hymns.[5]

The style thus responds to liturgical practice.

Andrewes indeed forms "hymns," or near lyrical bursts of song in such passages as the well-known statement that concludes his intercession in the Fourth Day:

> The brightness of the Lord our God be upon us,
> prosper Thou the work of our hands upon us,
> O prosper Thou our handy work.
> Be, Lord,
> within me to strengthen me,
> without me to guard me,
> over me to shelter me,
> beneath me to stablish me,
> before me to guide me,
> after me to forward me,
> round about me to secure me.[6]

In his confession in the "Order of Matin Prayer," we can see vividly Andrewes's management of this extraordinary style of reminiscence and participation, in which the form enriches the spontaneous affections of devotion and personal feeling. One prays in words that are common, yet curiously private:

---

5. See T. S. Eliot, *For Lancelot Andrewes: Essays on Style and Order* (1928; repr. London: Faber and Faber, 1970), 17–18, and Brightman (London: Methuen, 1903), 1.

6. Andrewes is quoted from J. H. Newman's translation, originally appearing in *Tracts for the Times*, no. 88 (London: Rivington, 1840), 54, 7.

> Essence beyond essence, Nature increate,
> Framer of the world,
> I set Thee, Lord, before my face,
> and I lift up my soul unto Thee.
> I worship Thee on my knees,
> and humble myself under Thy mighty hand.
> I stretch forth my hands unto Thee,
> my soul gaspeth unto Thee as a thirsty land.
> I smite on my breast
> and say with the Publican,
> God be merciful to me a sinner,
> the chief of sinners;
> to the sinner above the Publican,
> be merciful as to the Publican.
> Father of mercies,
> I beseech Thy fatherly affection,
> despise me not
> an unclean worm, a dead dog, a putrid corpse,
> despise not Thou the work of Thine own hands,
> despise not Thine own image
> though branded by sin.
> Lord, if Thou wilt, Thou canst make me clean,
> Lord, only say the word, and I shall be cleansed.

In such lines Andrewes really is writing religious poetry, embodying it with a liturgical setting, seemingly fixed yet expansive. Like Cosin after him, Andrewes lets a kind of liturgical worship regulate his feelings.

Although the form Andrewes uses in his *Devotions* is less traditionally liturgical than that which Cosin employs in his little office book, both books depend on the formularies of prayer; but neither Cosin nor Andrewes is principally a poet. Yet Andrewes is much affected by the rhythms of classical, and especially Hebrew verse, above all of the Psalter; and Cosin felt attracted also to the metrical compositions of medieval hymnody. Perhaps the pair's poetic as well as religious sensibilities may have been sharpened through the warmth of such relationships, but the great flowering of religious lyric poetry in England—and its indebtedness to liturgical practices and shapes—is naturally best illustrated by those, like John Donne, who deliberately elected also to write in verse, which is both more and less liturgically explicit.

We can see more easily the sense of this contrast or movement by recalling the sonnet or sonnetlike series of poems by writers close to one another in time and in faith: Robert Southwell (1561–1595), William Alabaster (1568–1640), and John Donne (1572–1631) shared an obvious joy in set forms of devotion, and they expressed these concerns in well-structured verse. Southwell's poetry is filled with vividly realized scenes, such as "The burning Babe," the passionate infant Christ who fills the poet with "sodaine heate" fueled by "wounding thornes," or the long "Saint Peters Complaint," "full fraught with grief." Perhaps his fourteen-poem "Sequence on the Virgin Mary and Christ" demonstrates most helpfully the compelling influence of liturgical design.

In this sequence, Southwell writes of Mary's conception, her nativity, her "spousals," her Annunciation ("Spell *Eva* backe and *Ave* shall you finde"), and at last her Assumption, necessarily combining her experience with that of her Son. Each of these sections is built on three six-line stanzas (except for "The Epiphanie," which contains four stanzas, or twenty-four lines). The effect achieved is similar to what Louis L. Martz describes in *The Poetry of Meditation*,[7] with the first stanza proposing the composition of place, the second, an analysis, the third, a colloquy or conversation, and the fourth, an application. The lyric on "The Nativity of Christ" thus calls on us to "Beholde the father, is his daughters sonne: / The bird that built the nest, is hatched therein"; then the poet proceeds to a second stanza that tries to understand these strange paradoxes and finally concludes with the confident request that "Gods gift am I, and none but God shall have me."[8]

The many sonnet sequences of the time dedicated to a secular mistress may have somewhat concealed these other sonnets devoted to the religious spirit. William Alabaster is another poet inspired to write of essential Christian scenes in liturgically significant ways. His sonnets are uneven in quality, but the best of them, as one in his series on "The Portrait of Christ's Death," demonstrate not only his concentration and skill but also his power to meditate on and internalize an outward event:

---

7. See *The Poetry of Meditation: A Study in English Religious Literature of the Seventeenth Century* (1954; rev. New Haven: Yale University Press, 1962), chap. 1 (esp. 39–43), and 111n.

8. Southwell's poetry is quoted from *The Poems of Robert Southwell, S.J.,* ed. James H. McDonald and Nancy Pollard Brown (Oxford: Clarendon Press, 1967).

> What should there be in Christ to give offence?
> His corded hands, why they for thee were bound,
> His mangled brows, why they for thee were crowned,
> His pierced breast, thy life did flow from thence.
> What though some arrows glance with violence
> From him to thee, shall this thy friendship wound?
> What though some stones upon thee do rebound,
> Shall such small fillips break thy patience?
> Those shafts which raze thy skin, ran through his heart;
> Those stones which touch thy hands, first broke his head;
> But those small drops of pain he doth impart
> To show what he did bear, what thou hast fled.
> And yet we grieve to suffer for his sake:
> 'Tis night, or else how could we so mistake?[9]

The theme of reciprocal and atoning grief anticipates such poems as Herbert's "The Bunch of Grapes," or "Affliction (I)": "I scarce beleeved, / Till grief did tell me roundly, that I lived." Alabaster's reflections are evidently also in much the same mode as Southwell's, or as Donne's, especially in his Holy Sonnets (especially the "penitential group"[10]), or in his notably liturgical "La Corona," "*this crown of prayer and praise,*" which celebrates in seven sonnets the coming of Christ, the Annunciation, the Nativity, the Presentation, the Crucifixion, the Resurrection, and the Ascension. Dame Helen Gardner noted the connection of the first poem in the "crown" with the Advent offices in the Roman Breviary;[11] but all of the poems in this series perform an interpretive ritual in a liturgical setting.

The impulse to write directly celebratory and liturgical verse appears everywhere among poets of this time. Herbert wrote of the major feasts commemorated in the Book of Common Prayer as well as

---

9. See *The Sonnets of William Alabaster,* ed. G. M. Story and Helen Gardner (London: Oxford University Press, 1959), xxxii–xxxiii, no. 7 of "The Portrait of Christ's Death."

10. Gardner links these four sonnets added in the 1635 edition of Donne's poems since they all deal with penitence. See *The Divine Poems,* 2d ed. (Oxford: Clarendon Press, 1978), 12–14. These are numbered 1, 5, 3, and 8 in H. J. C. Grierson's edition (1912; repr. Oxford: Clarendon Press, 1966). See also Roman Dubinski, "Donne's Holy Sonnets and the Seven Penitential Psalms," *Renaissance and Reformation* n.s., 10 (1986): 201–16.

11. See her edition of the *Divine Poems,* 57–58.

of the Virgin Mary, Mary Magdalene, and of the two dominical sacraments and the offices. Joseph Beaumont (1616–1699) wrote office hymns, baptismal and communion devotions, and poems for festivals and numerous saints, just as his friend Richard Crashaw (1612–1649), who compiled an office book, also wrote of the Assumption, of the "weeping motions" of Mary Magdalene, and, remarkably, of St. Teresa of Avila (three times), concluding the best of these Teresa poems, "The Flaming Heart," with a blazing outburst that he contains in the form of a litany ("By all thy dowr of Lights & Fires"). Similarly, much of Henry Vaughan's verse can best be understood through our recognition of his liturgical indebtedness, learned partly through his imitation of Herbert but mostly through his own design. Even Thomas Traherne (1637–1674), whose rhapsodic verse is often unmetrical as well as diffuse, tries to organize his worship into recognizable patterns. Thus we may read such "spontaneous" effusions as "Wonder" or "The Estate" as attempts to describe the meaning of the liturgy.

Poetry that refers to a liturgical setting or helps in its elaboration is sufficiently easy to define, but verse that seems more personal may still be deeply affected by an impulse toward formal worship. This may be the case with "A Nocturnall upon S. *Lucies* day, Being the shortest day" (written about 1617), included in the *Songs and Sonets* but probably imagined to be a solemn hymn to suit the canonical office of nocturn, a division of the traditional night office or "lauds," the first office (of seven) of the day. Donne begins,

>'Tis the yeares midnight, and it is the dayes,
>*Lucies*, who scarce seaven houres herself unmaskes,
>   The Sunne is spent, and now his flasks
>   Send forth light squibs, no constant rayes;
>   The world's whole sap is sunke:
>The generall balme th'hydroptique earth hath drunk,
>Whither, as to the beds-feet, life is shrunke,
>Dead and enterr'd; yet all these seeme to laugh,
>Compar'd with mee, who am their Epitaph.[12]

---

12. See Donne, *The Elegies and The Songs and Sonnets*, ed. Helen Gardner (Oxford: Clarendon Press, 1965), 84–85. Cf. Clarence H. Miller, "Donne's 'A Nocturnall upon S. Lucies Day' and the Nocturns of Matins," *Studies in English Literature* 6 (1966): 77–86.

Donne looks toward the whole world in which he wants to situate himself, discovering his own circumstances within it.[13] While the poet struggles to prepare himself—thus cast into desolation and emptiness—for the worship of this day by joining his life to whatever may yet survive, he finds in himself his own epitaph. The point is that this narrator measures his own experience by an external world of worship, of seasons, of potential life; and he discovers in his own special, internal world only a shadow of dawn, where the sun rises on others. Yet, paradoxically, he belongs to this larger community while being withdrawn from it. Such is the effect of liturgical worship, or the gathering up into a common petition the particular, diverse longings (or deprivations) of individuals. The St. Lucy's Day poem enables its speaker to celebrate his own worst loss.

Another example of this kind of liturgical writing may be drawn from Donne's *Divine Poems:* "Goodfriday, 1613. Riding Westward" assumes a devotional attitude appropriate to the present memory of the Passion. The poet is riding in a direction that seems to take him away from the sight of Christ's death:

>   . . . I am carryed towards the West
> This day, when my Soules forme bends toward the East.
>   (ll. 9–10)

But his life, while thus particularized, is not simply his own, for it must be common to all:

> Who sees Gods face, that is selfe life, must dye;
> What a death were it then to see God dye?
>   (ll. 17–18)

The poet of "Goodfriday" is discovering for himself the meaning of the Atonement, the sacrifice made for him and for all people who must be unworthy in order to deserve it. In the formal structure of the poem itself, the Crucifixion is represented; for midway, at lines 21–22, there is the question,

> Could I behold those hands which span the Poles,
> And tune all spheares at once, peirc'd with those holes?

---

13. Cf. my discussion of this poem in *The Sempiternal Season*, 4–6.

Liturgy, Worship, and the Sons of Light • 115

The outstretched arms, which would embrace the speaker, divide the poem horizontally, providing a cruciform design; what lies above the crossing describes the general "spectacle," and what now follows defines the special relationship of this person to it. The poem ends with a conventional prayer spoken by the narrator, but it is a prayer that he can say on behalf of all of us:

> Restore thine Image, so much, by thy grace,
> That thou may'st know mee, and I'll turne my face.
> (ll. 41–42)

Here is an implicitly liturgical poem that makes individual prayer possible within a carefully wrought form suitable for all times and individuals.[14]

The movement between verse that depends upon a liturgical setting and verse that grows into one—between what is "set" and what is "spontaneous"—may be further discovered in Herbert. His little poem on "Trinitie Sunday" is written for the feast day that celebrates a theological doctrine. Herbert reminds us of the Trinity in several ways, especially through the poetic structure itself:

> Lord, who hast form'd me out of mud,
> And hast redeem'd me through thy bloud,
> And sanctifi'd me to do good;
>
> Purge all my sinnes done heretofore:
> For I confesse my heavie score,
> And I will strive to sinne no more.
>
> Enrich my heart, mouth, hands in me,
> With faith, with hope, with charitie;
> That I may runne, rise, rest with thee.[15]

The poem is thick with threes: three stanzas of three lines in each, with sets of rhymes emphasizing the direction of Father, Son, and Spirit—with the associations of creator, redeemer, sanctifier ("mud," "bloud," "good"; "heretofore," "score," "no more"; "me," "charitie," "thee"),

---

14. See *Divine Poems*, ed. Gardner, 30–31.
15. See *The Works of George Herbert*, ed. F. E. Hutchinson (1941; repr. Oxford: Clarendon Press, 1959), 68.

though any set of three rhymes can be transposed, with the terms in any order. And key words in each stanza stress the one-in-three constitution of the Trinity: stanza 1 is the Father's, who *form'd, redeem'd, sanctifi'd;* stanza 2 is the Son's, who shows the poet how to *purge, confesse,* and *strive;* stanza 3 is the Spirit's, who enriches *heart* (of God = living), *mouth* (of Son = speaking), *hands* (of Spirit = enabling), with *faith, hope,* and *charity* (complemented by *run, rise,* and *rest*), each virtue pointing to a function of the three-in-one and one-in-three of the Trinity. The poem thus reads across and downward, reminding us throughout of the mysterious work of its subject, the poem as a whole seeming to state the Nicene or the Athanasian Creed succinctly.

Many of Herbert's poems are dedicated to a specific liturgical occasion, with celebration as the object of the verse. Other poems have no such external excuse, no previously determined occasion, and they would seem free to develop in their own way. "The Collar" is one such poem, which, in declaring (or having demanded) freedom discovers constraint; in supposing that worship is spontaneous the poet recognizes the inevitable pattern of devotion; and in avoiding the "calling" of God, he comes to hear it more clearly. We need to see "The Collar" again to realize its effect in the present context:

<pre>
        I struck ye board, & cryd, No more.
                I will abroad.
        What shall I euer sigh & pine?
    My lines & life are free: free as ye road
            Loose as ye wind, as large as store.   5
                Shall I be still in suit?
        Haue I no haruest but á thorne
        To lett mee blood & not restore,
        What I haue lost with cordiall fruit?
                    Sure there was wine   10
    Before my sighs did dry it. there was corne
            Before my teares did drowne it.
        Is the yeare onely lost to mee?
            Haue I no bayes to crowne it?
    No flowres, no garlands gay? all blasted?   15
                    All wasted?
        Not so my heart: but there is fruit,
                And thou hast hands.
</pre>

   Recouer all thy sigh-blowne age
On double pleasures. Leaue thy cold dispute   20
Of what is fitt, & not. forsake thy cage,
    Thy rope of sands,
W^{ch} petty thoughts haue made, & made to thee
  Good cable to enforce & draw,
     And be thy law,   25
While thou didst wink & wouldst not see.
    Away, Take Heed,
    I will abroad,
Call in thy deaths head there: ty up thy feares.
     He, y^t forbeares   30
  To suit & serue his need,
    Deserues his load.
But as I rau'd & grew more feirce & wild
    At euery word;
Me thoughts I heard one calling, Child!   35
  And I reply'd, My Lord.

I have quoted the Bodleian manuscript version because it makes a number of important adjustments to the appearance of the poem on the page, and it also gives some significant variant readings, different from the first printed version (1633), which most modern editions follow.[16] Above all, line 16, at the center of the poem, has a unique emphasis on account of its deep indentation: "All wasted?" is a forlorn question—and line; but the resolution of the poem turns on it, with the questions thereafter ceasing, and the raggedness of the meter and the rhyme scheme settling into the concluding composure of the last four lines. A curious feature of Herbert's poem is its tense. The narrator looks back on an event that has already happened: "I struck ye board, & cryd, No more." He has, in fact, resolved his difficulties; but in

---

  16. The transcription, from Bodleian MS Tanner 307, is the work of Mario A. Di Cesare; see his forthcoming edition of Herbert's *The Temple* (Binghamton, N.Y.: Medieval and Renaissance Texts and Studies). See F. E. Hutchinson's introduction to his edition of *The Works of George Herbert*, 1–lii, lxxii–lxxiv, and 153–54. Variants in the 1633 edition are as follows (given on the righthand side of the bracket): 1 more.] more, 3 What] What? 4 free:] free; 4 road] rode, 8 blood . . . restore,] bloud, . . . restore 11 it.] it: 17 so] so, 20 pleasures. Leaue] pleasures: leave 21 not. forsake] not forsake 24 cable] cable, 27 Away, Take Heed,] Away; take heed: 28 abroad,] abroad. 30 He, y^t] He that 33 wild] wilde, 34 word;] word, 35 Child!] *Childe:*

remembering them, he recreates conflicts that have passed. The poet is doing two things here of liturgical significance: he is imitating the spontaneous burst of emotion that he has felt in order to relive the painful feelings of the past in a new and continuing, momentaneous present; and he is, out of this "spontaneity," fashioning a generic statement for any individual who thinks that life is ensnaring. The poem builds (and is built) while it represents disintegration, resolving sadness into joy—both as a past and a present event. "The Collar" thus repeats and orders experience, and it therefore becomes as liturgical in its design and effect as any of those poems, such as "Trinitie Sunday," which already presume an explicit shape. Liturgy, indeed, defines and impels the religious lyric.[17]

There is no need to survey English religious lyrics of the late Renaissance in order to see their general indebtedness to liturgical rites and practices.[18] The impulse is obviously present wherever we look, whether in poetry that celebrates fixed occasions or in poetry that invents them—from "Trinitie Sunday," on the one hand, to "The Collar," on the other. It is this second kind of "invented" liturgical lyric that may be easiest to overlook because it seems unpremeditated, adventitious, or disordered—qualities one does not associate with liturgy. I have left to last, therefore, some discussion of the splendid lyrics of John Milton, whose skill at writing liturgical verse, especially of this voluntary and "natural" sort, has generally gone unremarked. One may think at first of Milton's great ode "On the Morning of Christ's Nativity," or "At a Solemn Music," or perhaps of *Lycidas*, or remember his life-long inter-

---

17. See Joseph H. Summers, *George Herbert: His Religion and Art* (1954; repr. London: Chatto and Windus, 1968), 90–92, who accurately analyzes the imitation of "disorder": "The poem contains all the elements of order in violent disorder. No line is unrhymed (a few rhymes occur as often as four times) and each line contains two, three, four, or five poetic feet. . . . If we consider that the first thirty-two lines represent eight quatrains, we discover six different patterns of rhyme (the only repeated one is the unformed *a b c d*) and seven patterns of line lengths. Until the final four lines, the poem dramatizes expertly and convincingly the revolt of the heart, and its imitation of colloquial speech almost convinces us of the justice of the cause. But the disorder of the poem provides a constant implicit criticism, and with the final lines we recogize that 'The Collar' is a narrative in past tense: the message for the present concerns the necessity of order" (92).

18. But see A. B. Chambers, *Transfigured Rites in Seventeenth-Century English Poetry* (Columbia: University of Missouri Press, 1992). Chambers's useful work is essentially just this kind of taxonomical study.

est in translating or adapting the Psalms.[19] While some or all of these works may disclose liturgical motives (though not all are really lyrics), I think Milton writes as a lyricist and liturgist most triumphantly in *Paradise Lost*. Barbara K. Lewalski has demonstrated convincingly that Milton employs a variety of genres in his great epic, embedding in it many lyric forms, in which "characters reveal their natures and their values through the lyrics they devise."[20] This is true, but I contend that most of these same lyrics are in form and intention acts of liturgical worship.

The six days' work of creation is described in such a way that each day becomes a separate hymn, reverberating to the sounds of glorious music. The sixth day, for example, ends with the familiar strains of angelic song. "Up he rode," Milton writes of the Creator,

> Follow'd with acclamation and the sound
> Symphonious of ten thousand Harps that tun'd
> Angelic harmonies: . . .
> . . . .
> Open, ye everlasting Gates, they sung,
> Open, ye Heav'ns, your living doors; let in
> The great Creator from his work return'd
> Magnificent . . .
> (*CPMP*, book VII, ll. 558–60, 565–68)[21]

And the "rest" of the seventh day is not kept in silence but in a mighty concert of music, while "of incense Clouds / Fuming from Golden Censers hid the Mount" (*CPMP*, book VII, ll. 599–600). Here there is an allusion to Psalm 24:9–10: "Lift up your heads, O ye gates, and be ye lift up, ye everlasting doors; and the King of glory shall come in," as well as reminiscences of the *Te Deum*, the ancient office hymn that appears in the order for morning prayer in the Book of Common Prayer: "To

19. See the authoritative study by Mary Ann Radzinowicz, *Milton's Epics and the Book of Psalms* (Princeton: Princeton University Press, 1989).
20. See Barbara K. Lewalski, "The Genres of *Paradise Lost*" in *The Cambridge Companion to Milton*, ed. Dennis Danielson (Cambridge: Cambridge University Press, 1989), 88, and cf. also her *Paradise Lost and the Rhetoric of Literary Forms* (Princeton: Princeton University Press, 1985).
21. Milton is quoted from the edition of *Complete Poems and Major Prose*, ed. Merritt Y. Hughes (New York: Odyssey Press, 1957). Hereafter references are cited as *CPMP*.

thee all Angels cry aloud, the Heavens and all the Powers therein. To thee Cherubim and Seraphim continually do cry, Holy, Holy, Holy, Lord God of hosts; Heaven and earth are full of the Majesty of thy glory."

Yet Adam and Eve's magnificent morning hymn in book 5 is the best example of liturgical worship that is not obviously determined to be so. The hymn is offered as if it might, too, be an appropriate canticle—this one recalling especially the *Benedicite, Omnia Opera* (or the apocryphal Song of the Three Children in the Book of Daniel), the hymn appointed for morning prayer in the Book of Common Prayer as an alternative to the *Te Deum:* "O all ye Works of the Lord, bless ye the Lord: praise him, and magnify him for ever"; and Milton also borrows phrases from Psalm 148. In spite of the disclaimer preceding the hymn that it is "unmeditated" or "prompt eloquence" (*CPMP*, book V, l. 149), this lyric has an admirable balance and finely wrought shape:

>These are thy glorious works, Parent of good,
>Almighty, thine this universal Frame,
>Thus wondrous fair; thyself how wondrous then!
>Unspeakable, who sit'st above these Heavens
>[5] To us invisible or dimly seen
>In these thy lowest works, yet these declare
>Thy goodness beyond thought, and Power Divine:
>Speak yee who best can tell, ye Sons of Light,
>Angels, for yee behold him, and with songs
>[10] And choral symphonies, Day without Night,
>Circle his Throne rejoicing, yee in Heav'n;
>On Earth join all ye Creatures to extol
>Him first, him last, him midst, and without end.
>Fairest of Stars, last in the train of Night,
>[15] If better thou belong not to the dawn,
>Sure pledge of day, that crown'st the smiling Morn
>With thy bright Circlet, praise him in thy Sphere
>While day arises, that sweet hour of Prime.
>Thou Sun, of this great World both Eye and Soul,
>[20] Acknowledge him thy Greater, sound his praise
>In thy eternal course, both when thou climb'st,
>And when high Noon hast gain'd, and when thou fall'st.

	Moon, that now meet'st the orient Sun, now fli'st
	With the fixt Stars, fixt in thir Orb that flies,
[25]	And yee five other wand'ring Fires that move
	In mystic Dance not without Song, resound
	His praise, who out of Darkness call'd up Light.
	Air, and ye Elements the eldest birth
	Of Nature's Womb, that in quaternion run
[30]	Perpetual Circle, multiform, and mix
	And nourish all things, let your ceaseless change
	Vary to our great Maker still new praise.
	Ye Mists and Exhalations that now rise
	From Hill or steaming Lake, dusky or grey,
[35]	Till the Sun paint your fleecy skirts with Gold,
	In honor to the World's great Author rise,
	Whether to deck with Clouds th'uncolor'd sky,
	Or wet the thirsty Earth with falling showers,
	Rising or falling still advance his praise.
[40]	His praise ye Winds, that from four Quarters blow,
	Breathe soft or loud; and wave your tops, ye Pines,
	With every Plant, in sign of Worship wave.
	Fountains and yee, that warble, as ye flow,
	Melodious murmurs, warbling tune his praise.
[45]	Join voices all ye living Souls; ye Birds,
	That singing up to Heaven Gate ascend,
	Bear on your wings and in your notes his praise;
	Yee that in Waters glide, and yee that walk
	The Earth, and stately tread, or lowly creep;
[50]	Witness if I be silent, Morn or Even,
	To Hill, or Valley, Fountain, or fresh shade
	Made vocal by my Song, and taught his praise.
	Hail universal Lord, be bounteous still
	To give us only good; and if the night
[55]	Have gather'd aught of evil or conceal'd,
	Disperse it, as now light dispels the dark.

(*CPMP*, book V, ll. 153–208)

This morning hymn (the evening is said to be the other time for such song), is carefully and symmetrically planned.[22] Adam and Eve praise

---

22. I am indebted to my colleague Lee M. Johnson for much of what follows, and

God in the first seven lines, even as they petition him in the final four [ll. 52–56]; thus they call on the angels, the "Sons of Light," for aid in their song. Now there are forty-five lines [ll. 8–52] descriptive of different orders of creation. These lines are balanced in two sections of twenty lines in each [ll. 8–27, 33–52], separated by a middle section of five lines [ll. 28–32]: the first section addresses the celestial universe; the middle section points to the elements of creation; and the last section provides more praise that rises from the earth. The middle section actually begins at the center of the passage, twenty-eight lines from the beginning and the same number from the end; but if we count from the eighth line, where this forty-five line passage begins, we reach "Perpetual Circle" [l. 30], the actual center of the passage.

The imagery throughout the whole hymn (sung at the canonical hour of Prime) depends upon circles, the sphere, the circlet, the orb, to which worship is rising, joining in ascent to "his praise," a notable phrase, occurring eight times, that spells out the motif of the song. This lyric, as we may surely style it, also invokes various kinds of light that put the end to all darkness: sun, eye and soul, noon, stars and moon, fires, sky. Finally, in the concluding four-line section, God is asked to disperse the brooding night, "as now light dispels the dark"; with "his praise" Adam and Eve and all of creation sing gloriously and melodiously, in words of consummate art and skill.

Milton's marvelous lyric is the manifestation of true prayer in a religious setting that brings forth abundance and exuberance. Yet this

---

to his "Language and the Illusion of Innocence in *Paradise Lost*," in *Of Poetry and Politics: New Essays on Milton and His World*, ed. P. G. Stanwood (Binghamton, N.Y.: Medieval and Renaissance Texts and Studies, forthcoming): "The entire passage [8–27] is encircled by the word 'Light' which serves as the end-word for lines [8] and [27]. The counterbalancing twenty-line section [33–52] on the terrestrial scale of creation uses the word 'praise' to end its major clauses, a praise that, according to other important words at the ends of lines, must 'rise' and 'ascend' as the passage touches on various aspects of earthly life associated with the springing forth of the morning light." See also Kathleen M. Swaim, who writes helpfully of the fundamental connections between the morning hymn, the Psalter, and the Book of Common Prayer in "The Morning Hymn of Praise in Book 5 of *Paradise Lost*," *Milton Quarterly* 22 (March 1988): 7–16: "By placing Adam and Eve's morning worship within a historical line, Davidic and liturgical, Milton might be said to validate the liturgy itself as well as to imply a legitimizing of Adam and Eve's spontaneous numbers" (11).

spontaneous liturgy, which is, of course, not spontaneous at all, becomes memorable because of its systematic ordering. Milton, through Adam and Eve, neatly regulates and organizes worship; instructed and accompanied by the Sons of Light, Adam and Eve have yet to know about formal prayer, but Milton is not so innocent, for he is quite conscious of the liturgical rightness of their song.

> **"ALL THINGS ARE BIGGE WITH JEST"**
> Wit as a Means of Grace

❋ ❋ ❋ *Judith Dundas* ❋ ❋ ❋

I

Given the identification of wit with levity, its relationship to faith was a controversial subject for seventeenth-century poets and critics. Nonetheless, the more imaginative religious poets knew the value of wit for the expression of their faith and did not hesitate to use it. Critics and poets with a narrower understanding were, on the other hand, inclined to see wit as not only a breach of decorum in religious poetry but as a sign of lack of faith. Such an assumption is implicit in Edmund Bolton's praise for Robert Southwell's poems as eschewing wit: "Never must be forgotten *St. Peter's Complaint*, and those other serious Poems said to be father *Southwell's;* the *English* whereof, as it is most proper, so the sharpness and Light of Wit is very rare in them."[1] Referring to the

---

1. *Hypercritica* (1612), in *Critical Essays of the Seventeenth Century*, ed. J. E. Spingarn, 2 vols. (Oxford: Clarendon Press, 1908–1909), 1:110.
 Modern criticism, though not religiously oriented, sometimes seems to reveal preconceptions not unlike those of Bolton. See, for example, a comment on ll. 3–4 of Herbert's "The Altar": "He is not being witty here; he is being sincere." (Richard Strier, *Love Known: Theology and Experience in George Herbert's Poetry*, [Chicago: University of Chicago Press, 1983], 193.) I would argue for the opposite: there can be no sincerity without wit.

sermons of a country parson, George Herbert could voice a similar prejudice against wit in a religious context: "The character of his Sermon is Holiness; he is not witty, or learned, or eloquent, but Holy."[2] It is the identification of wit with point and cleverness that evidently makes it out of place when what is called for is the simplicity of the Gospel.[3] Nevertheless, Herbert, like Donne and Marvell, demonstrates in his religious poetry that wit has a particular role to play in the conversion of sinners and may be decorous according to the principles of both art and religion.

When Herbert says that "All things are bigge with jest,"[4] his metaphor "bigge" represents all things as ready to give birth to the humor for which the poet serves as midwife. Here is the truth that must be brought to light, and the poet's wit is the instrument.

But considerations of audience also affect the use of wit in seventeenth-century religious poetry. If wit was out of place in preaching to a rural congregation, a gentleman addressing an educated audience was supposed to make light of his serious endeavors, as Sidney does in referring to his *Arcadia* as "but a trifle, and that triflingly handled," a playful toy.[5] Urbanity required such masking of purpose. A clear statement of the social value of wit appears in Henry Peacham's *The Compleat Gentleman:* "In your discourse be free and affable, giving entertainment in a sweete and liberall manner, and with a cheerefull courtesie, seasoning your talke at the table among grave and serious discourses, with conceipts of wit and pleasant invention, as ingenious Epigrammes, Emblems, Anagrammes, merry tales, wittie questions and answers."[6]

---

2. *A Priest to the Temple, or The Country Parson,* in *The Works of George Herbert,* ed. F. E. Hutchinson (Oxford: Clarendon, 1941), 233. Quotations from Herbert's poems are taken from this text.

3. For further examples relating to this issue, see my article "Levity and Grace: The Poetry of Sacred Wit," *Yearbook of English Studies,* 2 (1972), 93–102.

4. "The Church-porch," l. 239.

5. Sir Philip Sidney, Prefatory letter to his sister, the Countess of Pembroke. Cf. Milton's comment on the *Arcadia* as "a book in that kind full of worth and wit, but among religious thoughts and duties not worthy to be named. . . . " *Eikonoklastes,* in *John Milton: Complete Poems and Major Prose,* ed. Merritt Y. Hughes (New York: Odyssey Press, 1957), 793. Sidney would doubtless have agreed with this judgment of his work.

6. *The Compleat Gentleman* (1622), 196. For discussion of the courtly ideal, see Daniel Javitch, *Poetry and Courtliness in Renaissance England* (Princeton: Princeton University Press, 1978), and Marion White Singleton, *God's Courtier: Configuring a*

Milton's grander purposes disdained such displays of wit; the lyric poets of the seventeenth century, on the other hand, choosing a more intrinsically playful genre, were ready to speak in a language valued by their listeners. Herbert, in assessing his task of serving God, describes his own temperament: "My soul would stirre / And trade in courtesies and wit" ("Employment (II)," ll. 2–3). Elsewhere, he could dismiss "the wayes of Honour, what maintains / The quick returns of courtesie and wit" ("The Pearl," ll. 11–12).[7] Yet he, like Donne and Marvell, continues to appeal to the taste of his contemporaries for point and novelty of expression, even when explicitly renouncing wit. What these poets really articulate is a new decorum for religious poetry. As it takes over the witty man's form of expression, it makes of this expression a means of conversion. Wit becomes a net in which to catch sinners, making the poets fishers of men.[8]

Now decorum, according to Puttenham, "asketh one maner . . . in respect of the person who speakes: another of his to whom it is spoken: another of whom we speake: another of what we speake, and in what place and time and to what purpose."[9] It is to this overarching criterion that these poems are answerable as religious works of art. Their purpose renders their ambiguity, irony, indirection, playfulness—whatever terms we like to use—subordinate features, contingent on the poet's faith.

II

One of the challenges to the idea of decorum, especially in relationship to the urbanity of which I have spoken, is the childlike voice in many religious poems. Let us consider a figure that allows the poet

---

Different Grace in George Herbert's 'Temple' (Cambridge: Cambridge University Press, 1987).

7. I do not see the difference between these two poems as developmental but, rather, as representing different points of view that were available to Herbert to make use of in different poems. Contrast Singleton, *God's Courtier*, 131.

8. See *The Sermons of John Donne*, ed. George R. Potter and Evelyn M. Simpson, 10 vols. (Berkeley and Los Angeles: University of California Press, 1953–1962), 2:14, 287–310, on the text "And I will make you fishers of men."

9. *The Arte of English Poesie*, ed. G. D. Willcock and A. Walker (Cambridge: Cambridge University Press, 1936), 263.

both to preserve the rhetorical strength of his argument and to make room for the religiously childlike values of simplicity, innocence, and playfulness. I refer to *prosopopoeia*, or personification. Donne, for example, makes use of it in two of his Holy Sonnets, in one briefly, in one, throughout. In "Thou hast made me, and shall Thy work decay?," he introduces the image of a journey:

> I run to death, and death meets me as fast.
> And all my pleasures are like yesterday,
> I dare not move my dim eyes any way,
> Despair behind, and death before doth cast
> Such terror. . . . [10]

At first, the word *death* does not particularly suggest personification; but when it, along with despair, is given an action to perform, a fiction develops: "Despair behind and death before doth cast / Such terror. . . . " The traveler beset by these enemies, which are only phantasms, is a familiar theme in both literature and the visual arts—witness Dürer's *The Knight, Death, and the Devil*. But Donne, more overtly than Dürer, emphasizes the weakness and helplessness of the central figure—himself—so that he must turn to God for support: "Only thou art above, and when towards thee / By thy leave I can look, I rise again" (ll. 9–10). Conventional as Donne's personifications are, they represent the child's imagination, projecting into outward form what lies in the mind.

The other personification, in "Death be not proud" (Sonnet 6), reverses the strength of death relative to the speaker. Throughout this sonnet, the poet addresses death using *meiosis*, or the figure of belittlement, (Puttenham calls it "the disabler" [11]): "Thou art slave to fate, chance, kings, and desperate men, / And dost with poison, war, and sickness dwell. . . ." (ll. 9–10). The bad company death keeps reveals its weakness; its resemblance to sleep further diminishes its power; "And poppy, or charms can make us sleep as well, / And better than thy stroke. . . . " In one of Donne's sermons,[12] he notes that this analogy

---

10. Holy Sonnet 13, ll. 3–7. Quotations from Donne poems are taken from *John Donne*, ed. John Carey (Oxford: Oxford University Press, 1990).
11. *The Arte of English Poesie*, 219
12. *Sermons*, 8:7, 189–190, on the text "And when he had said this, he fell asleep."

between sleep and death only begins to flourish in the Christian era when the conviction of resurrection gives significance to the parallel: "One short sleep past, we wake eternally, / And death shall be no more, Death thou shalt die" (ll. 13–14). The taunting of death is a game played seriously, for its purpose is to alter the listener's perspective on what is most terrifying.

But Donne does not use *prosopopoeia* all that often; as we shall see, he prefers other forms of religious wit. Andrew Marvell, on the other hand, finds a particular use for this figure "to 'act out his meaning.'"[13] Indeed, his dialogues of "Soul and Body" and "A Dialogue between the Resolved Soul and Created Pleasure" give all the words to personifications. Winning by words becomes the game.

Both the Soul and the Body are witty in their imagery. The Soul speaks of being fettered "In feet, and manacled in hands," punning on the etymology of "fetter" and "manacle."[14] The Body, preferring to be an animal, explains that because the Soul makes it walk upright, "mine own precipice I go" (l. 14). They use playful arguments against each other in a parody of the medieval *débat*. Each tries to diminish the other by means of paradoxes, such as the Body's complaint that the Soul "Has made me live to let me die" (l. 18). Reluctantly, the Soul admits that all its care is bent "That to preserve, which me destroys" (l. 26); thus it is "shipwrecked into health again" (l. 30). The conclusion brings all paradoxes together by pointing to the Soul's animating and preserving role in relationship to the Body, and giving the Body, perversely, it might seem, the last word:

> What but a soul could have the wit
> To build me up for sin so fit?
> So architects do square and hew,
> Green trees that in the forest grew.
>   (ll. 41–44)

The architect is a noble artist and the one who must take charge of a work in its wholeness; but from the partial perspective of the Body, it is

---

13. See Rosemond Tuve, *Elizabethan and Metaphysical Imagery: Renaissance Poetic and Twentieth-Century Critics* (Chicago: University of Chicago Press, 1947), 94.

14. Quotations from Marvell's poems are taken from *Andrew Marvell: The Complete Poems,* ed. Elizabeth Story Donno (Harmondsworth: Penguin Books, 1972).

the Soul as architect who deprives the Body of the healthy animal life of instinct, making it only "for sin so fit." The complaint of the Body ends by putting the burden on the Soul. And indeed the very word *sin* as used by the Body makes the Soul responsible for its animal other half.

In "A Dialogue between the Resolved Soul and Created Pleasure," there are three speakers, as well as a chorus. The poem begins with a personifying address to the soul as a warrior, defended by faith:

> Courage, my Soul, now learn to wield
> The weight of thine immortal shield.
> Close on thy head thy helmet bright.
> Balance thy sword against the fight.
> See where an army, strong as fair,
> With silken banners spreads the air.
> Now, if thou be'st that thing divine,
> In this day's combat let it shine:
> And show that Nature wants an art
> To conquer one resolvèd heart.
> (ll. 1–10)

When the antagonists engage in their debate, the effect becomes even more masquelike than the suggestion here of a Minerva figure and an army "with silken banners." The poem is altogether more sensuous than the Body/Soul debate, leading quite naturally to the Chorus at the end.

An allusion by Pleasure to "Nature's banquet" serves as a reminder of a topos that appears, for example, in Shakespeare's *Venus and Adonis* and in Chapman's *Ovids Banquet of Sense:* "Lay aside that warlike crest, / And of Nature's banquet share."[15] Beginning with taste "the souls of fruits and flowers," we are led by Pleasure through experiences that appeal to touch, smell, sight, and hearing—from the lower senses to the higher. The longer speeches with the sensuous imagery are all given to Pleasure, and very lovely they are:

> Hark how music then prepares
> For thy stay these charming airs;

---

15. On the history of the topos, see Frank Kermode, "The Banquet of Sense," in *Shakespeare, Spenser, Donne: Renaissance Essays* (London: Routledge and Kegan Paul, 1971), 84–115.

> Which the posting winds recall,
> And suspend the river's fall.
> (ll. 37–40)

The Chorus, as in a masque, encourages the Soul in its resolve:

> Earth cannot show so brave a sight
> As when a single soul does fence
> The batteries of alluring sense,
> And heaven views it with delight.
>   Then persevere: for still new charges sound:
>   And if thou overcom'st, thou shalt be crowned.
> (ll. 45–50)

The next series of temptations, of beauty, money, fame, and knowledge, are as easily put by. Again the Chorus marks the end with a song, pronouncing the triumph of the Soul. If music and song are the most playful of poetry's attributes, then this example of Marvell's wit shows agonistic play at its most celebratory.

While Donne and Marvell use *prosopopoeia* only occasionally, it is a figure entirely at home in Herbert's poetry. He perfectly exemplifies the combined "seriousness of the child at play and the conscience of the artist."[16] Some examples are brief: "Wit fancies beautie, beautie raiseth wit: / The world is theirs; they two play out the game" ("Love (I)"). Herbert's own game is played more seriously than that of wit and beauty, for they are like chessmen in the moves he makes with them. But Sidney, explaining fiction in his *Apology for Poetry*, noted that we give names even to our chessmen: "And yet, methinks, he were a very partial champion of truth that would say we lied for giving a piece of wood the reverend title of bishop."[17] It is no diminution of poetry in Sidney's eyes to link it to the child's understanding of metaphor in order to show the adult the meaning of fiction: "What child is there that, coming to a play, and seeing *Thebes* written in great letters upon an old door, doth believe that it is Thebes?"[18] The simple act of

---

16. See Romano Guardini, *The Spirit of the Liturgy*, trans. Ada Land (New York: Sheed and Ward, 1940), 182.
17. *An Apology for Poetry: or, The Defence of Poetry*, ed. Geoffrey Shepherd (Manchester: Manchester University Press, 1965), 124.
18. Ibid.

turning abstractions into people becomes for Herbert paradigmatic of the fiction that is wittily invented to become a means of grace, not only for the reader but also for the poet himself.

In Herbert's "Love (III)," for example, the figure of Love speaks to the penitent sinner as to a child. It is an imaginary situation of question and answer, related to the catechism: "Love took my hand, and smiling did reply, / Who made the eyes but I?" (ll. 11–12). The pun "eye"/"I" gives a touch of playful wit that reinforces the "smiling"; and all this added to "quick-ey'd Love," a parody of the Love familiar to secular love poetry, makes a game of what has all the serious implications of a sinner at Holy Communion. The eyes here have achieved the simplicity of vision longed for in "Love (II)": "Our eies shall see thee, which before saw dust; / Dust blown by wit, till that they both were blinde" (ll. 9–10). It is not that wit is abandoned but that it has found a new voice in speaking with compassion toward human folly.

This new voice is heard, too, in "Humilitie," a poem that represents the Virtues as sitting hand in hand upon an azure throne and all the beasts, or passions, presenting "tokens of submission." Each one wants the peacock plume presented by the crow, and they quarrel over this emblem of pride. Humility makes the Virtues drive away the beasts till "the next Session-day." The little story ends with the playful decree that next time the beasts must pay double tribute. Through the wit of the invention, Herbert conveys the absurdity of pride.

As a priest, he knew the value of stories in preaching; personification and its capacity to turn into story came naturally to him. But he can also examine the attributes of a traditional personification such as Death. He does so more cheerfully than Robert Southwell or Lord Herbert of Cherbury or even Donne. Instead of Donne's *meiosis* in "Death be not proud," Herbert sings about the new vision of death that has come with the Christian faith: "But since our Saviours death did put some bloud / Into thy face; / Thou art grown fair and full of grace, / Much in request, much sought for as a good" ("Death," ll. 13–16). Having begun with the old view of Death as "an uncouth hideous thing," he ends joyfully: "When souls shall wear their new aray, / And all thy bones with beautie shall be clad" (ll. 19–20).

Over and over in his poems, Herbert influences our view of abstractions through his use of personification. He can put conscience in its place by saying, "Peace pratler" ("Conscience," l. 1), or he can tell a little fairy tale: "Joy, I did lock thee up: but some bad man / Hath let thee out again" ("The Bunch of Grapes, ll. 1–2). He can even reverse personification, turning man into something inanimate to show in a new light his purpose in the world: "To be a window, through thy grace" ("The Windows," l. 1). Herbert, in fact, makes a point of drawing attention to the co-presence of simplicity and wit in his poetry. In "The Church-porch," he completes the idea that "All things are bigge with jest," by telling both himself and his listeners that "nothing that's plain, / But may be wittie, if thou hast the vein" (ll. 239–40). Addressing God directly in "The Thanksgiving," he most clearly puts his wit in the divine service: "If thou shalt give me wit, it shall appeare, / If thou hast giv'n it me, 'tis here" (ll. 43–44).[19]

III

But besides wit exercised in the invention of personifications or in the redefining of them, there is a wit in using the figures of repetition. Repetition, says Puttenham, "doth much alter and affect the eare and also the mynde of the hearer, and therefore is counted a very brave figure both with the Poets and rhetoriciens."[20] In Herbert's "The Sacrifice," as in liturgical rites generally, the reiterated sounds induce an almost hypnotic state of calm, which contrasts markedly with the meaning of the refrain "Was ever grief like mine?" Each three-line stanza contains a paradox, of God's gifts and man's folly in refusing to take them; yet the incantatory effects of the verse and refrain, together with the conventionality of the images and ideas, make us engage in a ritual experience, rather than in a personal one.[21] It is communal, and it is musical, rather than analytical; it is not playful as personification is, but playful as the liturgy is in having no purpose other than to effect a state of mind in which grace may enter.[22]

If we turn from Herbert's long poem to Donne's much briefer *La Corona*, we find the same association of wit, repetition, and musical

---

19. Other examples include "The Posie" and "Jordan (I)" and "Jordan (II)."
20. *The Arte of English Poesie*, 198.
21. On "The Sacrifice," see Rosemond Tuve, *A Reading of George Herbert* (Chicago: University of Chicago Press, 1952), 19–99.
22. On the playfulness of the liturgy, see *The Spirit of the Liturgy,* chapter 5.

emphasis. Donne does not describe the struggle of the will (perhaps the reason this poem is less popular with critics than some others by Donne[23]) but celebrates the Christian story of salvation. This, one of the most beautiful of Donne's religious poems, makes repetition representative of the circle of faith. Within each sonnet are instances of *antimetabole*, or reversal of words: "The ends crown our works, but thou crown'st our ends" (I, l. 9). This use of the figure is both witty and illustrative of the paradoxes of faith. A similar circularity is conveyed by Donne's use of *adynaton*, a kind of impossibility, such as in his Annunciation sonnet when he addresses Mary: "thou / Wast in his mind, who is thy son, and brother, / Whom thou conceiv'st, conceived; yea, thou art now / Thy maker's maker, and thy father's mother" (II, ll. 9–12). Paradox, which Puttenham calls "the wonderer," is clearly a source of delight both to Donne and to his readers: "The Word but lately could not speak, and lo / It suddenly speaks wonders. . . . " (IV, ll. 5–6). Effectively, repetition underlines paradox:

> Whose creature Fate is, now prescribe a fate,
> Measuring self-life's infinity to a span,
> Nay, to an inch. Lo, where condemned he
> Bears his own cross, with pain, yet by and by
> When it bears him, he must bear more and die.
> ("Crucifying," ll. 7–11)

But, though repetitions point up paradox, they have so musical an effect that the paradox is almost transcended in the pleasure of the echoes. In this sequence of sonnets, linearity is turned to circularity by making the last line of each sonnet become the first line of the next (*anadiplosis*), and the last line of all, a repetition of the first of the sequence, all to confirm the title, *La Corona*, the wreath or crown.

The figure of *anadiplosis* is also used throughout Herbert's short poem "A Wreath," but since this is a personal prayer, the repetitions

---

23. Cf. Helen Gardner: "'*La Corona*' has been undervalued as a poem by comparison with the 'Holy Sonnets,' because the difference of intention behind the two sets of sonnets has not been recognized. The '*La Corona*' sonnets are inspired by liturgical prayer and praise—oral prayer; not by private meditation and the tradition of mental prayer" (Introduction to *John Donne: The Divine Poems* [Oxford: Clarendon Press, 1952], xxi).

have a less liturgical ring. While making his poem suggest circularity, he proclaims that life is straight and leads to God:

> A Wreathed garland of deserved praise,
> Of praise deserved, unto thee I give,
> I give to thee, who knowest all my wayes,
> My crooked winding wayes, wherein I live,
> Wherein I die, not live: for life is straight,
> Straight as a line, and ever tends to thee,
> To thee, who art more farre above deceit,
> Then deceit seems above simplicitie.
> Give me simplicitie, that I may live,
> So live and like, that I may know thy wayes,
> Know them and practise them: then shall I give
> For this poore wreath, give thee a crown of praise.
> (ll. 1–12)

The repetitions, of course, become a conceit as they illustrate the subject of the poem. Since straightness is set above "crooked winding wayes," however, the technique is used for opposite effect to that of Donne's "La Corona." In that poem, the mystery of the incarnation and redemption is expressed through circularity; in Herbert's poem, the subject is a manmade wreath, a crown that must give way to a heavenly tribute.[24] Yet even in rejecting his "poore wreath," Herbert gives it a musical sound.

A sense for a divinity in music, surpassing the discursive use of language, supports the value of liturgy. Donne's poem on the Sidneys' translation of the Psalms meditates on, and reflects, the idea of regulated worship: "In forms of joy and art doe re-reveale" (l. 34). Although his wit plays briefly with the thought of re-revelation, he finally subordinates it to the musical imagery appropriate to the Psalms. He begins the poem with a clear sense of human limits and of the powers of the intellect:

> Eternal God, (for whom who ever dare
> Seek new expressions, do the circle square,
> And thrust into strait corners of poor wit

24. Cf. Marvell's "A Coronet."

Thee, who art cornerless and infinite)
I would but blesse thy name, not name thee now. . . .
(ll. 1–5)

It takes wit to expose the ingenious arguments by which God, who is "cornerless and infinite," is thrust into "strait corners of poor wit." Here Donne's own wit, while praising God, laughs at theological definitions. To give wit its proper place in religious poetry is to dramatize the discrepancy between human understanding and the divine. Yet this step is mediate only; Donne's goal, like Herbert's, is to come to rest in the simplicities of praise: "may / These their sweet learned labours, all the way / Be as our tuning, that, when hence we part / We may fall in with them, and sing our part" (ll. 53–56).

IV

But for our part, we must still give some consideration to the mediate steps by which the poets seek to ascend the heavenly ladder. Of these, the one that has most caught the attention of critics from Dryden on is the witty conceit. A conscious pursuit of surprising analogies, the *discordia concors,* is the recognized characteristic of the so-called metaphysical poets. When Camden, in the early seventeenth century, wishing to praise English poets, notes that they "are as pregnant both in witty conceits and devises" as any,[25] we are reminded of the gradual identification of literary excellence with a certain kind of cleverness. How religious poets could turn this aesthetic category or artistic goal to a means of grace is worth exploring, especially in light of their frequent denunciations of wit.

Certainly the demand for point and paradox meant a constant search for witty conceits. As early as Gascoigne's *Certain Notes of Instruction* (1575), it had come to seem that literature lacking these qualities would be flat and without savor. Yet religious thinkers were concerned about the trend toward equating wit, originally the faculty of invention or even wisdom, with an apparently frivolous activity. C. S. Lewis, illustrating what he calls "the dangerous sense of the word," cites Hooker: "Sharp and subtle discourses of wit procure great applause, but being

---

25. William Camden, *Remaines concerning Britaine* (London, 1614), 316.

laid in the balance with that which the habit of sound experience plainly delivereth, they are overweighed."[26] It was necessary for religious poets to take this sense of the word and make it work for them, not as the opposite of wisdom and gravity but as a manifestation of the startling moment that reveals man to himself. If religious poetry is to catch the reader in its net, it too—at least, in the early seventeenth century—needs something of the sharp and piercing; if the world is, to some extent, the enemy, it must be countered in its own coin.

But wit can also perceive hidden resemblances and therefore prove the universe to have an invisible order of correspondences. In one of Donne's sermons, he compares the world to a sea in a series of analogies: it affords water, for example, but not to drink; it is apparently limitless, yet it is bounded by God's decree; it contains greater fish who devour the less, "and so doe the men of this world too." Above all, the sea is not a place of habitation "but a passage to our habitations." Concerned as he is to expatiate on the text that describes the calling of Peter and Andrew, Donne finds in the Gospel the very net that he himself would cast to catch the souls of his listeners. By finding analogies to confirm his argument, he exercises his wit, but not simply to win the admiration of these listeners: "Eloquence is not our net . . . only the Gospel is."[27]

Again using the sea as an analogy, Donne's elegy for Lady Markham makes a modification: "Man is the world, and death the ocean" (l. 1), which environs all. Having set up his analogy, he proceeds to describe the effects of death on Lady Markham as if she were a sculpted figure on a tomb:

> In her, this sea of death hath made no breach,
> But as the tide doth wash the slimy beach,
> And leaves embroidered works upon the sand,
> So is her flesh refined by death's cold hand.
> (ll. 17–20)

This, the most imaginative and musical part of the poem, conveys an image of death not unlike that on the famous tomb of Valentine Bal-

---

26. *Studies in Words*, 2d ed. (Cambridge: Cambridge University Press, 1967), 100.
27. *Sermons*, 2:14, 306–7.

biani, by Germain Pilon.[28] Instead of the horrors of decaying flesh, both the lower, *transi,* part of the tomb and the poem reveal death as refiner of the body. Metaphor here becomes an instrument of clarified perception.

More daring still are the metaphors of Herbert's "Church-monuments." Since Herbert is not commemorating one person, as Donne is in his elegy for Lady Markham, he is free from the requirements of praise and the need to mourn with patience. The decorum of his subject is different from that of Donne's. Just as Ben Jonson and Milton derided pyramids and monuments to commemorate the dead, so Herbert takes this well-worn theme and makes it startlingly new by his insistent repetitions, especially of the word *dust,* culminating in the image of the hourglass, and by his personifying method of mocking the transitoriness of monuments. He sends his body to school among them to

>   finde his birth
> Written in dustie heraldrie and lines;
> Which dissolution sure doth best discern,
> Comparing dust with dust, and earth with earth.
> These laugh at Jeat and Marble put for signes,
>
> To sever the good fellowship of dust,
> And spoil the meeting. What shall point out them,
> When they shall bow, and kneel, and fall down flat,
> To kisse those heaps, which now they have in trust?
> Deare flesh, while I do pray, learn here thy stemme
> And true descent . . .
>
> That flesh is but the glasse, which holds the dust
> That measures all our time; which also shall
> Be crumbled into dust. . . .
>   (ll. 8–22)

By a *catachresis,* or a shocking metaphor, he has the monuments "kiss" the dust. The remarkable use of enjambment and the repetitions of sound, such as "fall," "fat," "flesh," "fit," help to convey the inevitability with which sand runs through an hourglass. Even the twenty-

---

28. See Erwin Panofsky, *Tomb Sculpture: Four Lectures on Its Changing Aspects from Ancient Egypt to Bernini* (New York: Harry N. Abrams, 1964), 81

four lines of the poem represent the action of the hourglass. Although other seventeenth-century poets were also fond of this image, Herbert turns the body itself into an hourglass. Our time is "measured," but, typically, man refuses to recognize his limits, while at the same time constantly setting up self-imposed limits as containers for the spirit.

For all the containers with which man surrounds himself, Herbert has a favorite diminishing image, that of a box. It is a homely image of the sort he likes, stressing the limits of human existence. God has supplied us with two boxes for our life in this world: our bodies and the world of nature. Man himself, before the Fall, was "A box of jewels, shop of rarities" ("Miserie," l. 68), just as spring is "A box where sweets compacted lie" ("Vertue," l. 10). Yet so rich is the box image in ambiguity that Herbert can turn night into an "ebony box" ("Even-song," ll. 21–22), a kind of coffin, as well as a blessed antidote to the poison of thought.[29] The poet sees his own heart as a box containing anything but sweets:

> Since bloud is fittest, Lord, to write
> Thy sorrows in, and bloudie fight;
> My heart hath store, write there, where in
> One box doth lie both ink and sinne.
> ("Good Friday," ll. 21–24)

In "Mortification," Herbert spells out the consistency with which the box characterizes the human condition throughout the whole of life. The poem traces man from infancy on in terms of enclosures, from the swaddling bands "taken from a chest of sweets" (l. 2), to the "biere, / Which shall convey him to the house of death" (ll. 29–30). Between these poles man seeks a house;

> When man grows staid and wise,
> Getting a house and home, where he may move
> Within the circle of his breath,
> Schooling his eyes;
> That dumbe inclosure maketh love
> Unto the coffin, that attends his death.
> (ll. 19–24)

---

29. Cf. C. A. Patrides's edition of *The English Poems of George Herbert* (London: J. M. Dent, 1974) for a note on the idea that poisonous liquids "enclosed in a box of ebony were thought to be rendered harmless."

The title, "Mortification," sums up the message of the poem, that all the boxes within which man lives only prefigure "the house of death." By his use of the homely image of a box, Herbert wittily meets his own challenge to find "All things . . . bigge with jest." For how can one take seriously one's ownership of a house when it is thus put with all the other boxes within which the spirit seeks an illusory home? A Hamlet thinks he could be "bounded in a nutshell and count [himself] a king of infinite space, were it not that [he] has bad dreams."[30] The difficulty, as Herbert's poems likewise imply, is for man to realize his spiritual freedom within the various boxes by which he is surrounded.

Even within the human heart are boxes. Herbert explores them in "Confession," describing his masterliness in making chests, with a pun on the word *chest:* "within my heart I made / Closets; and in them many a chest; / And, like a master in my trade, / In those chests, boxes; in each box, a till" (ll. 2–5). But this compartmentalization is ineffectual: "Yet grief knows all, and enters when he will" (l. 6). To griefs and pains, "Closets are halls . . . and hearts, high-wayes" (l. 18). Indeed, fiction, the illusory, "Doth give a hold and handle to affliction" (l. 24) and, paradoxically, it is only the open breast without locks that can shut out the pain.

If the body is our chief box, our "poore cabinet of bone" ("Ungratefulnesse," l. 28), it has, however, the glory of imitating the Incarnation: "this box we know; / For we have all of us just such another." But the cabinet of the Trinity remains hidden from us, though in reality God has given this as one of his two boxes in exchange for one human heart. In this context, the humble box takes on a sublime significance and a mystery that unites human understanding to human incomprehension.

Architectural images simply magnify the box idea. When Herbert would praise man's gifts, he refers to him as "a stately habitation . . . all symmetrie, / Full of proportions, one limb to another, / And all to all the world besides" ("Man," ll. 13–15). In this palace, God is invited to dwell; but, perversely, man seeks to add balconies, terraces, weakening the original structure. Although sin, "combin'd with *Death* in a firm band / To raze the building to the very floore," *Love* and *Grace* "took *Glorie* by the hand, / And built a braver Palace then before" ("The

---

30. William Shakespeare, *Hamlet,* ed. Edward Hubler (New York: New American Library, 1963), 2.2.258–60.

World," ll. 16–20). Like Milton, Herbert thinks of God as the great architect, who builds "strong in a weak heart." The whole collection with the title *The Temple* alludes to the "frame and fabrick" within, not to the outward temples that are "Tombes for the dead, not temples fit for thee" ("Sion," l. 12 and l. 20). In using the word *temple*, Herbert has chosen a traditional metaphor, unlike his word *box*. Certainly he risked an indecorum in his choice of that word; but whimsically diminishing as it is, *box* has the effect of shocking the reader into a new awareness of the whole mystery of incarnation.

V

The power of images both to delight and to teach made them the chief weapon in the religious poet's armory. Rhetoricians never tired of commending them for their visual effect, calling them "readie pensils pliable to line out and shadow any maner of proportion in nature." But Peacham also notes their power to "minister a pleasure to the reader's wit."[31] It is this witty aspect of such metaphors as *catachresis* and *meiosis* that particularly distinguishes Donne and Herbert from the earlier Elizabethan poets. Closer to these older poets in his concern for the beautiful image is Andrew Marvell, but at the same time, he too seeks for novelty in his analogies. His emblematic poem "On a Drop of Dew" might seem to diminish man's pride by the analogy between the drop of dew and the human soul, but more important is the idea that both aspire heavenwards:

> See how the orient dew,
> Shed from the bosom of the morn
>   Into the blowing roses,
> Yet careless of its mansion new,
> For the clear region where 'twas born
>   Round in itself incloses:
>   And in its little globe's extent,
> Frames as it can its native element.
>   How it the purple flow'r does slight,

---

31. *The Garden of Eloquence* (1593) (Gainesville, Fla.: Scholars' Facsimiles and Reprints, 1954), 14, 13.

"All Things are Bigge with Jest" • 141

> Scarce touching where it lies,
> But gazing back upon the skies,
> Shines with a mournful light,
> Like its own tear. . . .
>
> (ll. 1–13)

The whole poem is whimsical as it develops the analogy, ending on a yet more gloriously whimsical analogy:

> Such did the Manna's sacred dew distill,
> White and entire, though congealed and chill,
> Congealed on Earth; but does, dissolving, run
> Into the glories of th'almighty sun.
>
> (ll. 37–40)

Marvell conveys his own pleasure in discovering hidden resemblances and turning them into a hymn of praise.

It is as if he believes that wit is needed to praise the divine playfulness. In "Bermudas," this aspect of God is to the fore:

> He hangs in shades the orange bright,
> Like golden lamps in a green night.
> And does in the pom'granates close,
> Jewels more rich than Ormus shows.
> He makes the figs our mouths to meet,
> And throws the melons at our feet.
>
> (ll. 17–22)

As the metaphors point to a God whose purpose is to give pleasure to man, so it should be part of man's religion to recognize the divine gifts. In Sidney's words, "problems . . . [or intellectual debate] from my reach do grow";[32] they cease to exist.

Marvell, the "easy philosopher," praises the masking by nature. In "Upon Appleton House," he pays tribute to the aptness of nature's disguising:

> And see how chance's better wit
> Could with a mask my studies hit!

---

32. *Astrophil and Stella*, 3.

> The oak leaves me embroider all,
> Between which caterpillars crawl:
> And ivy, with familiar trails,
> Me licks, and clasps, and curls, and hales.
> Under this antic cope I move
> Like some great prelate of the grove.
>
> (ll. 585–92)

God, too, engages in masking, as Donne implies by his reference to God's "vizard" and by the attention he gives to the enigmatic in divine expression, whether in nature or in the Bible.[33] But here Marvell's religious metaphors barely hint at the hidden God.

Poetry itself is another form of playful disguising, as Sidney never tires of pointing out with such expressions as "the masking raiment of poesy." Through poetry, everything can become a figure of significance; but it is the poet's wit that, maskingly, reveals the hidden resemblances and patterns that constitute significance. At the same time, the religious poet needs wit in more particular ways: to mock man's pretensions, to show that he moves "but on a point below" ("On a Drop of Dew," l. 25), or to praise the imagination of God. Critics who have admired the wit of seventeenth-century religious poets would agree with T. S. Eliot, that this wit is "as much a part of that period's religious intensity as of its levity."[34] Yet they have supplied no philosophical context within which to view the use of wit in religious poetry.

Perhaps we can find a beginning in Plato's words: "God alone is worthy of supreme seriousness, but man is made God's plaything, and that is the best part of him."[35] Marvell's "embroidered cope" can serve as a metaphor for all poetry made by poets who, while recognizing their priestly function, nevertheless "play" before the Lord. In Herbert's "all things are bigge with jest," we hear the echo of Socratic and Erasmian laughter. This is the levity that leaventh the whole lump.

---

33. "For now we see through a glasse darkly," in *The Sermons of John Donne*, 8:9, 219–36.

34. "A Note on Two Odes of Cowley," in *Seventeenth Century Studies Presented to Sir Herbert Grierson* (Oxford: Clarendon Press, 1938), 242.

35. *Laws*, viii, 803, cited in Johan Huizinga, *Homo Ludens: A Study of the Play-Element in Culture* (London: Routledge and Kegan Paul, 1950), 18.

CHRIST AND APOLLO IN THE SEVENTEENTH-CENTURY RELIGIOUS LYRIC

❀ ❀ ❀ *Stella P. Revard* ❀ ❀ ❀

Throughout the fifteenth and sixteenth centuries, Renaissance poets on the continent were creating a cult of Apollo, an Apollo, who is sometimes a secular god of poetry and at other times a transcendent god of light who sits at the right hand of the highest god. They handed down to poets of seventeenth-century England a figure who is both richly symbolic and problematical. As Apollo is the patron of poetry, the leader of the Muses, the holder of the golden lyre that symbolizes all art, he may be enthusiastically espoused and granted an honored part in poetry. At the beginning of the seventeenth century, a coterie of English poets dubbed the special room at the Mermaid Inn the Apollo room, where poets such as Herrick and Drayton gathered under the leadership of Ben Jonson and celebrated Apollo as the god of poetry. When Apollo appears as a rival lord of light in the religious poetry, however, he is a problematical figure. He must be either banished or suppressed or accommodated in some way to the Christian lord of light. Poets from Donne through Milton and Crashaw face the problem

I wish to thank Professors Phyllis Bober and Julia Gaisser, codirectors of a NEH Summer Seminar, held in Rome in 1990. I am indebted to their learning in Roman humanism, and to them I owe my introduction to the Vatican Apollo and the Renaissance cult of Apollo and the Muses.

of how to treat this other Apollo. Is he a symbol for Christ, or is he Christ's rival? The different religious and, to a degree, political orientations of the poets involved—Anglican, Puritan, or Roman Catholic—dictated different solutions to the problem, principally because the figure of Apollo had become by the seventeenth century a potent symbol in the iconography of the Roman Catholic Church and was becoming also a potent political symbol for the Stuart monarchy. Reactions to the Christianized and royalized Apollo intimately involved a poet's political and religious persuasion.

I

The linking of Apollo and Christ—and the Christianization of Apollo, the classical god of light or of the sun—has a long history that goes back to the early centuries of the Christian Church. In order to understand the reaction of seventeenth-century religious poets to the Christianized Apollo, it is useful to know something of this history. Both Christian and Neoplatonic writers, such as Synesius and Proclus, and Church Fathers, such as Gregory Nazianzen, associated Christ and Apollo as gods of light. In such hymns as Proclus's Hymn to the Sun the figures of Christ and Apollo begin to be most compellingly associated. The Greek Apollo—as archaic poets such as Pindar describe him—is the son of the highest god and has a prominent place next to his father in Olympus. As god of poetry he holds the golden lyre and leads the Muses (Pythia 1.1–2); he is also a prophet (Pythia 4.5–8), the allotter of disease and remedy (Pythia 5.60–62), the conqueror of the presumptuous giants (Pythia 8.17–18).[1] By the fifth century B.C. he was already a god who could come to stand beside Christ the prophet, Christ the lord, Christ the physician, and Christ the conqueror of Satan and his presumptuous angels. Later Greek religion added to Apollo's dominion the regency of the sun; he superseded the Greek Helios and Hyperion as the sun-god and took over their qualities. Hence, we find among Christian Neoplatonists such as Synesius and Neoplatonic universalists such as Proclus descriptions of Christ and Apollo that are very close. In Synesius's hymns the Son is the light from the foun-

---

1. Pindar, *Carmina*, ed. C. M. Bowra (Oxford: Oxford University Press, 1935).

tainhead, the founder of the universe, the wisdom of the Father's mind, and the splendor of his beauty.[2] We need only look back to the hymns and odes of Gregory Nazianzen and Clement of Alexandria to find similar descriptive epithets used for Christ. In a choral hymn, Clement addresses Christ as lord of all, the omnipotent word of the Father, the fountain of wisdom, the perpetual light. In his odes Gregory Nazianzen describes Christ as the word of God, present from the beginning, the light from light. Similar terms reappear in John of Damascus's "Hymn to the Theogonian," in which the Son is described as God's sacred word, radiant in light.[3]

The Neoplatonist Proclus (c. A.D. 410–485) was a universalist in religion, and he endeavored to move beyond sectarian boundaries to reach the philosophical principle that he felt was common to all religion, whether Greek or Christian or Hebraic. Proclus's Helios, addressed in Hymn 1, is neither the ancient Greek sun-god, Helios, nor the Romanized Apollo, god of the sun, but the lord of light, the intellectual soul and heart of healing and poetry. As such he has much in common with the Christian lord of light, the divine Son.[4] Both Synesius's and Proclus's hymns were popular with different groups in the Renaissance, for they appealed not only to Christian and Neoplatonic thinkers, but also to humanist poets, who saw in their hymns examples of poetry that successfully combined the pagan hymn-ode and the Christian hymn.[5]

---

2. See *The Essays and Hymns of Synesius of Cyrene*, trans. with introduction and notes by Augustine Fitzgerald (Oxford: Oxford University Press, 1930), 2:372–92. Synesius's account of the generation of the Son (in Hymns 2, 3, 4) especially borrows from Greek religion, Neoplatonism, and Gnosticism.

3. Clement of Alexandria, *Hymni in Christum* (Paris: Morel, 1598); Gregory Nazianzen in *Poetae Graeci Veteres*, ed. Petrus de la Rovière (Cologne, 1614), 185–89; John of Damascus in *Poetae Graecae Veteres*, 189–91.

4. See Proclus, *Inni* (Florence, 1929). Proclus appears in *Poetae Graeci Veteres, Carminis Heroici Scriptores, qui extant, Omnes* (Geneva, 1606). Proclus was born approximately the year that Synesius died and was like Synesius strongly influenced by Neoplatonism.

5. Synesius's hymns were first printed by Aldus in 1499, but they were reprinted throughout the sixteenth century, the two most important editions being those of Oporinus in Basel in 1567 and of H. Stephanus in Geneva in 1568. Oporinus's edition, which is edited by Canterus, includes selections of Synesius's other works; the hymns themselves, all ten of them, appear in the second part of the volume, with a separate title page. (Synesius, *Hymni carmine*, ed. Gulielmus Canterus [Basel:

From the early days of the Church, Apollo and Christ were also associated iconographically. A fourth-century mosaic found in the tomb of the Julii in the catacombs of the Vatican depicts Christ as a charioteer of the sun, his head encircled with a halo and his hand holding a globe.[6] Yet it was not until the Renaissance that Apollo was officially—as it were—brought into the Church. When Guiliano della Rovere was elevated in 1503 to the papacy and moved as Julius II from the confines of SS. Apostoli's in Rome to the Vatican, he took with him an ancient sculpture—a Roman copy of a Greek original—that probably had been dug up in a nearby garden and was to become the centerpiece of a vast Vatican courtyard. The sculpture is still at the Vatican in a more modest setting. The Apollo Belvedere, while still justly admired, no longer excites the religious passion, however, that it once did, when the son of the ancient god Jove came to make his home at the ecclesiastical center of Christianity, taking central place in the courtyard of the Vatican that the very Son of God—Christ himself—was to take at the apse of Julius's temple to the first pope, the Basilica of St. Peter that was then rising.

The adorning of the Vatican under the popes of the fifteenth and sixteenth centuries well illustrates the way in which Christian Rome was enthusiastically embracing its classical past. Newly recovered ancient statuary was installed, and Roman-style wall paintings were commissioned, depicting not only Christian but pagan mythological scenes in the same tableaux. Renaissance popes espoused in the visual arts a mythological mystique that attempted to unite ancient and modern Rome, and prominent in this mythological mystique was the use of the classical gods as metaphorical stand-ins for the Christian God. In the Vatican's Stanza della Segnatura, Raphael's *School of Athens* faces directly opposite his *Miracle of the Host* with its transformation of the elements into the body and blood of Christ. The third wall of Raphael's celebrated stanza attempts to unite classical and Christian, for on it both ancient and modern poets celebrate Apollo. So, in a fashion,

---

Oporinus, 1567]). Henry More translates hymns of Synesius. See *The Complete Poems of Dr. Henry More,* ed. Rev. Alexander B. Grosart (Edinburgh: Edinburgh University Press, 1878). There are some touches of Gnosticism and Mithraism in Synesius's descriptions of God. See *Essays and Hymns,* 2:481.

6. See James Lees-Milne, *Saint Peter's: The Story of Saint Peter's Basilica in Rome* (London: Hamish Hamilton, 1967), 68–69.

Apollo inevitably is linked to Christ. At the beginning of the sixteenth century, the Vatican was popularly called the "Hill of Apollo" because of the interest by Popes Sixtus IV, Alexander VI, Julius II, and Leo X in the cult of Apollo and the Muses. Julius II's installation of the statue of Apollo in the Belvedere Court simply crowned that interest.[7]

The Apollo Belvedere was a symbol not just of the syncretism of Christianity and classicism. Pope Julius II installed the Apollo in the Vatican as a sign of his power as well as his artistic taste. This is an active Apollo, repulsing his enemies, defeating the Python, defending his shrine at Delphi. The Belvedere symbolized an aggressive Catholicism. Sketches of it done by visiting artists were carried all over Europe. Filippino Lippi imitated it; Albrecht Dürer made it the model for his Sol-Apollo; Michelangelo, for his Christ. Francis I had it modeled in bronze for Fontainebleau, and so the symbol of the warring pope became a symbol for the warring French king.[8] Apollo was dear to the seventeenth-century pope, Maffeo Barberini, who had ascended to the papacy as Urban VIII in 1623. One of Urban's important imprese was the Apollonian laurel covered with bees, for Urban boasted himself a poet; the other important impresa was the rising sun. His motto, "Aliusque et Idem," was drawn from Horace's *Carmen Saeculare* to Apollo in recognition that Apollo was also Augustus Caesar's patron god. Both in the Vatican and in the Barberini palaces, Apollo and the sun are ubiquitous: in the radiant head of Apollo under the papal arms, in the ancient statue of Apollo in the landing of the palace, in the Apollo head above the fireplace of the salone, as well as the Belvedere Apollo, which Urban had inherited from Julius. As John Beldon Scott has pointed out, "Urban even had a wall in his apartment at the Vatican painted with a shining sun so that each morning he would be greeted by the light of his own impresa"—the Apollo-Sun.[9] Urban was clearly

---

7. Elisabeth Schröter, "Der Vatikan als Hügel Apollons und der Musen. Kunst und Panegyric von Nikolaus V bis Julius II," *Römische Quartalschrift für christliche Altertums Kunde und Kirchengeschichte* 74 (1979), 208–40. Deborah Brown, "The *Apollo Belvedere* and the Garden of Giuliano della Rovere at SS. Apostoli," *Journal of the Warburg and Courtauld Institutes* 49 (1986), 235–38.

8. Phyllis Pray Bober and Ruth Rubinstein, *Renaissance Artists & Antique Sculpture: A Handbook of Sources* (London: Harvey Miller Publishers, 1986), 28–29, 71–72.

9. See John Beldon Scott, *Images of Nepotism: The Painted Ceilings of Palazzo Barberini* (Princeton: Princeton University Press, 1991), 58, 70, 142. The sun was extraordinarily prominent both in Urban's natal chart and in the astrological chart that was

a pope in the style of Julius II, emulating him in both his collecting of antiquities and his pursuit of papal wars. With him Apollo was reigning once more in the Vatican.

II

It was the poets as well as the painters and sculptors who made possible the union of Apollo and Christ. One of the most important of these humanist poets was Michele Marullo, whose revival of the hymnode influenced the neo-Latin poets of his own and the next generation in Italy, the Pléiade in France, and, ultimately, the English poets at the end of the sixteenth century. Proficient in ancient Greek and with a comprehensive knowledge of Greek literature, including both the ancient hymns and Neoplatonic literature, Marullo was a direct link between the Renaissance and the ancient world. He wrote four books of *Hymni Naturales,* comprising hymns not only to deities of the Olympic pantheon, but also to Eternity, the Sun, other heavenly bodies, and Earth. Celebrating the interaction between the divine and the human, Marullo attempts to incorporate in his hymns elements from cult hymns to the Olympian gods, the Neoplatonic philosophical tradition, and contemporary astronomical poetry and to synthesize all this with Christianity.[10] His gods function as cult figures, as planetary influences, and as allegorical equivalents to the Christian Father, Son, and Spirit and the saints.

The Hymn to the Sun opens the third book of the *Hymni* and at 287 hexameter lines is the longest and most formal of the hymns, one of Marullo's richest and most syncretistic poems. Like Synesius and Pro-

---

drawn for his ascendancy to the papacy on August 6, 1623. Urban said that he was born and elected to rule (Scott, *Images of Nepotism,* 82). Also see Patricia Waddy, *Seventeenth-Century Roman Palaces: Use and the Art of the Plan* (Cambridge: MIT Press, 1990). Waddy notes that the Barberini had an ancient torso of Apollo to which they eventually commissioned the sculptor Giorgetti to add a head, arms, and legs. The renewed Apollo was eventually installed in a fountain court at the Barberini palace (257).

10. For commentary on Marullo's hymns, see Philip Ford, "The *Hymni Naturales* of Michael Marullus," *Acta Conventus Neo-Latini Bononiensis,* ed. R. J. Schoeck (Binghamton, N.Y.: Medieval and Renaissance Texts and Studies, 1985) 475–82; Pier Luigi Ciceri, "Michele Marullo e i suoi 'Hymni Naturales,'" in *Giornale Storia della letteratura italiana,* 64 (1914), 289–357.

clus, Marullo looks on Apollo-Sun's light as a generating force, and at the very outset of his hymn, he celebrates him as the deity who created the universe. A protogonos, who was generated prior to the birth of the earthly sun, he retains many of the characteristics of his preexistent state, not only bringing light physically and intellectually, but also, like Proclus's Helios, giving and sustaining life as well as promoting order and law.

> Solus inexhausta qui lampade cuncta gubernat,
> Sol pater—unde etiam Solem dixere priores,—
> Et patria longe moderatur imagine mundum,
> Idem rex hominum atque deum, pater omnibus idem.
>
> (Who alone governs, his torch altogether inextinguishable,
> Sun Father, whence to say even prior to the Sun,
> Who from afar controls the earth with his image,
> The same king of men and gods, the same father to all.)
>   (III. i, 20–23)[11]

Marullo's hymn is by no means unique in the Renaissance. Giovanni Pontano, Marullo's contemporary and friend, celebrates the Sun, describing in *Urania* his place in the universe as the father of all things and in a Sapphic ode,"Ad Solem," his function as the orderer of the cycles of days, months, years—the bringer of spring and the renewer of life. Both Pontano and Marullo adopt concepts from Proclus, from Synesius, and from Orphic religion. As in Proclus and Orphic religion, their Sun is the sower of souls, the fountain of all, the force necessary for life. His light causes things to grow, to turn green once more and to flower; he controls the return of spring and the regeneration of the earth, bringing form to the animals, strength to the mind of man. He divides time into years, months, days; fills everything with his holy light; and so controls human fate on the individual and on the societal level. Later humanistic poets follow Marullo and Pontano. Joannes Secundus's poem "De Sole" describes the sun as the fountain of all things, the investigator, founder, and spy of the earth, and the leader of

---

11. Quotations of Marullo are from *Michaelis Marulli Carmina*, ed. Alessandro Perosa (Zurich: Thesaurus Mundi, 1951). I have also consulted *Hymni et Epigrammata Marulli* (Florence, 1497); *Marulli Constantinopolitani Epigrammata & Hymni* (Paris: Andreas Wechelus, 1561).

the revolution of the years. Similar descriptions are found in the hymns to Apollo by Bernardo Tasso and Ippolito Capilupi. For Tasso, Apollo is the father of all things ("Gran Padre delle cose"), the god that dispels darkness and evil, and who is with his light the eternal eye of God ("Hymn to Light," *Odes* II. viii). For Ippolito Capilupi, Apollo is an intellective force, the Mind of the world. In his planetary aspect he is the bringer of day and night, hence the orderer of the diurnal regularity for human kind. Like Marullo, Ippolito thinks of the sun as the force that regulates the universe; he is the prince of stars, orderer of the nine orbs of planets and also of the sea and the land. Through his mastery of the art of music, he guides the universe in its eternal orbiting, as the lyre guides the feet of the chorus. Ippolito may here be remembering how the figure of the lyre functions in Pindar's Pythia 1. The tradition continues with Ronsard and the poets who followed him, notably François Habert, who composed a "Hymne du Soleil," celebrating the Sun as the soul of the universe. Humanist poets of the fifteenth and sixteenth centuries have brought down to the Renaissance a powerful figure in Apollo. More than ruler of the Sun, he is the intellective creator of the universe and hence a figure that, inevitably, is symbolic of Christ.[12] English poets such as Donne, Milton, and Crashaw, who were well versed in ancient literature and continental Latin writings, would have known both Synesius's and Proclus's hymns and those hymns and odes of Marullo and Pontano and those of later poets that imitate them. They may even have regarded these hymns as models for their own Christian verse.

III

How then are the English poets of the seventeenth century affected as they look on the figure of Apollo-Sun in Renaissance poetry and continental iconography? Since Christ himself had long been connected with the sun, the depiction of Christ as a lord of light or the pun on

12. Giovanni Pontano, "De Sole," *Pontani Opera* (Venice: Aldus, 1505); Giovanni Pontano, "Ad Solem," *Opera* (Venice: Aldus, 1518); Johannes Secundus, *Opera* (Paris, 1582), 11; Bernardo Tasso, *Rime*, 2 vols. (Bergamo, 1749); Ippolito Capilupi, "Ad Apollinem," *Capiluporum Carmina* (Rome, 1590); Pierre de Ronsard, *Les Hymnes de Pierre de Ronsard* (Paris, 1555); François Habert, "Hymne du Soleil," *Oeuvres Poétiques* (Paris, 1585), 30v–33r.

sun-son does not always have Apollonian associations. For hundreds of years, English poets had exploited the Christ's "son/sunship" before it became a staple for seventeenth-century religious poets. Hence, sometimes the pun calls to mind the classical Phoebus Apollo, sometimes merely the planet or star-sun. John Donne and George Herbert associate Christ and the sun without ever permitting the other sun-god to enter their poetry. Donne seems particularly inclined to the sun-son pun in poems that concern the Resurrection or Ascension. In the Ascension poem of the "La Corona" sequence, for example, Donne expresses "Joy at the'uprising of this Sunne, and Sonne" (l. 2).[13] In his unfinished poem "The Resurrection," Donne addresses the planetary sun, which was eclipsed at the Crucifixion, "Sleep sleep old Sun" (l. 1), telling that sun, "A better Sun rose before thee to day" (l. 4). More complicated is the use of the sun of "Goodfriday, 1613. Riding Westward"; the sun's course from east to west Donne mimicks, remarking that the other "sun" that has set in the east has reversed its physical course and the natural order: "by rising set,/ And by that setting endlesse day beget" (ll. 11–12). By contrasting the order of nature that the planetary sun and the divine son control, Donne alludes in a complex intellectual way to differences between the life-giving properties of the sun and the Son. His comparison-contrast recalls the vocabulary of the early Christian Fathers, who, without the benefit of the English pun, compared the Son and the sun as life-giving and light-giving forces. But Donne does not go further, however, either here or in "A Hymne to God the Father," in which Donne asks God to swear by himself that "at my death thy Sunne/ Shall shine as it shines now" (ll. 15–16). The sun-god Phoebus is not named and is denied as a deity in Donne's poems. He is implicitly present, however, in so sophisticated a poem as "Goodfriday, 1613. Riding Westward"; Donne declines to acknowledge that presence.

Similarly, in Herbert's *The Temple,* the bright beams of divinity belong only to the Son, not to an Apollo-Sun. In the poem "Easter," the Son rises before break of day: "The sunne arising in the East, / Though he give light, and the East perfume, / If they should offer to contest /

---

13. *The Complete Poetry of John Donne,* ed. John T. Shawcross (Garden City, N.Y.: Doubleday, Anchor Books, 1967), 337. All quotations from Donne are from this edition.

With Thy arising, they presume" ("Easter," "The Song," ll. 4–8).[14] Herbert describes the new light of the rays of the sun-Son in "Mattens" and calls the Son the lord of both day and night in "Even-song." But nowhere does he make the sun or Son directly Apollonian. Even in "Christmas," in which the genre of the Nativity hymn would seem most to suggest classical or Renaissance counterparts, the infant Christ only challenges the divinity of an earthly sun. The shepherds ask the sun to stay for the song that will celebrate the newborn infant, who clearly has taken over his powers:

> Shepherd and flock shall sing, and all my powers
>   Out-sing the daylight houres;
> Then we will chide the Sunne for letting Night
>   Take up his place and right:
> We sing one common Lord; wherefore he should
>   Himself the candle hold.
>
> I will go searching till I finde a sunne
>   Shall stay till we have done;
> A willing shiner, that shall shine as gladly
>   As frost-nipt sunnes look sadly:
> Then we will sing, and shine all our own day,
>   And one another pay.
>   (ll. 21–32)

While Donne and Herbert suppress the presence of Apollo as a sun-deity, Milton and Crashaw directly allude to Apollo's place as the "other" son of God and the ruler of the planetary sun. Milton and Crashaw were both devoted humanists who knew classical and neo-Latin literature, but one was a strongly anti-papal Protestant and the other, an enthusiastic convert to Catholicism. They were contemporaries whose different religious stances influenced them in the years that led up to and included the English Civil War to take completely different political stances as well. Crashaw was a celebrator of the Stuart monarchy during the 1630s; Milton, even as early as 1629, when his Nativity Ode was composed, was beginning to have grave doubts about the kingship of Charles I. As we shall see, their reactions to the

---

14. *The Poems of George Herbert*, ed. Arthur Waugh (Oxford: Oxford University Press, 1907).

figure of Apollo-Sun have much to do with both their religious and their political views.

Milton's Nativity Ode celebrates Christ as a lord of light—a new deity who supersedes Apollo-Sun and absorbs his characteristics, even as he denies him place, rudely dismissing him from his shrine. Crashaw's sequence of Christmastide poems— "Hymn in the Holy Nativity," "Hymn for New Year's Day," and "Hymne in the Glorious Epiphanie"—identifies Christ as a new sun-deity, but does not dismiss Apollo, as Milton does, in the final section of the Nativity Ode, in which he is exorcised with the other pagan deities. What do we make of this difference? Why does one seventeenth-century poet take the path of syncretism, while another seems both to embrace it and deny it? Why should Milton, who in the spring of 1629 was fervently welcoming Apollo as the harbinger of spring and urging him to warm his heart with his sunny rays and inspire his poetry, dislodge him from his shrine in the winter of the same year? This is the same Apollo, moreover, whom Milton makes the defender of the rewards of heavenly fame in "Lycidas." Still more perplexing is the accumulation of Apollonian allusions in the first part of the ode. Milton uses images of dawn and sunburst to suggest the majesty of Christ, characterizing him as a god of light sitting with "far-beaming blaze of Majesty . . . at Heav'n's high Council-Table . . . (in) the midst of Trinal Unity" (ll. 9–11), a description that recalls both the golden Apollo of antiquity, enthroned beside his father Zeus, and the god of light in the hymns and odes of Marullo, Pontano, and others.[15] As Christ comes into the world, the lesser sun, Milton tells us, hides his head. At first this contest between Son and Sun, who recognizes his inferiority to Christ, seems no more than the now familiar play that we have observed in both Donne and Herbert:

> The Sun himself withheld his wonted speed,
> And hid his head for shame,
> As his inferior flame,
>   The new enlight'n'd world no more should need;

---

15. *John Milton: Complete Poems and Major Prose,* ed. Merritt Y. Hughes (New York: Odyssey Press, 1957). All quotations of Milton are from this edition and are cited as *CPMP.*

> He saw a greater Sun appear
> Than his bright Throne, or burning Axletree could bear.
>
> (ll. 79–84)

Even though Milton does not name Apollo, the language of this description inevitably calls to mind Ovid's description of Apollo's bright throne and burning axle-tree. Further, the Apollo-Sun of the Renaissance hymns was a protogonos, like Christ, a creator who with first light framed the world and set the foundations of time in place, instituting the order of hours, days, and weeks that the planetary presence—the earthly sun—rules over. Milton tells us that Christ at his Incarnation brings about a new creation, like to, but now greater than that by which he laid the foundations of the world at the beginning. This creation too is heralded with light—the bright angels appear to the shepherds in a "Globe of circular light" (l. 110). The announcement of this new god of light means, of course, not only the banishment of the lesser sun but also of the lesser Apollo, the god who in the final section of the poem will leave his shrine at Delphos with a hollow shriek. No longer is the classical god of light a submerged presence in the Christian poem; he is directly named and exorcised. But we shall look more closely later at Milton's exorcism of Apollo with the other pagan gods.

Crashaw deals differently with Apollo and his place in the Christian poem. Like Milton, his sun-son parallels occur mostly in his Nativity and Epiphany, rather than in his Resurrection and the Ascension poems. He develops the comparison, in fact, in the sequence of Christmastide poems: "Hymn in the Holy Nativity," "Hymn for New Year's Day," and "Hymn in the Glorious Epiphanie." In "Hymn in the Holy Nativity," Christ is "love's Noon" or, as he appears in the earlier version, "Dayes King," the lord of light born before the sun arises: "In spite of Darknes, it was DAY. / It was THY day, SWEET! and did rise / Not from the EAST, but from thine EYES" (ll. 20–22).[16] It is Christ's birth that in Crashaw's poem assures salvation, which Crashaw describes as the "Bright dawn of our aeternall Day"; it is Christ's own light by which he is manifest in the world.

---

16. *The Complete Poetry of Richard Crashaw*, ed. George Walton Williams (Garden City, N.Y.: Doubleday, Anchor Books, 1970). All quotations of Crashaw are from this edition.

Complementary concepts occur in Crashaw's "Hymn to the Name of Jesus," in which Crashaw conceives of the name of Jesus in terms of the incarnation of creative light in the world. The holy doves that Crashaw invokes to help him sing the song are the "high-born Brood of Day," the "bright / Candidates of blissefull Light" (ll. 7–8). To invoke the very name of Christ is to invoke that light he brought with him when he first became man:

> Come lovely NAME! Appeare from forth the Bright
> >   Regions of peacefull Light
> Look from thine own Illustrious Home,
> Fair KING of NAMES, and come.
> Leave All thy native Glories in their Gorgeous Nest,
> And give thy Self a while The gracious Guest
> Of humble Soules . . .
> . . . .
> Come, lovely Name; life of our hope!
> Lo we hold our HEARTS wide ope!
> Unlock thy Cabinet of DAY
> Dearest Sweet, and come away.
> >   (ll. 115–21, 125–28)

There is a curious relationship between Crashaw's invocation of the name of Jesus and Milton's invocation of Christ himself in the Nativity Ode. Both poets envision Christ enthroned in light; both envision Christ's descent to the world at the Incarnation as the descent of that intellective, creative light with which he framed the world in the beginning. For Crashaw, Christ comes with daybreak to a dark world: "O see, The WEARY liddes of wakefull Hope / (LOVE'S Eastern windowes) All wide ope / With Curtains drawn / To catch The Day-break of Thy DAWN" (ll. 145–48). The coming of light is a process of intellective birth that shapes new thought; Christ is the "Womb of Day" in which "fair Conceptions" occur and from which "Bright Joyes" will be born. The name of Jesus contains, as it were, his identity as the creative lord. Those who bow to Jesus' name come also to know and understand the "dazeling light of [his] dread majesty" (l. 235). In this hymn, Crashaw is exploring the creative nature of Christ's light just as Marullo and Pontano in their philosophical hymns to the Sun were investigating the creative principle of Apollo as the lord of the sun. Like Milton, his focus is on Christ as the intellective principle of light and creation.

Both "Hymn for New Year's Day" and "Hymn in the Glorious Epiphanie" also look at Jesus in terms of light.[17] Like the Nativity hymn, which is a companion piece with these, the two hymns celebrate the "bright babe" whose Incarnation is the dawning of a new day. In "Hymn for New Year's Day" the sun is a "golden GOD" who attempts to rival the brightness of the Babe, but who, despite his attempt "to make himselfe rich in his rise," (l. 26) will be dark before "the Day / That breakes from one of these bright eyes" (ll. 27–28). All, in fact, will forsake the sun and in Christ's fairest eyes "find two [suns] for one" (l. 38). Is this mere extravagant compliment? I think not. Jesus is becoming, as the next hymn makes clear, the new sun-god.

Not only does the Epiphany hymn carry forth the light motif of these other hymns, it also deals rather explicitly with Jesus as an Apollonian deity, who takes place over from the earlier gods of light. "Hymne in the Glorious Epiphanie" involves the quest for a new "sun" to replace the old deities of sun that may no longer be worshipped.[18] The Magi and Dionysius the Areopagite are seekers among the gentiles who have worshipped the old deities: the Egyptian sun-god Osiris, the Persian Mithra. (The Greco-Roman gods—Apollo or Helios or Hyperion—are absent, significantly so, until the very end of the hymn.) In the first stanza, the kings greet the "Bright BABE," for whom the heavens now disinherit the world's former sun. He is the "DAY of Night," the "east of west," who with the brightness of his own star has made a day out of darkness. In the third chorus, the kings recognize that the Christ Child is the "little all," who contains within himself the creative center of the universe. He is the "All-circling point," the being who controls both the cycles of the time and of eternity that the worldly sun only seemed to control. The Christ of this poem, like the Christ of

---

17. For a discussion of the light imagery in this cycle of poems, see Diana Benet, "The Redemption of the Sun: Crashaw's Christmastide Poems," *Essays on Richard Crashaw*, ed. Robert M. Cooper (Salzburg: Institut für Anglistic und Amerikanistik, 1979), 129–44.

18. For discussion of this hymn, see Lorraine Roberts, "Crashaw's Epiphany Hymn: Faith out of Darkness," *"Bright Shootes of Everlastingnesse": The Seventeenth-Century Religious Lyric*, ed. Claude J. Summers and Ted-Larry Pebworth (Columbia: University of Missouri Press, 1987), 134–44; A. R. Cirillo, "Crashaw's 'Epiphany Hymn': The Dawn of Christian Time," *Studies in Philology* 67 (1970): 67–88.

Milton's Nativity Ode, is born into a time, season, and cycle governed by Nature and the Sun, that is, as Crashaw's kings explain, a "Time" that "is too narrow for thy YEAR" (l. 40). Contrasting the "Bright IDOL; Black IDOLATRY" (l. 51)—the "world's false light" (l. 48)—with the shading darkness that Christ—the new sun—has brought into the world, the kings bid farewell to the old gods and welcome Christ as the "deathles HEIR of all thy FATHER'S day" (l. 64). The old sun is associated with night and winter—death and sin; the new sun—Christ—brings a "gentler MORN, a juster sun" (l. 74).

At first, as it seems, Crashaw is dismissing the old deities, pronouncing the end both of false idols and false gods, just as Milton in his Nativity Ode declared that the oracles were dumb. No longer will the idols eclipse the light, but the Son, as he brings salvation at his Crucifixion, will eclipse the worldly sun, proving the triumph of his true light.

> That dark Day's clear doom shall define
> Whose is the Master FIRE, which sun should shine.
> That sable Judgment-seat shall by new lawes
> Decide and settle the Great cause
>   Of controverted light.
>   (ll. 143–47)

The eclipse at the Crucifixion is not only a moment of victory for the Son over the earthly sun, but also the event that converts the mystic Dionysius the Areopagite to Christianity: "Thus shall that reverend child of light, / By being scholler first of that new night, / Come forth Great master of the mystick day" (ll. 205–7).

In a curious way, however, the victory of the dark over the light does not dismiss darkness, but rather reunites darkness and light, pagan and Christian, the latter becoming the means of the former. As the kings explain, "the frugall negative light / Of a most wise and well-abused Night" is necessary to "read more legible thine originall Ray" (ll. 210–11).

> And make our Darknes serve THY day;
> Maintaining t'wixt thy world and ours
> A commerce of contrary powres,
>   A mutuall trade
>   'Twixt sun and SHADE
>   (ll. 212–16)

In order to see light, darkness must first be; in order to come to the true Sun, the worldly sun must first be dimmed. Rather than dismissing the earthly sun, Crashaw dresses him in the garments of the Son-Sun. The "delegated EYE of DAY" lays himself and his scepter in tribute before the Son-Sun; then undressing his "sacred unshorn treses" he lays down his "gorgeous tire / Of flame and fire" (ll. 241–42)—his robe, crown, gold, myrrh, and frankincense—before Christ. The glittering kings—the seekers of true light—those who were once part of pagan idolatry, merge in identity with the pagan Sun—the Osiris, the Mithra, and now the Apollo figure—who lays down his own light in order to be part of the reflected glory of the true Son-Sun. Christianity assimilates rather than destroys the idols that preceded it, just as the Son assimilates the Apollo figure. The final chorus makes this clear. The sun no longer has any pretense of being a rival to the Sun-Son. "His best ambition now," as Crashaw explains, "is but to be / Somthing a brighter SHADOW" of Christ. Like the Vatican Apollo, the Crashavian sun-god can coexist with the other sun as his symbol. With a "duteous Hand" he can point us "Home to our own sun / The world's and his HYPERION" (ll. 251–53). Hyperion in the usual classical myth is the older sun-god—the Titan that Apollo replaces in the new order. Crashaw here designates Hyperion as God, the original and irreplaceable deity. Crashaw's Apollo-Sun has only temporarily taken over the function of the Christian Hyperion, to whom he now restores his due honor. Crashaw's daring use of the name "Hyperion" for Christ shows us how well he understood that the cult of the Apollo-Sun in sixteenth- and seventeenth-century Rome was an attempt to syncretize classical antiquity and Christianity. When Renaissance poets and painters intellectualized the classical Apollo, they were attempting, just as Crashaw does in his Epiphany hymn, to demonstrate how Christianity drew from the religions that had preceded it. Both the Magi and Dionysius the Areopagite, whom Crashaw makes the spokesmen for his hymn, are moving from the serious mystical vision to an understanding of Christ. As the Neoplatonism of the Christian Synesius and the pagan Proclus is complementary, so too are the bright darkness and the dark light of the Magi and the Areopagite.

The complementary use of pagan and Christian motifs in Crashaw's poetry reminds us that in Rome and in England alike, there was extravagant use of classical models for Christian subjects. At approximately the same time that Crashaw was writing his poetry, Pope Urban VIII was directing the painting of the ceilings of the Barberini palace. As in his imprese and his adornment of the Vatican, the motif of Apollo-Sun was dominant. Particularly important was the sequence of paintings involving the triumph of Divine Wisdom and Divine Providence, both of whom are enthroned in bright circles of light. Andrea Sacchi's Divine Wisdom is seated on a cloudy throne, behind which is a bright disk of sun. On the ceiling of the salone, Cortona's Divine Providence is similarly enthroned. Cortona had originally, as Scott tells us, suggested using a majestic Jupiter to celebrate the triumphs of the Pope, but Urban had insisted on substituting Divine Providence, a figure who perfectly joins the classical and the Christian, and who is, moreover, crowned by a triumphant halo of the sun, Urban's own symbol.[19] It is this kind of syncretism that is perfectly represented in Crashaw's hymns.

IV

Milton's "via negativa" follows a different path. As Milton was composing the Apollo section of his Nativity Ode in December 1629, he was aware of the complex religious and political situation that was developing. Relationships with the Vatican as well as with Italy were becoming closer. Pope Urban was Henrietta Maria's godfather, and there had been negotiations with the Vatican at the time of the marriage. The Queen was constructing an elaborate chapel at St. James's Palace, and Charles, ever interested in continental art, had purchased the Gonzaga collection in 1628 with its superb Titians, Raphaels, and Tintorettos. In the next decade, Cardinal Francesco Barberini, the Pope's nephew, was to become the Queen's agent for purchasing art treasures in Italy.[20] In art as in life, Milton could recognize the encroaching influence of the Vatican Apollo.

In the Nativity Ode, Apollo is the first deity to be dismissed:

19. Scott, *Images of Nepotism,* 34–38, 175–76; Waddy, 218.
20. See John Bowle, *Charles I: A Biography* (Boston: Little, Brown, 1975), 123; Charles Carlton, *Charles I: The Personal Monarch* (London: Ark Paperbacks, 1984), 145.

> *Apollo* from his shrine
> Can no more divine,
> With hollow shriek the steep of *Delphos* leaving.
> No nightly trance, or breathed spell,
> Inspires the pale-ey'd Priest from the prophetic cell.
> (ll. 176–80)

As John Carey has pointed out, the exorcism and flight of the pagan gods and the cessation of the oracles are not uncommon poetic elements in the Nativity hymns of the sixteenth century, particularly among neo-Latin and Italian poets. In Torquato Tasso's "Nel giorno della Natività" Apollo is mute, no longer able to prophesy, and neither laurel nor oak gives off human voice. Carey suggests that Milton may have been remembering part of Tasso's poem as he composed his own hymn during the early hours of Christmas morning 1629.[21] I would like to suggest that Milton in this final passage of the poem was doing more than imitating his Italian and neo-Latin predecessors and that the presence of this passage of exorcism has particular meaning for a Protestant poet writing in 1629. For Milton was not so much proclaiming the ascendance of Christianity over paganism as he was asserting the ascendance of Protestantism over the Vatican and particularly over a Vatican that was beginning, as many Puritans feared, to have too much influence on the English court. In exorcising Apollo, he was exorcising the cult of Apollo that now was manifesting its presence in Charles's court.

It was not just papal Rome that had espoused Phoebus Apollo as its special symbol. The Sun-Kings of France from Francis I through Henri IV had displayed their magnificence by making Phoebus Apollo their god. When Phoebus Apollo comes to England, he is the emblem for James I. In Chapman's *The Memorable Masque*, performed before the King at White-Hall in February 1613, the Priests of the Sun address a song to Phoebus-James, "Rise rise, O Phoebus, ever rise . . . set set, great Sun, our rising love / Shall ever celebrate thy grace . . . be to earth her only light: All other kings, in thy beams met, / Are clouds and dark

---

21. See John Milton, *Complete Shorter Poems*, ed. John Carey (Burnt Mill, Harlow, Essex: Longman, 1971), 104n.

effects of night."²² In poems published in 1617 to celebrate James's return to England, James was described as an Apollo returning to the Muses, a sun-god giving light to his kingdom, which is dark in his absence. Even before Charles assumed the throne, he had assumed his father's mythological titles, appearing as a Phoebus scattering night in the poems written in 1623 to welcome him back from Spain to England.²³ So important is the Apollo figure for Charles I that he commissioned from Gerrit van Honhorst, a Dutch follower of Caravaggio, a painting of Apollo and Diana (completed in 1628), directing the artist to give King Apollo his own features, Diana Henrietta Maria's. This Apollo-Charles is enthroned receiving the homage of a Buckingham-Mercury and the Arts and routing Ignorance and Vice, just as the Christ of Milton's ode routs the pagan gods.²⁴

The year 1629 was an important one for Milton, who was turning twenty-one and was offering—as he told his friend Charles Diodati in "Elegia Sexta"—a birthday poem to Christ in English as the sign of his poetical maturity. The year was also a pivotal point in the developing political and religious crisis with King Charles. In March of 1629, Charles I had dissolved Parliament and those who called attention to the King's misdoings had been sent to the Tower. That Milton vividly remembered these events is attested by his reference to them in the sonnet he wrote some twelve to fourteen years later to Lady Margaret Ley, recalling the "sad breaking of that Parliament" (l. 5). He also describes them in some detail in *Eikonoklastes* in which he narrates Charles's successive encounters with Parliament, giving particular prominence to his dissolving of the 1629 Parliament.²⁵ Is the exorcism of Charles's alter ego Phoebus Apollo in Milton's Nativity Ode a special mark of that crisis?

---

22. George Chapman's *The Memorable Masque* (London, 1613). The masque concludes as Honour confers the "blessing of the golden age." Also see Jonson's *The Masque of Blackness*, in which James also appears as Phoebus.

23. *Iacobi Ara. Deo Reduci* (Oxford, 1617); *Carolus Redux* (Oxford, 1623).

24. See Christopher Lloyd, *The Royal Collection* (London: Sinclair-Stevenson, 1992), 39, 41, 81–84. The painting—a large canvas—is at Hampton Court Palace and depicts not only Apollo and Diana receiving the homage of Mercury and Grammar (the Duke and Duchess of Buckingham) and the other arts, but also the rout of Ignorance. The painting can be dated precisely since Buckingham was assassinated in 1628. The mythological scene of reception and rout is an interesting contrast to Milton's ode of advent and rout.

25. *Eikonoklastes* (London, 1650), 2. Milton alludes more than once in *Eikonoklastes* to Charles as the sun or Phoebus. He complains of Charles's comparing Stafford to

162 • Stella P. Revard

It has long been recognized that one of the literary models for Milton's Nativity Ode, particularly for its central section on the Age of Gold, is Vergil's Messianic eclogue, the fourth of the Bucolics. As Rosemond Tuve has pointed out, Christians since the age of Constantine looked on the child whose birth was prophesied in the eclogue as Christ and saw him as the restorer of the classical Age of Gold.[26] This eclogue was revived by the poets of sixteenth-century and seventeenth-century Italy, however, for a different purpose. The Age of Gold that the ancients had prophesied, the Renaissance popes were busily proclaiming had arrived. Alexander VI, conflating the bull imagery of his Borgia heritage from Spain with the Jovian bull and the Egyptian bull, was, in fact, announcing that a new god had arrived on earth—Horus to succeed the former Osiris.[27] Julius II, with his emblems of the Della Rovere oak and eagle, was prepared to be a new Jove on earth, just like his ancient predecessor Julius Caesar.[28] In a poem to Julius, Pietro Bembo declares that Julius's function is to bring back the Age of Gold; now that a new "Jove" is to rule on earth, the Jovian oak revives in the Della Rovere emblem, bringing back to the earth the age of law and probity and faith.[29] When Leo X, with his Medicean magnificence, succeeded Julius in 1513, it could be no other than Caesar Augustus on earth, an embodiment of the wisdom of the Age of Minerva.[30]

---

the sun, "which in all figurative use, and significance beares allusion to a King, not to a Subject" (20). He even challenges Charles's use of the name Phoebus, since "the whole course of his raign by an example of his own furnishing hath resembl'd *Phaeton* more then *Phoebus*" (105).

26. *Images and Themes in Five Poems by Milton* (Oxford: Oxford University Press, 1957).

27. Claudia Cieri Via, "*Sacra effigies e signa arcane:* la decorazione di Pinturicchio e scuola nell' appartamento Borgia in Vaticano," *Roma Centro Ideale della cultura dell' Antico nei Secoli XV e XVI,* ed. Silvia Danesi Squarzina (Rome, 1989), 185–200. Also see N. Randolph Parks, "On the Meaning Of Pinturicchio's Sala dei Santi," *Art History* 2 (1979), 291–317.

28. See John W. O'Malley, "Fulfillment of the Christian Golden Age under Pope Julius II: Text of a Discourse of Giles of Viterbo, 1507," *Traditio* 25 (1969), 265–338; also see John F. D'Amico, *Renaissance Humanism in Papal Rome: Humanists and Churchmen on the Eve of the Reformation* (Baltimore: Johns Hopkins Press, 1983).

29. Pietro Bembo, "Julii Secundi," *Carmina, Quinque Illustrium Poetarum* (Rome, 1753), 41.

30. See the epigram, "De suis temporibus," that Benedetto Lampridio wrote for the possesso of Leo X in 1513: "Olim habuit Cypris sua tempora: tempora Mauors / Olim habuit: sua nunc tempora Pallas habet." (Once Venus had her era; then Mars

One hundred years later, however, when Maffeo Barberini ascended to the papacy and began to emulate the splendor of the courts of Julius and Leo, it was he who was to inaugurate the Golden Age—the age, as Vergil's eclogue declares, when Apollo reigns. Urban and his nephew, Cardinal Francesco Barberini, were adorning both Rome's sacred buildings and private palaces with ancient art works and commissioning artists such as Bernini to create new works in imitation of antique statuary. Poets once more turned to Vergil's eclogue for their comparisons. The Jesuit neo-Latin poet Casimire Sarbiewski addressed an ode to this art-loving pope, proclaiming that Urban had renewed the Age of Saturn. The rivers of Italy flowed with milk and honey. Francesco Bracciolini composed twenty-three cantos on Urban's election to the papacy that concluded with Astraea descending to witness Urban's defeat of Envy and with the banishment of Error.[31]

This movement in Rome had a political and cultural counterpart in England. In Stuart masques, Astrea appears to announce the Age of Gold and to identify James as the one who is to preside over this golden era. Chapman's *The Memorable Masque* (1613) concluded as Honour confers the "blessing of the golden age" on England. In the 1620s Charles had assumed his father's place as ruler of the Age of Gold. But in December 1629 a new ruler was about to appear, for Henrietta Maria was bearing the heir to the throne. In November 1629 there were confident reports of Henrietta Maria's pregnancy, and Milton could not have failed to know of the coming event.[32] From the very beginning Prince Charles was associated with the "child" of the Vergilian eclogue. Charles's birth was to be proclaimed by a star, and he was to be compared to Christ himself. Poets led by Ben Jonson celebrated the Queen as a second Mary. The author of *Carolides*, the poets of the Cambridge and Oxford university collections, and finally Crashaw himself welcomed Prince Charles both as the child in the Vergilian

---

had his; now Pallas has her era.) in *Carmina Illustrium Poetarum Italorum*, ed. J. M. Toscanus (Paris, 1576), 1:152v.

31. Casimire Sarbiewski, *Lyricorum, Libri Tres* (Cologne, 1625), 187–195. See Scott, *Images of Nepotism*, 172–73.

32. See Elizabeth Hamilton, *Henrietta Maria* (London: Hamish Hamilton, 1976), 98; Carola Oman, *Henrietta Maria* (London: Hodder and Stoughton, rpt. 1951), 66–67. "The prospect of their Papist queen providing England with an heir had been resented by 'mutterers'" (67).

eclogue and as a new Phoebus.[33] Crashaw addresses the prince as the one who is about to establish an Age of Gold, as the descendant of a royal Phoebus and a royal Mars.

> Bright Charles! thou sweet dawn of a glorious day!
> Centre of those thy Grandsires (shall I say
> Henry and James? or, Mars or Phebus rather?)[34]

In December 1629 Milton was reacting to claims already current that the imminent royal birth would establish a Stuart Age of Gold by affirming that only the coming of the king of kings, only a reestablished Protestantism, could bring England her golden age. Christ must be reborn—not another Charles.

For Milton the term "the Age of Gold" had reverberations of millenarian promise.[35] As the angels in the Nativity Ode sing in praise of the new-born Son of God, the poet is so wrapped with their "holy Song" that he thinks "Time will run back, and fetch the age of gold" (l. 135). If that should happen, "speckl'd vanity" would die and "leprous sin" melt away (ll. 136–38), and "Truth and Justice then / Will down return to men" (ll. 141–42). He halts in the midst of his speculation to remark that the child who will bring salvation still lies in infancy; it is not yet time for the Age of Gold. If wisest Fate said no to the golden ages that Renaissance popes and English poets declared were imminent, the young Protestant poet in 1629 was quietly biding

---

33. Jonson's poem is on the Queen's lying-in, and he compares the two Marys. David Echlin was the Queen's physician, and he addresses the *Carolides* to King Charles. The title page of the work (published in 1630) declares that the Age of Saturn will return. The poem makes similar claims. The Oxford collection—*Britanniae Natalis*—was published in 1630; the Cambridge collection—*Genethliacum Illustrissimorum Principum Caroli & Mariae*—which celebrated the birth of Princess Mary also—in 1631.

34. Crashaw's poem appears in *Voces Votivae* (1640) a later university collection that celebrates the royal children.

35. Michael Wilding, *Dragons Teeth: Literature in the English Revolution* (Oxford: Clarendon Press, 1987). Michael Wilding has argued that the apocalyptic appeals in the Nativity Ode manifest an unusual sensitivity even in the prerevolutionary days to the political pressures about to erupt. It was almost as though Milton foresaw, Wilding says, as he described the rout of the pagan deities, "the parade of defeated bishops, clergy, and courtiers" that the Revolution would displace (14–16). Also see David Norbrook, *Poetry and Politics in the English Renaissance* (London: Routledge and Kegan Paul, 1984), 241–44.

his own and his countrymen's time. But by the mid-1640s, he was challenging Parliament to begin to build for that new age by refusing to enact laws of censorship that would only replicate what the worst Vatican repression had done in Rome. In *Areopagitica* the true English age of liberty from licensing was set against the Vatican imposition of Imprimaturs, and Milton specifically indicts Popes Martin V and Leo X together with the Council of Trent and the Spanish Inquisition for bringing about censorship (*CPMP,* 724). Further, Milton declares in *Areopagitica* that "God is decreeing to begin some new and great period in his Church, even to the reforming of reformation itself. What does he then but reveal himself to his servants, and, as his manner is, first to his Englishmen?" (*CPMP,* 743). Milton looked upon *Areopagitica* as an opportunity to contrast England and Italy and to proclaim the imminence of a "new and great period" about to begin—an Age of Gold perhaps. The Nativity Ode's apostrophe to this Age of Gold was Milton's first blast on the trumpet of prophecy.

When Milton silences Apollo at the beginning of the catalogue of routed deities, it is not Apollo the god of poetry or even Apollo the sun-god, but Apollo the prophet. He is intent on refuting the claims of Catholic Rome and Stuart England, silencing their prophecies as their gods. As the prophet of the new Protestantism, he declares, "The Oracles are dumb," and at the same time predicts the straitening of the old Dragon—who else but Rome?—under ground and the extinction of those gods that Renaissance Rome and Stuart England had so extravagantly revived to adorn their palaces and temples. Together with him go the nymphs that were so popular in Renaissance wall painting and the Roman gods of the hearth, the Lars and Lemurs, that were revived in Rome as Renaissance Italians celebrated their Roman heritage. The Egyptian deities that are prominent also in the catalogue of exorcised deities remind us that Renaissance popes such as Alexander VI, influenced perhaps by the writings of Annius and Giles of Viterbo, looked upon Egyptian Ammon, Hercules, Isis, and Osiris as counterparts to Hebraic and Christian figures. Alexander VI had celebrated his own "Egyptian" heritage by using the figures of Osiris and Isis in the wall decorations of the Borgia apartments.[36] Milton, in dismissing these

---

36. See Claudia Cieri Via, "*Sacra effigies e signa arcana,*" 185–200. Also see Barry Spurr, "Sable-Stoled Sorcerers," *Milton Quarterly* 26 (1992): 45–46.

pseudo-Christian substitutes, connects them with Moloch, Baal, and the crew of deities that the Israelites, like the current ruler and past rulers of the Vatican, falsely worship.[37] We should recall that in his early anti-papal Latin poem, "In Quintum Novembris," Milton depicts the Pope carrying idols—or as Milton calls them—gods made of bread—in procession about Rome and compares the chanting of the worshippers in procession to the cries of Bromius in the rites of Bacchus. The infant Jesus routs them as surely as Calvin and Luther and Zwingli rout Catholicism. The hymn closes with the earthly sun—no Apollonian god—about to declare the new day, dismissing the flocking shadows to an infernal jail.

At least one reader of the Nativity Ode understood quite well the implications of Milton's exorcism of Apollo. When William Blake illustrated the Apollo stanza of the Nativity Ode, he chose as his model for Apollo the Apollo Belvedere, demonstrating that he was an unusually astute interpreter of Milton. That Blake chose the celebrated Vatican Apollo as his model for Milton's Greek god is hardly accidental. For Blake the Belvedere Apollo with its perfect (but as he thought perverse) classical beauty symbolized Christianity's enslavement in the Renaissance to the mercantile and imperialistic ethics of classical art. Apollo's bow and quiver represent the militarism of Renaissance kings and popes, a militarism that debases art: "A Warlike State," said Blake, "never can produce Art. It will Rob & Plunder & accumulate into one place, & Translate & Copy & Buy & Sell, & Criticise, but not make."[38] About the column in Blake's picture a seductive serpent twines—representing the insidious power to corrupt that this beautiful image possesses. Blake understood that it is not an ancient pagan Apollo that Milton is exorcising but the Apollo that the Renaissance revived and revered and made a substitute for the true God.

As a humanist poet who looked back on the classical heritage that

---

37. C. W. R. D. Moseley argues that it is not an accident that in 1645 Milton prints immediately after the Nativity Ode the translations of Psalms 114 and 115 that he did at an early age and which were, even in his boyhood, scripture that Protestants looked to as celebration of the deliverance of the Reformed Church from the Egyptian or Babylonian capitivity of the Roman Catholic Church. See *The Poetic Birth: Milton's Poems of 1645* (Aldershot: Scolar Press, 1991), 88.

38. Raymond Lister, *The Paintings of William Blake* (Cambridge: Cambridge University Press, 1986), plate 51.

fellow Renaissance poets fostered, Milton often took the path of syncretism that he shuns here. The Apollo he dismisses in the Nativity Ode is not permanently exorcised from his poetry. He reappears in "Lycidas" as an honored voice. In *Paradise Lost* as Milton invokes God as light or as he makes Satan denounce the beams of the sun, we feel reverberations of a Christianized Apollo. In *Paradise Regained*, as the Son confronts Satan, Milton must once more deny Apollo as an oracular voice. When he wrote the Nativity Ode, Milton had not yet confronted in person the classicism of Renaissance Rome, visited the Vatican, or the Barberini palace with its extraordinary fresco of Divine Wisdom crowned with the Barberini sun, or confronted the presence of Apollo everywhere in Rome.

When Apollo appears in seventeenth-century poetry as god of poetry or as the wooer of the reluctant laurel, Milton and Crashaw, like most seventeenth-century poets, respond with enthusiasm or with wit to his deity. When as sun-god he casts over them the burning rays of his great axle-tree, they respond quite differently. In Milton and in Crashaw, we see the extremes of that response. As the great events of the 1640s often made poets choose sides, so many poets felt they could not swear allegiance both to the son of Zeus and the son of Jehovah. Often, as in other choices, the lots too were political. As a Catholic, Crashaw's choice of syncretism seems natural; as a Protestant, Milton denied Apollo divine authority in the Nativity Ode; as humanists, both assent to the power of the Apollo and classicism throughout their poetry.

DONNE, HERBERT, AND THE POSTMODERN MUSE

❖ ❖ ❖ R. V. Young, Jr. ❖ ❖ ❖

The scholarly attention still afforded the devotional poets of seventeenth-century England is somewhat anomalous: to a generation of critics who value "texts" to the extent that they can be made to yield grist for the mills of ideology, Holy Sonnets, "Sacred Poems and Private Ejaculations," and the like would seem to offer sparse gleanings. In an age that has witnessed the grand harvest of secularization, poets such as Donne and Herbert would seem to be of modest significance. Unlike Milton, whose influence was pervasive in the literature of subsequent generations, and who acted a substantial role in the great conflict of the century, the principal devotional poets of the seventeenth century lived in comparative obscurity, and their literary influence was negligible from the Restoration until recent times. Even John Donne, the most famous among them in his own day, is best known now for poems of profane love, which feed the current academic preoccupation with "gender" issues.

Since any contemporary interest in the likes of Donne and Herbert is surprising in itself, it is not surprising that this interest should assume the guises peculiar to contemporary academic thought. The method of reading their devotional poetry in terms of Protestant poetics, so much in vogue in recent years, deserves credit for restoring some sense of the force with which Christian doctrine was believed and contested during the seventeenth century. Yet upon close examination it often turns out that the Reformation is more valued as a revolutionary disruption of the traditional beliefs of Christendom than for its own doctrinal substance. Yet in its emphasis on the doctrinal strains generated by the radical impetus of the Reformation, Protestant poetics sheds light upon the intellectual and moral tensions that furnish the energy animating the rich and powerful Christian poetry of the age. The development of such a view is further reinforced by the aggressively anti-Christian approach to literature associated with most contemporary theory. While it is improbable that most critics who labor to prove that Herbert was a Calvinist (or Lutheran or Laudian) are themselves Calvinists (or Lutherans or Laudians), the critic who deconstructs "Affliction (I)" or who finds in the image of God in Donne's Holy Sonnets a sublimation of Stuart royal absolutism is quite likely to regard his own understanding of the human situation as a more adequate account of reality than any of the seventeenth-century versions of Christianity. In an odd way, poets like Donne and Herbert are honored by such efforts to subject their works to the hermeneutic demands of twentieth-century ideologies. What appears to be dismissive skepticism is covert acknowledgment of a text's power to resist interpretive assimilation, and it ought to endow with poignant immediacy our deliberations over the teaching and practice implicit in the devotional poetry of the past.

The extreme diversity of postmodernist reading is important, then, because it reminds us that the poems of Donne, Herbert, and their contemporaries are something more than so many carcasses spread out on a table for dissection; they are part of the intellectual drama of the seventeenth century. Although these devotional poets may seem to have been losers in their struggle against the secularization of the mind of Western man, the contest is not, perhaps, altogether played out, as current critical struggles over the devotional poems attest. Insofar as the Reformation is a crucial episode in the development of the modern world, the value that Protestant poetics places on its radical elements can be regarded as an attempt to accommodate the devotional poets to the secularism increasingly pervasive during the past three centuries. Because it emphasizes the shattering of the unity of Christendom along with the disruption of the continuity of Christian culture, Protestant poetics becomes the (possibly inadvertent) ally of postmodernism.[1] What the latter does overtly to poems from the past is done somewhat equivocally by the former, but the ultimate result is the same: texts that should challenge contemporary attitudes are rewoven to provide a comfortable fit.[2] What is finally at stake in our interpretation of the poetry of our ancestors is the judgment we pass on ourselves. The interaction between academic literary criticism and religious poetry furnishes a point at which scholarship touches the deepest concerns of our lives.

The particular significance of seventeenth-century devotional poetry for the literary theory of the postmodern era arises from the central importance of justification and grace among the contested issues of the Reformation era. For example, the assault upon the "bourgeois" notion of the self mounted by deconstructionists, Marxists, and various sorts of new historicists recalls the transformed conceptions of self that emerged during the religious crisis of the sixteenth and seventeenth centuries. There is no better example than the poetry of John Donne. As John Carey observes, "The Catholic notes in Donne's religious poems are remarkably clear and full. They are the work of a man who has renounced a religion to some manifestations of which he is still, at a profound level, attached." At the same time, Carey continues, Donne was by no means prepared to shoulder the spiritual burden of Calvin's complete teaching, which dominated the doctrine of the Church of England at the beginning of the seventeenth century: he was overcome by "a sense of his own isolation from the company of God's elect: he was outcast, a part of no whole." He tried to adapt the conscience of an anguished Catholic apostate to a theological scheme that focused obsessive scrutiny on the individual self, since saving faith is a trust in one's own salvation: "Justification by faith meant, in effect, justifica-

---

1. See Ilona Bell, "Revision and Revelation in Herbert's 'Affliction (I)'," *John Donne Journal* 3 (1984), 73–96, who expressly sets out to "suggest some similarities between Reformation Protestantism and modern literary theory which help to explain why Herbert's poetry has become so alluring" (74). Context makes it clear that she means *post*modern literary theory.

2. See Thomas M. Greene, "Anti-Hermeneutics: The Case of Shakespeare's Sonnet 129," in *The Vulnerable Text: Essays on Renaissance Literature* (New York: Columbia University Press, 1986), 159–74, for a salutary skepticism toward both the optimistic assumption that the original intention of a "remote" text can be wholly grasped, and the deconstructionist's assumption that this meaning is of no account.

tion by state of mind."[3] Donne thus becomes, as a result of his peculiar circumstances, a paradigm case of the alienation endemic to the period of the Protestant and Catholic Reformations. As a Catholic who abandoned the bitterly held faith of his Recusant family, Donne expresses an especially acute experience of the age's general sense of lost spiritual orientation. What the Reformation put into dispute was the means and nature of grace, that is, of the accessibility of God's saving power. In the Christian understanding of things, what must be saved is man's soul—his very individuality or self. Original Sin is, therefore, the primordial identity crisis.

Since the sixteenth century witnessed a massive challenge to the Church's traditional conception of grace, that essential element in the affirmation of personal identity, it is no wonder that Anne Ferry has been able to trace a deepening preoccupation with self—with the urge to articulate an "'inward' language" of the individual mind—in the English sonnet sequences of the century. In her chapter on Donne, she observes that *sincerity* is an issue in Donne's earliest and most liturgically oriented devotional poetry: "Reward my muses white sincerity," he cries in the first poem of *La Corona*, with "A crowne of Glory" (ll. 6–8). Likewise, in one of the last of his devotional sonnets, "Show me deare Christ, thy spouse," he is still worrying the issue of the true Church and the individual self's relation to it with daring yet uneasy ribaldry:

> Betray kind husband thy spouse to our sights,
> And let myne amorous soule court thy mild Dove,
> Who is most trew, and pleasing to thee, then
> When she'is embrac'd and open to most men.
> (ll. 11–14)

The poet who offers to seduce Jesus in "What if this present were the worlds last night?" here offers to cuckold him. "Here he pushes the convention to its most shocking limits," Ferry comments, "by taking literally the Church as bride of Christ, and then persuading him to

---

3. *John Donne: Life, Mind and Art* (New York and London: Oxford University Press, 1981), 51, 52, 57.

share her grace, understood as a euphemism for sexual favors, with the speaker."[4]

But of course Donne is not being literal so much as reminding us of the radical nature of the figure: sexual "grace" is itself a metaphor for *grace*—the ineffable, inconceivable gift by which God grants eternal life, an ongoing existence and identity to the soul or self. The "shocking" metaphor is intended to startle us into recognition of how very *different* God's love is from ours. We talk about it in our terms (we have no others) but in such a way that these terms are dismantled in paradox: His Bride shows her love in *promiscuous fidelity*. In thus teasing out the latent contradictions in what has become a routine analogy between human sexual love and the love of God both for the Church and for the individual soul, Donne anticipates what is sometimes seen as an exclusively postmodernist demystification of the self-present, speaking subject that deploys signification.

In a rather acid commentary on Donne's funeral sermon for King James, for example, Jonathan Goldberg remarks, "The text, composed of sliding signifiers, has its authority from something absent from it, the unmentioned Christ, the dead king." In Donne's text, Goldberg adds, God speaks only "through the king's preacher."[5] But, at least in some ways, Donne has already preempted this deconstructive gambit in the Holy Sonnets. The disclosure of the absence—the emptiness of self—behind the manipulative stratagems of the speaker's voice is a central theme. In the Holy Sonnets the failed courtier, the apostate Catholic, broken on the rack of frustrated ambition and fear of hell, discovers for himself the poignant wisdom of his favorite among the Church Fathers, St. Augustine: "And what man is even a man, when only a man?"[6] Even in one of the late sonnets, Donne manifests a vivid

---

4. *The "Inward" Language: Sonnets of Wyatt, Sidney, Shakespeare, Donne* (Chicago: University of Chicago Press, 1983), 223, 232. On "What if this present," see also R. V. Young, "Donne's Holy Sonnets and the Theology of Grace," in *"Bright Shootes of Everlastingnesse": The Seventeenth-Century Religious Lyric*, ed. Claude J. Summers and Ted-Larry Pebworth (Columbia: University of Missouri Press, 1987), 34–37. Donne's poems are quoted in this essay from *The Complete Poetry of John Donne*, ed. John T. Shawcross (Garden City, N.Y.: Doubleday, 1967).

5. *James I and the Politics of Literature: Jonson, Shakespeare, Donne, and Their Contemporaries* (Baltimore: Johns Hopkins University Press, 1983), 216–17.

6. *Confessiones* IV.1, Migne, *Patrologia Latina* 32.693: "Et quis homo est quilibet homo, cum sit homo?"

awareness of the inconsistency and insubstantiality, not only of the poetic persona, but also of the rôle of churchman and Christian:

> Oh, to vex me, contraryes meet in one:
> Inconstancy unnaturally hath begot
> A constant habit; that when I would not
> I change in vowes, and in devotione.
> (ll. 1–4)

In the Christian vision of reality, sin is privation, creeping nothingness; the speaker of this sonnet cannot find himself a sufficiently firm identity even to manage consistent prayer:

> I durst not view heaven yesterday; and to day
> In prayers, and flattering speaches I court God:
> To morrow, I quake with true feare of his rod.
> (ll. 9–11)

His efforts at devotion are no more than symptoms of the disease of sin, sporadic "devout fitts" of a "fantastique Ague"; hence it is only an acknowledgment of the reality of his situation when he admits, "Those are my best dayes, when I shake with feare" (ll. 12–14).

Donne is as aware as any deconstructionist that his own personal presence is insufficient to guarantee the significance of his signifiers. The purpose of the meditative techniques that furnish the structural principle of his Divine Poems is precisely to invoke the presence of God—in the argot of deconstruction, the "transcendental signified" that the "sliding signifiers" never manage to grasp. What is always sought but always doubtful in these poems is the confident assurance of the Real Presence of Christ in the Sacrament of the Altar. Although Donne retained his belief in the Real Presence from the religion of his youth, the ambiguity of Eucharistic doctrine in the Church of England must have been a source of anxiety for him. Hence it is not surprising that the Divine Poems, which eschew direct references to the Eucharist, are yet rife with liturgical overtones and images obliquely hinting at the concept of blood and sacrifice. Such notes are especially observable in the late devotional lyrics. In the first of the three sonnets unique to the Westmoreland MS. ("Since she whome I lovd"), there is a suggestion that the early death of Donne's wife—she was, intriguingly, in her thirty-third year—represents a sacrifice for his spiritual benefit: "And her Soule early into heaven ravished, / Wholy in heavenly things my mind is sett" (ll. 3–4). Thus taken up into heaven, Ann Donne is to be, like Beatrice, a stream revealing the fountainhead of love in God. The complex interchange of human and divine love then takes on the features of a private liturgical ritual:

> But though I have found thee, and though my thirst has fed,
> A holy thirsty dropsy melts mee yett.
> But why should I begg more Love, when as thou
> Dost woe my soule, for hers offring all thine.
>   (ll. 7–10)

The notion of sacrifice becomes explicit in "A Hymne to Christ, at the Authors last going into Germany," in which the poet's dead wife joins all his loved ones and even England itself in a great holocaust:

> I sacrifice this Iland unto thee,
> And all whom I lov'd there, and who lov'd mee;
> When I have put our seas twixt them and mee,
> Put thou thy sea betwixt my sinnes and thee.
> As the trees sap doth seeke the root below
> In winter, in my winter now I goe,
>   Where none but thee, th'Eternall root of true Love I may know.
>   (ll. 7–14)

What is sought by this exchange is an intense, consuming, and exclusive love relationship with God:

>   As thou
>   Art jealous, Lord, so I am now,
>   Thou lov'st not, till from loving more, thou free
>   My soule: Who ever gives, takes libertie:
>   O, if thou car'st not whom I love alas, thou lov'st not mee.
>   (ll. 17–21)

This meditation on sacrifice and abandonment closes with an appeal for a "Divorce to All"—a longing for death: "To see God only, I goe out of sight: / And to scape stormy dayes, I chuse an Everlasting night" (ll. 22, 27–28).

This hymn has been a puzzling poem for modern criticism. In her commentary Helen Gardner maintains that Donne has distorted an Augustinian motif: "The prayer to be freed from 'loving more' than Christ echoes Augustine: 'Minus te amat qui tecum aliquid amat, quod non propter te amat' (*Confessions,* x.29). But the conceit of Christ as a lover who should be jealous, since all true lovers are so, is Donne's own." In fact, the jealousy of God is scriptural: it is announced in the giving of the law (Exod. 20.5, 34.14; Deut. 4.24; etc.); and surely Our Lord's own words provide some basis for Donne's hyperbole: "If any man come to me, and hate not his father, and mother, and wife, and children, and brethren, and sisters, yea, and his own life also, he cannot be my disciple" (Luke 14.26). Still, Gardner feels that there is an "uncharacteristic" morbidity in this hymn and in the sonnet on his wife's death, and she ascribes it to his grief and sees a resurgence of mood after his return from the German journey.[7] More recent commentators have been less charitable. For Aers and Kress, the "Hymne" marks Donne out as "a Moloch-worshipper" who sacrifices others in un-Christian fashion rather than relinquishing his own ambitions and desires.[8] This bit of simplistic literalism would not require notice, except that it does touch an important facet of this troubled poem, as well as the sonnet on the death of Donne's wife, remarked with more subtlety by John Carey. The sonnet, Carey observes, is a testimony—"outstandingly honest, and poignant in its honesty"—to Donne's consuming sense that he is insufficiently loved, and that God's love is not enough. God is "jealous" not only of Donne's wife but also of the Catholic Church, "where 'saints and Angels' were worshipped (so Protestants said)."[9] Carey finds the same expression of dissatisfaction in the "Hymne," along with a reminiscence of Donne's "martyred kinsman Sir Thomas More," whose *Utopia* anticipated Donne in recommending dark churches. In the end the poem discloses "both the majestic finality of pagan suicide and the Christian martyr's thirst for union with God."[10]

---

7. Helen Gardner, ed., *John Donne: The Divine Poems,* 2d ed. (Oxford: Clarendon Press, 1978), 107.
8. David Aers and Gunther Kress, "Vexatious Contraries: A Reading of Donne's Poetry," *Literature, Language and Society in England 1580–1680,* ed. David Aers, Bob Hodge, and Gunther Kress (Totowa, N.J.: Barnes and Noble Books, 1981), 71.
9. *John Donne,* 59.
10. Ibid., 218–19.

John Carey is a shrewd critic, but he sees Donne's angst only from the outside and, in a fashion typical of much current criticism, underestimates its depth. The tensions between pagan pride and Christian humility, between worldly ambition and personal renunciation, are the common themes of Christian spiritual struggle. Donne, however, bears the marks of a soul lost in a theological wilderness: the invocation of "Everlasting night" at the close of the "Hymne" represents a Kierkegaardian leap of "faith alone" by a man who has been deprived of the concrete and efficacious symbols of his boyhood religion. Likewise, the uncontrolled talk of sacrifice in the poem's second stanza evinces a preoccupation with Catholic theological language without its substance and gives at least a shadow of plausibility to the extravagant claims of Aers and Kress: if the body of the Son is not on the altar as a sacrifice to the Father, then *what* is to be offered, and to whom? As Malcolm Ross notes, "Donne has the Thomist feeling for society as an organism," which is not sustained by a corresponding faith in the Communion of the Saints as a present reality, because the indispensable foundation for the unity of Christ's mystical Body is the reality of his sacramental body in the Eucharist.[11]

Postmodern theory is thus anticipated and eluded by Donne's meditative poetry with its coy relation to St. Ignatius Loyola's *Spiritual Exercises,* designed to maintain the disciplined meditator's sense of the divine presence under any circumstances. Donne joined with St. Ignatius, and with St. Augustine and St. Thomas Aquinas before him, in an ironic, preemptive agreement with a dictum of Jacques Derrida: "Only infinite being can reduce the difference in presence. In that sense, the name of God, at least as it is pronounced within classical rationalism, is the name of indifference itself."[12] It is, of course, precisely the "infinite being" of God that transcends the "differance" (to invoke Derrida's [mis]spelling) of the spatiotemporal. This transcendence is preeminently true of Christ's Real Presence in the sacrament of the Eucharist, understood in terms of Transubstantiation, in which the words of consecration enact the transformation of the elements of bread and wine into the actual body and blood of Christ and thus

11. *Poetry and Dogma: The Transfiguration of Eucharistic Symbols in Seventeenth-Century English Poetry* (1954; rpt. New York: Octagon Books, 1969), 167.
12. *Of Grammatology,* trans. Gayatri Chakravorty Spivak (Baltimore: Johns Hopkins University Press, 1974), 71.

present what they *represent*. The drama of Donne's Divine Poems arises from his simultaneous rejection of and fascination with this mode of divine presence and means of grace, as he stands on the brink of the abyss between the analogical realm of Catholic Christianity and the deconstructed world of contemporary literary theory.

Unencumbered by the personal baggage of Donne's Recusant upbringing, George Herbert seems to rest more securely within the fold of the Church of England as a Reformation institution. A result has been an ever more confidently relentless effort to assimilate his devotional poetry to a radically Protestant understanding of grace and the sacraments. Ironically, this attempt at an old-fashioned historical interpretation only succeeds in delivering the poet to the custody of postmodernism. If the Calvinist or Lutheran view that the grace of regeneration amounts to no more than the sheer imputation of righteousness to a human soul that remains essentially corrupt is also Herbert's view, then interpretations of *The Temple* must finally end up with the perspective of Stanley Fish and Barbara Harman. Indeed, the antihumanism of postmodernist theory seems an apt secular counterpart for the antihumanism that Richard Strier finds at the heart of the Protestant Reformation.[13] In both the current ideological and the older theological schemes, the "fiction" of a coherent self, of personal human identity, is swept away. According to Harman, the speech of the poems of *The Temple* marks an assertion by the speaker of self-manifestation since speech insists upon the presence of the speaker; however, the

---

13. On the antihumanism of the Protestant Reformation, in addition to Bell, "Revision and Revelation," see Richard Strier, *Love Known: Theology and Experience in George Herbert's Poetry* (Chicago: University of Chicago Press, 1983), 1–4, 21, as well as Strier, "Ironic Humanism in *The Temple*," in *"Too Rich to Clothe the Sunne": Essays on George Herbert*, ed. Claude J. Summers and Ted-Larry Pebworth (Pittsburg: University of Pittsburg Press, 1980), 33–52. For the Reformation view that grace does not transform human nature, see Luther's *Commentary on Galatians*, in *Martin Luther: Selections from His Writings*, ed. John Dillenberger (Garden City, N.Y.: Doubleday, 1961), 129: "So we shroud ourselves under the covering of Christ's flesh, . . . lest God should see our sin." See also John Calvin, *Institutes of the Christian Religion* 3.xi.23, trans. Henry Beveridge (Grand Rapids, Michigan: W. B. Eerdmans Publishing Co., 1957), 2:58: "This is equivalent to saying that man is not just in himself, but that the righteousness of Christ is communicated to him by imputation. . . . Thus vanishes the absurd dogma, that man is justified by faith, inasmuch as it brings him under the influence of the Spirit of God by whom he is rendered righteous."

effort is repeatedly frustrated: "Though the speaker of 'The Holdfast' is aggressive about self-assertion, he is blocked three times by an interlocutor who is clearly less interested in rejecting the speaker's admittedly flawed positions than in rejecting, and finally preempting, speech itself."[14] Strier likewise sees "The Holdfast" as "a quintessential Herbert poem" in its dramatization of "the Reformation doctrine of grace" and "the strangeness and wonder of faith alone."[15] But while both Harman and Strier see the poem as a denial of any human complacency or self-sufficiency, for the former this is a matter of desperation, for the latter of praise and celebration.

Neither reading, however, attends adequately to the exact text of the poem or to its broader Christian context. As the poem opens, the speaker is gently rebuked in his proud resolve first to be strictly obedient to God's laws, second to trust absolutely in God, and finally even to confess his trust:

> Then I confesse that he my succour is:
> But to have nought is ours, not to confesse
>   That we have nought. I stood amaz'd at this,
>   Much troubled, till I heard a friend expresse,
> That all things were more ours by being his.
>   What Adam had, and forfeited for all,
>   Christ keepeth now, who cannot fail or fall.[16]
>   (ll. 8–14)

The key line is 12: "That all things were *more ours* [my emphasis] by being his." Strier maintains that "more ours" means *"more secure,"*[17] but there is no warrant for the words not meaning what they actually say. Because we are children of Adam by nature, we inherit his sin; that is, his loss, his nothingness, for evil in the Christian view of it has no substantial being. "Therefore, if things are deprived of all good," St.

---

14. *Costly Monuments: Representations of the Self in George Herbert's Poetry* (Cambridge: Harvard University Press, 1982), 41, 43, 51. See Jacques Derrida, *Speech and Phenomena and Other Essays on Husserl's Theory of Signs*, trans. David B. Allison (Evanston, Ill.: Northwestern University Press, 1973), 48–59, for the dismantling of self-presence in speech.

15. *Love Known*, 67, 73.

16. Herbert is quoted from *The Works of George Herbert*, ed. F. E. Hutchinson (Oxford: Clarendon Press, 1941).

17. *Love Known*, 72.

Augustine remarks, "they are altogether nonexistent: therefore so long as they exist, they are good: therefore whatever things are, are good. And that evil whose origin I was seeking is not a substance; because if it were a substance, it would be good."[18] It is not man's human nature as such that is evil, but the loss of that nature and the defacement of the divine image in which it was made. Adam lost the purity of original being, and man has no source of being in himself: "all things" can *only* be "more ours by being his" because we and they can only be *at all* by being his. Only the participation by grace in the Incarnation—in God made man—restores human identity and makes a "coherent self" possible as anything but a fiction.

Harman is, then, perfectly correct in saying that "Affliction (I)" is the "story" of a man who has come to learn that he is "utterly without means," that in the world of his own self, "there *never were* either means or possibilities—only the illusion of them." She is surely wrong, however, to say that God "cross-biases" the speaker "not because he has specific plans which counter the plans one has for oneself," but rather His whole purpose lies in "countering every attempt by the self to have plans, to determine who he is, to define the terms of existence."[19] God's plan for man is, to the contrary, quite specific, and it is intended to enable him "to determine who he is, to define the terms of existence," in the only way possible: "Thou shalt love the Lord thy God with all thy heart, and with all thy soul, and with all thy mind" (Matt. 22.37). Man, despite his sinfulness, Augustine explains, is still part of God's creation and he is moved to praise: "You made us for yourself, and our hearts are restless until we rest in you."[20]

Now "Affliction (I)" is a poem about a restless heart that desires to

---

18. *Confessiones* VII.xii.18, Migne, *Patrologia Latina,* 32.743: "Ergo si omni bono privabuntur, omnino nulla erunt: ergo quamdiu sunt, bona sunt: ergo quaecumque sunt, bona sunt. Malumque illud quod quaerebam unde esset, non est substantia; quia si substantia esset, bonum esset."

19. *Costly Monuments,* 90, 95. Cf. Bell, 86.

20. *Confessiones,* I.i.1., *Patrologia* 32.661: "et tamen laudare te vult homo, aliqua portio creaturae tuae. Tu excitas, ut laudare te delectet; quia fecisti nos ad te, et inquietum est cor nostrum, donec requiescat in te." Gene Edward Veith, *Reformation Spiritually: The Religion of George Herbert* (Lewisburg, Pa.: Bucknell University Press, 1985), 45, says that Reformation theologians, unlike Aquinas, deny that man truly desires God. On this point, as on so many, Augustine has more in common with St. Thomas than with the supposedly "Augustinian" Reformation.

praise but is "cross-biased" not by God but by its own sinful nature. The speaker is not sinful because he wishes to define a coherent self; it is the incoherence and inconstancy of his selfish complaining that is the most notable manifestation of his sinfulness. As in "The Collar" the speaker cannot decide whether he is a retiring scholar or an ambitious worldling, a servant of God or a servant of self:

> What pleasures could I want, whose King I served,
>   Where joyes my fellows were?
> Thus argu'd into hopes, my thoughts reserved
>   No place for grief or fear.
> . . . .
> Whereas my birth and spirit rather took
>   The way that takes the town;
> Thou didst betray me to a lingring book
>   And wrap me in a gown.
>   (ll. 13–16, 37–40)

His desire to be a tree, so that at least he might be useful (ll. 57–60) shows the impulse to praise inherent in man as "a part of God's creation," but his restless discontent reveals the effect of sin—the inability to settle into a rôle or coherent identity: "Well, I will change the service, and go seek / Some other master out" (ll. 63–64). It is only God's grace, his love for man, that enables the speaker to fulfill his nature and create a true, consistent self out of the chaos of sin—hence the paradoxical closing couplet of "Affliction (I)": "Ah my deare God! though I am clean forgot, / Let me not love thee, if I love thee not" (ll. 65–66). The *Confessions* once again provide a pertinent gloss on *The Temple*: "What am I to you," Augustine writes, "that you command me to love you, and grow angry with me unless I do so, and threaten great miseries? Is it a small misery itself, if I do not love you?"[21] Herbert similarly suggests that, for man, not to love God is tantamount to forgetting himself completely or to being completely forgotten by God; for

---

21. *Confessiones* I.v.5, *Patrologia* 32.663: "Quid tibi sum ipse, ut amari te jubeas a me, et nisi faciam irascaris mihi, et mineris ingentes miserias? Parvane ipsa est, si non amem te?" The many parallels between *The Temple* and the *Confessions* would make an interesting study. For general similarities between Herbert and Augustine, see Mark Taylor, *The Soul in Paraphrase: George Herbert's Poetics* (The Hague: Mouton Press, 1974), 1–8.

not to love God is not to exist fully. Nothing is worse than not loving God because it is the love of God that fulfills human nature and makes possible the only complete self available to a human being: "Our hearts are restless until we rest in you." At the end of "Affliction (I)," the speaker finally realizes that all the other miseries mentioned here (and in other poems of complaint) are insignificant by comparison. The afflictions visited upon him are not God's way of thwarting or reducing the self, but of saving it, of enabling the self to exist in the only way possible for a creature necessarily dependent upon the will of its creator.

Grace, then, is God's gift to the soul of the capacity to love Him, because the only freedom available to a contingent will that is not self-destructive is freely to conform to the divine will. Such submission of the mind and will to God is evidently appalling to Stanley Fish, who maintains that "The Flower" is characteristic of Herbert's demand that we "experience the full force of this admission in all its humiliating implications":[22]

> We say amisse,
> This or that is:
> Thy word is all, if we could spell.
> (ll. 19–21)

Fish, however, has mistaken humility for humiliation. "There is nothing easy about the 'letting go' this poetry requires of us," he continues. "We are, after all, being asked to acquiesce in the discarding of those very habits of thought and mind that preserve our dignity by implying our independence."[23] But here Fish misses the point of the poem: there is no humiliation in "discarding" what are merely illusions, given man's ontological status as a contingent creature. Moreover, though man has no dignity or independence apart from God, dignity and independence are precisely the gifts of God's grace: *The Temple*, Herbert says, is

---

22. *Self-Consuming Artifacts: The Experience of Seventeenth-Century Literature* (Berkeley and Los Angeles: University of California Press, 1972), 156.
23. Ibid., 157. Cf. Robert B. Shaw, *The Call of God: The Theme of Vocation in the Poetry of Donne and Herbert*, (Cambridge, Mass.: Cowley, 1981) 104: "Fish's reading of the poems makes them into barren exercises in dialectic. Seeing the poems as 'self-consuming,' he would have us experience a sense of void upon coming to the end of one. It would be truer to Herbert's thought, as I understand it, if we experienced instead a sense of divine plenitude."

"a picture of the many spiritual conflicts that have past betwixt God and my Soul, before I could subject mine to the will of Jesus *my Master: in whose service I have now found Perfect freedom.*"[24] In whose *service* I have now found perfect *freedom*! In "The Flower" Herbert makes good the paradox, and the feat of style by which he evokes the sense of *grace*, with all its resonances, is one of the great achievements of English lyric poetry:

> And now in age I bud again,
> After so many deaths I live and write;
> I once more smell the dew and rain,
> And relish versing: O my onely light,
>   It cannot be
>   That I am he
> On whom thy tempests fell all night.
>   (ll. 36–42)

Above all, Fish's view of this poem as a "self-consuming artifact" mistakes its tone. As Anthony Low observes, "'The Flower' devotes proportionately more time to winter and change than to spring. . . . Yet critics rightly read the poem as a brilliant expression of joy."[25] This apparent disproportion is so effective because it is faithful to the reality of the human situation, which, in its fallen unregenerate state, is wholly lacking in the "dignity" of independence. From one viewpoint, it seems that we are tossed incomprehensibly by the "power" of an arbitrary master:

> These are thy wonders, Lord of power,
> Killing and quickning, bringing down to hell
>   And up to heaven in an houre;
> Making a chiming of a passing-bell.
>   We say amisse,
>   This or that is:
> Thy word is all, if we could spell.

. . . .

24. Izaak Walton, *The Lives of John Donne, Sir Henry Wotton, Richard Hooker, George Herbert, and Robert Sanderson* (London: Oxford University Press, 1927), 14.

25. *Love's Architecture: Devotional Modes in Seventeenth-Century English Poetry* (New York: New York University Press, 1978), 112.

> These are thy wonders, Lord of love,
> To make us see we are but flowers that glide:
> Which when we once can finde and prove,
> Thou hast a garden for us, where to bide.
> Who would be more,
> Swelling through store,
> Forfeit their Paradise by their pride.
> (ll. 15–21, 43–49)

In both stanzas the possibility of damnation is raised, but this, far from dampening the joyousness of the poem, heightens it. The sense of release is intensified by the reminders of the grim reality of human nature—sin and its consequences—from which we are delivered by God's grace. Moreover, it is not a matter of the obliteration of human personality or will; it is rather a matter of "letting go" of illusions. It is the "Lord of love" who *makes us see*, but *we* must still "finde and prove." Far from diminishing individual identity, grace enhances and fulfills it, enabling us to see ourselves and God truly—to see things as they really are. That is why Herbert found "perfect freedom" in the "service" of Christ. As Rosalie Colie remarks, "The indefinable 'something' of *logos* once understood, all things become clear—the last shall be first, the small great, the least thing sufficient for total content."[26] Herbert's viewpoint is quite compatible with a famous utterance of St. Thomas Aquinas: "For since grace does not take away nature, but perfects it, it is proper that natural reason serve faith just as the natural inclination of the will is subject to charity."[27]

Of course Herbert and St. Thomas were both acquainted with the recalcitrance of human nature; both knew that while grace could finally perfect human nature, nature could never adequately express or manifest grace. But though natural responses to grace are all defective and must be finally relinquished, they are not, for all that, meaningless or contemptible. "The Forerunners" is, then, neither a "self-consuming artifact" nor a poem of puritan iconoclasm, as Richard Strier maintains.[28] One does not

---

26. *Paradoxica Epidemica: The Renaissance Tradition of Paradox* (1966; rpt. Hamden, Conn.: Shoestring Press, 1976), 214–15.
27. *Summa Theologiae* I.1.8, 3d ed. (Madrid: BAC, 1961), I.11: "Cum enim gratia non tollat naturam, sed perficiat, oportet quod naturalis ratio subserviat fidei; sicut et naturalis inclinatio voluntatis obsequitur caritati."
28. *Love Known*, 217.

write a *poem* regretfully taking leave of poetry, if poetry is not better than a trivial diversion. The worst that Herbert says about poetry is that it, like any created art, falls infinitely short of its divine object:

> Yet if you go, I passe not; take your way:
> For, *Thou are still my God*, is all that ye
> Perhaps with more embellishment can say.
> (ll. 31–33)

Such regret offers a rather mild renunciation next to St. Thomas's notorious leavetaking from theology: "All that I have written seems to me nothing but straw—compared with what I have seen and what has been revealed to me." The key word here is "compared," which suggests, as Josef Pieper points out, that "the fragmentary character of the *Summa Theologica* is an inherent part of its statement."[29] The incompleteness of *The Temple*, its reiterated intimations that the poetry is quite inadequate to cope with its subject, is likewise an inherent part of its statement.

Thus Herbert, like St. Thomas, has anticipated (or even preempted) critics like Stanley Fish. To be sure, the latter rightly observes "that both as a poem and as an experience, *The Temple* is unfinished"[30]—but only insofar as it is the work of the poet alone. But it does not follow that such a poem as "The Forerunners" is a "powerful comment on the difficulty, if not the impossibility, of the self-consuming enterprise of Herbert's art."[31] It is not as if Herbert has grimly surrendered an otherwise complete human poetic achievement to the whims of a ferocious Calvinist God. Right from the start, in the prefatory verses to *The Temple*, the poet acknowledges that in surrendering the poems to God they are completed and the purpose of the volume attained:

> *Lord, my first fruits present themselves to thee:*
> *Yet not mine neither: for from thee they came,*
> *And must return.*
> ("The Dedication," ll. 1–3)

---

29. *Guide to Thomas Aquinas,* trans. Richard and Clara Winston (1962; rpt. New York: Mentor-Omega, 1964), 139.

30. *The Living Temple: George Herbert and Catechizing* (Berkeley and Los Angeles: University of California Press, 1978), 157.

31. *Self-Consuming Artifacts,* 223.

Grace is here understood as a reciprocity between God and man, enabling and fulfilling fragmentary human nature. If it is drained out of Herbert's poems, then we are left not even with Fish's reading of "The Forerunners" (and "Love [III]") as an episode of devastating mortification; we are left, finally, with Jonathan Goldberg's reading of "The Bag":

> The death of Jesus, in which this story—and all utterance—occurs is the movement of words that do not arrive at final signification, and that (by telling three stories at once) derive from an origin in repetition that must, perforce, de-originate all utterance and replace/displace it within the already written. In this "strange storie" the very notions of fullness, origin, presence, and Being (of all that supposedly inheres in voice) are replaced by spacing (literally, the making of space), repetitive motion, tracing, dissolution, undoing: death. The "being" of writing.[32]

This particular "utterance" borders on gibberish, and yet the tortured style is appropriate to the death-obsessed postmodernist perspective; if there is no divine grace, no sacramental quality transforming our lives and works, then *The Temple* ("and all utterance") can be nothing but "the movement of words that do not arrive at final signification." If there is no intelligible relationship between the spear-wound in Christ's side and a mail pouch, then the following stanza from "The Bag" is indeed mere "writing" without the live meaning of voice:

> If ye have any thing to send or write,
>   I have no bag, but here is room:
> Unto my Fathers hands and sight,
>   Beleeve me, it shall safely come.
> That I shall minde, what you impart,
> Look, you may put it very neare my heart.
>   (ll. 31–36)

Goldberg's point is that we should not "beleeve"—much less believe *in*—the voice represented here just because it is re-presented rather than actually present. Of course, as he sees it, unmediated presence, the fullness of being, is always already deferred by the "spacing" and "tracing" and such that are generated by the differential play of signifiers.

---

32. *Voice Terminal Echo: Postmodernism and English Renaissance Texts* (New York and London: Methuen, 1986), 121.

But there is no need to assume that the *difference* (or "differance") between identity and analogy implies sheer meaningless equivocation, or that meaning is generated by, and hence locked up within, the prison house of language. In the first place, Christianity begins with the assumption that our ordinary ways of knowing and speaking will never bring us to the Transcendental Signified. "Beleeve me" in Herbert's context means to have faith, and "faith is the substance of things hoped for, the evidence of things that appear not" (Heb. 11.1). "Christ is the way, the door: the dead letter kept in circulation and kept from arrival at anything more or less than endless supplementation," Goldberg complains.[33] The sort of "arrival" in which signifier and signified converge, however, would preempt faith by ordinary human knowledge; words would no longer be images or representations of the Word because there would be no *difference,* and it is the difference between the divine original and the human imitation that preserves the fragile dignity and independence of the latter.

In the final stanza of "The Bag," the voice that Herbert attributes to Christ assures us that, although our temporal, contingent world is separate from his, the wound in his side provides a portal between the two realms:

> Or if hereafter any of my friends
>   Will use me in this kinde, the doore
> Shall still be open; what he sends
> I will present, and somewhat more,
> Not to his hurt. Sighs will convey
> Any thing to me. Harke, Despair away.
>   (ll. 37–42)

The grace of Christ communicates "somewhat more" than our bare words; in fact, words are not even necessary: "Sighs will convey/ Any thing to me." Herbert's poem cannot give us the actual or present voice of Christ, but it intimates more than the bare writing on the page: it evokes a voice that points beyond itself. In typical postmodernist fashion, Goldberg would reduce language to the mere mechanics of writing, spacing, repetitive motion, tracing—which indeed portend dissolution, undoing, and death. But serious attention to "The Bag" reveals

---

33. Ibid., 123.

how it transcends the physical inscription of its characters. The first two words of the poem are "Away despair!"; the last two are "Despair away." As the eye traverses the forty-two intervening lines, it "makes space" and time elapses in the course of "repetitive motion." Yet the poem ends where it began—not in time and space, but in memory enhanced by language, language that is something other than material marks on a page, language that delivers what is recognizably the *same* poem in an unlimited number of printed copies and manuscripts. "The Bag" is not literally the voice of Christ, but the form comprising those letters constitutes a structure that provides an imaginative experience of that voice. Like the wound in Christ's side that it describes, it is a *door still open* to the sources of meaning.

The devotional poetry of Donne and Herbert continues to fascinate (and the same could be said about that of their successors Richard Crashaw and Henry Vaughan) because it addresses essentially the same issue that holds a central place among the deliberations of contemporary literary theory: the capacity of the speaking self to define its identity in meaningful utterance and the relationship between the words of its discourse and an absolute source of significance. One of the chief dramas of the past several centuries has been the development of a thoroughly secularized culture in the Western world, of a culture that asserts the self-sufficiency, morally and intellectually, of the individual. This modern autonomous self, free of creaturely status, utterer of its own original Logos, has been the chief target of deconstruction and other postmodern modes of interpretation. A residual "logocentricism" reveals that modern humanism, however secular in name, is still covertly tied to the idea of God, the Transcendental Signified, in its privileging of speech over writing, in its unseemly longing for Truth. Now if postmodernism attacks modern humanism for clinging to elements of theism, poets like Donne and Herbert, at the threshold of the modern world, wrote in resistance to what they sensed as an incipient abandonment of God. The deconstructionist and the devotional poet are thus alike in deploring the secular humanist's illusion of self-sufficiency; both note his failure to get along without God. The confrontation between seventeenth-century devotional poetry and contemporary literary theory is, then, an academic version of the conflict between faith and unbelief; and for this reason its outcome has more than academic interest.

THE POETRY OF MEDITATION
Searching the Memory

❋ ❋ ❋ Louis L. Martz ❋ ❋ ❋

With any mention of memory, students of religious literature are likely to think of the great discourse on the power of memory in Augustine's *Confessions*. Memory is "an awesome thing," he says, "deep and boundless and manifold in being! And this thing is the mind, and this am I myself." The "fields and caves and caverns" of the memory, he adds, are "innumerable and innumerably filled with all varieties of innumerable things," and "through all these I run, I fly here and there, and I penetrate into them as far as I can, and there is no end to them."[1] At the same time, with regard to meditation, one is bound to think of the essential part that memory plays in the meditative exercises of the Late Renaissance, the first of the three powers of the soul in Augustinian theology, the power that recalls the dramatic composition of place and moves onward toward the understanding and the will.

Since this memoir is in large part an exercise in understanding, it seems appropriate to begin with a place: a classroom in which about a dozen students are reading Donne's *Anniversaries* in the context of the New Criticism, to which the discussion-leader (myself) is deeply de-

---

1. Augustine, *The Confessions of St. Augustine* 10.17, trans. John K. Ryan (Garden City, N.Y.: Doubleday, Image Books, 1960), 246.

voted. In the search for organic form that characterizes this mode of criticism, the class gradually discovers that the *First Anniversary* (as the refrain indicates) is divided into five main sections, while each of these sections seems to be subdivided into three parts. Similarly, though not identically, the *Second Anniversary* seems (as the side-notes indicate) to be divided into seven main parts, which are also subdivided into three parts. The group can think of no poetical precedent for such construction; yet Renaissance writers relied on precedents. What forerunning form or tradition could have suggested such construction to Donne? Perhaps the model might have come from traditions in medieval religious writing? So the leader of the discussion asks a colleague, Robert Menner, the Old English scholar, whether he knows of any such structures in medieval literature. The scholar knows of none, but he has a Jesuit father in his graduate class, and he will ask him whether he knows of any such traditions. The Jesuit smiles and says, "Yes, I practice such exercises quite frequently." And he recommends reading the third volume of Pierre Pourrat's *Christian Spirituality* to find out about the widespread practice of spiritual exercises on the Continent during the sixteenth and seventeenth centuries.

Pourrat's book came as a revelation, for my Evangelical upbringing and later affiliation with the Congregational Church had left me utterly unacquainted with this cultural development that flourished under the impulse of the Counter-Reformation during the time of Donne. It seemed that scholars of English Literature had, we might say, marginalized this movement, as its Catholic followers in England had certainly been oppressed, or suppressed, by authority. Still, the England of Donne's day was close to all developments in Continental religion and literature. Was it possible that High Church or moderate members of the Church of England knew of these spiritual exercises flourishing on the Continent? And could these exercises provide, perhaps, a precedent for Donne's *Anniversaries* and the peculiar dynamic of his Holy Sonnets? So *The Poetry of Meditation* began slowly to take shape, over a period of seven or eight years, and was finally published in 1954.

This was not simply a matter of scholarly research. During those years I was reading widely in the New Criticism and was teaching a course called "Problems in Poetry," which dealt with the principles and practices of this kind of criticism as represented in the writings of I. A. Richards, G. Wilson Knight, L. C. Knights, R. P. Blackmur, William Empson, F. R. Leavis, D. A. Traversi, Kenneth Burke, René Wellek, Allen Tate, Cleanth Brooks, Robert Penn Warren, and, of course, T. S. Eliot. The whole movement, as these names indicate, was much more varied and international than current attacks upon it would imply. Its center lay in the belief that the power of a literary work, with all its internal resistances and ambiguities, would best be conveyed by close attention to the subtle affiliations of its words, through imagery, allusion, sound, tone, and speaker.

None of this was necessarily opposed to historical scholarship. How could it be, when the prime instrument for these critics was the *OED*—originally known as "A New English Dictionary on Historical Principles Founded Mainly on the Materials Collected by The Philological Society"! But the attacks of some of the New Critics upon irrelevant historical and biographical research had certainly led many of the older scholars to mistrust and denounce the New Criticism. "I think it's dreadful," one of my older colleagues said to me, "how you young fellows are going off a-whoring after I. A. Richards." (I didn't realize at the time that he was echoing the biblical prophets.) But it seemed to these young fellows that the New Critics were only saying that the literary work should *control* the ways in which historical scholarship should be used in interpreting the work. Later critics of the New Critics have misunderstood the meaning of phrases like "The Verbal Icon" or "The Well-Wrought Urn." After all, a Russian icon represents a concentration of Russian Orthodox religion, and a Grecian urn, as Keats knew, includes vivid episodes from Greek religion on its surfaces. The Icon and the Urn are the vessels of history: they are, to shift the metaphor, lenses through which society and history may be revealed, microscopically or telescopically, as the revelation transcends (while including) society and history.

In any case, in the early days of the New Criticism, many of us could see no reason to abdicate the responsibility to perform historical scholarship, so long as this scholarship served as an aid to interpretation of the words. This becomes clear if one rereads that classic and controversial essay, "The Intentional Fallacy," written by the Aristotle of the New Criticism, William Wimsatt, in collaboration with his philosopher-friend, Monroe Beardsley. Meaning, they say, "is discovered through the semantics and syntax of a poem, through our habitual knowledge of the language, through grammars, dictionaries, and all the literature which is the source of dictionaries, in general through all that makes a language and culture."[2] *All that makes a language and culture.* Surely that all-inclusive conclusion allows for the possibility of creating a cultural poetics.

All of us then were well aware, as Donne was—and how could it be otherwise with the heirs of the Great Depression and the Second World War?—aware of the constant threat of disintegration in the social, political, ethical, and religious life of the Late Renaissance—and of similar issues in our own day. Nevertheless, like Donne, we believed that the search for the metaphysical One was worth the effort, that the quest for what Yeats called "Unity of Being" could be, and should be pursued—and that the study of literature could play a major role in that quest. But how could the verbal pursuit of unity in a poem in any way relate to history, to politics, to ordinary life? The answer was implicit in the writings of I. A. Richards, whose psychological principles of literary study and value underlie the critical approach of Brooks and Warren.

The core of it all lay in Richards's view of "The Interinanimation of Words," best set forth in his *Philosophy of Rhetoric* (1936), but implicit in all his earlier books. His famous terms *vehicle* and *tenor* were part of his argument that "metaphor is the omnipresent principle of language," not something specially limited to poetry. As his exploration of the nature of metaphor proceeds, Richards says:

> We find that all the questions that matter in literary history and criticism take on a new interest and a wider relevance to human needs. In asking how language works we ask about how thought and feeling and all the other modes of the mind's activity proceed, about how we are to learn to live and how that 'greatest thing of all,' a command of metaphor—which is great only because it is a command of life—may best, in spite of Aristotle, 'be imparted to another.'[3]

---

2. Originally published in *Sewanee Review* 54 (1946): 468–88, included in Wimsatt's collection *The Verbal Icon: Studies in the Meaning of Poetry* (Lexington: University of Kentucky Press, 1954), 10.

3. *The Philosophy of Rhetoric* (New York and London: Oxford University Press, 1936), 92, 95. Hereafter, references to this work are cited as *PR*.

A command of metaphor is a command of life! How strange it is, in view of this, to hear it said that the views of the New Critics were divorced from concern with life and consisted in a "formalism" that severed text from context. But we saw then what Richards meant. He had an absolute, unshakable belief in the power of language as the unique instrument possessed by human beings, an instrument that could, when rightly managed, lead to the ordering and enrichment of the individual mind and hence onward to the ordering and enrichment of society at large. Words, he declared, "are the meeting points at which regions of experience which can never combine in sensation or intuition, come together. They are the occasion and the means of that growth which is the mind's endless endeavour to order itself. That is why we have language. It is no mere signalling system. It is the instrument of all our distinctively human development." (*PR*, 131) Transferred from the secular to the religious realm, this is not far from the logocentric view with which Donne closes the *Second Anniversary*, addressing the immortal "Shee," the image of the redeemed soul:

> Since his will is, that to posteritee,
> Thou shouldst for life, and death, a patterne bee,
> And that the world should notice have of this,
> The purpose, and th'Autority is his;
> Thou art the Proclamation; and I ame
> The Trumpet, at whose voice the people came.

It is no accident, then, that the first modern defence of Donne's *First Anniversary* should have been published by Richards in 1942, under the title, "The Interactions of Words," and that it should have appeared in a volume edited by one of the New Critics, Allen Tate.[4] It is furthermore no accident that the first edition of *The Poetry of Meditation* contained two references to Richards, along with two sizeable quotations from R. P. Blackmur. The first of the quotations from Blackmur formed the epigraph for part 1 of the book in its first edition (the second edition replaced this with a quotation from Donne—a substitution I now regret). "The life we all live," Blackmur wrote, "is not alone enough of a subject for the serious artist; it must be life with a leaning, life with a tendency to shape itself only in certain forms, to afford its most lucid

---

4. *The Language of Poetry* (Princeton: Princeton University Press, 1942), 65–87.

revelations only in certain lights." He is preparing to defend Yeats's use of magical symbols in his poetry, especially the occult symbolism of Yeats's *A Vision*, the poet's personal handbook for his meditations. "If our final interest, either as poets or as readers, is in the reality declared when the forms have been removed and the lights taken away, yet we can never come to the reality at all without the first advantage of the form and lights." This mode of defence seemed to justify a study of the Renaissance "Art of Meditation" as a form and light that could increase our understanding of seventeenth-century religious poetry. And again, at the close of chapter 1 ("The Method of Meditation") Blackmur appears, discussing Yeats: "It is the very purpose of a supernaturally derived discipline, as used in poetry," he says, "to set the substance of natural life apart, to give it a form, a meaning, and a value which cannot be evaded . . . for the poet the discipline, far from seeming secondary, had an extraordinary structural, seminal, and substantial importance to the degree that without it he could hardly have written at all."[5] This, I thought, was exactly the way in which the discipline of religious meditation may have played its role in the creation of seventeenth-century poetry.

What I am saying, then, is that, unconsciously or half-consciously, it was the principles of the New Criticism that led to my interest in exploring the imaginative structures created by the Art of Meditation, for such meditation seemed to encourage a dramatic action of the senses and the "whole soul"—an internal action of the sort that the New Criticism admired. *The Poetry of Meditation*, then, might be called a work of New Critical Historicism, and it is far from being alone in its kind.[6] I think of the writings of Maynard Mack on Pope, of C. L. Barber's *Shakespeare's Festive Comedy*, of Joseph Summers's book on George Herbert, of Meyer Abrams's writings on the Romantics, and of Robert Penn Warren's long and learned essay on "The Ancient Mariner."

In pursuing its study of context, the book develops a method of presentation that may have some affinity with the current New Historicism: poetry and prose flow together, as passages from the meditative

---

5. R. P. Blackmur, *The Expense of Greatness* (New York: Arrow Editions, 1940), 75–76.

6. References to *The Poetry of Meditation: A Study in English Religious Poetry of the Seventeenth Century* are cited as *PM*.

handbooks, not usually regarded as canonical, are given side by side with poetry by Donne, Herbert, and Crashaw—poetry that is privileged only by its greater verbal power. The effect, as I now look back upon the book, is to suggest an unbreakable continuum in the religious consciousness of the time, both English and Continental—an effect supported by the writings of Edward Wilson and Terence Cave, as they have later studied the impact of meditation upon the poetry of Spain and France.[7] Every quotation in the book is literature, some more powerful than others, but all are imbued with the same incentive: to draw together the senses and the "powers of the soul" toward one incandescent moment—of grief, of joy, of love. So the book bears a title with deliberate ambiguity: the *poetry* of the act of meditation: the *poiesis*, the creative power implied in the process of meditation, and the ultimate efflorescence of that process in what we ordinarily call poetry—by Donne, Herbert, and their fellows.

I seem to have realized that the single-minded pursuit of one strand in the complex culture of the Renaissance was likely to produce an effect of over-emphasis, for the last sentence of the introduction reads: "All our studies are partial; all need to be set together for a full view of literature. The present study is focused on one aspect of the period; my aim is to convince the reader that this is one among the several necessary methods of approaching a full understanding of English literature in the seventeenth century" (*PM*, 22). But, alas, the momentum of the whole book has led some readers to overlook this cautionary admission, and no wonder, for at the very outset appears the rash suggestion (assertion?): "The 'poetry of meditation,' I believe, would be a more accurate, a more flexible, a more helpful term, both historically and critically, than the much debated term 'metaphysical poetry'" (*PM*, 4). I should have said, "a more helpful term" when applied to *religious* poetry. I have since on several occasions recanted that statement, as in an essay of 1959: "The term 'meditative,' as I [now!] see it, does not serve to replace the term 'metaphysical'; it rather intersects the term

---

7. Edward M. Wilson, "A Key to Calderón's *Psalle et sile*" (1959) and "Spanish and English religious poetry of the seventeenth century" (1958); included in the memorial collection *Spanish and English Literature of the 16th and 17th Centuries: Studies in Discretion, Illusion, and Mutuality* (Cambridge: Cambridge University Press, 1980); Terence C. Cave, *Devotional Poetry in France c. 1570–1613* (Cambridge: Cambridge University Press, 1969).

'metaphysical,' and serves a different purpose by associating Donne with a powerful tradition in European religious life."[8]

Throughout the book, from time to time, an awareness of other factors in the poetry is shown, as in the treatment of Donne's "La Corona," in which the discussion shows that poetical, liturgical, and meditative traditions are all involved. But most of all, the chapters on George Herbert seem eager to stress the many elements that entered into the fabric of *The Temple*. Nevertheless, in chapter 7, the opening (ten-page) emphasis on the analogy between Herbert and François de Sales (reinforced by a handsome engraving of the saint) has had the effect of overpowering the subsequent twenty-three pages, which treat in detail Herbert's kinship with Sidney's sonnets, with Sidney's version of the Psalms, and with psalmody in general, along with the statement: "The history of English religious poetry in the sixteenth and seventeenth centuries can never be accurately recorded without remembering that for the devout poet of the time the greatest examples of religious poetry lay in the Bible" (*PM*, 278). "It is hardly too much to say," I added, "that the 'Church' is a book of seventeenth-century psalmody,"—a "book of personal psalms" in which Herbert seems to have "taken special pains to include at least one example of every kind of short poem popular in his day, along with at least one example of every kind of devotional practice" (*PM*, 280–81). I do not think, then, that the book neglected the other sources of poetic inspiration cultivated by English Protestants.

It never occurred to me to point out that Herbert was a Protestant; I took this for granted. The point in stressing the analogy with François de Sales (and in calling attention to Herbert's "great esteme" for Savonarola's *De Simplicitate Christianae Vitae*) was that the Protestantism

---

8. "Donne and the Meditative Tradition," *Thought* 34 (1959): 269–78; included in *The Poem of the Mind* (New York and London: Oxford University Press, 1966), under the title: "John Donne: A Valediction," 21–32. See also the opening pages of "John Donne: The Meditative Voice," *Massachusetts Review* 1 (1960), 326–42 (included in *Poem of the Mind*). See the extended efforts to distinguish between the terms *meditative* and *metaphysical* in the introduction to *The Meditative Poem: An Anthology of Seventeenth-Century Verse* (Garden City, N.Y.: Doubleday, Anchor Books, 1963 (included in revised form in *Poem of the Mind*); and, finally, the long introduction to *The Anchor Anthology of Seventeenth-Century Verse*, vol. 1 (Garden City, N.Y.: Doubleday, Anchor Books, 1969); currently published by Norton under the title *English Seventeenth-Century Verse*.

of George Herbert was broad enough to include elements of devotion cultivated by Roman Catholic writers. This thesis has recently been given additional support by the appearance of Paul Stanwood's edition of Jeremy Taylor's *Holy Living*, which calls attention to the fact that Taylor concludes his treatise with a sizeable quotation from a source cited in the margin: "L'Eveque de Gènève, introd. à la vie dévote"—François de Sales, *Introduction to the Devout Life*, not John Calvin of Geneva, but the *Bishop* of Geneva. Of course Taylor, like Herbert, is a firm Protestant, as he shows by attacking the doctrine of transubstantiation and other Catholic beliefs. Nevertheless, the conclusion of his treatise stresses the importance of partaking of "the Lords Supper," by which, it is clear, he believes that a Real Presence is communicated: "In the act of receiving," he writes, we should believe the elements of the communion "not to be common bread and wine, but holy in their use, holy in their signification, holy in their change, and holy in their effect." "Dispute not," he adds, "concerning the secret of the mystery, and the nicety of the manner of Christ's presence: it is sufficient to thee that Christ shall be present to thy soul, as an instrument of grace."[9]

George Herbert, in the final version of *The Temple*, is presenting the same view of the efficacy of the Lord's Supper, as I have tried to show in a recent essay.[10] The argument (*PM*, chap. 8) that *The Temple* is unified by what the age called "mental communion" is therefore valid, I think, in spite of efforts to play down the Eucharistic presence in favor of Calvinist theology. But the Calvinist view, ably presented by Barbara Lewalski, Richard Strier,[11] and others, has shown a serious

---

9. *Holy Living and Holy Dying*, ed. P. G. Stanwood, 2 vols. (Oxford: Clarendon Press, 1989), 1:262. Stanwood notes, "Of the many devotional manuals in print by 1650, the *Introduction* has most relevance to *Holy Living*, for it is the work with which the latter has most in common in terms of tone and style; it is also the only contemporary devotional work from which Taylor quotes" (xxxvii). For the larger significance of this parallel see my review in *Modern Philology*, 90 (1992): 258–62.

10. See "The Generous Ambiguity of Herbert's *Temple*," in *A Fine Tuning: Studies of the Religious Poetry of Herbert and Milton*, ed. Mary A. Maleski (Binghamton, N.Y.: MRTS, 1989), 31–56; included in the collection *From Renaissance to Baroque: Essays on Literature and Art* (Columbia: University of Missouri Press, 1991). The collection also includes a revised version of the 1972 lecture in revision, "Donne's *Anniversaries* Revisited," published by Agnes Scott College in 1973.

11. Barbara Kiefer Lewalski, *Protestant Poetics and the Seventeenth-Century Religious Lyric* (Princeton: Princeton University Press, 1979); Richard Strier, *Love Known: Theology and Experience in George Herbert's Poetry* (Chicago: University of Chicago Press, 1983).

weakness in the way in which the book aligns Herbert with Salesian devotion to the Eucharist: the chapter does not consider the important theological differences between Roman Catholic and Protestant doctrine (or rather doctrines) of the Lord's Supper, which ranged from Jeremy Taylor's belief that, in a way not to be debated, the Real Presence is still allied with the elements of the sacrament, through Calvin's view that Christ exerts a spiritual presence from his place in Heaven, on to the extreme Zwinglian view that the sacrament is only a memorial, a pledge of faith. These differences were moderated by the impact of Lutheranism. It is surprising that recent writers on the influence of Calvinism tend to treat this doctrine as identical with Lutheranism. But there is a powerful distinction to be made. Lutheranism, through its doctrine of consubstantiation (which, unlike Calvinism, allowed Christ to be bodily present at more than one place at the same time) maintained the sense of a Real Presence at the Communion service; hence the word *messe* or even *missa* could be retained, along with a vernacular ritual, priestly garments, and the rich music of organ and choir—all serving to celebrate the divine presence. One might say that the crucial difference between Lutheranism and Calvinism is represented by the contrast between Bach's B-Minor Mass and the psalm-singing of Calvinist Geneva and dissenting congregations in England. In many ways the Church of England, with its Book of Common Prayer and its moderated ritual (both constantly under attack by strict Calvinists), is closer to Lutheranism than it is to Calvinism.

Still, the current concern with Calvinism is important, for it presents another strand in the complex culture of the Late Renaissance, a strand that should not, I think, be regarded as canceling out the presence of elements adapted from Catholicism, but rather as tempering those elements, working in concert with them, or questioning them in ways that sometimes create a dramatic tension in the poetry of the time. That is why, in reviewing Barbara Lewalski's *Protestant Poetics*, I made this suggestion: "The peculiar power that developed in English religious poetry of this era seems to result from the impingement of *two* Continental forces upon the ground of the old religion as established in England before the reign of Henry VIII. Reformed doctrines were colliding with, sometimes coalescing with, always modifying, the meditative and devotional practices nourished by the Counter-Reformation, in a struggle taking place upon the ground of an ancient

Catholicism deeply rooted in the popular consciousness."[12] This is a view that bears some affinity with the New Historicism, although my old historicism, intent on exploring the *poiesis* of organic unity, did not concern itself with seeing the Art of Meditation as an instrument of political and ecclesiastical power, as in some hands it surely was.

I could defend my book's lack of concern for political and theological issues by arguing that it was studying the structure of meditation, and that the basic structure remained intact, even when Catholic treatises from Spain were published in London, "purged of Popish errors." The *method* was neutral: it remained valid as long as free will could make the effort to restore, in some degree, the three-fold Image of God that constituted the human soul, in the theology of Augustine's *De Trinitate:* Memory, Understanding, and Will. When the doctrine of Predestination, derived in large part from other writings of Augustine, took away the freedom of the will and placed the soul's whole future in the hands of God, the three powers of the inward trinity lost the motive to function as accessories in the process of salvation. Thus Calvinist meditation tended to rely on other modes of thought: the search for "evidences of election," expressions of love and gratitude when one became convinced of election—or, as Bunyan so vividly demonstrates, expressions of horror and anguish when one feared inescapable reprobation. It is significant that in 1650 Richard Baxter, himself a free-will man, should in the *Saints Everlasting Rest* show his fellow dissenters how to use the powers of the soul in methodical meditation upon the joys of heaven—in a work that became one of the most popular works of the late seventeenth century.

Like the Bible itself, the richly varied and experimental works of Augustine could lead in different and even conflicting directions. Thus *The Paradise Within* (1964) explores the role of "Augustinian meditation," with its basically Platonic orientation, in the works of Vaughan and Traherne. This was not a matter of associating these writers with medieval sources, although the study of Traherne relied heavily upon Bonaventure's *Journey of the Mind*. The Platonic aspects of the Augustinian tradition were very much alive in the middle of the seventeenth century, as a result of the revival of interest in Platonism, a reaction against the forces of Calvinism. *The Paradise Within* explored the differ-

---

12. "Meditation as Poetic Strategy," *Modern Philology* 80 (1982), 168–74; see 169.

ences between Augustinian and Ignatian meditation, in a work concerned with Protestant development of meditation upon the three Books cultivated by the Augustinian tradition: the Bible, the Book of Nature, and the Book of the Soul—books to which the Protestant turned when Calvinist theology had diminished the significance of the Sacrament of the Altar. These aspects of seventeenth-century Protestant devotion have been further explored in relation to Vaughan and Rembrandt in a recent essay included in the collection *From Renaissance to Baroque*.

It was unfortunate that immersion in administrative duties delayed the appearance of *The Paradise Within* for ten years; it was meant to follow quickly upon the suggestion of a sequel contained in the introduction to *The Poetry of Meditation*. And indeed much of it was written during a leave of absence in 1955–1956. If it had appeared in 1957 it might have helped to dispel an impression that I was proceeding with too exclusive an emphasis upon Counter-Reformation forces. But two developments had already alerted me to the importance of paying more attention to Puritan devotional practices. In the 1950s I was asked to provide a foreword to Donald Stanford's edition (1960) of the poems of the New England Calvinist Edward Taylor. This commission resulted in a twenty-five-page essay on Taylor's *Preparatory Meditations*, an essay that seems to be well-known among students of American Colonial poetry, but not so well-known among students of British literature. Later on, one of my graduate students, Milo Kaufmann, through his dissertation on John Bunyan, convinced me that Calvinists had far more areas of devotional practice than I had allowed. His book *The Pilgrim's Progress and Traditions in Puritan Meditation* (1966) provided a strong corrective and compensation for my rather tart treatment of English Puritan writers. I would argue, though, that my reliance on Richard Baxter's testimony was not wholly misguided. Baxter was a powerful witness, and when he says that the devotional life of dissenters needs the help of methodical meditation by all the powers of the soul, we can believe that he knows the needs of his people. Still, I should not have spoken of "the Puritan mistrust of all sensory aids to devotion" (*PM*, 164). Some sensory aids were always available: meditation on "the creatures," on the "occasions" of daily life, and most important, on the imagery provided by the Bible, as witnessed by Edward Taylor's meditations on the Song of Songs. In my anthology, *The Meditative Poem* (1963), I included poems by Taylor as the close of the meditative tradition that had begun, as I saw it, with Robert Southwell and William Alabaster—the latter a newcomer to the canon whose Ignatian qualities are described in the long preface to the second (slightly revised) edition of *The Poetry of Meditation.*

What, then, does this searching of the memory reveal? I would conclude that the basic argument of *The Poetry of Meditation* is still valid, but that it needs, and has been subjected to, constant modification and supplementation, by others as well as by myself. No book or article can stand fast in its particular moment. Critical and historical writings should, I think, constitute an ever-present process of revision, rethinking, as new students, new colleagues, new books, new articles, and new personal experiences all come together to inspire modification of one's previous position. And so it seems right to conclude, as I began, with a quotation from Augustine concerning the power of memory, which I hope has here led to some understanding:

> There too I encounter myself and recall myself, and what, and when, and where I did some deed, and how I was affected when I did it. There are all those things which I remember either as experienced by me or as taken on trust from others. From that same abundant stock, also, I combine one and another of the likenesses of things . . . with things past, and from them I meditate upon future actions, events and hopes, and all these again as though they were actually present.[13]

---

13. *Confessions* 10.8.

JOHN DONNE
"The Holy Ghost is Amorous in His Metaphors"

❖ ❖ ❖ Anthony Low ❖ ❖ ❖

It is a "widely publicized observation that Donne expresses religion through human love," as Winfried Schleiner has remarked.[1] In a sermon preached before the King at Whitehall on February 24, 1625/26, Donne indicates why he found the language of sexual love appropriate in speaking about divine matters:

> And would GOD pretend to send thee a *gracious Messadge,* and send thee a *Divorce?* GOD is *Love,* and the *Holy Ghost* is amorous in his *Metaphors;* everie where his *Scriptures* abound with the notions of *Love,* of *Spouse,* and *Husband,* and *Marriadge Songs,* and *Marriadge Supper,* and *Marriadge-Bedde.* But for words of *Separation,* and *Divorce,* of *Spirituall Divorce* for ever, of any soule formerly taken in Marriadge, this very word *Divorce,* is but *twice* read in the *Scriptures;* once in this *Text;* and heere *God* dis-avowes it; For when hee says, *Where is the Bill,* hee meanes there is no such *Bill.*[2]

---

1. *The Imagery of John Donne's Sermons* (Providence: Brown University Press, 1970), 158. Schleiner discusses this "field of imagery" only briefly (157–58).
2. *The Sermons of John Donne,* ed. Evelyn M. Simpson and George R. Potter (Berkeley and Los Angeles: University of California Press, 1954) 7:87–88; hereafter references are cited as *Sermons.* It is sometimes said that Protestants, or Anglicans, used

There is ample biblical precedent in speaking about both the love between God and man and the love between God and his Church in sexual and marital terms. In this instance, Donne's sermon speaks of an indissoluble marriage between God and the soul.[3] And, of course, although he invokes the authority of the Bible directly here, there is also an ancient tradition of writings based on these originary biblical metaphors—hermeneutical, theological, devotional, and literary—on which Donne also drew.

Having considered Donne's secular love poetry at length elsewhere,[4] I would like now to consider how his divine poems are related to his secular love poems and to those of other poets in the tradition. There has been a variety of approaches to Donne's use of human love in his divine poems, ranging from Freudian debunking to respectful admiration, and from emphasis on continuity to emphasis on difference.[5]

---

the scriptural marriage-metaphor only of Christ and his Church, not of Christ and the individual soul; see, e.g., Bruce Henricksen, "Donne's Orthodoxy," *Texas Studies in Literature and Language* 14 (1972): 5–16. This distinction is not correct; both usages are common. As this passage illustrates, Donne speaks of God marrying the soul—as did many other Protestant writers.

3. In the light of the whole sermon and of Donne's other writings, marriage without divorce probably does not imply irresistible election but confidence that God will never reject a soul arbitrarily. Luther uses quite a different trope for the divine-human relationship: "Thus the human will is like a beast of burden. If God rides it, it wills and goes whence God wills. . . . If Satan rides, it wills and goes where Satan wills. Nor may it choose. . . . But the riders themselves contend who shall have it and hold it," Erasmus and Luther, *Discourse on Free Will*, trans. Ernst F. Winter (New York: Frederick Ungar, 1961), 112.

4. See "Donne and the Reinvention of Love," *English Literary Renaissance* 20 (1990): 465–86; also "Love and Science: Cultural Change in Donne's *Songs and Sonnets*," *Studies in the Literary Imagination* 22 (1989): 5–16.

5. For a reading which argues that "Show me deare Christ" "enacts Freud's thesis that religious 'ideology' is a form of sexual sublimation," see Robert Bagg, "The Electromagnet and the Shred of Platinum," *Arion* 8 (1969): 420. Wilbur Sanders writes, "In Donne's best religious poetry there is no shallow antithesis between the natural man and religious man, but a deep continuity" (*John Donne's Poetry* [Cambridge: Cambridge University Press, 1971], 110). Robert Nye argues for a "consistent" Donne whose secular and religious poetry alike concern "the problem of . . . how to love well" ("The body is his book: the poetry of John Donne," *Critical Quarterly* 14 [1972]: 352). A. J. Smith argues that Donne was the last poet to hold together two areas of experience that later diverged: "After Donne, sexual love offered no way" to seek ultimate truths ("The Failure of Love: Love Lyrics after Donne," in *Metaphysical Poetry*, ed. Malcolm Bradbury and David Palmer, Stratford-Upon-Avon Studies 11 [London: Edward Arnold, 1970], 52, 71). Robert S. Jackson,

No exploration of love in the seventeenth century will be adequate unless one takes sacred love into account, since, although religious concerns do not generally loom as large in our eyes as they did in earlier times, sacred love represents an important aspect of cultural developments and changing attitudes. In the seventeenth century, nearly everything, personal or political, social or psychological, was filtered through, and colored by, religious experience, which, as Helen C. White once so aptly argued, and as many critics have since confirmed, was a central concern of the times.[6] Although sacred love was paramount, it cannot be fully understood without considering its sometimes complicated connections with secular love.

Critics of seventeenth-century literature have often remarked on the resemblances as well as the tensions between sacred devotional and secular love poetry. We know that sacred and secular loves have often been in conflict, but that in the expression they seem to include many of the same feelings and emotions and to employ many of the same images. Even at the highest level of religious verse, for example in the poems of St. John of the Cross, such connections are often easily visible. We might take our departure from Freud and the twentieth century and posit that religious love is human love "sublimated"—that is, deflected onto other, ghostlier, finally imaginary objects.[7] Or we might prefer Robert Southwell's earlier argument that religious love is human love raised and redirected toward a higher object: "Passions I allow,

---

who finds continuity in Donne's progress from proverbial Jack Donne to Dr. Donne, gives useful biblical sources for the marriage metaphor in "Show me deare Christ" (*John Donne's Christian Vocation* [Evanston: Northwestern University Press, 1970], 146–78). Among numerous other studies, see A. L. French, "The Psychopathology of Donne's Holy Sonnets," *Critical Review* 13 (1970): 111–24; Lindsay A. Mann, "The Marriage Analogue of Letter and Spirit in Donne's Devotional Prose," *Journal of English and Germanic Philology* 70 (1971): 607–16; Kitty Datta, "Love and Asceticism in Donne's Poetry: The Divine Analogy," *Critical Quarterly* 19 (1977): 5–25.

6. Helen C. White, *English Devotional Literature [Prose], 1600–1640*, University of Wisconsin Studies in Language and Literature, 29 (Madison: University of Wisconsin Press, 1931), 10. See also Debora Shuger's persuasive recent case for the centrality of religious attitudes in relation to politics and culture, in *Habits of Thought in the English Renaissance: Religion, Politics, and the Dominant Culture* (Berkeley and Los Angeles: University of California Press, 1990). The many studies of such historians as Christopher Hill and Steven E. Ozment offer further cases in point.

7. I take Freud as the most representative and influential analytical figure of our century, but much the same might be said concerning the relation of the sacred, for example, to Lacan's "objet a" or to Winnicott's separation from the mother.

and loves I approve, onely I would wishe that men would alter their object and better their intent. For passions being sequels of our nature, and alloted unto us as the handmaides of reason: there can be no doubt, but that as their author is good, and their end godly: so ther use tempered in the meane, implieth no offence."[8] The chief practical difference between these two views, seventeenth-century and modern, results from their origins in two opposing sets of assumptions: either that God is real and worthy of love above all other objects, or that he is imaginary, no more than an illusory projection of thwarted or repressed love. Both views posit some degree of continuity between the secular and the sacred. The drawback of the modern view, when dealing with some early religious verse (Donne's and Crashaw's especially), is that it too often results in prematurely patronizing and reductionist conclusions.

It is not within the scope of a merely critical study to prove or to declare which of these views is finally correct. It is useful to remind ourselves of them, however, in order to be conscious of potential blind spots. I would argue that (as is often the case) the best procedure is to suspend disbelief at least long enough to make a thorough effort to understand and to work through the worldviews of the earlier writers under consideration, feeling free to use modern insights to intervene and interpret, but not to block out, older views. And we always reserve the right to reassume our private or contemporary opinions at the close of the excursion—or perhaps to decide that past writers had a better grip on some matters than we do. In any case, most readers will reserve the right to make their own decisions.

In what sense might we say that Donne's divine poems are "sacred parodies" of his secular love lyrics? Donne struggled with Petrarchism in the *Songs and Sonets*, and in the course of this struggle he invented new ways of thinking about love. Did his struggles and discoveries carry over significantly into his religious verse? Are his metaphors for divine love in the Holy Sonnets based only on biblical models, or do they also parody conventional love poetry? And do they imitate, qualify, or dismiss what Donne had learned from experience with his wife,

---

8. *Marie Magdalens Funeral Teares* (London, 1591), Preface, Cited by Louis L. Martz, *The Wit of Love: Donne, Carew, Crashaw, Marvell* (Notre Dame: University of Notre Dame Press, 1969), 141.

"she whome I lovd," or with his other "profane mistresses"?[9] If so, what kind of relationship do we find in the divine poems between Donne's speaker and his God?

Two critical comments offer a useful starting point in understanding the nature of love in Donne's divine poetry. Mario Praz writes that Donne "uses the elements of the Petrarchan subject matter, but in a bizarre, unorthodox way."[10] And Carol M. Sicherman notes that "although involved in an inward crisis, [Donne's] speaker always conducts his self-examination in relation to another being, either a woman or God."[11] As Donne himself says, relationships are critical in defining the persons who are related. At Paul's Cross, on the anniversary of the King's accession on March 24, 1616/17, he respectfully preaches to the Lords of the Council that, just as there can be no subjects without a king, so there can be no king without subjects. The principle applies even to the Divine Persons within the Holy Trinity: "God could not be a father without a Son, nor the Holy Ghost *Spiratus sine spirante*. As in Divinity, so in Humanity too, *Relations* constitute one another, King and subject come at once and together into consideration" (*Sermons*, 1:184).

"*Relations* constitute one another." These relations are prior to what we would call the individual identities of the persons involved.

> As he that would vow a fast, till he had found in nature, whether the Egge, or the Hen were the first in the world, might perchance starve himself; so that King, or that subject, which would forbear to do their several duties, till they had found which of them were most necessary to one another, might starve one another; for, King and subjects are Relatives, and cannot be considered in execution of their duties, but together. (*Sermons*, 1:183–84)

---

9. All quotations from the divine poems in this essay are from *John Donne: The Divine Poems*, ed. Helen Gardner, 2d ed. (Oxford: Clarendon Press, 1978). The two quotations are from "Since she whome I lovd" (l. 1) and "What if this present were the worlds last night?" (l. 10). Hereafter references are cited as *DP*.

10. *Mnemosyne: The Parallel Between Literature and the Visual Arts*, Bollingen Series 35.16 (Princeton: Princeton University Press, 1970), 97. Praz does not explain this passing comment apart from comparing the poems to Michelangelo's anteroom to the Laurentian Library and stressing dialectic reversal.

11. "Donne's Discoveries," *Studies in English Literature, 1500–1900* 11 (1971), 69 (author's abstract).

True, Donne here emphasizes public and not private relationships ("in execution of their duties"), but he also finds an analogy between social relationships and the "familial" relationships within the Godhead itself. And, however much the law might elaborate on the distinction between the King's two bodies, public and private realms were inextricably connected, as so many literary-historical studies have recently demonstrated. In the ordinary thinking of the time, even in the case of a king, the essential identity of the self and, reciprocally, of the other, depend on that person's relationship with the other. Indeed, what we think of as the very "nature" of the phenomenal or "objective" world always depends on our relationship with it, on our cultural bias, on the way—normally largely unconscious—we perceive it.[12] Subject and object define themselves in one another.

Three of the significant ways in which Donne relates to God in the divine poems are as king, master, and father. These three relationships are so closely interconnected with one another as to be almost wholly inseparable and indistinguishable. "Father, part of his double interest / Unto thy kingdome, thy Sonne gives to mee" (ll. 1–2). In this sonnet, God is king, father, and property owner, as well as creator. In "Oh my blacke Soule," God is a great king against whom the soul has committed treason. In "Batter my heart," he is a king who has left a deputy to command his city. In "I am a little world," he is lord of a "house," which the poet wants to join, that is, he is head of a family, tribe, or nation. In "Oh, to vex me," he bears the "rod" or scepter of authority, the sign of his ability to punish his subjects. The anxious speaker assiduously courts him, "In prayers, and flattering speeches." These images reflect some aspects of Donne's complex and often passionate relationship with the Father God. Debora Shuger documents the extent of this relationship throughout the Sermons, uncovering in the process the sometimes almost unbearable intensity of feeling with which Donne confronted his Omnipotent Father.[13]

---

12. See Low, "Donne and the Reinvention of Love"; and for further illustration, "Agricultural Reform and the Love Poems of Thomas Carew; With an Instance from Lovelace," in *Culture and Cultivation in Early Modern England: Writing and the Land*, ed. Michael Leslie and Timothy Raylor (Leicester: Leicester University Press, 1992), 63–80.

13. See Shuger, *Habits of Thought*, who shows the importance of the father-king relationship in a number of writers, of whom Donne is decidedly the most extraordinary.

But, strong as Donne's feelings are toward the figure of the authoritative father, the strongest emotion in his divine poems, especially the Holy Sonnets, is probably that between man and woman, husband and wife. Donne himself says, as we might expect, that, other than divine love,

> The highest degree of other love, is the love of woman: Which love, when it is rightly placed upon one woman, it is dignified by the Apostle with the highest comparison, *Husbands love your wives, as Christ loved his Church:* And God himself forbad not that this love should be great enough to change natural affection, *Relinquet patrem,* (for this, a man shall leave his Father) yea, to change nature it self, *caro una,* two shall be one.[14] (*Sermons*, 1:199)

Thus, on the authority of Genesis, Donne explicitly ranks the love of a husband for his wife above a son's love for his father, indeed above any other kind of human love. As we shall see, however, Donne does not succeed in bringing together the love of woman with the love of God without experiencing agonizing inner conflicts and difficulties, which his poems reflect. These poems are far from being pious exercises in the established conventions about love. The focus of Donne's inner psychological or spiritual tensions is on the speaker's sexual identity—on his confusion between what amount to conflicting roles. In the divine poems, Donne is both an insistently masculine seeker after mistresses or truths and the necessarily feminine and passive recipient of God's love.

"A Hymne to Christ, at the Authors last going into Germany" is among the most powerful of Donne's divine love poems. It begins with a typological metaphor, in which he compares his voyage across the Channel to Noah's preservation from the flood, which was traditionally understood to typify the passage of the Church and its members through the perils of a threatening world, as well as to typify any individual's particular experience in perilous times.[15]

---

14. "Two shall be one": here Donne refers more immediately to Christian theology and canon law than to Neoplatonic mysticism. See, e.g., St. Thomas Aquinas, *Summa*, trans. Fathers of the English Dominican Province, 3 vols. (New York: Benziger Brothers, 1948) 3:2762–2770 (Supplement, Q. 55); "carnal intercourse is the cause of affinity" (2764; Q. 55, Art. 3).

15. For general background, see Don Cameron Allen, *The Legend of Noah: Renaissance Rationalism in Art, Science, and Letters* (Urbana: University of Illinois Press,

> In what torne ship soever I embarke,
> That ship shall be my embleme of thy Arke;
> What sea soever swallow mee, that flood
> Shall be to mee an embleme of thy blood;
> Though thou with clouds of anger do disguise
> Thy face; yet through that maske I know those eyes,
>   Which, though they turne away sometimes, they never will despise.
>
> (ll. 1–7)

The universal typology of Noah's ark, which Donne understands to be an emblem of salvation linking the two covenants, he also applies specifically to his own threatened situation. Amid ominous threats of outward danger and of inward guilt, there flashes forth in his imagination a strong suggestion of recuperative love, in the powerful phrase, "I know those eyes." As yet, this is a love unspecified, although there are unavoidable suggestions both of a lord's or a father's anger toward his servant or child and of coquetry with a masked lover of indeterminate sex. Although the masking presumably derives from the biblical metaphor of God's turning away his face, to which Donne later alludes (l. 7), it more immediately provokes thoughts of casual courtship or flirtation, which, in turn, are belied by the seriousness of the speaker's response: "I know those eyes."

In the second stanza, Donne offers to give up all of his other loves and allegiances for the sole love of Christ:

> I sacrifice this Iland unto thee,
> And all whom I lov'd there, and who lov'd mee;
> When I have put our seas twixt them and mee,
> Put thou thy sea betwixt my sinnes and thee.
> As the trees sap doth seeke the root below

1963); for concise background on the typological tradition, see David Shelley Berkeley, *Inwrought with Figures Dim: A Reading of Milton's "Lycidas"* (The Hague: Mouton, 1974), 113–64. On individual typology, see Barbara Kiefer Lewalski, *Protestant Poetics and the Seventeenth-Century Religious Lyric* (Princeton: Princeton University Press, 1979). Donne's "speaker imagines himself a new Noah about to experience a new Flood in a new Ark" (280). I would only dispute Lewalski's view, however, that this form of typology (foreshadowing the individual Christian's experience) is uniquely "Protestant." Application to the self is common in earlier Catholic and in Counter-Reformation spirituality.

> In winter, in my winter now I goe,
> Where none but thee, th'Eternall root of true love I may know.
>
> (ll. 8–14)

There is some echo here of the First Commandment: "Thou shalt have no other gods before me" (Exod. 20.3). There is a closer echo of God's pronouncement on marriage in Genesis. And there is an even closer echo of Matthew, in which Jesus, who first quotes the Genesis text (Matt. 19.5), a little later bases a new saying on it: "And every one that hath forsaken houses, or brethren, or sisters, or father, or mother, or wife, or children, or lands, for my name's sake, shall receive an hundredfold, and shall inherit everlasting life" (Matt. 19.29). Precisely as in this invitation, Donne's pledge to love Christ above all other loves derives from the marriage vow. To love Christ is the new ultimate: he is "th'Eternall root of true love."

The third stanza, like the second, echoes the Commandments: "For I the Lord thy God am a Jealous God" (Exod. 20.5). But this jealousy sounds a note distinctly marital and sexual. It builds on the disparate biblical texts to the point where Gardner, who certainly knew these texts, is nonetheless moved to call it "Donne's own" conceit (*DP*, 107):

> Nor thou nor thy religion dost controule,
> The amorousnesse of an harmonious Soule,
> But thou would'st have that love thy selfe: As thou
> Art jealous, Lord, so I am jealous now,
> Thou lov'st not, till from loving more, thou free
> My soule: Who ever gives, takes libertie:
>   O, if thou car'st not whom I love, alas, thou lov'st not mee.
>
> Seale then this bill of my Divorce to All,
> On whom those fainter beames of love did fall;
> Marry those loves, which in youth scatter'd bee
> On Fame, Wit, Hopes (false mistresses) to thee.
> Churches are best for Prayer, that have least light:
> To see God only, I goe out of sight:
>   And to scape stormy dayes, I chuse an Everlasting night.
>
> (ll. 15–28)

The last stanza amounts to a pledge of marriage. Donne will divorce the world and all lesser loves to unite himself indissolubly with God.

The biblical tradition is that God is the bridegroom and the soul is the bride. Donne recognizes this polarity of the metaphorical sexes when he plays, in part, the conventional woman's role. He teases and provokes through jealousy; he pleads to be loved; he admits that God must be the one to act, to "free" his soul, to remove him from his attachments to the world, to "Seale" the bill of divorce which Donne himself is powerless to effect. Yet even in this moment of "feminine" passivity and surrender, Donne evokes the reverse polarity of the sexual metaphor. He remains a man, married to "false mistresses."

These mistresses compete with God for his love. By the logic of the metaphor, then, God momentarily becomes a woman, the true bride as opposed to the false mistresses. The implications are disturbing: not just because God is thus seen under a female metaphor—after all, orthodox Medieval and Renaissance writers often picture him under the metaphor of a nursing mother[16]—but because, in terms of the hierarchical thought of Donne's age, God as bride would be viewed as hierarchically inferior to the speaker. The metaphor thus makes God greater than various created "goods" but still apparently less than Donne himself. These sexual confusions are not especially prominent in the "Hymne to Christ," and might easily be overlooked. But they account for some of the underlying tension and uneasiness (which many readers have found even in the three hymns) and for Donne's inability quite to resign himself in this poem to an appropriately passive role. He admits that he must seek aid and permission before he can possibly be divorced and remarried. Yet, even to the last, we find him boldly plunging into action and taking control of the situation: "To see God only, I goe out of sight: / And to scape stormy dayes, I chuse an Everlasting night" (ll. 27–28). Donne's flamboyant closing gesture underlines and sets its seal to the hymn's magnificent poetry;

---

16. Female imagery for God is collected in many feminist studies, which, however, sometimes implicate earlier writers in the struggle for dominance. For helpful comment, see Caroline Walker Bynum, "The Body of Christ in the Later Middle Ages: A Reply to Leo Steinberg," *Renaissance Quarterly* 39 (1986): 399–439. Usually mother and nursing images emphasize God's tenderness and the soul's trusting reliance. A significant biblical source is Isaiah 49:15. I cite the previous verse to show how easily the image emerges from that of God as Israel's husband: "But Zion said, The Lord hath forsaken me, and my Lord hath forgotten me. Can a woman forget her sucking child, that she should not have compassion on the son of her womb? yea, they may forget, yet will I not forget thee."

but this same gesture undermines the hymn's effectiveness as a work of exemplary devotion.

Of course, there is inevitably some degree of ambiguity or paradox when a male speaker assumes a female role. The more patriarchal the society, the greater the inversion demanded. Yet many other male writers—Crashaw, for example, or St. Francis de Sales—settle into the role with no apparent uneasiness. Christianity is fundamentally posited on the basis of such humbling reversals and willing self-immolations. The case is different with Donne, whose insistent masculinity has so often been noticed by critics of the *Songs and Sonets*. As early as 1633, in "An Elegie upon the death of the Deane of Pauls," Thomas Carew admires Donne for committing "holy Rapes upon our Will," for opening "a Mine / Of rich and pregnant phansie," and most famously for founding "a line / Of masculine expression" (ll. 17, 37–39). Many other religious writers of the time, from Catholics to Puritans, easily resign themselves to God's love and play the female part when they invoke the marriage trope,[17] but not even with the all-desirable prospect of union with God in mind can Donne surrender easily to the imperatives of this metaphorical role reversal. For him the relinquishment of his usually dominant and aggressively masculine stance is never anything but uncomfortable. In the greatest of his *Songs and Sonets*, his will to dominate dissolves into timeless moments of equal sharing and of intimate mutuality, but never into passivity, still less into a posture of admitted inferiority.

Although there is room in sacred love for some degree of mutuality or reciprocity, equality is clearly no more workable than superiority as a suitable stance for loving God. Many of the *Songs and Sonets* offer moments of intense, timeless transcendence—but not transcendence of a religious, or at least of a specifically Christian, description.[18] Indeed, in such poems as "The Anniversarie," "A nocturnall upon S. *Lucies* day," and "The Relique," Donne treats the love of God and human love as mutually exclusive and fundamentally incompatible. In these poems God's eternity must wait on the private eternity of the

---

17. This is notably true of Crashaw; see Maureen Sabine, *Feminine Engendered Faith: The Poetry of John Donne and Richard Crashaw* (London: Macmillan, 1992), and the chapter on Crashaw in Anthony Low, *The Reinvention of Love: Poetry, Politics and Culture from Sidney to Milton* (Cambridge: Cambridge University Press, forthcoming).

18. For discussion of this point, see "Donne and the Reinvention of Love."

two lovers. From them society and children are excluded. The sacrament of marriage goes unmentioned. As idealistic and "spiritual" as Donne's love may be in the *Songs and Sonets,* it never claims to represent part of a continuous Neoplatonic ladder leading upward to the pure love of the Christian God. So the road from the *Songs and Sonets* to the Holy Sonnets is much more difficult and discontinuous than it might first appear. Although Donne's ideal secular love incorporates many of the qualities, feelings, and attitudes of religion, it represents an early forerunner of "natural supernaturalism," which cannot lead spontaneously to sacred Christian love.

Donne directly confronts the difficulties of moving from human to divine love in the first of the three late Holy Sonnets from the Westmoreland manuscript. He tries to postulate an easy transference, but the inward tensions soon grow evident:

> Since she whome I lov'd, hath payd her last debt
> To Nature, and to hers, and my good is dead,
> And her soule early'into heaven ravished,
> Wholy in heavenly things my mind is sett.
> Here the admyring her my mind did whett
> To seeke thee God; so streames do shew the head,
> But though I'have found thee,'and thou my thirst hast fed,
> A holy thirsty dropsy melts mee yett.
>
> (ll. 1–8)

The first quatrain is ambiguous about Donne's love for God. It implies at least the possibility that there was no room in him for divine love until his wife died. But it also suggests that her ravishment into heaven has directed his mind upward, and thus that love for her has led him to love for God. This suggestion is strongly confirmed in the second quatrain, in which the speaker argues that human love has "whett" his love for God and that she belongs to the same stream of love that leads back to its source in the Godhead. But these positive affirmations are somewhat blunted by the admission that he still thirsts, under a kind of love that increases his desire rather than satisfies it. Thus Donne implies the absence, not the presence, of the divine object of his love. As yet, the metaphor of thirst may be read simply as a measure of the infinite gulf between man and God. It represents, nonetheless, a retreat from or a severe qualification of his argument for simple continuity.

As yet there is nothing in the imagery to indicate a polarity of sexes between the speaker and his God, except that God takes the place formerly occupied by his wife. The sestet formally introduces the traditional marriage trope, with God as suitor and lover, only to proceed immediately to qualify and confuse it:

> But why should I begg more love, when as thou
> Doest wooe my soule, for hers offring all thine:
> And dost not only feare least I allow
> My love to saints and Angels, things divine,
> But in thy tender jealosy dost doubt
> Least the World, fleshe, yea Devill putt thee out.
> (ll. 9–14)

God as lover actively "wooe[s]" Donne's feminine soul. Then he immediately seems to switch roles, playing the conventional woman's part and passively "offring" himself in place of Donne's wife. In the rest of the sestet, the sexual roles become entirely uncertain. God is said to fear that Donne may "allow" his love to saints and angels, whether as lover or object of love is uncertain, although the Anglican prohibition against praying to the saints on which Donne plays would suggest that the forbidden role must be the former and not the latter. In the same way, love for the world, the flesh, and the devil implies Donne's love for them, but that they should "putt" God "out" seems, in turn, to render him their passive object. What is clear enough, at any rate, is that nothing is clear or easy for Donne in this new love relationship. The marriage trope fragments and breaks into confusing pieces. Donne simply cannot effect the kind of direct, simple transference of love from his wife to his God that he momentarily promised with such assurance, nor can he borrow and build upon the biblical marriage trope without running immediately into confusion and, as in the "Hymne to Christ," severe difficulty in accepting the indicated passive female role. Perhaps the speaker's most convincing statement is that "A holy thirst dropsy melts mee yett." That is, he is consumed with unsatisfied, perhaps never to be satisfied, desire. He is engaged in an endless and possibly hopeless quest. In this regard, he much more closely resembles the disappointed lover of the Petrarchan tradition—which Donne himself had earlier helped to overthrow—than the happy, mutual lover of the *Songs and Sonets*.

The second of the Westmoreland sonnets is considerably more conflicted and disturbing than the first:

> Show me deare Christ, thy spouse, so bright and cleare.
> What, is it she, which on the other shore
> Goes richly painted? or which rob'd and tore
> Laments and mournes in Germany and here?
> Sleepes she a thousand, then peepes up one yeare?
> Is she selfe truth and errs? now new, now'outwore?
> Doth shee,'and did she, and shall she evermore
> On one, on seaven, or on no hill appeare?
> Dwells she with us, or like adventuring knights
> First travaile we to seeke and then make love?
> Betray kind husband thy spouse to our sights,
> And let myne amorous soule court thy mild Dove,
> Who is most trew, and pleasing to thee, then
> When she'is embrac'd and open to most men.

There is no need to point out how anxious and disturbed Donne is about the life-and-death question of identifying the true Church, the Bride of Christ, and of discriminating it from false, harlot Churches, whether Catholic or Puritan. As many critics have pointed out, it is far from certain whether Donne thinks that a true Church exists in this world to be found, or whether the Anglican Church to which he now belonged escapes his general censure. Most of all, the shocking image of God as a complacent husband, prostituting his wife to as many men as possible, has proven difficult for many critics, who have tried to bring it back within the bounds of acceptable, traditional metaphorical discourse. The underlying source of the indecorum, however, has not yet been noticed.

The fundamental difficulty and source of unease in "Show me deare Christ" is that Donne has crossed the wires between the two traditional versions of the biblical marriage trope: the marriage between Christ and his Church, and the marriage between God and the soul. On its surface, from its opening words, the sonnet seems to be based only on the marriage of Christ and his Church. The problem is simply to discriminate between the true bride of Christ and the false harlots who may seduce the unwary. But the sestet unexpectedly introduces a version of the individual marriage trope: "Dwells she with us, or like adventuring knights / First travaile we to seeke and then make love?" Donne substitutes the Church for God as an intermediary in the usual trope, however, and incorporates additional imagery from the courtly romance love tradition.

The soul is a questing, masculine knight; the object of its love is a maiden, who must first be actively sought and courted before she can be loved. The result of Donne's having introduced this strange variant of the biblical metaphors into the poem is that we soon find that we have on our hands a ménage-à-trois, if not worse. Christ and the speaker have essentially been transformed into rivals for the lady's affections. Donne has, in fact, presumptuously inserted himself (and us as readers and presumed fellow members of the Anglican Church) into the ancient marriage trope, as an additional husband. In spite of all the sexual and marital imagery, love between the speaker and Christ finds no logical place in the poem. Instead, the Church is their common wife. Donne has promoted himself from the normal position of sonship in a mother Church to the position of co-husband with God. Of course, we presume this not to have been his intention. But, once more, great difficulties arise because Donne simply cannot allow himself to relinquish his habitually masculine role. "First travaile we to seeke and then make love." "[L]et myne amorous soule court thy mild Dove." At most, Donne concedes that he must seek God's permission to go on playing the lover's part.

The individual marriage trope plays a part in several of the twelve sonnets printed in 1633 and the four added in 1635. In "As due by many titles," it is implied by the rivalry between God and the devil, who has usurped, stolen, "nay ravish[ed]" (l. 10) what belongs to God—although marriage is not cited among the eight or more "titles" God has in him. The trope is characteristically reversed in "What if this present were the worlds last night?," in which the bloody face of the crucified Christ becomes a potential rival of "all my profane mistresses" (l. 10) and remains, implicitly, the feminine object of Donne's still masculine (and touchingly Petrarchan) love: "This beauteous forme assures a pitious minde" (l. 14). The trope appears very tenuously in "I am a little world made cunningly," in which he asks that God burn the fires of lust and envy out of his soul "with a fiery zeale / Of thee'and thy house, which doth in eating heale" (ll. 13–14). This sonnet is almost an instance of Donne playing the passive role of love object to the end. Perhaps he can do so precisely because the sexual or marital implications are so tenuous. For Donne speaks of "zeale," not love, and makes envy equal to lust among his prior sins. Moreover, zeal implies an active response to the divine fires.

In one of the four 1635 sonnets, intertwined sacred and secular love imagery permeates the entire poem. These two loves are in one sense treated as opposites, for one is idolatrous, the other, true. At the same time, they are treated as precisely alike. Unexpectedly, in this sonnet, which is probably among the last that he wrote among the first sixteen, Donne presents the two loves, sacred and profane, as essentially Petrarchan, and, at least up until the present time, as equally unrequited:

> O might those sighes and teares returne againe
> Into my breast and eyes, which I have spent,
> That I might in this holy discontent
> Mourne with some fruit, as I have mourn'd in vaine;
> In my Idolatry what showres of raine
> Mine eyes did waste? what griefs my heart did rent?
> That sufferance was my sinne, now I repent;
> Because I did suffer'I must suffer paine.
> Th'hydroptique drunkard, and night-scouting thiefe,
> The itchy Lecher, and selfe tickling proud
> Have the remembrance of past joyes, for reliefe
> Of comming ills. To (poore) me is allow'd
> No ease; for, long, yet vehement griefe hath beene
> Th'effect and cause, the punishment and sinne.

Here, surprisingly, Donne does not accuse himself of lust for mistresses or the world. He is neither drunkard, nor thief, nor lecher, nor proud man; for they, at least, can comfort themselves with having gained something, with "remembrance of past joyes" to repay them for some of the suffering of repentance. To the contrary, the speaker in this poem has sinned precisely as a Petrarchan lover. He has mourned in vain, he has wasted his sighs and tears without return, he has suffered from a "vehement griefe" that is both cause and effect, "punishment and sinne." His was a fruitless and empty love, lacking even the rewards of lust. Now Donne hopes that he may, in "this holy discontent / Mourne with some fruit, as I have mourn'd in vaine." But no such fruit, no such return of love, is yet evident anywhere in the poem. There is nothing to differentiate Donne's "holy discontent" from his former "Idolatry," except for his prayerful plea for a change of objects, which is less a prayer than a lover's vain complaint to an absent God, who seems as distant and unobtainable as any Petrarchan mistress.

The only divine poem in which Donne assumes the female part unequivocally to the end is "Batter my heart." Critics have often commented on this poem as among the most powerful and brilliant as well as among the most disturbing of the Holy Sonnets. It is powerful in part precisely because it is so disturbing. Once more, Donne characteristically makes great poetry from a devotional stance that is troubled and internally conflicted:

> Batter my heart, three person'd God; for, you
> As yet but knocke, breathe, shine, and seeke to mend;
> That I may rise, and stand, o'erthrow mee,'and bend
> Your force, to breake, blowe, burn and make me new.
> I, like an usurpt towne, to'another due,
> Labour to'admit you, but Oh, to no end,
> Reason your viceroy in mee, mee should defend,
> But is captiv'd, and proves weake or untrue,
> Yet dearely'I love you, and would be lov'd faine,
> But am betroth'd unto your enemie,
> Divorce mee,'untie, or breake that knot againe,
> Take mee to you, imprison mee, for I
> Except you'enthrall mee, never shall be free,
> Nor ever chast, except you ravish mee.

As many explications have argued, there is a three-part development of the imagery in this sonnet: the prayer for destruction and remaking, the prayer for relief of the besieged town usurped by Satan, and the prayer for a forcible divorce from Satan and a divine ravishment. But as other explications have argued, there is also continuity in the imagery. The divine rape that closes the poem casts its influence backward, so that one cannot read the poem a second time without reading sexual implications from the beginning. The summary meaning of the poem is that Donne cannot surrender himself to God. He must be forced, broken, burned, entirely remade, taken by storm, broken away from his marriage to Satan, the knot cut, imprisoned, enthralled, and raped. The poem's power depends on the poet's utter resistance to a role he knows he must but cannot play: that of spouse to God. He must be beaten into submission, because in no other way can he find it within himself to submit to the woman's role.

This is imagery likely to trouble nearly any reader, from a traditional Christian to, say, a feminist-materialist. That Donne wishes to turn the violence against himself does not make it much prettier. If this is Christian devotion, it is surely devotion at the extreme verge of the permissible. Some critics have explained the speaker's inability to act or to exert his will in any way, even with God's loving help, as an instance of the Calvinist strain in Donne's thinking. The logic of the imagery, however, argues against that explanation. If we restate what Donne asks of God in Calvinist terminology, it seems to be that God should violently tear him from a state of hopeless reprobation to election—which no Calvinist of his time would have thought possible. Such theological speculations cannot be entirely excluded. Yet they do not, in themselves, explain why Donne had so much more trouble than any of his contemporaries—many of whom embraced Calvinism far more openly and completely than he ever did—in surrendering himself, here and elsewhere, to the terms of the biblical marriage trope. The simpler explanation is that, unless forced—even when putting himself under conditions of extreme psychological pressure—Donne simply cannot submit to the woman's passive role.

For the convenience of the argument, I have looked at these poems in approximately the reverse of their chronological order. The main body of the Holy Sonnets was probably written about 1609, the Westmoreland sonnets, or at least "Since she whome I lovd," after his wife's death in 1617, and "A Hymne to Christ" in 1619. But the imagery in these various poems reveals no noticeable evolution in Donne's general attitude toward or treatment of the marriage trope. In some poems, he escapes the feminine imperative in one way; in others he escapes it in another. In none does he simply and gracefully surrender. Donne was ordained on January 23, 1614/15, so at least two of these poems, and probably also "Showe me Deare Christ," were written after he joined the Anglican ministry. The only other poem certainly written after Donne's ordination that makes significant religious use of sexual imagery is "To Mr. Tilman after he had taken orders." Donne does not employ the marriage trope, but he does use several related metaphors that cast some light on his feelings about sexual role reversal.

Donne sympathizes with Tilman on his joining the profession to which Donne also belongs. (Donne's tone is very much that implied by today's colloquial saying: "Welcome to the club.") He makes much of the "Lay-scornings" (l. 3) and worldly "disrespect" (l. 35) that render a minister's office shameful. Donne's underlying argument is that a Christian should accept this worldly shame and glory in it.[19] Therefore, it may be inferred that many of the images he introduces in the course of his argument carry a paradoxical burden combining feelings of worldly shame and compensatory heavenly glory:

> Let then the world thy calling disrespect,
> But goe thou on, and pitty their neglect.
> What function is so noble, as to bee
> Embassadour to God and destinie?
> (ll. 35–38)

Donne then illustrates his point in a striking trope that compares the office of minister to the Virgin Mary:

> *Maries* prerogative was to beare Christ, so
> 'Tis preachers to convey him, for they doe
> As Angels out of clouds, from Pulpits speake;
> And blesse the poore beneath, the lame, the weake.
> (ll. 41–44)

The further comparison of the preacher to angels in clouds attenuates the impact of the first simile. Still we are left with the thought that preaching a sermon is like, or is a furthering of, Mary's giving birth to the Savior. Implicit in the comparison is the common view that ordinary childbirth, which falls under the curse, is shameful—yet Mary's acceptance of humiliation brings salvation. Hers is a glorious "prerogative."

If Donne safely skirts the implications of this metaphor, which has the preacher giving a kind of birth to his God,[20] the same cannot be said of the trope with which the poem ends:

---

19. For more on Donne's Pauline treatment of worldly shame in "To Mr. Tilman," see Anthony Low, *The Georgic Revolution* (Princeton: Princeton University Press, 1985), 182–83.

20. Although the relations implied by the Church as Mother and Bride have dominated theology and tradition, Donne's images are not wholly without prece-

> These are thy titles and preheminences,
> In whom must meet Gods graces, mens offences,
> And so the heavens which beget all things here,
> And th'earth our mother, which these things doth beare,
> Both these in thee, are in thy Calling knit,
> And make thee now a blest Hermaphrodite.
>
> (ll. 49–54)

Here the priest, as mediator between heaven and earth, is God's hermaphrodite, male and female, shameful and "blest," doubly a parent of his flock. Although, as Helen Gardner notes (*DP*, 102), hermaphrodite is "used figuratively at this period for any striking conjunction of opposites," the "wit of this climax" lies in Donne's near literalization of the sexual metaphor in its unexpected context. The metaphor shows, with those we have discussed before, that Donne did not hesitate to use almost any variation of sexual imagery in his religious poems. He hesitated, rather, to play a passive part, to surrender himself to the divine lover.

In his sermon of 1626, cited near the beginning of this essay, Donne recognizes the central significance of the marriage trope in describing the individual's relation to God, as sanctioned by many passages in the Bible. Yet to offer up his soul as the willing bride of God is a trope representing a devotional practice from which—although he often touches on it or narrowly skirts it—he nearly always turns away as soon as it comes to the point of personal surrender. Donne's experience with human love enabled him to write some of the best and most innovative love lyrics in the language. But that experience did not carry over successfully into the divine poems. He could surrender himself to an unspecified, Romantic feeling of transcendence and of participation in something larger than himself—to what in more recent times has sometimes been called the "oceanic feeling," but he could not surrender himself to a specific, personal, masculine Christian God.

Instead, we find Donne in some poems reverting to sterile Petrarch-

---

dent. St. Paul addresses his followers as "My little children, of whom I travail in birth again until Christ be formed in you" (Gal. 4:19). Also, "I write not these things to shame you, but as my beloved sons I warn you. For though ye have ten thousand instructors in Christ, yet have ye not many fathers: for in Christ Jesus I have begotten you through the gospel" (1 Cor. 4:14–15).

ism and in others wrestling with biblical passages he could confidently recommend to others but not bear to apply to himself. As I have several times suggested in the course of the discussion, the result is that love in his religious poems is powerful, moving, shocking, memorable, but (to borrow a phrase of his time) seldom worthy of imitation. Donne's inner struggles remain unresolved. His inability to break through the barrier between himself and a state of peaceful and loving receptivity to God is clearly revealed in the mounting tensions and the outrageous conclusions of such poems as "Batter my heart" and "Show me deare Christ." His efforts to resolve his psychological conflicts, to accommodate his aggressive personality to a passive devotional stance based on an ancient system of religious metaphor, repeatedly fail. But the issue of his struggle is strong, admirable poetry.

The failure of love in Donne's divine poems meant that, in spite of his generally high contemporary reputation as Dean of St. Paul's and as a poet, he had far less direct influence on the devotional poets who followed him than George Herbert. His contemporaries and major successors admired his divine poems but did not closely imitate them. The preferred pattern among devotional poets of the century is doubt followed by faith and questions followed by answers—not struggle followed by failure or prayer followed by silence. It is doubtful that Donne (unlike some writers of today) intended such a result. But the poems he produced speak strongly to the troubled and disillusioned religious sensibilities of later ages: to Gerard Manley Hopkins in the "terrible" sonnets, to T. S. Eliot before his public conversion, to the many modern composers who have set his Holy Sonnets to music, and to many others of our century who have found God harder to reach than Donne's contemporaries did. Still more, perhaps, he speaks to those who live in the absence of God and find all talk of "relation" inconceivable in such a context.

"SHOWING HOLY"
Herbert and the Rhetoric of Sanctity

❋ ❋ ❋ Christopher Hodgkins ❋ ❋ ❋

> Would you have me
> False to my nature? Rather say I play
> The man I am.
> —*Coriolanus* 3.2.13–15

In chapter 7 of *The Countrey Parson,* George Herbert discusses particular ways for a preacher to maintain the attention, fervor, and submission of his rural congregation. The onetime University Orator of Cambridge warns, not without a note of frustration, that "countrey people" are "thick, and heavy, and hard to raise to a poynt of Zeal, and fervency, and need a mountaine of fire to kindle them."[1] So to spark them, he suggests a variety of effective apostrophes, exclamations, and scattered "irradiations," concluding with a sampler of dazzling finishes. Having spread these gems before the reader, he steps back, like a jeweler, to a professional distance. "Such discourses," he adds, "shew very Holy" (*W*, 234).

By this point in *The Countrey Parson,* we have already heard a good

---

1. *The Works of George Herbert,* ed. F. E. Hutchinson, rev. ed. (Oxford: Clarendon Press, 1964), 233. All subsequent citations of Herbert's works are from this edition, abbreviated as *W,* with page numbers noted parenthetically in the text.

deal about "showing holy." In the previous chapter, "The Parson Praying," the minister when leading worship "composeth himselfe to all possible reverence; lifting up his heart and hands, and eyes, and using all other gestures which may express a hearty, and unfeyned devotion." To promote such unfeigned expressions, Herbert gives some notably histrionic advice: the parson's praying voice should be "humble, his words treatable, and slow; yet not so slow neither, as to let the fervency of the supplicant hang and dy between speaking, but with a grave livelinesse, between fear and zeal, pausing yet pressing, he performes his duty." From his parishioners the parson expects the same consciousness of role: he "exacts of them all possible reverence . . . causing them, when they sit, or stand, or kneel, to do all in a straight and steady posture . . . answering aloud both Amen, and all other answers, which are the Clerks and peoples part" (W, 231).

Such spiritual histrionics have never been without their moral dangers, as any number of recent, well-publicized ministerial scandals have reminded us. Religious discourse, when appropriated by skilled and unscrupulous performers, can convincingly whiten the sepulcher. And Renaissance writers were keenly aware that the self-effacing language of piety can be both self-justifying and self-authorizing: Molière's Tartuffe abhors his flesh in public so that, unimpeded, he can gratify it in private; Shakespeare's Richard III steals "old ends out of holy writ" and, prayer book in hand, seeks the even darker satisfactions of sheer dominion. It is a story at least as old as that of Cain's false sacrifice.

To mention notorious religious hypocrites, real or imagined, in connection with "the holy Mr. Herbert" is unpalatable. Certainly not the slightest innuendo of sensuality will stick to him; this country preacher was no Elmer Gantry. Yet the deeper question of Herbert's sincerity should not be dismissed out of hand. By his own account he was a naturally ambitious man, even fiercely so, yet in courtly terms he was a major failure; thus it would be hard to overestimate the resentment that a might-have-been privy councillor could feel while ebbing out his days in vanishingly obscure Bemerton. Nor should we underestimate the role that Herbert's former courtliness played in shaping his ideals of the pastoral office. Indeed, noting his courtly past seems crucial to comprehending him, both as priest and as poet. Cristina Malcolmson suggests that "Herbert may have understood his transition from urban gentleman to country parson as primarily a shift from a social to an ecclesiastical elite"; thus, she argues, *The Countrey Parson* is a kind of courtesy book for clergy that also "provides an alternate reading of Herbert's life in which 'failure' is redefined as a willing renunciation."[2] Michael C. Schoenfeldt claims further that the rhetorical self-consciousness of courtly language is fundamental to Herbert's poetry. His poems "reveal the glimmers of aggression and manipulation couched in the most apparently humble and benign social maneuvers. The fact that God is the audience . . . amplifies rather than silences the echoes of persuasion and resistance."[3] Herbert left a great deal behind in going from court to country, but he seems to have brought a good deal with him as well.

Elitist, aggressive, manipulative, maneuvering—all of these terms cast a worrisome shadow on *The Countrey Parson*, with its frequent emphasis on pastoral surveillance and control over the parish. In "The Parson in Circuit," "The Parson in Sentinell," "The Parson's Eye," and "The Parson's Surveys," the ideal pastor is virtually ubiquitous, discovering "vicious persons," rebuking idlers, and compelling participation in parish activities. In fact, Herbert recommends that in most cases the parson come upon his people unexpected, so that he will find them "naturally as they are, wallowing in the midst of their affairs, whereas on Sundays it is easie for them to compose themselves to order" (W, 247). One can imagine a surprised and discomposed parishioner renaming any of these chapters "The Parson Prying." Is it possible to see a link between the parson's "showing holy" and his omnipresence in others' affairs? The pulpit, Herbert says, is the parson's "joy and throne" (W, 232); is it also his stage and his observation platform?[4] Does he dazzle and bully these "thick and heavy" country people by

---

2. "George Herbert's *Country Parson* and the Character of Social Identity," *Studies in Philology* 85 (1988): 253, 247. Malcolmson argues that Herbert's main concern is for the parson, in both his preaching and his life, to make visible this inner quality of holiness. It is this holiness, says Malcolmson, that enables the parson to circumvent the class system by establishing his hierarchical authority on spiritual grounds. I agree with her, but I emphasize Herbert's probable debt as a pastoral theorist to the moderate Elizabethan Puritan William Perkins.

3. *Prayer and Power: George Herbert and Renaissance Courtship* (Chicago: University of Chicago Press, 1991), 4.

4. Stanley Fish advances such an argument in an as-yet-unpublished paper entitled "Herbert's Hypocrisy," delivered at Chicago's Newberry Library in 1989.

orchestrating his motions, expressions, voice, and words like so many players? Does he do so to wring from them the guilt, self-immolation, gratitude, and sweet acquiescence that he, "in God's stead," so relishes?

I would argue that Herbert is more compelling as man and poet for having known such temptations intimately, and for sometimes having succumbed. His stuff was, after all, "flesh, not brasse." Yet to read Herbert as a high-order hypocrite would be, in the end, profoundly misleading, for two reasons. First, the element of truth to be winnowed from such a view—that Herbert knew and loved the histrionic ways of power—should not obscure the fact that throughout both *The Temple* and *The Countrey Parson,* such ways are usually presented in order to be criticized, undermined, or overthrown. Second, all that Herbert has to say about "showing holy" identifies him with a preaching tradition—exemplified by William Perkins's *Arte of Prophecying*—that sought the clearest and simplest signs for communicating the preacher's inner life to his hearers. This tradition assumed that inner reality preceded outward "show" and militated against pulpit hypocrisy by insisting that words be matched by everyday deeds. Furthermore, the preacher, according to both Perkins and Herbert, is not only watcher, but watched: he is under the people's, and God's, surveillance—in and out of church. If the parson is acting a role, it is the most rigorous kind of "method" acting imaginable; for he must immerse himself in the part twenty-four hours a day, day after day, for the rest of his life.

The Humiliation of Eloquence

Herbert's natural love for the ostentatious show of "great place" is well documented in a letter to his stepfather, Sir John Danvers, written in September 1619, about his desire for appointment as University Orator:

> The Orator's place . . . is the finest place in the University, though not the gainfullest; . . . for the Orator writes all the University Letters, makes all the Orations, be it to King, Prince, or whatever comes to the University; to requite these pains, he takes place next the Doctors, is at all their Assemblies and Meetings, and sits above the Proctors, . . . and such like Gaynesses, which will please a young man well (*W,* 369–70).

As F. E. Hutchinson notes, the Oratorship was, because of its visibility, generally regarded as a stepping-stone to courtly power as secretary of state (*W*, xxvii).

That the poetry of *The Temple* is permeated by references to courtly show and power relations has been amply demonstrated by Schoenfeldt.[5] These secular performance strategies are frequently invoked not only in the shrewd and prudential "Church-porch" but also in the devotional lyrics of "The Church." The speaker of "The Pearl. Matt. xiii.45" (*W*, 88)—reasonably identifiable with Herbert himself—claims to know

> the wayes of Honour, what maintains
> The quick returns of courtesie and wit:
> In vies of favours whether partie gains,
> When glorie swells the heart, and moldeth it
> To all expressions both of hand and eye. . . .
> (ll. 11–15)

He is at pains to tell us that his love for God is not the product of naïveté; he understands as well as anyone the high stakes involved when wits exchange ripostes in the presence of their betters, and how to keep score by observing the sinuous and minute interplay of pun, glance, and gesture. Yet he also knows what most gallants do not: that he has become lost in the worldly maze. In this spiritual labyrinth, his serpentine wisdom is useless, merely "groveling wit"; only divine grace, in the form of the "silk twist let down" from the heavenly court, can guide him out (ll. 37–40).

Herbert repeats this rejection of theatrical courtly wit in "The Quidditie" and "The Posie" (*W*, 69, 182), relying instead on biblical terseness; and in "The Quip" (*W*, 110) he movingly dramatizes the consolations of scripture in the wake of his failed career. This latter poem presents a parade of cavalier tormenters so vividly that the sympathetic reader

---

5. In addition to *Prayer and Power*, see "Standing on Ceremony: The Comedy of Manners in Herbert's 'Love (III),'" in Claude J. Summers and Ted-Larry Pebworth, *"Bright Shootes of Everlastingnesse": The Seventeenth-Century Religious Lyric* (Columbia: University of Missouri Press, 1987), 116–33; and "'Subject to Ev'ry Mounters Bended Knee': Herbert and Authority," in *The Historical Renaissance: New Essays on Tudor and Stuart Literature and Culture*, ed. Heather Dubrow and Richard Strier (Chicago: University of Chicago Press, 1988), 242–69.

naturally casts around for the retaliatory barb, only to be brought up short by each stanza's psalmic refrain—*"But thou shalt answer, Lord, for me"*—and, at the end, by the apparent blandness of the "quip" sought from Christ—"say, I am thine" (l. 23). If we had hoped for the retort courteous, what we get is language stripped of all ornament and display, relying fully for its power on the identity of the One to whom it refers.

"The Answer" (*W*, 169), like "The Quip," is set in circumstances of courtly failure, as the speaker again builds expectation of a flamboyant reply that will shut the mouths of his detractors—who claim, significantly, that he brags without real "prosecution." This expectation of a quip is heightened by the English sonnet form, with its concluding lines often reserved for ironic reversal. But the couplet falls flat; instead of the anticipated arch rejoinder, we get an admission of ignorance: "to all, that so / Show me, and set me, I have one reply, / Which they that know the rest, know more then I" (ll. 12–14)—to paraphrase, "if others have information about my future, I wish they would tell *me*." The speaker's dishevelment is palpable. The possibility of a pun on "the rest"—as not only "the remainder of my life," but also as a spiritual quietude—reintroduces a note of cleverness, but it does not compensate for the reader's raised and then disappointed anticipation.

Yet Herbert's criticism of rhetorical ostentation goes beyond such explicit rejections of courtly wordplay. He is even more frequently concerned with the ways that the human will to power conspires with or is cloaked by specifically religious language. At times this criticism takes the relatively mild—and often noted—form of pointing to the limitations of all language in the presence of God. So in "Prayer (I)" (*W*, 51), Herbert circles the looming immensity of this spiritual experience in an ascending spiral of metaphors, all of them as remarkable for their brilliant particularity as for their bewildering diversity. Then, with the imageless generality of "something understood" (l. 14), he comments ironically on the preceding struggle at definition. Without rejecting the attempt, he implies that even at its dazzling best, this process can only bring us to know our ignorance and to rely on God's omniscience. Prayer is not incidentally, but essentially, "something understood"; indeed it is the only kind of communication that truly is understood since the divine Understander knows immediately, without the creaturely need for analogies. Similarly, the speaker in "Easter"

(*W*, 41), having gathered his poetical garlands to meet the rising Christ, finds that Jesus, like the sun, "wast up by break of day, / And brought'st thy sweets along with thee" (ll. 21–22)—that Christ needs no praise to celebrate his triumphs, but contains his own self-sufficient glory, to which the awed worshiper may hope to be admitted. Thus in both poems, Herbert revels in language while pointing emphatically beyond it.

Often, however, Herbert thematizes linguistic limitation more violently, pruning and even killing his flowers of devotion. "Jordan (I)" and "Jordan (II)" (*W*, 56, 102) present his best-known disavowals of "false hair" and "trim invention" when speaking to and about God. The latter poem addresses more directly the issue of "showing holy." Here he pillories the religious poet's continual nemesis: the preening self-absorption that weaves its way like flame into the fabric of his verse, consuming that which it had seemed to ornament. The sonnet by Sidney that Herbert parodies—"Loving in truth, and fain in verse my love to show"—rejects the laboriously rhetorical self as merely silly; Herbert works the greatest of his changes on the original by portraying this rhetorical self as insidiously corrupting. By the end, the poet's initial intentions are so fully compromised that the poem must itself be taken over in the last lines by the remedial voice of the plain-speaking "friend," whose presence banishes *"all this long pretence."*

This attack on devotional eloquence is yet more emphatic elsewhere. In "Deniall" (*W*, 79), it intrudes deeply into the very fabric of the poem. "When my devotions could not pierce / Thy silent eares," begins the speaker, complaining of God's unresponsiveness in relatively smooth iambics, "Then was my heart broken, as was my verse." This third line enacts brokenness, stumbling from trochee to iamb to trochee before the caesura. As we read on, we find that within each stanza, no two lines are the same length, and few of the final lines rhyme, either with preceding lines or with each other—although "But no hearing" receives monotonous repetition at the ends of stanzas 3 and 4. The ultimate "chiming" of the last two lines in rhyme, expressing as they do hope for restored harmony with God, depend for their effect on the demonstrable disharmony that precedes them.

In "Grief" (*W*, 164), the speaker furthers this attack on pious display, questioning the sincerity of any person whose anguish "allows him musick and a ryme" (l. 17). This speaker himself had begun histrionically by calling, like Lear on the heath, for "all the watry things" of earth—springs, clouds, rain, rivers—to supply his eyes with tears. However, he has found his own eloquent outpouring in verse to be "too wise / For my rough sorrows: cease, be dumbe and mute," he commands, seeking a formlessness of expression that "excludes both measure, tune, and rhyme" (ll. 13–14, 17). The final fragment of a line provides what amounts to an alternate, "sincere," unpoetic poem—"Alas, my God!" Like Colin Clout in Spenser's first eclogue, this speaker has deliberately shattered his pipes.

But Herbert most profoundly subverts the language of conventional piety in those poems that leave their zealously religious speakers either sputtering or wordless. Among these are some of Herbert's most-discussed lyrics: "The Thanksgiving," "The Holdfast," and "Love (III)." Richard Strier has written that each of these poems is about God's *agape* love violating human reason and decorum;[6] and all of these violations are evidenced, in one way or another, by the breakdown of language. In "The Thanksgiving" (*W*, 35), the speaker's calculating, self-assertive devotion leads him to seek ways of paying back Christ's many unsolicited gifts. Like the persona of "Jordan (II)," his brain runs with ideas, and these flow freely along the well-worn channels of traditional asceticism—voluntary poverty, celibacy, endowment of chapel and "spittle," hostility to "the world." But his logorrhea is twice dammed—and damned—by the measureless obstacle of Christ's passion. At first, the persona manages to skirt the monolith—"But of that anon, / When with the other I have done" (ll. 29–30)—yet only temporarily. After the further euphoric rush of lines 31–48, his fluency is brought to a final, dead stop: "Then for thy passion—I will do for that— / Alas my God, I know not what" (ll. 49–50). It is left to the succeeding poem, "The Reprisall" (*W*, 36), to break the silence and state the lesson, that "there is no dealing with thy mighty passion" (l. 2).

The speaker of "The Holdfast" (*W*, 143) learns a similar lesson about "dealing," and is silenced by it as well. He too is ostentatiously serious about his religious duties, and given to self-assured speech acts—he

---

6. See *Love Known: Theology and Experience in George Herbert's Poetry* (Chicago: University of Chicago Press, 1983), 49–54 for "The Thanksgiving," 65–74 for "The Holdfast," and 73–83 for "Love (III)."

threatens, trusts, and confesses vociferously in the first two quatrains as if his words were meritorious works. But his assertions are repeatedly interrupted by a "friend" with an ever more confounding message: not only do all religious deeds lack saving merit, but even the words of faith are useless in themselves. "But to have nought is ours," says the friend, "not to confess / That we have nought" (ll. 9–10). All of his avenues of action blocked, the persona stands dumbfounded, "amaz'd at this, / Much troubled" (ll. 10–11). It is at this nadir of silence that the sonnet turns; the speaker becomes a hearer, and for the first time hears the Good News as good news: that "all things"—both the words and deeds of faith—are "more ours by being his [Christ's]" (l. 12). To be "in Christ" is to speak and act, not out of anxious ambition, but out of grateful security.

Herbert dramatizes this lesson most famously in "Love (III)" (W, 188). As in "The Holdfast," the speaker threatens to be more strict with himself than God would be, repeatedly (and amusingly) voicing his scrupulous objections to being allowed into the heavenly banquet. However, here his interlocutor is not a schoolmasterish (albeit benevolent) "friend," but Love himself, urgent with sweet hospitality. The "guiltie" speaker is even witty at his own expense; when Love asks if he lacks anything, he replies with a kind of synecdoche, treating the whole as if it were the part: "A guest, I answer'd, worthy to be here" (l. 7). "I don't have a lack; I am a lack," he says. But although he repeatedly refuses grace with such obstinate self-abnegation, grace is finally as irresistible as a host who will not take no for an answer. When the guest finally falls silent to "sit and eat" (l. 18), the silence is neither apoplectic nor befuddled; it is the silence of a hungry man at a feast.

The Preacher: Observer and Observed

So the lyrics of *The Temple* treat in abundant and diverse ways the humiliation of eloquence, and of language itself, in the presence of the divine Word. However, "The Parson Preaching" is not about being silent in the pulpit, but rather about performing impressively from it. The parson "procures attention by all possible art," says Herbert, "both by earnestnesse of speech ... and by a diligent, and busy cast of eye on his auditors." (W, 232–33). Everything that he says and does is carefully calculated to affect his hearers and to observe that effect. Even in Herbert's poetry his sudden silences and fragmented sentences can be classified as rhetorical devices with their own Greek names: *aporia, aposiopesis, parenthesis, anacoluthon.* All can be prescribed, like drugs, to produce particular results. What, after all, are we to make of this studied plainness?

Herbert was certainly not alone in his concern for "showing holy." In fact, the phrase itself, and nearly everything that he has to say about homiletics, strongly suggests a direct debt to Elizabethan England's master preacher, William Perkins. In *The Arte of Prophecying* (1592), Perkins writes that for sermonizing "two things are required: the hiding of human wisdom and the demonstration or showing of the Spirit." "This demonstration," he goes on to say, "is either in speech or in gesture." On the one hand, the preacher's speech must be "spiritual and gracious . . . simple and perspicuous." Although extensive reading and careful exegesis are necessary preparation for preaching, nevertheless "neither the words of arts, nor Greek and Latin phrases and quirks must be intermingled in the sermon . . . it is also a point of art to conceal art."[7] In other words, as Herbert writes, the parson preaching "is not witty, or learned, or eloquent, but Holy" (*W*, 233).

On the other hand, Perkins's "showing of the Spirit" also means mastering the language of gesture. As if he were blocking a scene in a play, Perkins directs the posture and movements of God's would-be "grave messenger": "It is fit . . . that the trunk or stalk of the body being erect and quiet, all the other parts, as the arm, the hand, the face and eyes, have such motions as may express and (as it were) utter the godly affections of the heart." Since motions and expressions can "utter" truth, Perkins even provides a brief lexicon of gesture: "The lifting up

---

7. In *The Workes of . . . William Perkins* (London: 1626), 2:670. Translated by Thomas Tuke, the original Latin *Ars Praedicandi* was published in 1592 and became almost immediately the definitive homiletic manual by an English Protestant. Perkins was a standard-bearer of English Calvinism and a moderate Puritan who sought reform within the Established Church, largely by promoting the sort of plain, "godly" preaching that his treatise defines. It is almost certain that Herbert would have read Perkins's Latin works while a divinity student at Cambridge in Trinity College, then a Calvinist center. He also may have read Tuke's translation while ministering at Bemerton. Either possibility would account for the remarkable similarities not only in thought, but also in wording, between his and Perkins's work on preaching.

of the eye and hand signifieth confidence, the casting down of the eyes signifieth sorrow and heaviness."[8] So, both in word and in action, he defines what Herbert was later to call a new rhetorical "Character of Holiness"—a character, writes Herbert, "that *Hermogenes* never dream'd of, and therefore he could give no precepts thereof" (*W*, 233).

But by supplying this lack with such abundant attention to externals and pragmatics, Perkins and Herbert would seem to create great potential for abuse—especially when we consider their insistence on pastoral authority. Protestants frequently derided Roman Catholic priests as mere "players," yet we see how easily the charge of histrionics might double back on the accusers: Beware the speaker, we may well think, who produces a prepared text, puts it aside as if on impulse, and promises to speak from the heart.[9] Perkins, and Herbert after him, perceived this dangerous space between action and intention where hypocrisies breed and grow. Indeed, they were preoccupied, if not obsessed by it, because their theory of preaching, for all of its concern about performance, was profoundly expressionist. Before "showing holy," writes Herbert, parsons must prepare "by dipping, and seasoning all our words and sentences in our hearts, before they come into our mouths, truly affecting, and cordially expressing all that we say; so that the auditors may plainly perceive that every word is hart-deep" (*W*, 233). Perkins writes similarly: "Wood that is capable of fire doth not burn unless fire be put to it: and he must first be godly affected himself who would stir up godly affections in other men." Thus the charlatan who masters the words and gestures of holiness in order to cover his sins receives Perkins's harsh and solemn condemnation: it is "execrable in the sight of God that godly speech should be conjoined with an ungodly life"; the secretly or openly wicked minister "is not worthy to stand before the face of the most holy and the almighty God."[10]

It is hardly surprising to find sincerity praised and hypocrisy denounced in a pastoral manual; no doubt duplicity is more effectively practiced than preached. The remarkable fact about Perkins's, and especially Herbert's, treatments of hypocrisy is that, for them, the hypocrite's

---

8. *Workes*, 2:672.

9. See Jonas Barish, *The Anti-Theatrical Prejudice* (Berkeley and Los Angeles: University of California Press, 1981), 162. See also Philip Edwards, et al., eds., *The "Revels" History of Drama in English* (London: Methuen, 1981), 1613–1660, 4:64.

10. *Workes*, 2:671.

problem is not too *much* attention to outward performance, but too *little*. This fact may seem strange given their concern for "hart-deep" devotion, but it becomes intelligible as part of their larger faith that, sooner or later, a tree will be known by its fruit. The bad clerical apple may shine for a time, but the worms will out. It is probably because of this belief that Herbert portrays in harrowing detail God's chosen engine against aspiring impostors: the stifling, busybody country parish.

If, as has been suggested, the parson's office is a kind of observation platform from which he surveys his people, Herbert would make him fully aware that the lines of sight run in both directions—and that the Argus-eyed gaze from the pew can be withering. If a man wishes to master the role, he must first be "an absolute Master and commander of himself," especially "in those things which are most apt to scandalize his Parish," for the congregation's eyes are everywhere. When he is counting his tithes, they are there: "Countrey people live hardly . . . and consequently knowing the price of mony, are offended much with any, who by hard usage increase their travell [travail]"; therefore "the Countrey Parson is very circumspect in avoiding all covetousnesse" (*W*, 227). When he is considering whether to marry, they are there: he would rather be single for devotion's sake; but, "as the temper of his Parish may be, where he may have occasion to converse with women, and that among suspicious men, . . . he is rather married" (*W*, 237). When he is drawing up a guest list for dinner, they are there, or want to be: "Having then invited some of his Parish, hee taketh his times to do the like to the rest . . . because countrey people are very observant of such things, and will not be perswaded, but being not invited, they are hated" (*W*, 243). They are there when he is arbitrating disputes, so he calls in other wise heads to give their opinions first, and thus make things pass "with more authority, and lesse envy" (*W*, 260). They are there when he is joking, so he seldom jokes, except as a "key to do good"; they are there when he is thinking of a drink, so he avoids this "most popular vice; into which if he come . . . he disableth himself of authority to reprove them" (*W*, 268, 227). The congregational eyes—as well as its fingers and nose—are upon him even when he dresses in the morning: since "disorders" of apparel are "very manifest," his clothing must be "plaine, but reverend, and clean, without spots or dust, or smell" (*W*, 228). There is much of the courtier's sensibility in Herbert's awareness that public people have no real privacy, that everything they do is cause for comment. The parson must run a virtually epic gauntlet of scrutiny. Only a deceiver of equally epic endurance could hold up under such a communal inquisition, and by doing so probably would win sympathy, if not admiration, from the hypocrite in us all.

Yet by multiplying these examples—of which I have cited not the half—Herbert drives home the point that ultimately the parson's authority depends not on his official status, but on his personal integrity; and in the enforced intimacy of a rural village, integrity cannot be put on with the preacher's robes. Country people may be "thick, and heavy" —and petty—but they are shrewd; if the parson is not honest, says Herbert, "he wil quickly be discovered, and disregarded: neither will they beleeve him in the pulpit, whom they cannot trust in his Conversation" (*W*, 228). "Conversation," in its richer archaic sense, joins words and deeds. Similarly, in "The Windows" (*W*, 67–68),

> Doctrine and life, colours and light, in one
>   When they combine and mingle, bring
> A strong regard and aw: but speech alone
>   Doth vanish like a flaring thing,
>   And in the eare, not conscience ring.
>   (ll. 11–15)

Every preacher should know that his auditors can hear more convivial and less demanding liars at the alehouse.

So for all of Herbert's apparent commitment to the elite status of the pastor's office, he nevertheless knows that the parson's actual power in the parish is constituted by an implicit but exacting social contract.[11] He "disableth himself of his authority" when he breaks this contract through his sins, which, he says, "make all equall, whom they finde together" (*W*, 227). In such straitened circumstances, under so much surveillance, the satisfactions of lording it over the likes of Bemerton would seem meager indeed.

---

11. For a fuller account of Herbert's belief in a Tudor Protestant model of class interdependence and mutual obligation, see Christopher Hodgkins, "'Betwixt This World and That of Grace': Herbert and the Church in Society," in *Authority, Church, and Society in George Herbert: Return to the Middle Way* (Columbia: University of Missouri Press, 1993), 181–209. In "The Parson's Surveys," Herbert promotes an extensive program for national regeneration through spiritual revival at the parish level. He presents the country parson as the chief local catalyst for social reformation and cohesion; therefore, the parson bears great responsibility to the community and to God.

Divine Surveillance

That *The Countrey Parson* raises so many hedges against clerical duplicity and arrogance argues that Herbert was himself well acquainted with these temptations. There is a psychologically suggestive pattern observable throughout the book, but particularly in "The Parson's Surveys": Herbert was a "younger son" of the nobility, and he inveighs against "loose" younger sons; he for years lacked "employment," and he attacks the great national sin of "Idlenesse"; he had been a finely dressing gentlemen, and he scolds ostentatious "Gallants"; he had been an ambitious courtier, and he calls the court a place of eminent ill (W, 277, 274, 275, 277). It is, of course, axiomatic that hypocrites cry out against their favorite sins; however, it is also true that converts, religious or otherwise, often feel the most vehemence against their own past sins—more even than seasoned veterans, because converts have the bitterness of direct experience in their mouths. So it may be that when Herbert seems most the busybody, he is preaching as much to himself as to the people. In medical terms, it is as though, having survived a disease, Herbert sets out to cure his parish.

Such an analogy is appropriate, because, in his emphasis on vigilance, Herbert is imagining the country parson not as a prison warden, but as a parent and spiritual physician. "When any sinns, he hateth him not as an officer, but pityes him as a Father" (W, 250), for sin afflicts the sinner. Significantly, one of the manual's longest chapters (besides "The Parson's Surveys") is "The Parson's Dexterity in applying of Remedies" (W, 280–83). Here, having surveyed the people, the parson diagnoses their most common distempers of soul—complacency, atheism, and despair—and administers their particular cures. As in "The Parson Preaching," Herbert's prescriptions take the form of suggested speeches: the comfortable he would afflict with an exhortation to judge themselves, lest they be judged; and those afflicted with atheism he would comfort with friendly observations about God's marvelous providence. With those near despair, the parson acts strikingly like the Host of "Love (III)": his quick and comprehensive eye takes in the parishioners' spiritual condition, but he refuses either to minimize their sinfulness or acquiesce in their self-contempt. Instead, he shows them, in effect, that the God who sees their sins has borne the blame.

So, for Herbert, the mutual surveillance of parson and people is redeemed by a kind of gracious divine surveillance. God's quick, all-seeing eye is a loving eye, and a powerful eye as well, capable not only of penetrating but also regenerating with a glance, and, in the end, of "look[ing] us out of pain" ("The Glance," W, 171–72, l. 21). Herbert believed that, under God, it is the parson's omnipresent diligence that spreads spiritual healing, regeneration, and compassion among his normally inquisitorial flock. Their natural watchfulness will always exist as a sobering check against pastoral malpractice, but when transformed by grace, it will express itself as shrewd charity—the sort that discerns between sins and foibles, confronting the former, and winking at the latter. Because it is the parson's work that produces this change, Herbert's entire pastoral theory finally stands or falls on the parson's regenerate state. If he is not himself "hart-deep," he cannot hope to mediate such a communal transformation. Introducing *The Countrey Parson*, Herbert thanks God "who giveth mee my Desires and Performances" (W, 224); but throughout, the book teaches that if the parson lacks true desires, his performances are unlikely to stir anything but amusement, pity, or contempt.

It is possible to hear in Herbert's aside about "showing holy" the voice of the cynical rhetorical manipulator, just as it is possible to hear in his remarks about "thick and heavy" country folk an elitist sneer. However, given Herbert's oratorical training, his relatively great birth, and his former courtly ambitions, what seems truly remarkable is not that he was to some degree a manipulator and a snob—what would we expect?—but that he came so far and so deliberately toward humility.

And, at least in Herbert's remarks about homiletic technique, it is not necessary to hear any note of hypocrisy at all. The primary imagined audience of this chapter is probably the exact opposite of a hypocrite: that is, the earnest novice in his first pulpit, sincere of heart but tied of tongue. To such a struggling young preacher, groping for clear words and gestures to express his inner zeal and kindle others to it, Herbert—like Perkins before him—gives a wealth of hearteningly specific advice. "They listened to this. They understood this. They responded to this." It is as if he were to say, "Be true to your nature: play the man you are—or rather, the man whom God is making you."

OPENING THE RELIGIOUS LYRIC
Crashaw's Ritual, Liminal, and Visual Wounds

❀ ❀ ❀ *Eugene R. Cunnar* ❀ ❀ ❀

Of all the seventeenth-century religious lyrics, those written by Richard Crashaw have been subjected to the most adverse criticism. In particular, his lyrics on Christ's Passion and wounds have generated negative responses from the time of their publication through the twentieth century. In part, these negative reactions are the result of Protestant reactions to Crashaw's Counter-Reformation Catholic imagery and theology, which has been perceived as grotesque and bizzare by numerous readers.[1] Robert Adams's comment on "On our crucified Lord Naked, and bloody" is typical: "Nothing from one point of view, could be more disgusting and grotesque. Yet how else to convey the combination of sacred, spiritual preciousness with the vulgar, social utility."[2] Adams's sense of condemnation and wonder have caused other critics to find ways to explain or justify Crashaw's imagery. Frank J. Fabry explains the images of wounds as displaying clinical

1. For an overview, see Lorraine M. Roberts and John R. Roberts, "Crashavian Criticism: A Brief Interpretive History," in *New Perspectives on the Life and Art of Richard Crashaw,* ed. John R. Roberts (Columbia: University of Missouri Press, 1990), 1–29.
2. "Taste and Bad Taste in Metaphysical Poetry: Richard Crashaw and Dylan Thomas," *Hudson Review* 8 (1955): 67.

realism.[3] Patrick Grant perceives such imagery as being a deliberate strategy in imitation of Capuchin devotional practices, designed to shock the reader into accepting spiritualized meanings.[4] Vera J. Camden interprets Crashaw's images of bloody wounds psychoanalytically, seeing in that imagery elements of castration fears and oral repression that manifest themselves in thought typical of unconscious association.[5] Basically, this poem and others like it have been criticized as being disjunctive, that is, the relationship between imagery and concept is not clear, and it is difficult to visualize what are commonly thought to be perverse or grotesque images, even on a psychological level. The power of Crashaw's imagery to generate such diverse approaches and generally negative responses suggests the powerful effect Crashaw's images had for both contemporary readers and later readers. In this essay, I want to explore the reasons and sources for the power of those images by reexamining and recontextualizing them in terms of ritual liminality, theology, and the visual arts. In doing so, I plan to explain how a limited, narrow view of the religious lyric, especially Crashaw's, prevents us from understanding historical responses to those lyrics and their baroque imagery.

As we now know, religious lyrics were not just transcendent and autonomous aesthetic objects, but instead were frequently involved in the religiopolitics surrounding an author and his audiences, as Claude J. Summers points out in his essay. Moreover, the religious lyric did not just reflect an author's personal religious views; it often engaged his audience and society in debate designed to change views. Subsequently, any given religious lyric might be problematic in exhibiting tensions and contradictions in the author and his or her society.[6] Richard Cra-

---

3. "Crashaw's 'On the Wounds of our Crucified Lord,'" *Concerning Poetry* 10 (1977): 53.

4. *Images and Ideas in Literature of the English Renaissance* (Amherst: University of Massachusetts Press, 1979), 90–92, 113–20.

5. "Richard Crashaw's Poetry: The Imagery of Bleeding Wounds," *American Imago* 40 (1983): 258.

6. For a thoughtful account of the religious lyric in these terms, see Michael C. Schoenfeldt, *Prayer and Power: George Herbert and Renaissance Courtship* (Chicago: University of Chicago Press, 1991); Jonathan Goldberg, "Herbert's 'Decay' and the Articulation of History," *Southern Review: Literary and Interdisciplinary Essays* 18 (1985): 3–21; Sidney Gottlieb, "Herbert's Case of 'Conscience': Public or Private Poem?," *Studies in English Literature, 1500–1900* 25 (1985): 109–26; Claude J. Sum-

shaw's religious lyrics are no exception. Crashaw's religious poems, especially those we designate as reflecting Counter-Reformation Catholic sensibilities, are intimately involved in the poet's personal religious struggles as well as contemporary religiopolitical debates. During the civil war period, Crashaw lost his university appointment because of his Anglo-Catholic religious beliefs and practices. Subsequently, he converted to Catholicism, was forced into exile, and revised a number of his poems to reflect distinct and overt Catholic beliefs. Moreover, Crashaw was seriously involved in ritual practices that approximated Catholic worship. Consequently, his mature religious lyrics are imbued with ritual or liturgical structures and images that generated varying religiopolitical responses, especially negative ones from Puritans.[7]

The ritual setting of Crashaw's poems has been ignored for the most part, yet that setting is central to understanding how the poet conceived of his work and how his contemporaries variously responded to his work.[8] Secular and sacred ritual was of central importance in seventeenth-century England and was the subject of serious controversy as Puritans, Anglicans, and Catholics debated over the religious, social, and political implications of ritual.[9] On a larger level, this debate raised

---

mers and Ted-Larry Pebworth, "Herbert, Vaughan, and Public Concerns in Private Modes," *George Herbert Journal* 3 (1979/1980): 1–21, and "The Politics of *The Temple*: 'The British Church' and 'The Familie,'" *George Herbert Journal* 8, no. 1 (1984): 1–15.

7. For more detailed accounts of these aspects of Crashaw, see Eugene R. Cunnar, "Crashaw's Hymn 'TO THE NAME ABOVE EVERY NAME': Background and Meaning," in *Essays on Richard Crashaw*, ed. Robert M. Cooper (Salzburg: Institut für Anglistik und Amerikanistik, 1979), 102–44.

8. Several scholars have pointed to Crashaw's use of ritual, but they have not developed a comprehensive view of that ritual. See Walter R. Davis, "The Meditative Hymnody of Richard Crashaw," *ELH* 50 (1982): 107–29; Paul G. Stanwood, "Time and Liturgy in Donne, Crashaw, and T. S. Eliot," *Mosaic* 12 (1979): 105; Elizabeth H. Hageman, "Calendrical Symbolism and the Unity of Crashaw's *Carmen Deo Nostro*," *Studies in Philology* 77 (1980): 161–79; and Cunnar, "Crashaw's Hymn to the Name."

9. Useful overviews are Leah S. Marcus, *The Politics of Mirth: Jonson, Herrick, Milton, Marvell, and the Defense of Old Holiday Pastimes* (Chicago: University of Chicago Press, 1986); Horton Davies, *Worship and Theology in England: From Andrewes to Baxter and Fox, 1603–1690* (Princeton: Princeton University Press, 1975), 2:215–52; David Cressy, *Bonfires & Bells: National Memory and the Protestant Calendar in Elizabethan and Stuart England* (Berkeley and Los Angeles: University of California Press, 1989); Donald F. E. Weissman, *Ritual Brotherhood in Renaissance Florence* (New

some interesting problems for the religious lyric written in a liturgical mode, that is, a lyric that imitates aspects—themes, structures, images—of a particular rite. If the liturgical event were experienced by the poet, how did the ritual experience influence the poetry's imagery and structure? Inversely, how did the liturgical experience influence the reader's response to a poem? Did readers perceive theological or sociopolitical functions in religious poems? And what was the ritual experience understood historically? Even though clearly central to any understanding of the multiple meanings of religious lyrics, these questions are rarely posed, particularly about a given poet or work. In order to understand how and why ritual could exert a strong influence on both a poet and the reader, I want to examine a few of Crashaw's ritualized poems through Victor Turner's analysis of ritual as a creative and dynamic form of social drama.

For Turner, rituals are one of the ways in which individuals and societies mediate social and personal conflict. Following van Gennep's concept of rites of passage as involving three stages (separation, limen, and reaggregation), Turner reconceptualizes ritual as a dynamic, transformative force in society. Instead of perceiving ritual as dull, mechanical, repetitious behavior, Turner analyzes ritual as providing the seedbed for creative endeavor. According to Turner, the dynamic, transformative power of ritual occurs in the liminal phase, in which ritual participants are "betwixt and between the positions assigned and arrayed by law, custom, convention, and ceremonial."[10] During this period, participants experience the multivocality of ritual symbols structured along oretic and ideational poles. Symbols clustering around the oretic pole tend to be sensory, natural, physiological, and visual, while symbols on the ideational side are cognitive, intellectual, and cosmic. According to Turner, one of the major reasons the power of ritual is not understood is that most analyses of ritual only account for the normative, or cognitive, side of the symbol while failing to understand the oretic, or physiological, pole.[11] In particular, oretic images of bodily

---

York: Academic Press, 1982); and Richard C. Trexler, *Public Life in Renaissance Florence* (New York: Academic Press, 1980).

10. *The Ritual Process: Structure and Anti-Structure* (Ithaca: Cornell University Press, 1969), 95. See also *The Forest of Symbols: Aspects of Ndembu Ritual* (Ithaca: Cornell University Press, 1967), for discussion of ritual symbols.

11. *The Forest of Symbols*, 20–47. The cognitive side of the symbol would include

parts and biological processes are conceived of as sources of regenerative power. In the exchange between oretic and ideological poles of the ritual symbol, Turner explains, "The biological referents are ennobled and the normative referents are charged with emotional significance."[12] In this state, ritual participants often experience the inversion of normative values or blur and merge traditional distinctions and oppositions, such as life and death, male and female, sacred and secular. Freed from the constraints of their previous status, ritual participants may experience the symbolic death of self as they generate new concepts and metaphors from the dominant symbols as a combination of visual, auditory, tactile, spatial, and visceral modes of perception that lead to a new conception of the self. Often, Turner says, these "factors or elements of culture may be recombined in numerous, often grotesque ways, grotesque because they are arrayed in terms of possible or fantasied rather than experienced combinations."[13] Because the liminal state is highly subjunctive, it allows participants to experience doctrinal abstractions as if they were real; or, as Turner says, "*All* the senses of participants and performers may be engaged; they *hear* music and prayers, *see* visual symbols, *taste* consecrated foods, *smell* incense, and *touch* sacred persons and objects."[14] In other words, Turner's concept of multivocal ritual symbols includes the physiological and natural processes to which they refer as a lived experience by the ritual participant. The sheer grossness of the liminally experienced ritual

---

the literary tradition behind it, which does not necessarily explain emotional responses to the symbol. Moreover, Turner, *From Ritual to Theatre: The Human Seriousness of Play* (New York: Performing Arts Journal Publications, 1982), 37–40, argues that the Protestant Reformation brought with it a breakdown in the understanding of the ritual symbol, especially in the Protestant preference for the normative pole of the symbol.

12. *Dramas, Fields, and Metaphors: Symbolic Action in Human Society* (Ithaca: Corneil University Press, 1974), 55.

13. *From Ritual to Theatre*, 27.

14. Victor Turner, "Social Dramas and Stories About Them," *Critical Inquiry* 7 (1980): 162. Further scientific research in neurobiology confirms Turner's concepts, showing that in the liminal state worshipers experience altered states of consciousness and actual psychophysiological changes. See Eugene d'Aquili, "Human Ceremonial Ritual and the Modulation of Aggression," *Zygon* 20 (1985): 21–30; and Barbara Lex, "The Neurobiology of Ritual Trance," in *The Spectrum of Ritual: A Biogenetic Structural Analysis*, ed. Eugene G. d'Aquili, Charles D. Laughlin, Jr., and John McManus (New York: Columbia University Press, 1979), 117–51.

242 • Eugene R. Cunnar

image combines with its spiritual or theological meanings within the ritual performance, producing in ritual participants new meanings and new metaphors as well as "anti-structure," the potential subversiveness inherent in the liminal state. This experience, in turn, leads the ritual participant to *communitas,* the egalitarian relationship shared by those stripped of power, status, and self during the liminal phase. Consequently, ritual is always potentially a transformative and creative experience that binds groups together as it simultaneously allows for creative and social change.[15] Moreover, the powerfully affective experience of ritual liminality may be transferred to other media, such as poems, paintings, and plays, which Turner calls liminoid genres, that have the potential for re-creating liminality within them and, thus, may also embed political action and social change.[16] This is the kind of broadly applicable model of ritual that has not been applied to Crashaw's religious and liturgical poems.[17]

If we take Crashaw's "On the wounds of our crucified Lord" as representative of his poems treating Christ's wounds, then I believe a reevaluation of the poem from Turner's concept of ritual will provide a new way of perceiving it as functioning within a complex social drama in which its imagery, generally thought to be grotesque, becomes understandable within its cultural framework. Crashaw's political and religious disenfranchisement corresponds to Turner's concept of social drama, which includes breach, crisis, redress, and either reintegration or permanent breach.[18] Ritual mediates this process. Consequently, in his ritual practices, Crashaw experienced liminality as a state that not only mediated his own personal religious crisis, but also allowed him to create liturgically mimetic poems out of ritual liminality. As a person displaced from his preferred ritual practices, Crashaw experienced the marginality characteristic of the liminal state. "Betwixt and between" Anglicanism and Catholicism, Crashaw turned to Catholic ritual as the means of mediating his own religious crisis. It is a measure

---

15. For discussion of the political implications of ritual, see *Dramas, Fields, and Metaphors,* 60–97.

16. *From Ritual to Theatre,* 32–33, 52.

17. See my "Crashaw's 'Sancta Maria Dolorum': Controversy and Coherence," in *New Perspectives,* 118–20.

18. See "Social Dramas and Stories About Them," 141–68. For historical case studies of ritual mediating social conflict, see Weissman, *Ritual Brotherhood,* 80–95.

of the power of his poetic talent that he tapped this liminal experience to create images that would engage his reader in the movement from liminality to *communitas,* the bonding of those that shared values. In articulating the liminal state, Crashaw also exhibited the potential to subvert normal Anglican beliefs and ritual practices. Consequently, his ritual poems are more than personal religious lyrics embodying a transcendent, mystical attitude divorced from the sociopolitical realities of his world. They are also poems that examine the sociopolitical context of the rituals he engages, especially his concern for the shared religious values of the disenfranchised, worshipping community to which he converted. Understandably, those who did not share the poet's religious values, which were perceived as upholding forms of absolutism in politics and religion, reacted negatively, criticizing the religious content of poems in terms of aesthetic weakness or psychological perversity, including the charge that the poet was effeminate.

I

Crashaw's poem on the crucified Christ focuses on a dominant liturgical symbol that Catholics and Protestants debated over in terms of the Eucharist. Both groups argued over more than just the theology of the Eucharist. As John Bossy and others have shown, the Catholic Mass as a social institution was thought to embody within it the model of social and political structures governing the secular world.[19] With the advent of the Counter-Reformation and the employment of the new baroque style, Catholicism and the Mass were perceived by Protestants as upholding idolatrous and absolutist values that they abhorred.[20] As a major event in Christian theology, the Crucifixion involves a social drama that has the potential to change the secular world. On another level, the Crucifixion functions as a ritual of rever-

19. See John Bossy, "The Mass as a Social Institution 1200–1700," *Past & Present* 100 (1983): 29–61, and *Christianity in the West 1400–1700* (Oxford: Oxford University Press, 1985) and Jean Delumeau, *Catholicism between Luther and Voltaire: A New View of the Counter-Reformation* (Philadelphia: Westminster Press, 1977).

20. For discussion, see A. D. Wright, *The Counter-Reformation: Catholic Europe and the Non-Christian World* (New York: St. Martin's, 1982), 223–63; and José Antonio Maravall, *Culture of the Baroque: Analysis of a Historical Structure* (Minneapolis: University of Minnesota Press, 1986).

sal in which the eternal God submits to death, and the receiving Christian gains eternal life by eating Christ in the Communion ritual. As such, the Eucharist invokes the liminal characteristics of weakness and humility leading to ecstasy and the gaining of spiritual power.[21] Christ's vulnerability and passivity were frequently identified as positive female attributes, constituting the essence of humanity, virtue, and charity that were to be emulated by the ritual participant. In this tradition, the wounded and bleeding Christ was conceived of as a nurturing mother, whose breasts/wounds provided spiritual nourishment.[22] In the ritual and devotional traditions, the oretic imagery of wounds merges with the normative imagery of the Eucharist and transubstantiation, producing a powerful emotive and bonding experience in the worshiper. These and other liminal concepts of status and gender reversal, which paradoxically elevated the low and displaced, were articulated in the liturgy and theology of the wounds from which Crashaw draws for his own imagery.

The theology of wounds emphasizes the wounds as portals or liminal passageways through which the worshiper is invited to enter in order to see Christ's heart sacrificed for the sinner. The concept of threshold or passage through Christ's wounds as a frame is made explicit in Augustine, who, in explicating the gospel of John, explains the wounds as liminal passages:

> "But one of the soldiers with a spear laid open His side, and forthwith came there out blood and water." A suggestive word was made use of by the evangelist, in not saying pierced, or wounded His side, or anything else, but "opened" that thereby, in a sense, the gate of life might be thrown open, from whence have flowed forth the sacraments of the Church, without which there is no entrance to the life which is the true life. That blood was shed for the remission of sins; that water it is that makes up the health-giving cup, and supplies at once the laver of baptism and water for drinking. This was announced

---

21. For Turner's application of his theories to Christianity, see Victor Turner and Edith Turner, *Image and Pilgrimage in Christian Culture: Anthropological Perspectives* (New York: Columbia University Press, 1978; and Victor Turner, "Ritual, Tribal and Catholic," *Worship* 50 (1976): 504–26.

22. For this tradition, see Caroline Walker Bynum, *Jesus as Mother: Studies in the Spirituality of the High Middle Ages* (Berkeley and Los Angeles: University of California Press, 1982.)

beforehand, when Noah was commanded to make a door in the side of the Ark . . . and by the Church was prefigured. . . . O death, whereby the dead are raised anew to life! What can be purer than such blood? What more health-giving than such a wound?[23]

Augustine's explanation of Christ's wounds as liminal openings—thresholds to be crossed—becomes a standard feature in later devotions to the wounds.

The medieval Mass of the Five Wounds was popularly called the *Humiliavat* from the opening of the office: "Our Lord Jesus Christ humbled himself, and became obedient unto death, even the death of the cross."[24] During the Counter-Reformation, devotion to the five wounds was renewed as part of the Tridentine Church's new emphasis on the Eucharist and became popular with confraternities devoted to the wounds.[25] The Mass is found in the *Sarum Missal*, a source with which Crashaw was familiar. The sequence, *Anima Christi*, makes explicit reference to Christ's liminal wounds:

> O Good Jesu, hear me
> Within Thy wounds hide me,
> Suffer me not to be separated from Thee.[26]

Numerous materials developed for use in the Mass as homilies or as matter for private devotions. St. Bernard of Clairvaux established much of the theological and emotional meanings attributed to the wounds in his allegorical sermons based on the *Song of Songs*. In explaining the *Song of Songs* 2.13–14, Bernard says,

> And there is no lack of clefts by which they poured out. They pierced his hands and feet, they gored his side with a lance, and through

---

23. *Homilies on the Gospel of John*, ed. Philip Schaff (Grand Rapids, Mich.: Eerdmans, 1956), 434–5.

24. See *The Sarum Missal*, trans. Frederick E. Warren (London: De La More Press, 1911), 2:64–70.

25. For the history and popularity of the Mass and related devotions, see "Wounds of Our Lord," *The New Catholic Encyclopedia* (New York: McGraw-Hill, 1967), 14:1035–37; Emile Mâle, *Religious Art in France: The Late Middle Ages*, trans. Marthiel Matthews (Princeton: Princeton University Press, 1967), 99–116; and Douglas Gray, "The Five Wounds of Our Lord," *Notes & Queries* n.s. 10 (1963): 50–51, 82–89, 127–34, 163–68.

26. *The Old Catholic Missal* (1909; rpt. New York: AMS, 1969), 18.

these fissures I can suck honey from the rock and oil from the flinty stones—I can taste and see that the Lord is good. He was thinking thoughts of peace and I did not know it. "For who has the mind of the Lord, or who has been his counsellors?" But the nail that pierced him has become for me a key unlocking the sight of the Lord's will. Why should I not gaze through the cleft? The nail cries out, the wound cries out that God is truly in Christ, reconcilling the world to himself. "The iron pierced his soul" and his heart was drawn near, so that he is no longer one who cannot sympathize with my weaknesses. The secret of his heart is laid open through the clefts of his body; that mighty mystery of loving is laid open, laid open to the tender mercies of our God, in which the morning sun from on high has risen upon us. Surely his heart is laid open through his wounds! Where more clearly than in your wounds does the evidence shine that you, Lord, "are good and forgiving, abounding in steadfast love?"[27]

Bernard's explanation of the wounds not only places them within the popular theology of charity, but also articulates the sensory and synaesthetic responses to the ritual of a worshiper. Following the liminal patterns of a ritual of reversal, Bernard links Christ's wounds to the bridegroom's breasts in the *Song of Songs,* in which reciprocal nourishment of the soul is achieved. Christ's breasts bleed blood and water in an exchange with the bride (or the Virgin), who provided the Christ child with the nourishment of her breasts.[28] The lactating Virgin subsequently becomes a maternal image of the Church, whose role is to provide spiritual nourishment to souls while Christ becomes a spiritual mother.[29] In this complex of multivocal images, the reader/worshiper is invited to suck Christ's wounds, enter those wounds, and see through them to Christ's sacrificial heart so that an appropriate sense of humility and love may be experienced.

Along similar lines, St. Bonaventure also explains Christ's wounds from a liminal perspective. In his *Stimulus Divini amoris,* a work made available to English Catholics for devotion, he says that Christ's wounds

---

27. *On the Song of Songs III,* trans. Kilian Walsh and Irene M. Edmonds (Kalamazoo, Mich.: Cistercian Publications, 1979), 141–50.

28. See Bynum, *Jesus as Mother,* 115–19; Barbara G. Lane, *The Altar and the Altarpiece: Sacramental Themes in Early Netherlandish Painting* (New York: Harper and Row, 1984), 1–11.

29. Bynum, *Jesus as Mother,* 120–25; Marina Warner, *Alone of All of Her Sex: The Myth and the Cult of the Virgin Mary* (New York: Pocket Books, 1976), 192–205.

"are alwayes open, and by *them* I will enter againe into his wombe; and I will do this so often, until such time as I am so united *unto* him, as that I can never more be separated from him."[30] For Bonaventure, the eucharistic wounds are the open "gates of Paradise." He tells the worshiper who adores them that you "will willingly have the doores of his wounds (after you have once entered into them) shutt and lockt upon you, that may go forth no more from *theme*."[31] Subsequently, the wounds become the means to instill love and charity in the worshiper: "O wounds, wounding with your love heate as obdurate, as the very stones; inflaming with your heate, mindes as cold as ice."[32]

Bonaventure's meditations on the Passion and the wounds reflect the liminal experience of ritual in his creation of new and unique metaphors to describe the salvific effect of the wounds. In *The Mystical Vine*, he calls Christ the rose of love and his wounds become bleeding roses:

> Let the torrents of this blood crimson our rose, for here is love the most ardent, and passion the reddest in its glow. It is in the depth of the passion that we should see the depth of the love; in this redness of the passion that we should see the fire of the rose of love. . . . For as the rose throughout the chill of night is closed, but in the warmth of the rising sun unfurls again in full joy, so the delight-giving Flower of heaven, Jesus most beautiful. . . . Behold how the crimsoned Jesus blossomed forth in this rose. . . . Examine the wound of His side, for the rose is still there. . . . How manifold and well adorned is this rose with its innumerable petals.[33]

The transformation of the wounds into roses and rose petals is not grotesque, but instead typical of the creative influence of ritual liminality. In *On the Perfection of Life*, Bonaventure urges his reader to experience the Crucifixion as a liminal event:

> *See in His hands the print of the nails,* with the Apostle Thomas, not only . . . put your hand into His side, but enter with your whole being through the door of His side into Jesus's heart itself. There, trans-

---

30. *Stimulus Divini amoris: That Is, The Goade of Divine Love* (Douay, 1642), 12.
31. *Stimulus Divini amoris*, 15.
32. *Stimulus Divini amoris*, 18.
33. *The Works of Bonaventure: Cardinal, Seraphic Doctor, and Saint*, trans. Jose de Vinck (Paterson, N.J.: St. Anthony Guild Press, 1960), 1:199–201.

> formed into Christ by your burning love for the Crucified, pierced by the nails of the fear of God, wounded by the spear of superabounding love, transfixed by the sword of intimate compassion, seek nothing, desire nothing, wish for no consolation, other than to be able to die with Christ on the cross. Then you may cry out with the Apostle Paul: *With Christ, I am nailed to the cross. It is now no longer I that live, but Christ lives in me.*[34]

In entering the wounds, one loses the worldly and sinful self in order to be reborn in Christ. Bonaventure's liminal response to the wounds appealed to Crashaw, who also sought to negate the worldly self through ritual.[35]

St. Catherine of Siena provides another typically liminal response to Christ's wounds in her visionary accounts of union with Christ. In an account of one of her visions of the five wounds, Christ comes to her and

> tenderly placed his right hand on her neck, and drew her toward the wound in his side. "Drink daughter, from my side," he said, "and by that draught your soul shall become enraptured with such delight that your very body, which for my sake you have denied, shall be inundated with its overflowing goodness." Drawn close . . . to the outlet of the Fountain of Life, she fastened her lips upon that sacred wound, and still more eagerly the mouth of her soul, and there she slaked her thirst.[36]

In another vision Christ appears to her as a nourishing and lactating mother, who, she says,

> showed me his most sacred side from afar and I cried from the intensity of my longing to put my mouth to the sacred wound. After he had laughed for a little while at my tears—at last that is what he

---

34. *Works*, 1:239–40.

35. Crashaw's motto was "Live Jesus, Live, and let it bee / My life to dye, for love of thee," placed at the beginning of *Steps to the Temple*. See Richard Crashaw, *The Complete Poetry of Richard Crashaw,* ed. George Walton Williams (Garden City, N.Y.: Doubleday, 1970), 1. All subsequent references to Crashaw's poetry are to this edition.

36. Raymond of Capua, *Life of Catherine,* trans. Conleth Kearns (Wilmington: Glazier, 1980), 155–56. For discussion, see Caroline Walker Bynum, *Holy Feast and Holy Fast: The Religious Significance of Food to Medieval Women* (Berkeley and Los Angeles: University of California Press, 1987), 165–82.

seemed to do—he came up to me, clasped my soul in his arms, and put my mouth to where his most sacred wound was, that is to say, the wound in his side. Then with its great longing my soul entered right into that wound and found such sweetness and such knowledge of the Divinity there that if you could ever appreciate it you would marvel that my heart did not break, and wonder how ever I managed to go on living in that body in such excess of ardour and love.[37]

Such accounts of drinking from or entering Christ's wounds may seem particularly perverse to modern sensibilities, but they were quite common as part of the liminal response to ritual or intense private meditation and devotion. Indeed, the Counter-Reformation Church encouraged both the experience and the depiction of such responses, the former through its new emphasis on the sacraments experienced liturgically and the latter in the religious art commissioned as altarpieces.

Several Counter-Reformational devotional and meditative works were translated for English Catholics as a means for them to maintain their faith. Any number of these works reflected strong ritual liminality as a way of maintaining *communitas* in trying times. Following Bernard and Bonaventure, writers like Juan de Avila and Luis de la Puente advocated an affective and liminal imagery associated with Christ's wounds.[38] Luis de Granada provides a summary of much of the liminal imagery associated with Christ's wounds, of which he says,

> From thence issued water, and bloude, wherewith are washed the sinnes of the worlde. O river that ronnest out of paradise, and waterest with thy streames all the face of the earth! O wounds of the pretious syde of my sweete Saviour, made rather with his fervent love towardes mankinde, than with the sharpe iron of the cruell speare! O gate of heaven! O windowe of paradise! O place of refuge! . . . O nest of clene doves! O flourishing bed of the spouse of Salomon! Al haile O wounde of the pretious syde of our savior, that woundest the hartes of devout persons! O strooke that strikes the soules of the just! O rose of unspeakable bewtie! O rubie of inestimable price! O entrance into the harte of my sweete Saviour Jesus Christ! . . . Throughe thee doe all

---

37. Raymond of Capua, *The Life of St. Catherine of Siena*, trans. George Lamb (London: Haverill Press, 1960), 173.

38. See Juan de Avila, *Certain Selected Epistles* (Rouenl, 1631), 22; Juan de Avila, *The Audi Fidia, or A Rich cabinet full of Spirituall Jewells* (St. Omer, 1620), 392; Luis de la Puente, *Meditations upon Mysteries of the Holy Faith* (St. Omer, 1619), 321.

living thinges enter into the Arcke of the true Noe, to be preserved from the floude.... Through thee doe sinners enter into heaven.... Open o moat, loving Lorde, I beseache thee, this gate unto me: receave my harte into this most delitefull habitation: give me passadge through the same into the tender bowell of thy love.[39]

The obvious eucharistic implications in the liminal imagery of the wounds is made explicit by other Catholic writers, such as Fulvio Androzzi, who tells his reader to "Consider so ofte as thou receavest this holy sacrament, thou layst thy mouthe to the wounds of our Saviours side."[40] The complex of images developed around the five wounds also included perceiving the nails as writing instruments as well as the keys making salvation accessible.[41]

When we consider the complex merging of liminal images and theological meanings surrounding Christ's wounds, we can begin to perceive just how powerful the response to such strong and "grotesque" visual imagery was for the contemporary worshiper. The liminal images of Christ's wounds generated in the liturgy and meditative tradition were adapted by painters in their creation of altarpieces and other religious paintings celebrating the wounds as part of the Tridentine Church's emphasis on the Eucharist and the concept of transubtantiation. Innumerable artworks depict the bruised Christ displaying his wounds (*ostentatio vulnerum*), often combined with the concepts of the *arma Christi, imago pietatis*, the Man of Sorrows, and the Fountain of Life.[42] Typical of such works is Murillo's altarpiece for the Capuchin

---

39. *Of Prayer and Meditation* (Douai, 1612), 130–31. See also for similar imagery, Luis de Granada, *A Spiritual Doctrine* (Louvan, 1599), 99.

40. *Certaine devout considerations of frequenting the Blessed Sacrament* (Douay, 1615), 9. See also Fulvio Androzzi, *Meditations upon the Passion of Our Lord* (Douay, 1606), 93; Pierre Cotton, *The Interior Occupation of the Soule* (Douay, 1612), 11.

41. For this and other aspects of passion iconography, see F. P. Pickering, *Literature and Art in the Middle Ages* (Coral Gables: University of Miami Press, 1970); James H. Marrow, *Passion Iconography in Northern European Art of the Late Middle Ages and Early Renaissance: A Study of the Transformation of Sacred Metaphor into Descriptive Narrative* (Kortrijik, Belgium: Van Ghemmert Pub. Co., 1979); John V. Fleming, *From Bonaventure to Bellini: An Essay in Franciscan Exegesis* (Princeton: Princeton University Press, 1982), 12–13, 135; Albert C. Labriola, "Herbert, Crashaw and the *Schola Cordis* Tradition," *George Herbert Journal* 2, no. 1 (1978): 13–23; and Albert C. Labriola, "Richard Crashaw's *Schola Cordis* Poetry," in *Essays on Richard Crashaw*, 1–13.

42. For this iconography and numerous examples, see Gertrud Schiller, *Iconogra-*

Church in Seville, depicting St. Francis and the crucified Christ as an invitation to the viewer to enter the wounds and discover Christ's sacred heart now manifested in the Eucharist. Not only were Christ's wounds a reminder of his willing sacrifice, but they were also associated with the concepts of *Ecclesia*, compassion and charity, and the *sponsa* of Christ. Frequently painters depicted the parallel offerings of Christ and Mary, that is, Christ offers his wounds and Mary offers her breast in an act of double intercession.[43] Ludovico Gimigani's *The Vision of St. Catherine* depicts the saint literally drinking from the eucharistic wound in Christ's side. Similarly, Rubens's *Descent from the Cross* (1617) portrays St. John with his mouth juxtaposed against the wound in an act of eucharistic drinking, while Mary Magdalene kisses Christ's wounded hand (Fig. 1).

II

Within this larger tradition of Christ's wounds, Crashaw writes his "On the wounds of our crucified Lord" as a liminal response to his meditation on or his ritual experience of the liturgy of the wounds. While the tradition provides a clear indication as to how worshipers were to respond emotionally and theologically to the wounds, it is my contention that Crashaw's poem reflects his own liminal experience of the liturgy of the wounds and that that experience accounts for his unique handling of metaphors. Crashaw consistently frames his poems liturgically, as indicated either by titles referring to liturgical feasts or by their setting within the liturgical cycle. Crashaw was not just imitating a liturgical feast's structure and themes; he was also re-creating its powerful liminal state and, thus, opening up the religious lyric to new social, psychological, and theological dimensions. While a liturgy has

---

phy of Christian Art, trans. Janet Seligman (Greenwich, Conn.: New York Graphic Society, 1972), 2:88–229.

43. For these concepts, see Schiller, *Iconography*, 2:164– 211, 224–6; Caroline Walker Bynum, "The Female Body and Religious Practice in the Late Middle Ages," in *Fragments for a History of the Human Body*, eds. Michel Feher, Ramona Naddaff, and Nadia Tazi (Cambridge: MIT Press, 1989), 175–82; Barbara G. Lane, "The 'Symbolic Crucifixion' in the Hours of Catherine of Cleves," *Oud Holland* 86 (1973): 4–26; and John B. Knipping, *Iconography of the Counter-Reformation in the Netherlands: Heaven on Earth* (Nieuwkoop: B. de Graf, 1974), 2:263–76.

Fig. 1 Peter Paul Rubens, *Descent from the Cross*, 1617 (Giraudon/Art Resource, N.Y., Lille, Musee des Beaux-Arts)

an invariant order reflecting veritable theological truths, it is the individual experience of those truths in the liminal state that actually leads to transformations in the individual and group. In creating a poetic liturgy, the poet was inviting the reader to share through the poems the same powerful and affective experience of ritual liminality that he had experienced. Ritual liminality becomes both the creative source and the mediating agent for the poet's own religious vision. Subsequently, in reading the poem, the reader reexperiences the dynamic and transformative effects of the liturgy. Because Crashaw was recreating Catholic theology and liturgy, his ability to capture liminality made his poems particularly offensive to Protestants (Calvinists), who disagreed with that theology and also feared the liminal power of Catholic ritual images to convert the unwary or unsuspecting Protestant. Moreover, as Turner explains, the typical Puritan/Protestant response to theological or ritual symbols was to focus on the normative or cognitive element. Consequently, interpretations of Crashaw's liminal imagery from this perspective misreads a significant and valid part of meaning.[44]

Early in his career, Crashaw displays familiarity with the tradition of the wounds of love. In the dedicatory poem to his sacred epigrams he explains his own transformation of Cupid from a god of secular love into the God of sacred love:

> ["]O Love, who possess the sacred rites of a harmless quiver, your arrow does not burn except in a chaste heart. O Boy, pierce me whom you pierce with a well-aimed arrow. O may your quiver become light because of me. Thence also each thing thirsts and drinks, drinks and thirsts forever: forever may my heart thirst and forever may it drink. Pierce this heart, Boy. You are present very little in these *thorns,* much in the sharp point of *nail* or *spear,* more with the whole *cross,* or most of all at last you transfix this heart with your very presence. Pierce [me], Boy. O may your bow have proclaimed this eternal aim: may the heavier breath of your shaft whizz to this mark. O if a fiercer wing should bear any dart for you, may it have this path of the old wound to go. Whatever is the crowd, whatever is the throng in your quiver, this nest will hold those wounding birds well. O may you ever be so savage in this war against me! Never may you enter this breast [as] a gentler foe. How I wish I might lie well torn apart in this fight! How

---

44. Turner and Turner, *Dramas, Fields, and Metaphors,* 250, 277, 285.

very whole I will be with a torn heart!" These are my wishes. These too are the wishes of my little book. May these be yours, Reader; if you wish to be mine. If you wish to be mine; to be mine (Reader) your eyes [should be] chaste, but not, I pray, too dry. For let this [book] of mine have met you with damp wings (with blood or with tears may it flow). Everything opens with the tree and is closed with nails and spear: will your fountain be idle in [filling] the rivers? If this little [book] of mine has gone to you on a great stream of blood, will you deny it your waters, cruel one? Ah cruel man! Whoever does not want my loves, except dry-eyed, let him deny there is here cause for his tears. Often here will he have loved either the waters of Magdalene or the floods; . . . . [45]

Crashaw's invocation of the wounds of love not only employs the related conceit of the nails or instruments of the Passion as writing instruments that wound the sinful soul, but also reflects the liminality of conversion. Crashaw makes it clear that he wants his own words as instruments of passion to move the reader's heart to humility and love of God expressed through tears that become the reader's reciprocal sacrifice.[46]

Crashaw's religious poems cannot and should not be divorced from his own ritual experiences. Even early in his career, Crashaw displayed a clear preference for elaborate ritual. Benjamin Lany, Master of Pembroke College when Crashaw entered, reintroduced enhanced ceremony in the college chapel as part of the Laudian reforms. Lany revived kneeling for Communion, the elevation of the host, and fixed, railed altars that were decorated. At Peterhouse, Crashaw served first under Matthew Wren, a strong supporter of Laud and a noted liturgist, who introduced a Latin liturgy and other liturgical elaborations. These reforms triggered attacks by Puritans, who condemned such ritual practices as Catholic.[47] Wren was followed by John Cosin, who had stressed the need for more elaborate public ritual in his *A Collec-*

---

45. *Complete Poetry,* 644, 646.
46. For Crashaw's use of nails or instruments of the Passion as writing instruments, see Eugene R. Cunnar, "Crashaw's 'Sancta Maria Dolorum': Controversy and Coherence," in *New Perspectives,* 99–126.
47. See Alfred Walker, *Peterhouse* (Cambridge: W. Heffer and Sons, 1935), 52–60; Austin Warren, *Richard Crashaw: A Study in Baroque Sensibility* (Ann Arbor: University of Michigan Press, 1939), 31–56, and "Crashaw's Residence at Peterhouse," [London] *Times Literary Supplement,* November 3, 1932, 815, and "Richard Crashaw, 'Catechist and Curate,'" *Modern Philology* 32 (1935): 261–69.

tion of Private Devotions in the Practice of the Ancient Church, called *The Hours of Prayer*, a work based in part on the old Sarum usage.[48] Cosin continued Wren's beautification program, including decorating the chapel with paintings and stained glass windows.[49] The ceiling was painted sky-blue with sunbursts in the compartments. Directly above the altar was a dove representing the Holy Ghost, and above the dove were cherubims. Behind the altar were painted hangings with eagles and the words *In quod cupiant Angeli*. The east window above the altar contained a painting based on Rubens's *Le Coup de Lance*, showing the wound in Christ's side. The other windows were of stained glass and contained events from the life of Christ. In addition, there was a painting of St. Gregory, probably displayed during Communion, especially if it were a painting of the "Mass of St. Gregory," a popular Catholic theme emphasizing transubstantiation in the Eucharist. Above the chancel were inscribed the words *Hic locus Domus dei, nil aliud, et Porta Coeli*. These architectural changes and decorations emphasized the rituals taking place in the chapel as liminal or threshold events, whereby the worshiper crossed the threshold, entered into sacred space, and experienced contact with God.

Thomas Pocklington, a Laudian, describes the new enhanced ritual in another chapel that underwent beautification, stating that worshipers

> take their absolution on their knees, at, or neare the *Altar*, when they were reconciled to the Sacraments, and this absolution they received not *ad limina Ecclesia* in the porch, where they cast themselves downe, no nor yet in the body of the Church, or any other part of the Church, but only at or neare the *Altar*.[50]

---

48. *A Collection of Private Devotions*, ed. P. G. Stanwood (Oxford: Clarendon Press, 1967), 13–14.

49. For Cosin's program of liturgical beautification and detailed accounts of the chapel, see John G. Hoffman, "John Cosin's Cure of Souls: Parish Priest at Brancepeth and Elwick, County Durham," *Durham University Journal* 71, n.s. 40 (1978): 73–83, and "The Arminian and the Iconoclast: The Dispute between John Cosin and Peter Smart," *Historical Magazine of the Protestant Episcopal Church* 48 (1979): 279–301, and "The Puritan Revolution and the 'Beauty of Holiness' at Cambridge: The Case of John Cosin, Master of Peterhouse and Vice-Chancellor of the University," *Proceedings of the Cambridge Antiquarian Society* 72 (1982–83): 94–105; Allan Pritchard, "Puritan Charges Against Crashaw and Beaumont," [London] *Times Literary Supplement*, July 2, 1964, 578.

50. *Altare Christianum: or, The dead Vicars Plea*, 2nd. ed. (London, 1637), 11.

Pocklington cites St. Charles Borromeo in support of his concept of the sacred space of the church and altar and then describes a chapel he saw, explaining that,

> for besides the *Altar* so furnished, there are to bee seene many goodly pictures, which cannot but strike beholders with thoughts of piety and devotion at their entrance into so holy a place; as the picture of the Passion, and likewise of the Holy Apostles, together with a faire Crucifix, and an *Blessed lady*, and Saint *John* set up in painted glasse in the east window just over the *Holy table*, or sacred *Altar*.[51]

The combination of beautified and enhanced ritual and religious paintings—liminal phenomena—allows Pocklington to accept the Catholic doctrine of the Eucharist, which doctrine he prefers to the Protestant doctrine.[52]

Crashaw was in residence at Pembroke and Peterhouse during these liturgical reforms and actively supported them. Like Andrewes, Lany, Wren, and Cosin, Crashaw believed in high and ceremonial styles of public ritual as a means of demonstrating the proper love and adoration of God. Moreover, Crashaw was reputed to be an excellent musician and painter. In the latter capacity he may even have executed one or more of the approximately sixty religious paintings that William Dowsing reported destroyed in 1643 in Little St. Mary's, where Crashaw served as curate.[53] We know that Crashaw practiced all-night vigils and engaged in other forms of ritual practices that the Puritans deemed popish. These ritual practices were largely responsible for his expulsion from his university position and his exile to Holland. In a number of poems, he praises the new decorations and the enhanced rituals in these churchs. What is particularly revealing about these early praises of ritual is the poet's understanding of the power of ritual liminality. In a dedicatory poem praising Lany in his collection of sacred epigrams, Crashaw perceives the newly enhanced ritual as a form of liminality:

51. *Altare Christianum*, 34, 87.
52. *Altare Christianum*, 48.
53. See Richard Crashaw, *The Poems English Latin and Greek of Richard Crashaw*, ed. L. C. Martin (Oxford: Clarendon Press, 1957), xxv, xxii, for Dowsing's findings and for an account of the Peterhouse records, showing that around 1635 picture frames were purchased for Crashaw.

>   Nempe hanc ipse Deus, Deus
> Hanc ara, per te pulchra, diem tibi
> Tuam refundit, obvióque
>   It radio tibi se colenti.
>
> Ecce, ecce! sacro in limine, dum pio
> Multúmque prono poplite amas humum,
>   Altaria annuunt ab alto;
>   Et refluis tibi plaudit alis
>
> Pulchro incalescens officio, puer
> Quicunque crispo sydere crinium
>   Vultúque non fatente terram,
>   Currit ibi roseus satelles.
>   (ll. 29–40)
>
>   (Indeed God himself, God,
> the altar, beautiful through your efforts,
> returns this day to you and comes
> with glory to meet you, his worshiper.
>
> Look, look! On the sacred threshold while you [touch]
> the great earth on pious bended knee,
> the altars nod approval from on high;
> with outstretched wings [the boy] applauds you
>
> and glowing from his lovely duty the boy
> with the curly glory of his hair
> and a face which does not bespeak the earth
> runs about there as a rosy attendant.)

Crashaw extols the altar as a sacred threshold through which the Eucharist is celebrated and through which the worshiper passes to heaven. As Lany kneels at the altar in prayer and liturgical celebration, he brings the heavenly liturgy down to earth. The angels or cherubs, who were painted behind and above the altar, represent the divine aid, who, along with the Holy Spirit, assist the priest in celebrating the Mass.[54] From the beginning of his career, this experience of ritual liminality, in which the senses and creativity are heightened, shapes and mediates Crashaw's religious vision and his poetry.

---

54. Henry FitzSimon, *The Justification and Exposition of the Divine Sacrifice of the Masse* (Douai, 1611), 81–85. See also Lane, *Altar and Altarpiece*, 40–49.

The combination of enhanced ritual, including the presence of religious paintings, exerted a strong influence on Crashaw and his poetry. In his early epigram, "I *am the Doore,*" he provides a clear statement of liminality. Writing out of the theology of wounds, he states,

> And now th'art set wide ope, The Speare's sad Art,
> Lo! hath unlockt thee at the very Heart:
> Hee to himselfe (I feare the worse)
>   And his owne hope
> Hath *shut* these Doores of Heaven, that durst
>   Thus set them *ope.*[55]

The sense of Christ's wounds as liminal passages to salvation also seem to have helped Crashaw in his own conversion, which may be seen as a profound liminal event. In his "Letter to the Countess of Denbigh urging her to convert," the poet treats the conversion experience in terms of liminality:

> What Heav'n-beseiged Heart is this
> Stands Trembling at the Gate of Blisse:
> Holds fast the Door, yet dares not venture
> Fairly to open and to enter?
> Whose definition is, A Doubt
> 'Twixt Life and Death, 'twixt In and Out,
> Ah! Linger not, lov'd Soul: A slow
> And late Consent was a long No.
> . . . .
> Say, lingring Fair, why comes the Birth
> Of your brave Soul so slowly forth?
> Plead your Pretences, (O you strong
> In weaknesse) why you chuse so long
> In Labour of your self to ly,
> Not daring quite to Live nor Die.
>   (ll. 1–8, 15–20)

Crashaw urges the Countess to cross the threshold and undergo liminal conversion, by which she will experience strength in her weakness. The liminal moment "'Twixt Life and Death" was one Crashaw was

---

55. *Complete Poetry,* 17. See also the Latin version, 347.

well familiar with through his own participation in and performance of ritual. When Peterhouse was investigated in 1641 for sanctioning Catholic practices, Crashaw was singled out for his ritual practices. In part, the report states that,

> Mr Crashaw fellow of Peterhouse in a speech made in that Colledge Chappell *Die Annunciationis 1638* is credibly reported to have turned himselfe to the picture of the Virgine Mary & to have used these words *Hanc adoremus, colamus hanc,* That is rather probable because his practices in little St Maryes, where he is Curat are superstitious [.] On every Sunday & on many holy dayes he hath a Communion (when the parish is both poore and of small extent) what this Implyes those know who are not ignorant of the popish doctrine of private masses, The Church plate he hath exchanged for a covered bowle made after his owne devising, on the cup is the full portraiture of Christ with these words, This is my blood indeede. Soe likewise on the lipp of the Cover are these words, This is my body indeed, on the top of the cover is a Crosse. Before he officiates at the Communion he washeth his hands in the vestry where is a table set Altarwise towards the East, and puts on a fresh paire of shoe which are appropriated to the Altar. All the remainder of wyne after he hath made his low incurvation he drinks off & picks vp the crummes which remaine of the bread. In his Catechise he told the people that god had set apart one part of the Church & that was the place where the Altar stood calling it *Sancta Sanctorum,* and that he puts much holineese in that place appeares from hence, that hee permitts not the Clerke to come within the railes & hath converted a carpet which cost 8li into a foot carpet to tread vpon when offices are performed at the Altar.[56]

The picture of Crashaw as a priest that emerges here is one of a man who has moved beyond Anglican theology and is engaged in Catholic ritual and eucharistic practices that in themselves are profoundly liminal.

Subsequently, if we reexamine another of Crashaw's epigrams from this perspective, then we may be able to see that it is only "grotesque" from a limited and narrow view of ritual poetry. The epigram, "Luke 11, *Blessed be the paps which Thou hast sucked,*" has become infamous for what is mistakenly thought to be its perverted sexual implications. The epigram reads,

56. Cited in Pritchard, "Puritan Charges," 578.

> Suppose he had been Tabled at thy Teates,
> Thy hunger feels not what he eates:
> Hee'l have his Teat e're long (a bloody one)
> The Mother then must suck the Son.[57]

Read against the theology of the wounds and the profound gender reversal that most likely came about from the liminal experience, this poem simply merges oretic and normative ritual imagery in order to emphasize the salvific effect of the Eucharist. Moreover, the mother in Luke 11 becomes a positive and parallel image of the nourishing Christ.

Crashaw's "On the wounds of our crucified Lord" also demonstrates how the ritual experience of liminality can shape and influence a poem. Like other poems, past readings have tended to be based on analyzing only the normative pole of the symbols and not their oretic counterpart. Moreover, this poem could well have been conceived of during one of Crashaw's performances of ritual in which liminality would engender a new combination of the liturgical elements and symbols experienced. The opening stanza presents the reader with images of paradoxical transformation and transpositions that seem almost perverse or grotesque in their execution:

> O these wakefull wounds of thine!
>   Are they Mouthes? or are they eyes?
> Be they Mouthes, or be they eyne,
>   Each bleeding part some one supplies.
>   (ll. 1–4)

The perception of Christ's wounds as mouths and eyes is far from perverse in the theology and ritual of the wounds. Crashaw begins his poem by emphasizing the oretic pole of the Crucifixion. In ritual liminality the oretic side of a symbol may appear gross or grotesque to those who do not accept its values or do not experience it ritually. Crashaw does not leave his image at this level, but instead treats it as if it were experienced liminally by creating an exchange of meanings through the eucharistic frame that serves as the normative pole for the imagery. These imagistic transpositions echo the type of imagery expe-

---

57. *Complete Poetry,* 14. Williams's commentary summarizes the misreadings and points to Crashaw's use of theology of the wounds.

rienced in ritual liminality and prepare the reader to participate in the eucharistic meaning of the wounds. Christ's wounds as mouths that are eyes serve as thresholds, drawing the reader to enter and experience the meaning of Christ's suffering that is celebrated in the Eucharist.

In the second stanza, the poet begins to juxtapose Mary Magdalene's perspective on the Crucifixion and wounds with that of the reader:

> Lo! a mouth, whose full-bloom'd lips
> At too deare a rate are roses.
> Lo! a blood-shot eye! that weepes
> And many a cruell teare discloses.
>   (ll. 5–10)

While the images allude to the long tradition of imagery associated with the theology of wounds, Crashaw presents them through a unique liminal transposition in which Christ's wound becomes a mouth, then roses, and then the Magdalene's eyes, which weep teares as her mouth prepares to kiss the wounds. The two participants in this eucharistic scene are transposed and simultaneously merged in acts of reciprocal love. Here, Crashaw modifies the traditional depiction of the double intercession by substituting the Magdalene for the Virgin in that it is the Magdalene's acts of humility and penance that respond to and parallel Christ's sacrificial act of love.

The dynamic ritually induced imagistic transformations may be compared to similar ones written by La Ceppède, who also discussed, following St. Bernard, Christ's wounds as liminal openings. In one of his poems on the wounds he develops the following imagistic transformation of the wounds:

> Deux des cés trous gardez en l'immortalitié
> Nous marquent de vos mains la liberalité
> Par eux cherront sur nous tous vos riches hyacinthes.
>
> Et les trois serviront de trois jours à nos yeux
> Pour (mesme avant sortir des mortels Labyrinthes)
> Par iceux oeillader vos secrets dans les Cieux.
>
> (Two of these holes which you will keep in your
> immortal form are the sign for us of your hands'
> generosity: through them will fall on us all your
> rich hyacinths.

> And the three holes will serve as three windows for our eyes so that (even before passing through death's labyrinth) we may glimpse through them your secrets in Heaven.)[58]

La Ceppède's imagistic transformations compare the wounds to hyacinths and windows through which the reader is to view Christ's sacrifice and its meanings.

What makes Crashaw's imagery even more complex and emotionally intense is his juxtaposition of meanings or referents upon the same image, just as one who experiences the multivocal ritual symbol. Specifically, Crashaw juxtaposes images and theological meanings associated with Mary Magdalene, the penitent and converted sinner, with those of Christ and the Virgin. This liminal moment of conversion typically is what appealed to and guided Crashaw's religious sensibility. Accordingly, he projects a liminal juxtaposition that creates a sense of gender reversal in the poem, whereby Christ takes on positive feminine characteristics by shedding his nourishing blood and tears. For the Tridentine Church, Mary Magdalene's was the epitome of the perfect meditative life, in which salvation is achieved through penance and spiritual love. The moment of her conversion represented the critical event in the development of the individual spiritual life.[59] Crashaw converges, transposes, and interpenetrates these images in an affective and sacramental form of *ut pictura poesis,* designed to soften or wound the reader's heart in a reciprocal act of charity.

Crashaw was familiar with the theology associated with the Magdalene as presented in his famous poem "The Weeper."[60] In the hymns and sequences used in her feast and Mass appear numerous images analogous to Crashaw's. In her liturgy she is celebrated as an example of repentance and conversion whom God views with love. The hymn, *Summi Parentis Unice,* provides not only justification for Crashaw's

---

58. Jean Ive La Ceppède, *Les Théoremes sur le Sacré Mystère de Nostre Rédemption* (Geneva: Librairie Droz, 1966), 293.

59. For the complex history and iconography of the Magdalene, see Majorie M. Malvern, *Venus in Sackcloth: The Magdalen's Origins and Metamorphoses* (Carbondale: Southern Illinois University Press, 1975), and Victor Saxer, *Le Culte de Marie Madeleine en Occident, dès Origenes à la Fin du Moyen-Age* (Paris: Clarereuill, 1959).

60. See Robert M. Cooper, *An Essay on the Art of Richard Crashaw* (Salzburg: Institut für Anglistik und Amerikanistik, 1982), 38–65, for a cogent analysis of the poem and its critical treatment.

unique visual perspective, but also other elements of his imagery. The hymn opens by establishing a God's eye perspective:

> Son of the Highest! deign to cast
> On us a pitying eye;
> Thou, who repentant Magdalene
> Didst call to endless joy.[61]

Christ, from his elevated perspective on the cross, looks down at the Magdalene. Subsequently, she is associated with eye and tear imagery, as in *O Maria, nole flere*, one of the hymns used in the *Sarum Breviary* for her feast:

> Whence thy grief and lamentation?
>   Lift, faint soul, thy heart on high;
> Seek not memory's consolation,
>   Jesus, whom thou lov'st, is nigh:
> Dost though seek thy Lord? thou hast him,
>   Though unseen by human eye.[62]

As the first to recognize the risen Christ, she is praised for her special spiritual vision.

Her conversion from sinner to saint is expressed in *Summi Parentis Unice* as:

> The gem is found, and cleansed from mire,
> Doth all the stars outshine.
> (RB 4:697)

And in the hymn, *Pater superni luminis*, the moment of her conversion is described as an act of visual reciprocity:

> Father of lights! one glance of thine,
> Whose eyes the universe control,
> Fills Magdalene with holy love,
> And melts the ice within her soul.
> (RB 4:692)

---

61. *Roman Breviary in English*, ed. Joseph A. Nelson (New York: Benzinger, 1950), 4:697. Subsequent citations to this edition will be made in the text as *RB*.
62. *The Diurnal after the Use of the Illustrious Church of Salisbury*, ed. G. H. Palmer (St. Mary's Convent: Wantage, 1921), 213.

In the other numerous hymns written for her, she is compared to jewels, light, and roses.[63] Her washing of Christ's feet with her tears and hair is usually juxtaposed with Christ's washing away of her sins with his blood, as in *Summi Parentis Unice*:

> O Jesu! balm of every wound!
> The sinner's only stay!
> Wash thou in Magdalene's pure tears
> Our guilty spots away.
> (RB 4:697)

Whereas the hymn provides a normative interpretation of the Magdalenes's actions, Crashaw captures the liminal aspects of her conversion and compassion.

Crashaw merges and transposes these images as he depicts the Magdalene's response to Christ's crucifixion. The deliberate multivocality of the images allows the reader to identify with the penitent and humble Magdalene and, thus, participate by shedding tears as she did:

> O thou that on this foot hast laid
> Many a kisse, and many a Teare,
> Now thou shal't have all repaid,
> Whatsoe're thy charges were.
> (ll. 9–12)

Although this stanza implicitly invokes the sexuality of the Magdalene, theologically the lines allude to a standard theory of atonement as a business transaction and to Magdalene's role as penitent sinner and convert, who out of love washed and kissed Christ's feet and then repeated the act at the Crucifixion for which she received forgiveness of her sins.[64]

The fourth stanza reverts to the opening imagery by discussing the wounds in Christ's feet as mouth and eyes:

---

63. For a thorough discussion of Magdalene imagery, see Joseph Szövérffy, "'Peccatrix Quondam Femina': A Survey of Mary Magdalen Hymns," *Traditio* 19 (1963): 79–146.

64. Farby, 53–55, discusses some of the sexual implications in the lines. For the atonement as a business transaction, see C. A. Patrides, *Milton and the Christian Tradition* (Hamden, Conn.: Archon, 1979), 121–52.

> This foot hath got a Mouth and lippes,
>   To pay the sweet summe of thy kisses:
> To pay thy Teares, and Eye that weeps
>   In stead of Teares such Gems as this is.
>   (ll. 13–16)

Christ's wounds become a mouth reciprocating the Magdalene's kiss, and his eyes weep gemlike blood.[65] The affective import of this act of reciprocal love is to urge the reader to imitate the penitent Magdalene by shedding tears of love, that is, to share in her liminal moment of conversion.

The transposition of wounds, mouths, and eyes engages the reader in the type of multiple perspectives common to liminal perception. As a point of comparison, one might look at Alabaster's poem on tears in which he points out the proper way to view the Crucifixion:

> When without tears I look on Christ, I see
> Only a story of some passion,
> Which any common eye may wonder on;
> But if I look through tears Christ smiles on me.
> Yea, there I see myself, and from that tree
> He bendeth down to my devotion,
> And from his side the blood doth spin, whereon
> My heart, my mouth, mine eyes still sucking be;
> Like as in optick works, one thing appears
> In open gaze, in closer otherwise.
> Then since tears see the best, I ask in tears,
> Lord, either thaw mine eyes to tears, or freeze
> My tears to eyes, or let my heart tears bleed,
> Or bring where eyes, nor tears, nor blood shall need.[66]

Alabaster's use of an anamorphic perspective wittily points out how the Crucifixion, when viewed with the common eye, is only a story,

---

65. On Christ's blood as gems, see Mâle, *Late Middle Ages*, 100–101.
66. *The Sonnets of William Alabaster*, ed. G. M. Story and Helen Gardner (Oxford: Oxford University Press, 1959), 39. For a discussion of the literature of tears, see Louis L. Martz, *The Poetry of Meditation: A Study in English Religious Literature of the Seventeenth Century*, 2d ed. (New Haven: Yale University Press, 1962), 119–210; and Joan Hartwig, "Tears as a Way of Seeing," in *On the Celebrated and Neglected Poems of Andrew Marvell*, ed. Claude J. Summers and Ted-Larry Pebworth (Columbia: University of Missouri Press, 1992), 70–85.

but when it is viewed through the tears of humility and penance, that is, from a changed perspective, one sees the act of love in the eucharistic sacrifice. Similarly, Crashaw shifts perspectives, providing a liminal view of the Crucifixion through Magdalene's tears that merge into Christ's sacrificial wounds, which become, in turn, eyes that weep blood.

Crashaw's imagery and liturgical framing finds a parallel in Rubens's *Descent from the Cross* (1617), which served as the high altarpiece in the Capuchin monastery in Lille.[67] In this painting, nine persons surround Christ's body as it is lowered from the cross. Rubens interprets Christ's Crucifixion and wounds within the Franciscan tradition of Bonaventure and the Cistercian tradition of Bernard, in which Christ's wounding is the emergent moment of the Church and her sacraments. Moreover, he also composes the altarpiece as a liminal response to the Eucharist in that the frame invites the worshiper/viewer to cross the threshold into the sacred scene that is being reenacted on the altar.[68] The action of receiving Christ's body becomes the community of the faithful now receiving that body in the Eucharist. As Christ's body is lowered, the faithful reach upward to receive him. Mary Magdalene, in the lower foreground, is about to press her lips to Christ's wounded hand as her tears mingle with his blood. St. John, in the red clothing, holds up the weight of Christ's body in a stance that is explained by St. Francis de Sales, who states that John should be painted at Christ's breast because

> he was like a beloved child placed on its mother's breast, which is fed there with her milk even while asleep, and sleeps while being fed. O God, what delight was it for this Benjamin, this child of Savior's joy, to sleep thus in the arms of his father, who on the next day gave him, as "Benoni, child of pain," to be his own Mother's sweet bosom! Noth-

---

67. For a discussion of Rubens's descent paintings, see Jan Bialostocki, "The Descent from the Cross in Works by Peter Paul Rubens and His Studio," *Art Bulletin* 46 (1964): 511–24: and John R. Martin, ed., *Rubens: The Antwerp Altarpiece* (New York: Norton, 1969).

68. On the liminal qualities in Renaissance architectural enframements, see Marcia Kupfer, "Spiritual Passage and Pictorial Strategy in the Romanesque Frescoes at Vicq," *Art Bulletin* 68 (1986): 35–53; Karl M. Birkmeyer, "The Arch Motif in Netherlandish Painting of the Fifteenth Century," *Art Bulletin* 43 (1961): 1–20, 99–112; and Margaret English Frazer, "Church Doors and the Gates of Paradise: Byzantine Bronze Doors in Italy," *Dumbarton Oaks Papers* 27 (1973): 147–48.

ing is more desireable to a little child, whether awake or asleep, than his father's bosom and his mother's heart.[69]

Consequently, Rubens places John's head near Christ's wound in the side so that it appears that he is about to drink the blood as a child would suckle his mother. For Rubens, as for Crashaw, Christ becomes the nourishing mother, providing eucharistic food to the faithful.

Crashaw, who may have seen similar compositions, echoes Rubens's liminal interpretation of the Crucifixion with his own liturgical framing of the event. In the last stanza of the poem, Crashaw concludes:

> The difference onely this appeares,
>   (Nor can the change offend)
> The debt is paid in *Ruby*-Teares,
>   Which thou in Pearles did'st lend.
>   (ll. 17–20)

To repay Christ's sacrifice the reader can, like the Magdalene, show repentance and partake of the Eucharist, which, in this instance, Crashaw's imagery makes clear is the "bloody sacrifice" so objected to by Protestants, who perceived Catholicism as theologically and politicaily subversive of their values. Christ's blood as "*Ruby*-Teares" and Magdalene's tears as "Pearles" are placed in parallel positions of intercession so that their affective relationship becomes that of the Church and the sinner, who still perceives Christ's wounds in the Eucharist. For Crashaw, Christ's wounds are the entrance to the temple of the heart, that liminal space in which love moves and converts the poet and reader. Moreover, it is the poet's own experience of ritual liminality that allows him to create daring and affective images of love and sacrifice as wounds that are eyes and mouths. It is precisely that ritual experience that allows Crashaw to open up the religious lyric to new dimensions not available to his contemporary Protestant poets.

---

69. *On the Love of God*, trans. John K. Ryan (Garden City, N.Y.: Doubleday, 1963), 291.

THE SEVENTEENTH-CENTURY ENGLISH RELIGIOUS LYRIC
A Selective Bibliography of Modern Criticism 1952–1990

❈ ❈ ❈

The following bibliography is selective, not comprehensive, and includes modern critical studies of religious lyricists of the late sixteenth and seventeenth centuries. The bibliography begins in 1952, the date of the publication of Helen Gardner's very influential edition of Donne's divine poems, and ends with 1990 because more recent studies were not always available and because bibliographical aids after this year were very incomplete. I have listed items chronologically so that by glancing through the bibliography the reader will be able to obtain some sense of the various shifts and developments that have occurred in modern criticism during the years covered by this bibliography. The focus of this bibliography is primarily on the following as religious poets: John Donne, George Herbert, Richard Crashaw, Ben Jonson, Robert Herrick, Henry King, Henry Vaughan, William Alabaster, Thomas Traherne, Barnabe Barnes, Henry Constable, Henry Colman, Gertrude More, and Andrew Marvell. I have included also Robert Southwell, even though he was put to death in 1595, since he stands at the beginning of the period during which the religious lyric flourished. The bibliography does not include biographical works unless there is considerable discussion of the religious lyric or of the poet as religious lyricist, nor does it include short notes, very brief explications, reviews, textbooks, or doctoral dissertations. It also does not include studies of religious, philosophical, and theological verse that is not lyrical; thus Milton has not been included since, strictly speaking, he did not write religious lyrics.

Abbreviations of Titles of Journals

ABR	*American Benedictine Review*
ArlQ	*Arlington Quarterly*
Assays	*Assays: Critical Approaches to Medieval and Renaissance Texts*
BSE	*Brno Studies in English*
BSEAA	*Bulletin de la Société d'Études Anglo-Américaines des 17 et 18 Siècles*
BuR	*Bucknell Review*
BUSE	*Boston University Studies in English*
CahiersE	*Cahiers Elisabéthains: Etudes sur la Pré-Renaissance et la Renaissance Anglaises*
C&L	*Christianity and Literature*
CE	*College English*
Cithara	*Cithara: Essays in the Judaeo-Christian Tradition*
CL	*Comparative Literature* (Eugene, Oreg.)
CLAJ	*College Language Association Journal*
CollL	*College Literature*
Costerus	*Costerus: Essays in English and American Language and Literature*
CP	*Concerning Poetry* (Bellingham, Wash.)
CQ	*The Cambridge Quarterly*
CR	*The Critical Review* (Canberra, Australia)
Criticism	*Criticism: A Quarterly for Literature and the Arts* (Detroit, Mich.)
Crosscurrents	*Cross Currents*
CSR	*Christian Scholar's Review*
DR	*Dalhousie Review*
DUJ	*Durham University Journal*

Selective Bibliography • 271

EIC	*Essays in Criticism: A Quarterly Journal of Literary Criticism* (Oxford, England)
EAS	*Essays in Arts and Sciences*
EIRC	*Explorations in Renaissance Culture*
ELH	
ELN	*English Language Notes* (Boulder, Colo.)
ELR	*English Literary Renaissance*
ELWIU	*Essays in Literature* (Macomb, Ill.)
EM	*English Miscellany*
Emblematica	*Emblematica: An Interdisciplinary Journal of Emblem Studies*
ES	*English Studies: A Journal of English Language and Literature* (Lisse, The Netherlands)
ESC	*English Studies in Canada*
GHJ	*George Herbert Journal*
GorR	*Gordon Review*
HLQ	*Huntington Library Quarterly: A Journal for the History and Interpretation of English and American Civilization*
HSL	*University of Hartford Studies in Literature: A Journal of Interdisciplinary Criticism*
HTR	*Harvard Theological Review*
HUSL	*Hebrew University Studies in Literature and the Arts*
JAAC	*Journal of Aesthetics and Art Criticism*
JDJ	*John Donne Journal: Studies in the Age of Donne*
JEP	*Journal of Evolutionary Psychology*
JEGP	*Journal of English and Germanic Philology*
JMRS	*Journal of Medieval and Renaissance Studies*
JWCI	*Journal of the Warburg and Courtauld Institutes*
KN	*Kwartalnik Neofilologiczny* (Warsaw, Poland)
KPAB	*Kentucky Philological Association Bulletin*
KR	*Kenyon Review*
Lang&S	*Language and Style: An International Journal*
LHR	*Lock Haven Review* (Lock Haven State College, Penn.)
LCrit	*The Literary Criterion* (Mysore, India)
McNR	*McNeese Review*
MHLS	*Mid-Hudson Language Studies*
MichQR	*Michigan Quarterly Review*
MLQ	*Modern Language Quarterly*
MLR	*The Modern Language Review*

MLS	*Modern Language Studies*
Mosaic	*Mosaic: A Journal for the Interdisciplinary Study of Literature*
MP	*Modern Philology: A Journal Devoted to Research in Medieval and Modern Literature*
MQR	*Michigan Quarterly Review*
MR	*Massachusetts Review: A Quarterly of Literature, the Arts and Public Affairs* (Amherst, Mass.)
MysticsQ	*Mystics Quarterly*
NDEJ	*Notre Dame English Journal: A Journal of Religion and Literature*
Neophil	*Neophilologus* (Groningen, Netherlands)
PCP	*Pacific Coast Philology*
PLL	*Papers on Language and Literature: A Journal for Scholars and Critics of Language and Literature*
PMLA	*Publications of the Modern Language Association of America*
POMPA	*Publications of the Mississippi Philological Assn.*
PPMRC	*Proceedings of the PMR Conference: Annual Publication of the International Patristic, Mediaeval and Renaissance Conference*
PQ	*Philological Quarterly* (Iowa City, Iowa)
Ren&R	*Renaissance and Reformation/ Renaissance et Réforme*
Renascence	*Renascence: Essays on Value in Literature*
RenP	*Renaissance Papers*
RenQ	*Renaissance Quarterly*
RES	*Review of English Studies: A Quarterly Journal of English Literature and the English Language*
RoHum	*Roczniki Humanistyczne* (Lubin, Poland)
SAQ	*South Atlantic Quarterly*
SCen	*The Seventeenth Century*
SCN	*Seventeenth-Century News*
SCRev	*South Central Review: The Journal of the South Central Modern Language Association*
SEL	*Studies in English Literature, 1500–1900*
SELit	*Studies in English Literature* (Tokyo, Japan)
SMlit	*Studies in Mystical Literature* (Taiwan, Republic of China)
SMy	*Studia Mystica*
SN	*Studia Neophilologica: A Journal of Germanic and Romance Languages and Literature*
SoAR	*South Atlantic Review*

SoQ	*The Southern Quarterly: A Journal of the Arts in the South* (Hattiesburg, Miss.)
SoRA	*Southern Review: Literary and Interdisciplinary Essays* (Adelaide, Australia)
SP	*Studies in Philology*
SR	*Sewanee Review*
SRen	*Studies in the Renaissance*
Style	*Style* (Dekalb, Ill.)
Thoth	*Thoth: Department of English, Syracuse U.*
Thought	*Thought: A Review of Culture and Idea*
TLS	*[London] Times Literary Supplement*
TSE	*Tulane Studies in English*
TSLL	*Texas Studies in Literature and Language: A Journal of the Humanities*
UES	*Unisa English Studies: Journal of the Department of English*
UTQ	*University of Toronto Quarterly*
WascanaR	*Wascana Review*
YES	*Yearbook of English Studies*

1952

Bewley, Marius. "Religious Cynicism in Donne's Poetry." *KR* 14:619–46.

Davison, Dennis. Introduction to *Andrew Marvell: Selected Poetry and Prose,* edited by Dennis Davison, 13–61. (Life, Literature and Thought Library) London: George G. Harrap.

Gardner, Helen. Introduction to *John Donne: The Divine Poems,* edited with Introduction and Commentary by Helen Gardner, xv-lv. (Oxford English Texts.) Oxford: Clarendon Press. (Reprinted, 1959; 2d edition, 1978.)

Tuve, Rosemond. *A Reading of George Herbert.* Chicago: University of Chicago Press; London: Faber and Faber; Toronto: W. J. Gage. 215p. (Reprinted several times.)

1953

Bethell, S. L. "The Theology of Henry and Thomas Vaughan." *Theology* 56:137–43.

Mourgues, Odette de. *Metaphysical Baroque & Précieux Poetry.* Oxford: Clarendon Press. vii, 184p.

Peter, John. "Crashaw and 'The Weeper.'" *Scrutiny* 19:258–73.

Turnell, Martin. "Baroque Art and Poetry." *Commonweal* 56:146–49.

1954

Bottrall, Margaret. *George Herbert.* London: John Murray. 153p. (Reprinted several times.)

Hunt, Clay. *Donne's Poetry: Essays in Literary Analysis.* New Haven: Yale University Press; London: Geoffrey Cumberlege, Oxford University Press. xiii, 256p. (Reprinted, 1956.)

McCann, Eleanor. "Donne and Saint Teresa on the Ecstasy." *HLQ* 17:125–32.

Martz, Louis L. *The Poetry of Meditation: A Study in English Religious Literature of the Seventeenth Century.* (Yale Studies in English, 125.) New Haven: Yale University Press; London: Oxford University Press. xiv, 375p. (Revised edition, 1962; reprinted several times.)

Oliver, H. J. "The Mysticism of Henry Vaughan: A Reply." *JEGP* 53:352–60.

Ross, Malcolm Mackenzie. *Poetry and Dogma: The Transfiguration of Eucharistic Symbols in Seventeenth Century English Poetry.* New Brunswick: Rutgers University Press. xii, 256p. (Reprinted, 1969.)

Summers, Joseph H. *George Herbert: His Religion and Art.* Cambridge, Mass.: Harvard University Press; London: Chatto & Windus. 247p. (Reprinted, 1968; reprinted, Binghamton, N.Y.: MRTS, 1981.)

1955

Esch, Arno. *Englische religiöse Lyrik des 17. Jahrhunderts: Studien zu Donne, Herbert, Crashaw, Vaughan.* (Buchreihe der Anglia Zeitschrift für englische Philologie, 5.) Tübingen: Max Niemeyer. xi, 225p.

Manning, Stephen. "The Meaning of 'The Weeper.'" *ELH* 22:34–47.

Sells, Arthur Lytton. "Southwell," in *The Italian Influence in English Poetry: From Chaucer to Southwell*, 306–35. Bloomington: Indiana University Press.

Whitaker, Thomas R. "Herrick and the Fruits of the Garden." *ELH* 22:16–33.

1956

Collmer, Robert G. "Crashaw's 'Death More Misticall and High.'" *JEGP* 55:373–80.

Denonain, Jean-Jacques. *Thèmes et formes de la poésie "métaphysique": Étude d'un aspect de la littérature anglaise au dix-septième siècle.* (Publications de la Faculté des Lettres d'Alger, 28.) Paris: Presses Universitaires de France. 548p.

Enright, D. J. "George Herbert and the Devotional Poets," in *From Donne to Marvell*, 142–59. (The Pelican Guide to English Literature, edited by Boris Ford, vol. 3.) London: Penguin Books.

Farnham, Anthony E. "Saint Teresa and the Coy Mistress." *Boston University Studies in English* no. 2: 226–39.

Gardner, Helen. "The Historical Sense," in *The Limits of Criticism: Reflections on the Interpretation of Poetry and Scripture*, 40–63. London: Oxford University Press.

1957

Dabrowska, Claire G. "Robert Southwell, 1561[?]–1595: A Reevaluation." *RoHum* 6:5–51.

Novarr, David. "The Dating of Donne's *La Corona*." *PQ* 36:259–65.

1958

Praz, Mario. "The Flaming Heart: Richard Crashaw and the Baroque," in *The Flaming Heart: Essays on Crashaw, Machiavelli, and Other Studies in the Relations between Italian and English Literature from Chaucer to T. S. Eliot*, 204–63. (Doubleday Anchor Books.) Garden City: Doubleday.

Wallace, John Malcolm. "Thomas Traherne and the Structure of Meditation." *ELH* 25:79–89.

Wilson, Edward M. "Spanish and English Poetry of the Seventeenth Century." *Journal of Ecclesiastical History* 9:38–53.

1959

Campbell, Lily B. *Divine Poetry and Drama in Sixteenth-Century England.* Cambridge: Cambridge University Press; Berkeley and Los Angeles: University of California Press. viii, 268p.

Farnham, Fern. "The Imagery of Henry Vaughan's 'The Night.'" *PQ* 38:425–35.

Garner, Ross. *Henry Vaughan: Experience and the Tradition.* Chicago: University of Chicago Press. viii, 176p.

Martz, Louis L. "Donne and the Meditative Tradition." *Thought* 34:269–78. (Reprinted in *Essential Articles for the Study of John Donne's Poetry*, edited by John R. Roberts [1975], 142–49; also reprinted as "John Donne: A Valediction" in *The Poem of the Mind* [1966], 21–32.)

Peterson, Douglas L. "John Donne's *Holy Sonnets* and the Anglican Doctrine of Contrition." *SP* 56:504–18. (Reprinted in *Essential Articles for the Study of John Donne's Poetry*, edited by John R. Roberts [1975], 313–23.)

Story, G. M. "General Introduction," in *The Sonnets of William Alabaster*, edited by G. M. Story and Helen Gardner, xi-xliii. (Oxford English Monographs, gen. eds. J. R. R. Tolkien, Herbert Davis, Helen Gardner.) Oxford: Oxford University Press.

Tuve, Rosemond. "George Herbert and *Caritas.*" *JWCI* 22:303–31. (Reprinted in *Essays by Rosemond Tuve*, edited by Thomas P. Roche, Jr. [1970], 167–206.)

1960

Allen, Don Cameron. "George Herbert: 'The Rose'" and "Henry Vaughan: 'Cock Crowing,'" in *Image and Meaning: Metaphoric Traditions in Renaissance Poetry*, 102–14; 226–41. Baltimore: Johns Hopkins Press. (Revised and enlarged, 1968.)

Chambers, A. B. "The Meaning of the 'Temple' in Donne's *La Corona.*" *JEGP* 59:212–17. (Reprinted in *Essential Articles for the Study of John Donne's Poetry*, edited by John R. Roberts [1975], 349–52.)

Claydon, Margaret. *Richard Crashaw's Paraphrases of the Vexilla Regis, Stabat Mater, Adoro Te, Lauda Sion, Dies Irae, O Gloriosa Domina.* Washington, D. C.: The Catholic University of America Press. vii, 167p.

Ellrodt, Robert. *L'Inspiration personnelle et l'esprit du temps chez les poètes métaphysiques anglais.* Paris: José Corti. 2 parts in 3 vols. 459p., 491p., 435p.

Grenander, M. E. "Holy Sonnets 8 and 17: John Donne." *BUSE* 4:95–105. (Reprinted in *Essential Articles for the Study of John Donne's Poetry,* edited by John R. Roberts [1975], 324–32.)

Grundy, Joan. Introduction to *The Poems of Henry Constable,* edited by Joan Grundy, 15–105. (Liverpool English Texts and Studies, gen. ed. Kenneth Muir.) Liverpool: Liverpool University Press. 261p.

Hughes, Richard E. "Conceptual Form and Varieties of Religious Experience in the Poetry of George Herbert." *Greyfriar: Siena Studies in Literature* 3:3–12.

Knieger, Bernard. "The Religious Verse of George Herbert." *CLAJ* 4:138–47.

Martz, Louis L. "John Donne: the Meditative Voice." *MR* 1:326–42. (Reprinted in *The Poem of the Mind* [1966], 3–20.)

Montgomery, Robert L., Jr. "The Province of Allegory in George Herbert's Verse." *TSLL* 1:457–72. (Reprinted in *Essential Articles for the Study of George Herbert's Poetry,* edited by John R. Roberts [1979], 114–28.)

Pettet, E. C. *Of Paradise and Light: A Study of Vaughan's "Silex Scintillans."* Cambridge: Cambridge University Press. x, 216p.

Roberts, John R. "The Influence of *The Spiritual Exercises* of St. Ignatius on the Nativity Poems of Robert Southwell." *JEGP* 59:450–56.

Rosenberg, John D. "Marvell and the Christian Idiom." *BUSE* 4:152–61.

Stambler, Elizabeth. "The Unity of Herbert's 'Temple.'" *Crosscurrents* 10:251–66. (Reprinted in *Essential Articles for the Study of George Herbert's Poetry,* edited by John R. Roberts [1979], 328–50.)

White, Helen C. *Poetry and Prayer.* (Wimmer Lecture 8.) Latrobe, Pa.: Archabbey Press. viii, 59p.

1961

Archer, Stanley. "Meditation and the Structure of Donne's 'Holy Sonnets.'" *ELH* 28:137–47.

Chambers, A. B. "Goodfriday, 1613. Riding Westward: The Poem and the Tradition." *ELH* 28:31–53.

Collmer, Robert G. "The Meditation on Death and Its Appearance in Metaphysical Poetry." *Neophil* 45:323–33.

Hart, Jeffrey. "Herbert's *The Collar* Re-Read." *BUSE* 5:65–73.

Hughes, Richard E. "George Herbert's Rhetorical World." *Criticism* 3:86–94. (Reprinted in *Essential Articles for the Study of George Herbert's Poetry,* edited by John R. Roberts [1979], 105–13.)

Knowles, David. *The English Mystical Tradition.* London: Burns & Oates. viii, 197p.

McCann, Eleanor. "Oxymora in Spanish Mystics and English Metaphysical Writers." *CL* 13:16–25.

Morris, Harry. "*In Articulo Mortis.*" *TSE* 11:21–37.

Olson, Paul A. "Vaughan's *The World:* The Pattern of Meaning and the Tradition." *CL* 13:26–32.

Rickey, Mary Ellen. *Rhyme and Meaning in Richard Crashaw.* Lexington: University of Kentucky Press. 98p. (Reprinted, New York: Haskell House, 1973.)

Tuve, Rosemond. "Sacred 'Parody' of Love Poetry, and Herbert." *SRen* 8:249–90. (Reprinted in *Essays by Rosemond Tuve,* edited by Thomas P. Roche, Jr. [1970], 207–51; *Essential Articles for the Study of George Herbert's Poetry,* edited by John R. Roberts [1979], 129–59.)

Warnke, Frank J. *European Metaphysical Poetry.* (The Elizabethan Club Series, 2.) New Haven: Yale University Press. xi, 317p.

1962

Bowers, Fredson. "Henry Vaughan's Multiple Time Scheme." *MLQ* 23:291–96. (Reprinted in *Essential Articles for the Study of Henry Vaughan,* edited by Alan Rudrum [1987], 91–97.)

———. "Herbert's Sequential Imagery: 'The Temper.'" *MP* 59:202–13. (Reprinted in *Essential Articles for the Study of George Herbert's Poetry,* edited by John R. Roberts [1979], 231–48.)

Durr, R. A. *On the Mystical Poetry of Henry Vaughan.* Cambridge, Mass.: Harvard University Press. xxi, 178p.

Eliot, T. S. *George Herbert.* (Writers and Their Works, no. 152.) London: Longmans, Green. 36p. (Reprinted, 1968; first American edition, 1964.)

Hardy, John Edward. "Andrew Marvell's 'The Coronet': The Frame of

Curiosity," in *The Curious Frame: Seven Poems in Text and Context*, 45–60. Notre Dame, Ind.: University of Notre Dame Press.

Rickey, Mary Ellen. "Vaughan, *The Temple*, and Poetic Form." *SP* 59:162–70.

Simmonds, James D. "Vaughan's Masterpiece and Its Critics: 'The World' Reevaluated." *SEL* 2:77–93.

Starkman, Miriam K. "*Noble Numbers* and the Poetry of Devotion," in *Reason and the Imagination: Studies in the History of Ideas, 1600–1800*, edited by J. A. Mazzeo, 1–27. New York: Columbia University Press; London: Routledge & Kegan Paul.

Swardson, H. R. *Poetry and the Fountain of Light: Observations on the Conflict between Christian and Classical Traditions in Seventeenth-Century Poetry*. Columbia: University of Missouri Press. 167p.

Walker, John David. "The Architectonics of George Herbert's *The Temple*." *ELH* 29:289–305.

White, Helen C. "The Contemplative Element in Robert Southwell," *Catholic Historical Review* 48:1–11.

1963

Cohen, J. M. *The Baroque Lyric*. London: Hutchinson University Library. 207p.

Colie, R. L. "*Logos* in *The Temple:* George Herbert and the Shape of Content." *JWCI* 26:327–42.

Cubeta, Paul M. "Ben Jonson's Religious Lyrics." *JEGP* 62:96–110.

Garner, Ross. *The Unprofitable Servant in Henry Vaughan*. (University of Nebraska Studies, n.s. 29.) Lincoln: University of Nebraska Press. 61p.

Hastings, Robert. "'Easter Wings' as a Model of Herbert's Method." *Thoth* 4:15–23.

Kawasaki, Toshihiko. "From Southwell to Donne." *SELit* 39:11–31.

Martz, Louis L. "Henry Vaughan: The Man Within." *PMLA* 78:40–49. (Reprinted in *Essential Articles for the Study of Henry Vaughan*, edited by Alan Rudrum [1987], 98–120.)

Maurer, Warren R. "Spee, Southwell, and the Poetry of Meditation." *CL* 15:15–22.

Rudrum, Alan. "Henry Vaughan and the Theme of Transfiguration." *SoRA* 1:54–68.

Simmonds, James D. "Vaughan's 'The Book': Hermetic or Meditative?" *Neophil* 47:320–28.

Williams, George Walton. *Image and Symbol in the Sacred Poetry of Richard Crashaw.* Columbia: University of South Carolina Press. ix, 151p.

1964

Berman, Ronald. *Henry King and the Seventeenth Century.* London: Chatto & Windus. 160p.

Blanchard, Margaret M. "The Leap into Darkness: Donne, Herbert, and God." *Renascence* 17:38–50.

Edwards, Philip. "Who Wrote 'The Passionate Man's Pilgrimage'?" *ELR* 4:83–97. (Discusses Southwell.)

Fisch, Harold. *Jerusalem and Albion: The Hebraic Factor in Seventeenth-Century Literature.* New York: Schocken Books. ix, 301p.

Hughes, Richard E. "George Herbert and the Incarnation." *Cithara* 4:22–32. (Reprinted in *Essential Articles for the Study of George Herbert's Poetry*, edited by John R. Roberts [1979], 52–62.)

Martz, Louis L. *The Paradise Within: Studies in Vaughan, Traherne, and Milton.* New Haven: Yale University Press. xix, 217p.

Salter, K. W. *Thomas Traherne: Mystic and Poet.* New York: Barnes & Noble. 142p.

Warnke, Frank J. "Sacred Play: Baroque Poetic Style." *JAAC* 22:455–64.

White, Helen C. "Southwell: Metaphysical and Baroque." *MP* 61:159–68.

1965

Collmer, Robert G. "The Function of Death in Certain Metaphysical Poems." *McNR* 16:25–32. (Reprinted in *BSE* 6 [1966]: 147–54.)

Crum, Margaret. "The Poems," in *The Poems of Henry King*, edited by Margaret Crum, 27–47. Oxford: Clarendon Press.

Endicott [Patterson], Annabel M. "The Structure of George Herbert's *Temple*: A Reconsideration." *UTQ* 34:226–37. (Reprinted in *Essential*

Articles for the Study of George Herbert's Poetry, edited by John R. Roberts [1979], 351–62.)

Greenwood, E. B. "George Herbert's Sonnet 'Prayer': A Stylistic Study." *EIC* 15:27–45. (Partly reprinted in *George Herbert and the Seventeenth-Century Religious Poets: Authoritative Texts/Criticism,* edited by Mario A. Di Cesare [1978], 249– 55.)

MacCaffrey, Isabel G. "The Meditative Paradigm." *ELH* 32:388–407.

Ostriker, Alicia. "Song and Speech in the Metrics of George Herbert." *PMLA* 80:62–68. (Reprinted in *Essential Articles for the Study of George Herbert's Poetry,* edited by John R. Roberts [1979], 298–310.)

Woodhouse, A. S. P. "Elizabethan Religion and Poetry: Spenser and Southwell" and "The Seventeenth Century: Donne and His Successors," in *The Poet and His Faith: Religion and Poetry in England from Spenser to Eliot and Auden,* 11–41; 42–89. Chicago: University of Chicago Press.

1966

Brown, Nancy Pollard. "The Structure of Southwell's 'Saint Peter's Complaint.'" *MLR* 61:3–11.

Chambers, Leland H. "Henry Vaughan's Allusive Technique: Biblical Allusions in 'The Night.'" *MLQ* 27:371–87.

Colie, Rosalie L. *Paradoxia Epidemica: The Renaissance Tradition of Paradox.* Princeton: Princeton University Press. xx, 553p.

Gardner, Helen. "The Titles of Donne's Poems," in *Friendship's Garland: Essays Presented to Mario Praz on His Seventieth Birthday,* edited by Vittorio Gabrielli, 1:189–207. (Storia e letteratura: Raccolta di studi e testi, 106.) Rome: Edizioni di storia e letteratura.

King, James Roy. "Pilgrimage to Paradise: Center of Vaughan's Religious World," in *Studies in Six 17th Century Writers,* 121–37. Athens: Ohio University Press.

Knieger, Bernard. "The Purchase-Sale: Patterns of Business Imagery in the Poetry of George Herbert." *SEL* 6:111–24.

Leishman, J. B. "'Religious' Poems," in *The Art of Marvell's Poetry,* 193–220. London: Hutchinson.

McGill, William J., Jr. "George Herbert's View of the Eucharist." *LHR* 8:16–24.

Martz, Louis L. "Meditative Action and 'The Metaphysick Style,'" in *The Poem of the Mind: Essays on Poetry, English and American*, 33–53. New York: Oxford University Press; London: Hutchinson. (First appeared, in a shorter version, in the introduction to *The Meditative Poem: An Anthology of Seventeenth-Century Verse* [1963].)

Rickey, Mary Ellen. *Utmost Art: Complexity in the Verse of George Herbert.* Lexington: University of Kentucky Press. xv, 200p.

Rollin, Roger B. *Robert Herrick.* (Twayne's English Authors Series, no. 34.) New York: Twayne Publishers; London: Bailey Bros. 231p. (Revised edition, 1992.)

Stewart, Stanley. *The Enclosed Garden: The Tradition and the Image in Seventeenth-Century Poetry.* Madison: University of Wisconsin Press. xiv, 226p.

1967

Brown, Nancy Pollard. General introduction to *The Poems of Robert Southwell, S. J.,* edited by James H. McDonald and Nancy Pollard Brown, xv-xxxiv. Oxford: Clarendon Press.

Chambers, Leland. "In Defense of 'The Weeper.'" *PLL* 3:111–21.

Marilla, E. L. "The Mysticism of Henry Vaughan: Some Observations." *RES* 18:164–66.

Milward, Peter. *Christian Themes in English Literature.* Tokyo: Kenkyuska. xvi, 269p. (Reprinted, Folcroft, Pa.: Folcroft Press, 1970, 1971.)

Peterson, Douglas L. *The English Lyric from Wyatt to Donne: A History of the Plain and Eloquent Styles.* Princeton: Princeton University Press. vi, 391p.

Reilly, R. J. "God, Man, and Literature." *Thought* 42:561–83.

Sandbank, S. "Henry Vaughan's Apology for Darkness." *SEL* 7:141–52. (Reprinted in *Essential Articles for the Study of Henry Vaughan*, edited by Alan Rudrum [1987], 128–40.)

Ziegelmaier, Gregory. "Liturgical Symbol and Reality in the Poetry of George Herbert." *ABR* 18:344–53.

1968

Baker-Smith, Dominic. "John Donne and the Mysterium Crucis." *EM* 19:65–82.

Bradford, Melvin E. A. "Henry Vaughan's 'The Night': A Consideration of Metaphor and Meditation." *ArlQ* 1:209–22.

Buckley, Vincent. *Poetry and the Sacred*. New York: Barnes & Noble; London: Chatto & Windus. 244p.

Carnes, Valerie. "The Unity of George Herbert's *The Temple:* A Reconsideration." *ELH* 35:505–26. (Reprinted in *Essential Articles for the Study of George Herbert's Poetry,* edited by John R. Roberts [1979], 505–26.)

Chambers, Leland H. "Vaughan's 'The World': The Limits of Extrinsic Criticism." *SEL* 8:137–50.

Daly, Peter M. "Southwell's 'Burning Babe' and the Emblematic Practice." *WascanaR* 3, no. 2: 29–44.

Goldknopf, David. "The Disintegration of Symbol in a Meditative Poet." *CE* 30:48–59.

Grant, Patrick. "Hermetic Philosophy and the Nature of Man in Vaughan's *Silex Scintillans*." *JEGP* 67:406–22.

Hanley, Sara William. "Temples in *The Temple:* George Herbert's Study of the Church." *SEL* 8:121–35.

Howard, Thomas T. "Herbert and Crashaw: Notes on Meditative Focus." *GorR* 11:79–98.

Hughes, Richard E. *The Progress of the Soul: The Interior Career of John Donne*. New York: William Morrow; Toronto: George J. McLeod. 316p.

Spitz, Leona. "Process and Stasis: Aspects of Nature in Vaughan and Marvell." *HLQ* 32 (1968–1969): 135–47.

Stein, Arnold. *George Herbert's Lyrics*. Baltimore: Johns Hopkins Press, xliv, 221p.

Whitlock, Baird W. "The Baroque Characteristics of the Poetry of George Herbert." *Cithara* 7:30–40.

1969

Asals, Heather. "The Voice of George Herbert's 'The Church.'" *ELH* 36:511–28. (Reprinted in *Essential Articles for the Study of George Herbert's Poetry,* edited by John R. Roberts [1979], 393–407.)

Cave, Terence C. *Devotional Poetry in France c. 1570–1613*. Cambridge: Cambridge University Press. xvi, 356p.

Clements, Arthur L. *The Mystical Poetry of Thomas Traherne.* Cambridge, Mass.: Harvard University Press. x, 232p.

Davidson, Clifford. "Barnabe Barnes" *A Divine Centurie of Spirituall Sonnets. LHR* 11:3–16.

Dolan, Paul J. "Herbert's Dialogue with God." *Anglican Theological Review* 51:125–32.

Fraser, Russell. "On Metaphor, Mysticism, and Science." *MichQR* 8:49–57.

Martz, Louis L. *The Wit of Love: Donne, Carew, Crashaw, Marvell.* (University of Notre Dame Ward-Phillips Lectures in English Language and Literature, vol. 3.) Notre Dame, Ind.: University of Notre Dame Press. xv, 216p.

Merrill, Thomas F. "'The Sacrifice' and the Structure of Religious Language." *Lang&S* 2:275–87.

Miner, Earl. *The Metaphysical Mode from Donne to Cowley.* Princeton: Princeton University Press. xix, 291p.

Nelly, Una. *The Poet Donne: A Study in His Dialectic Method.* Cork, Ireland: Cork University Press. 165p.

Rudrum, Alan. "Vaughan's 'The Night': Some Hermetic Notes." *MLR* 64:11–19. (Reprinted in *Essential Articles for the Study of Henry Vaughan,* edited by Alan Rudrum [1987], 141–53.)

Schten, Carolyn A. "Southwell's 'Christs Bloody Sweat': A Meditation on the Mass." *EM* 20:75–80.

Strier, Richard. "Crashaw's Other Voice." *SEL* 9:135–51.

1970

Berthoff, Ann E. *The Resolved Soul: A Study of Marvell's Major Poems.* Princeton: Princeton University Press. xiii, 243p.

Brooks, Cleanth. "Henry Vaughan: Quietism and Mysticism," in *Essays in Honor of Esmond Linworth Marilla,* edited by Thomas Austin Kirby and William John Olive, 3–26. Baton Rouge: Louisiana State University Press.

Carpenter, Margaret. "From Herbert to Marvell: Poetics in 'A Wreath' and 'The Coronet.'" *JEGP* 69:50–62.

Cirillo, A. R. "Crashaw's 'Epiphany Hymn': The Dawn of Christian Time." *SP* 67:67–88.

Cullen, Patrick. "Andrew Marvell: The Christian Lyrics: Pastoral and Anti-Pastoral," in *Spenser, Marvell, and Renaissance Pastoral*, 151–82. Cambridge, Mass.: Harvard University Press.

Ellrodt, Robert. "George Herbert and the Religious Lyric," in *English Poetry and Prose, 1540–1674*, edited by Christopher Ricks, 173–205. (History of Literature in the English Language, vol. 2.) London: Barrie & Jenkins. (Paperback edition, Sphere Books, 1970; reprinted in *Essential Articles for the Study of George Herbert's Poetry*, edited by John R. Roberts [1979], 3–32; reprinted in *New History of Literature*, vol. 2, edited by Christopher Ricks [1987], 171–200.)

Gallagher, Michael P. "Rhetoric, Style, and George Herbert." *ELH* 37:495–516.

Halewood, William H. *The Poetry of Grace: Reformation Themes and Structures in English Seventeenth-Century Poetry*. New Haven: Yale University Press. xii, 180p.

Jackson, Robert S. *John Donne's Christian Vocation*. Evanston: Northwestern University Press. viii, 192p.

Jacobus, Lee A. "Richard Crashaw as Mannerist." *BuR* 18, no. 3: 79–88.

Mahood, M. M. "Something Understood: The Nature of Herbert's Wit," in *Metaphysical Poetry*, edited by Malcolm Bradbury and David Palmer, 123–47. (Stratford-upon-Avon Studies, 11.) London: Edward Arnold, Ltd.; New York: St. Martin's Press. (Reprinted, 1971.)

Martz, Louis L. "The Action of the Self: Devotional Poetry in the Seventeenth Century," in *Metaphysical Poetry*, edited by Malcolm Bradbury and David Palmer, 101–21. (Stratford-upon-Avon Studies, 11.) London: Edward Arnold, Ltd.; New York: St. Martin's Press. (Reprinted, 1971.)

Petersson, Robert T. *The Art of Ecstasy: Teresa, Bernini, and Crashaw*. London: Routledge & Kegan Paul. xv, 160p.

Sherrington, Alison J. *Mystical Symbolism in the Poetry of Thomas Traherne*. St. Lucia, Queensland: University of Queensland Press. viii, 136p.

Stewart, Stanley. *The Expanded Voice: The Art of Thomas Traherne*. San Marino: The Huntington Library. ix, 235p.

Summers, Joseph H. *The Heirs of Donne and Jonson*. London: Chatto & Windus; New York: Oxford University Press. 198p.

Wilson, Gayle E. "A Characteristic of Vaughan's Style and Two Meditative Poems: 'Corruption' and 'Day of Judgement.'" *Style* 4:119–31.

1971

Berman, Ronald. "Herrick's Secular Poetry." *ES* 52:20–30. (Reprinted in *Ben Jonson and the Cavalier Poets*, edited by Hugh Maclean [1974], 529–40.)

Bertonasco, Marc F. *Crashaw and the Baroque*. Tuscaloosa: University of Alabama Press. vii, 158p.

Day, Malcolm M. "'Naked Truth' and the Language of Thomas Traherne." *SP* 68:305–25.

Duvall, Robert. "The Biblical Character of Henry Vaughan's *Silex Scintillans*." *PCP* 6:13–19.

Festugière, A. J. *George Herbert, poète, saint, anglican (1593–1633)*. (Études de théologie et d'histoire de la spiritualité, 18.) Paris: Librairie philosophique J. Vrin. 349p.

Gardner, Helen. "Religious Poetry," in *Religion and Literature*, 121–94. New York: Oxford University Press; London: Faber and Faber. (Reprinted, 1983.)

Goldberg, Jonathan S. "Donne's Journey East: Aspects of a Seventeenth-Century Trope." *SP* 68:470–83.

———. "The Typology of 'Musicks Empire.'" *TSLL* 13:421–30.

Grant, Patrick. "Augustinian Spirituality and the *Holy Sonnets* of John Donne." *ELH* 38:542–61.

———. "Original Sin and the Fall of Man in Thomas Traherne." *ELH* 38:40–61.

Kay, W. David. "The Christian Wisdom of Ben Jonson's 'On My First Sonne.'" *SEL* 11:125–36.

Kimmey, John L. "Order and Form in Herrick's *Hesperides*." *JEGP* 70:255–68.

Lerner, Laurence. "Pastoral *versus* Christianity (Nature in Marvell)," in *Seven Studies in English for Dorothy Cavers*, edited by Gildas Roberts, 20–43. Capetown: Purnell & Sons. (Reprinted in *The Uses of Nostalgia: Studies in Pastoral Poetry* [London: Chatto & Windus; New York: Schocken Books, 1972], 181–96.)

Sanders, Wilbur. *John Donne's Poetry*. London: Cambridge University Press. vi, 160p. (Reprinted, 1974.)

Stewart, Stanley. "Marvell and the *Ars Moriendi*," in *Seventeenth-Century Imagery: Essays on Uses of Figurative Language from Donne to*

Farquhar, edited by Earl Miner, 133–50. Berkeley and Los Angeles: University of California Press.

Toliver, Harold E. *Pastoral Forms and Attitudes.* Berkeley and Los Angeles: University of California Press. viii, 391p.

Wellington, James W. "The Litany in Cranmer and Donne." *SP* 68:177–99.

1972

Anderson, Donald K., Jr. "Donne's 'Hymne to God my God, in my sicknesse' and the T-in-O Maps," in *Essays in the Renaissance in Honor of Allan H. Gilbert,* edited by Philip J. Traci and Marilyn L. Williamson, *SAQ* 71:465–72.

Brown, C. C., and W. P. Ingoldsby, "George Herbert's 'Easter Wings.'" *HLQ* 35:131–42. (Reprinted in *Essential Articles for the Study of George Herbert's Poetry,* edited by John R. Roberts [1979], 461–72.)

Carrive, Lucien. *La poésie religieuse anglaise entre 1625 et 1640: Contributions à l'étude de la sensibilité religieuse à l'âge d'or de l'anglicanisme.* Vol. 1. Caen: Assoc. des Pubs. de la Faculté des Lettres et Sciences Humaines de l'Université de Caen. 546p.

Dundas, Judith. "Levity and Grace: The Poetry of Sacred Wit." *YES* 2:93–102.

Fish, Stanley E. "Letting Go: The Dialectic of the Self in Herbert's Poetry," in *Self-Consuming Artifacts: The Experience of Seventeenth-Century Literature,* 156–223. Berkeley and Los Angeles: University of California Press.

Freer, Coburn. *Music for a King: George Herbert's Style and the Metrical Psalms.* Baltimore: Johns Hopkins University Press. xiv, 252p.

Kremen, Kathryn R. *The Imagination of the Resurrection: The Poetic Continuity of a Religious Motif in Donne, Blake, and Yeats.* Lewisburg, Pa.: Bucknell University Press. 344p.

Lessenich, Rolf P. "Henry Vaughan's Poem 'Regeneration.'" *SN* 44:76–89.

Patrides, C. A. *The Grand Design of God: The Literary Form of the Christian View of History.* (Ideas and Forms in English Literature, edited by John Lawler.) London: Routledge & Kegan Paul; Toronto and

Buffalo: University of Toronto Press. (Revised and much expanded version of *The Phoenix and the Ladder: The Rise and Decline of the Christian View of History* [1964].)

Sandler, Florence. "'Solomon vbique regnet': Herbert's Use of the Images of the New Covenant." *PLL* 8:147–58. (Reprinted in *Essential Articles for the Study of George Herbert's Poetry*, edited by John R. Roberts [1979], 258–67.)

Scupholme, A. C. "Anglican Wit: An Anniversary Study of John Donne: 1" and "'Fraited with Salvation': An Anniversary Study of John Donne: 2." *Theology* 75:21–26, 72–78.

Simmonds, James D. *Masques of God: Form and Theme in the Poetry of Henry Vaughan.* Pittsburgh: University of Pittsburgh Press. xi, 255p.

Underwood, Horace H. "Time and Space in the Poetry of Vaughan." *SP* 69:231–41.

Warnke, Frank J. *Versions of Baroque: European Literature in the Seventeenth Century.* New Haven: Yale University Press. xi, 229p.

1973

Christopher, Georgia B. "In Arcadia, Calvin . . . : A Study of Nature in Henry Vaughan." *SP* 70:408–26. (Reprinted in *Essential Articles for the Study of Henry Vaughan*, edited by Alan Rudrum [1987], 170–88.)

Clements, A. L. "Theme, Tone, and Tradition in George Herbert's Poetry." *ELR* 3:264–83. (Reprinted in *Essential Articles for the Study of George Herbert's Poetry*, edited by John R. Roberts [1979], 33–51.)

Friedman, Donald M. "Memory and the Art of Salvation in Donne's Good Friday Poem." *ELR* 3:418–42.

King, Bruce. "A Reading of Marvell's 'The Coronet.'" *MLR* 68:741–49.

Mulder, John R. "George Herbert's *The Temple:* Design and Methodology." *SCN* 31:37–45.

Paynter, Mary. "'Sinne and Love': Thematic Patterns in George Herbert's Lyrics." *YES* 3:85–93.

1974

Adkins, Joan F., and J. H. Adamson. "Via Negativa: Spanish Mystics and English Poets." *LCrit* 11:43–57.

Blanch, Robert J. "Fear and Despair in Donne's *Holy Sonnets.*" *ABR* 25:476–84.
Brooks, Cleanth. "Religion and Literature." *SR* 82:93–107.
Deming, Robert H. *Ceremony and Art: Robert Herrick's Poetry.* (De proprietatibus litterarum, edited by C. H. Van Schooneveld, Series Practica, 64.) The Hague: Mouton. 176p.
DeNeef, A. Leigh. *"This Poetick Liturgie": Robert Herrick's Ceremonial Mode.* Durham: Duke University Press. vii, 200p.
Grant, Patrick. *The Transformation of Sin: Studies in Donne, Herbert, Vaughan, and Traherne.* Montreal: McGill-Queen's University Press; Amherst: University of Massachusetts Press. xiii, 240p.
Higbie, Robert. "Images of Enclosure in George Herbert's *The Temple.*" *TSLL* 15:627–38. (Reprinted in *Essential Articles for the Study of George Herbert's Poetry,* edited by John R. Roberts [1979], 268–79.)
Kerrigan, William W. "The Fearful Accommodations of John Donne." *ELR* 4:337–63.
McCanles, Michael. "The Rhetoric of the Sublime in Crashaw's Poetry," in *The Rhetoric of Renaissance Poetry from Wyatt to Milton,* edited by Thomas O. Sloan and Raymond B. Waddington, 189–211. Berkeley and Los Angeles: University of California Press.
McFarland, Ronald E. "Thanksgiving in Seventeenth-Century Poetry." *Albion* (Washington State University Press) 6:294–306.
McGuire, Philip C. "Private Prayer and English Poetry in the Early Seventeenth Century." *SEL* 14:63–77.
Patrides, C. A. *"A Crown of Praise:* The Poetry of Herbert," in *The English Poems of George Herbert,* edited by C. A. Patrides, 6–25. London, Melbourne and Toronto: J. M. Dent & Sons. (First American edition: Totowa, N.J.: Rowman and Littlefield, 1975.) (Reprinted several times.)
Roston, Murray. *The Soul of Wit: A Study of John Donne.* Oxford: Clarendon Press. 236p.
Sandler, Florence. "The Ascents of the Spirit: Henry Vaughan on the Atonement." *JEGP* 73:209–26.
Segel, Harold B. *The Baroque Poem: A Comparative Survey.* New York: E. P. Dutton. xx, 328p.
Sellin, Paul R. "The Hidden God: Reformation Awe in Renaissance English Literature," in *The Darker Vision of the Renaissance: Beyond the Fields of Reason,* edited, with introduction by Robert S. Kinsman,

147–96. (UCLA Center for Medieval and Renaissance Studies, Contributions VI.) Berkeley and Los Angeles: University of California Press.

Taylor, Mark. *The Soul in Paraphrase: George Herbert's Poetics.* (De proprietatibus litterarum: Series Practica, 92.) The Hague and Paris: Mouton. vii, 127p.

Thekla, Sister. *George Herbert: Idea and Image.* Buckinghamshire, England: Greek Orthodox Monastery of the Assumption, Filgrave, Newport Pagnell. 308p.

Tsur, Reuven. "Poem, Prayer & Meditation: An Exercise in Literary Semantics." *Style* 8:405–24.

1975

Bellette, Antony F. "'Little Worlds Made Cunningly': Significant Form in Donne's *Holy Sonnets* and 'Goodfriday, 1613. Riding Westward.'" *SP* 72:322–47.

Bozanich, Robert. "Donne and Ecclesiastes." *PMLA* 90:270–76.

Cathcart, Dwight. *Doubting Conscience: Donne and the Poetry of Moral Argument.* Ann Arbor: University of Michigan Press. 199p.

Chambers, A. B. "Christmas: The Liturgy of the Church and the English Verse of the Renaissance," in *Literary Monographs,* vol. 6, edited by Eric Rothstein and Joseph Anthony Wittreich, Jr., 109–53. Madison: University of Wisconsin Press.

———. "Herrick and the Trans-shifting of Time." *SP* 72:85–114.

Davies, Horton. *Worship and Theology in England: From Andrewes to Baxter and Fox, 1603–1690.* (Worship and Theology in England, vol. 2.) Princeton: Princeton University Press. xxiii, 592p.

Ferrari, Ferruccio. *La poesia religiosa inglese del seicento.* (Biblioteca di cultura contemporanea, 115.) Messina and Florence: Casa editrice G. D'Anna. 202p.

Galdon, Joseph A. *Typology and Seventeenth-Century Literature.* (De proprietatibus litterarum, edited by C. H. Van Schooneveld, Series Maior, 28.) The Hague and Paris: Mouton. 164p.

Lewalski, Barbara Kiefer. "Typology and Poetry: A Consideration of Herbert, Vaughan, and Marvell," in *Illustrious Evidence: Approaches to English Literature of the Early Seventeenth Century,* edited, with an introduction by Earl Miner, 41–69. Berkeley and Los Angeles: University of California Press.

Lottes, Wolfgang. "Henry Hawkins and *Partheneia Sacra*." *RES* 26:144–53; 271–86.

McCanles, Michael. "The Dialectical Structure of the Metaphysical Lyric: Donne, Herbert, Marvell," in *Dialectical Criticism and Renaissance Literature*, 54–117. Berkeley and Los Angeles: University of California Press.

McLaughlin, Elizabeth, and Gail Thomas. "Communion in *The Temple*." *SEL* 15:111–24.

Nestrick, William. "George Herbert: The Giver and the Gift." *Ploughshares* 2, n. 4: 187–205.

Scallon, Joseph D. *The Poetry of Robert Southwell, S. J.* (Salzburg Studies in English Literature, Elizabethan & Renaissance Studies, edited by James Hogg, no. 11.) Salzburg: Institut für Anglistik und Amerikanistik, Universität Salzburg. xiv, 235p.

Summers, Claude J., and Ted-Larry Pebworth. "Vaughan's Temple in Nature and the Context of 'Regeneration.'" *JEGP* 74:351–60. (Reprinted in *Essential Articles for the Study of Henry Vaughan*, edited by Alan Rudrum [1987], 215–25.)

Vendler, Helen. *The Poetry of George Herbert*. Cambridge, Mass.: Harvard University Press. 303p.

Wanamaker, Melissa C. *Discordia Concors: The Wit of Metaphysical Poetry*. (National University Publications: Literary Criticism Series, gen. ed. John E. Becker.) Port Washington, N.Y.: Kennikat Press. x, 166p.

1976

Asals, Heather. "King Solomon in the Land of the *Hesperides*." *TSLL* 18:362–80.

Fuzier, Jean. "Donne sonnettiste: Les Holy Sonnets et la tradition européene," in *De Shakespeare à T. S. Eliot: Mélanges offerts à Henri Fluchère*, edited by Marie-Jeanne Durry, Robert Ellrodt, and Marie-Thérèse Jones-Davies, 153–71. (Études anglaises, 63.) Paris: Didier.

Merrill, Thomas F. *Christian Criticism: A Study of Literary God-Talk*. Amsterdam: Rodopi N. V. 201p.

Raynaud, Claudine. "The Garden of Eden in Marvell's Poetry." *CahiersE* 10:13-32.

Selkin, Carl M. "The Language of Vision: Traherne's Cataloguing Style." *ELR* 6:92-104.

Stringer, Gary. "Donne's Religious *Personae:* A Response." *SoQ* 14:191-94. (See Helen S. Thomas below.)

Thomas, Helen S. "The Concept of the *Persona* in John Donne's Religious Poetry." *SoQ* 14:183-89. (See Gary Stringer above.)

Wall, John N., Jr. "Donne's Wit of Redemption: The Drama of Prayer in the *Holy Sonnets.*" *SP* 73:189-203.

Warren, Austin. "Herrick Revisited." *MQR* 15:245-67.

Wyly, Thomas J. "Vaughan's 'Regeneration' Reconsidered." *PQ* 55:340-53.

1977

Archer, Stanley. "The Archetypical Journey Motif in Donne's Divine Poems," in *New Essays on Donne,* edited by Gary Stringer, 173-91. (Salzburg Studies in English Literature, Elizabethan & Renaissance, edited by James Hogg, no. 57.) Salzburg: Institut für Englische Sprache und Literatur, Universität Salzburg.

Asals, Heather. "David's Successors: Forms of Joy and Art." *PPMRC* 2:31-37.

Bell, Ilona. "'Setting Foot into Divinity': George Herbert and the English Reformation." *MLQ* 38:219-41. (Reprinted in *Essential Articles for the Study of the Poetry of George Herbert's Poetry,* edited by John R. Roberts [1979], 63-83.)

Brunner, Larry. "Herbert's 'Affliction' (I) and 'The Flower': Studies in the Theme of Christian Refinement." *C&L* 26, no. 3:18-28.

Chambers, A. B. "*La Corona:* Philosophic, Sacred, and Poetic Uses of Time," in *New Essays on Donne,* edited by Gary Stringer, 140-72. (Salzburg Studies in English Literature, Elizabethan & Renaissance, edited by James Hogg, no. 57.) Salzburg: Institut für Englische Sprache und Literatur, Universität Salzburg.

Charles, Amy. *A Life of George Herbert.* Ithaca: Cornell University Press. 242p.

El-Gabalawy, Saad. "George Herbert and the Emblem Books." *EM* 26:173–84.

Fabry, Frank J. "Crashaw's 'On the Wounds of our Crucified Lord.'" *CP* 10, no. 1: 51–58.

Gallagher, Philip J. "George Herbert's 'The Forerunners.'" *ELN* 15:14–18.

Harnack, Andrew. "Robert Southwell's 'The Burning Babe' and the Typology of Christmastide." *KPAB* 4:25–30.

King, Bruce. *Marvell's Allegorical Poetry.* Cambridge, England: Oleander Press. 208p.

Lewalski, Barbara Kiefer. "Typological Symbolism and the 'Progress of the Soul,' in Seventeenth-Century Literature," in *Literary Uses of Typology from the Late Middle Ages to the Present*, edited by Earl Miner, 79–114. Princeton: Princeton University Press.

Marcus, Leah Sinanoglou. "Herrick's *Noble Numbers* and the Politics of Playfulness." *ELR* 7:108–26.

Patterson, Annabel. "*Bermudas* and *The Coronet*: Marvell's Protestant Poetics." *ELH* 44:478–99.

Pequigney, Joseph. "Marvell's 'Soul' Poetry," in *Tercentenary Essays in Honor of Andrew Marvell*, edited by Kenneth Friedenreich, 76–104. Hamden, Conn.: Archon Books.

Smalling, Michael. "Donne's Medieval Aesthetics and His Use of Morally Distant *Personae:* Two Questions, One Answer," in *New Essays on Donne*, edited by Gary Stringer, 74–109. (Salzburg Studies in English Literature, Elizabethan & Renaissance, edited by James Hogg, no. 57.) Salzburg: Institut für Englische Sprache und Literatur, Universität Salzburg.

Sobosan, Jeffrey G. "Call and Response—The Vision of God in John Donne and George Herbert." *Religious Studies* 13:395–407.

1978

Bloomer, Peggy Ann. "A Re-examination of Donne's 'La Corona.'" *EAS* 7:37–44.

Cain, T. G. S. "'*Times trans-shifting*': Herrick in Meditation," in *"Trust to Good Verses": Herrick Tercentenary Essays*, edited by Roger B. Rollin and J. Max Patrick, 103–23. Pittsburgh: University of Pittsburgh Press. vi, 291p.

Charles, Amy. "Touching David's Harp: George Herbert and Ralph Knevet." *GHJ* 2, no. 1: 54–69.

Corthell, Ronald J. "Joseph Hall and Protestant Meditation." *TSLL* 20:367–85.

Delany, Veronica. General introduction to *The Poems of Patrick Cary, with Biographical and Critical Introduction*, edited by Sister Veronica Delany, xiii-lxxxi. Oxford: Clarendon Press.

Ellrodt, Robert. "Marvell's Mind and Mystery," in *Approaches to Marvell: The York Tercentenary Lectures*, edited by C. A. Patrides, 216–33. London, Henley, and Boston: Routledge & Kegan Paul.

Fish, Stanley E. *The Living Temple: George Herbert and Catechizing*. Berkeley and Los Angeles: University of California Press. ix, 201p.

Friedenreich, Kenneth. *Henry Vaughan*. (Twayne English Authors Series, 226, edited by Sylvia E. Bowman.) Boston: Twayne Publishers. 180p.

Gilman, Ernest B. "The Pauline Perspective in Donne, Herbert, and Greville," in *The Curious Perspective: Literary and Pictorial Wit in the Seventeenth Century*, 167–203. New Haven: Yale University Press.

Labriola, Albert C. "Herbert, Crashaw, and the *Schola Cordis* Tradition." *GHJ* 2, no. 1: 13–23.

Leigh, David J. "Donne's 'A Hymne to God the Father': New Dimensions." *SP* 75:84–92.

Lewalski, Barbara Kiefer. "Emblems and the Religious Lyric: George Herbert and Protestant Emblematics." *HUSL* 6:32–56.

———. "Marvell as Religious Poet," in *Approaches to Marvell: The York Tercentenary Lectures*, edited by C. A. Patrides, 251–79. London, Henley, and Boston: Routledge & Kegan Paul.

Low, Anthony. *Love's Architecture: Devotional Modes in Seventeenth-Century English Poetry*. (The Gotham Library Series.) New York: New York University Press. xix, 307p.

———. "Metaphysical Poets and Devotional Poets," in *George Herbert and the Seventeenth-Century Religious Poets: Authoritative Texts/Criticism*, edited by Mario A. Di Cesare, 221–32. (A Norton Critical Edition.) New York: W. W. Norton.

Marcus, Leah Sinanoglou. *Childhood and Cultural Despair: A Theme and Variations in Seventeenth-Century Literature*. Pittsburgh: University of Pittsburgh Press. xii, 305p.

Mollenkott, Virginia Ramey. "Herrick and the Cleansing of Perception," in *"Trust to Good Verses": Herrick Tercentenary Essays*, edited by Roger B. Rollin and J. Max Patrick, 197–209. Pittsburgh: University of Pittsburgh Press. vi, 291p.

Nania, John, and P. J. Klemp. "John Donne's *La Corona:* A Second Structure." *Ren&R* n.s. 2: 49–54.

Oram, William. "Herrick's Use of Sacred Materials," in *"Trust to Good Verses": Herrick Tercentenary Essays*, edited by Roger B. Rollin and J. Max Patrick, 211–18. Pittsburgh: University of Pittsburgh Press. vi, 291p.

Strier, Richard. "Changing the Object: Herbert and Excess." *GHJ* 2, no 1: 24–37.

Summers, Claude J. "Herrick's Political Poetry: The Strategies of His Art," in *"Trust to Good Verses": Herrick Tercentenary Essays*, edited by Roger B. Rollin and J. Max Patrick, 171–83. Pittsburgh: University of Pittsburgh Press. vi, 291p.

Summers, Joseph H. "From 'Josephs coat' to 'A true Hymne.'" *GHJ* 2, no. 1: 1–12.

1979

Asals, Heather A. R. "Crashaw's Participles and the 'Chiaroscuro' of Ontological Language," in *Essays on Richard Crashaw*, edited by Robert M. Cooper, 35–49. (Salzburg Studies in English Literature, Elizabethan & Renaissance Studies, ed. James Hogg, no. 83.) Salzburg: Institut für Anglistik und Amerikanistik, Universität Salzburg. i, 264p.

———. "John Donne and the Grammar of Redemption." *ESC* 5:125–39.

Benet, Diana. "The Redemption of the Sun: Crashaw's Christmastide Poems," in *Essays on Richard Crashaw*, edited by Robert M. Cooper, 129–44. (Salzburg Studies in English Literature, Elizabethan & Renaissance Studies, ed. James Hogg, no. 83.) Salzburg: Institut für Anglistik und Amerikanistik, Universität Salzburg. i, 264p.

Bertonasco, Marc F. "A Jungian Reading of Crashaw's 'The Flaming Heart,'" in *Essays on Richard Crashaw*, edited by Robert M. Cooper, 224–64. (Salzburg Studies in English Literature, Elizabethan & Renaissance Studies, ed. James Hogg, no. 83.) Salzburg: Institut für Anglistik und Amerikanistik, Universität Salzburg. i, 264p.

Bienz, John. "George Herbert and the Man of Sorrows." *HSL* 11:173-84.

Booty, John E. "George Herbert: *The Temple* and *The Book of Common Prayer.*" *Mosaic* 12:75-90.

Cunnar, Eugene R. "Crashaw's Hymn 'To the Name Above Every Name': Background and Meaning," in *Essays on Richard Crashaw*, edited by Robert M. Cooper, 102-28. (Salzburg Studies in English Literature, Elizabethan & Renaissance Studies, ed. James Hogg, no. 83.) Salzburg: Institut für Anglistik und Amerikanistik, Universität Salzburg. i, 264p.

Engel, Wilson F., III. "Christ in the Winepress: Backgrounds of a Sacred Image." *GHJ* 3, nos. 1 & 2 (1979-1980): 45-63.

Grant, Patrick. "Richard Crashaw and the Capucins [sic]": Images and the Force of Belief," in *Images and Ideas in Literature of the English Renaissance*, 89-128. Amherst: University of Massachusetts Press.

Hahn, Thomas. "The Antecedents of Donne's Holy Sonnet 11." *ABR* 30:69-79.

Hilyard, Joseph P. "The Negative Wayfarers of Richard Crashaw's 'A Hymn in the Glorious Epiphanie,'" in *Essays on Richard Crashaw*, edited by Robert M. Cooper, 169-95. (Salzburg Studies in English Literature, Elizabethan & Renaissance Studies, ed. James Hogg, no. 83.) Salzburg: Institut für Anglistik und Amerikanistik, Universität Salzburg. i, 264p.

Labriola, Albert C. "Richard Crashaw's *Schola Cordis* Poetry," in *Essays on Richard Crashaw*, edited by Robert M. Cooper, 1-13. (Salzburg Studies in English Literature, Elizabethan & Renaissance Studies, ed. James Hogg, no. 83.) Salzburg: Institut für Anglistik und Amerikanistik, Universität Salzburg. i, 264p.

Lewalski, Barbara Kiefer. *Protestant Poetics and the Seventeenth-Century Religious Lyric.* Princeton: Princeton University Press. xiv, 536p.

Miller, Edmund. *Drudgerie Divine: The Rhetoric of God and Man in George Herbert.* (Salzburg Studies in English Literature, Elizabethan & Renaissance Studies, edited by James Hogg, no. 84.) Salzburg: Institut für Anglistik und Amerikanistik, Universität Salzburg. x, 250p.

———. "Sensual Imagery in the Devotional Poetry of Robert Herrick." *C&L* 28:24-33.

Ottenhoff, John H. "Herbert's Sonnets." *GHJ* 2, no. 2: 1–14.
Pollock, John J. "A Mystical Impulse in Donne's Devotional Poetry." *SMy* 2:17–24.
Sherwood, Terry G. "Conversion Psychology in John Donne's Good Friday Poem." *HTR* 72:101–22.
Stanwood, P. G. "Time and Liturgy in Donne, Crashaw, and T. S. Eliot." *Mosaic* 12:91–105.
Steanson, Karen E. Introduction to *Henry Colman: Divine Meditations (1640)*, edited with Introduction and Commentary by Karen E. Steanson, 3–52. (The Elizabethan Club Series, 6.) New Haven: Yale University Press.
Strier, Richard. "Herbert and Tears." *ELH* 46:221–47.
———. "'To All Angels and Saints': Herbert's Puritan Poem." *MP* 77:132–45.
Summers, Claude J., and Ted-Larry Pebworth. "Herbert, Vaughan, and Public Concerns in Private Modes." *GHJ* 3, nos. 1 & 2 (1979–1980): 1–21.
Todd, Richard. "The Passion Poems of George Herbert," in *From Caxton to Beckett: Essays Presented to W. H. Toppen on the Occasion of His Seventieth Birthday*, edited by Jacques B. H. Alblas and Richard Todd, with a foreword by A. J. Fry, 31–59. (*Costerus* n.s. 23.) Amsterdam: Rodopi.

1980

Bell, Ilona. "The Double Pleasures of Herbert's 'Collar,'" in *"Too Rich to Clothe the Sunne": Essays on George Herbert*, edited by Claude J. Summers and Ted-Larry Pebworth, 77–88. Pittsburgh: University of Pittsburgh Press. xvi, 260p.
Boulger, James D. *The Calvinist Temper in English Poetry*. (De proprietatibus litterarum, Series Maior 21, edited by C. H. van Schooneveld.) The Hague, Paris, New York: Mouton Publishers. xii, 498p.
Crane, David. "Catholicism and Rhetoric in Southwell, Crashaw, Dryden, and Pope." *Recusant History* 15:239–58.
Di Cesare, Mario A. "Herbert's 'Prayer (I)' and the Gospel of John," in *"Too Rich to Clothe the Sunne": Essays on George Herbert*, edited by

Claude J. Summers and Ted-Larry Pebworth, 101–12. Pittsburgh: University of Pittsburgh Press. xvi, 260p.

Dubinski, R. R. "Donne's 'La Corona' and Christ's Mediatorial Office." *Ren&R* n.s. 4: 203–08.

Edgecombe, Rodney. *"Sweetnesse readie penn'd": Imagery, Syntax and Metrics in the Poetry of George Herbert.* (Salzburg Studies in English Literature, Elizabethan and Renaissance Studies, edited by James Hogg, 84:2.) Salzburg: Institut für Anglistik und Amerikanistik, Universität Salzburg. iii, 180p.

Ellrodt, Robert. "Angels and the Poetic Imagination from Donne to Traherne," In *English Renaissance Studies Presented to Dame Helen Gardner in Honour of her Seventieth Birthday*, edited by John Carey, 164–79. Oxford: Clarendon Press.

Elsky, Martin. "History, Liturgy, and Point of View in Protestant Meditative Poetry." *SP* 77:67–83.

Fiore, Peter A. "The Nativity Theme in Late Renaissance Minor Devotional Verse." *WascanaR* 15:3–19.

Fowler, Anne C. "'With Care and Courage': Herbert's *'Affliction'* Poems," in *"Too Rich to Clothe the Sunne": Essays on George Herbert*, edited by Claude J. Summers and Ted-Larry Pebworth, 129–45. Pittsburgh: University of Pittsburgh Press. xvi, 260p.

Guibbory, Achsah. "John Donne and Memory as 'the Art of *Salvation.*'" *HLQ* 43:261–74.

Hageman, Elizabeth H. "Calendrical Symbolism and the Unity of Crashaw's *Carmen Deo Nostro.*" *SP* 77:161–79.

Hermann, John P. "Herbert's 'Superliminare' and the Tradition of Warning in Mystical Literature." *GHJ* 4, no. 1: 1–10.

Hinman, Robert B. "The 'Verser' at *The Temple* Door: Herbert's 'The Church-porch,'" in *"Too Rich to Clothe the Sunne": Essays on George Herbert*, edited by Claude J. Summers and Ted-Larry Pebworth, 55–75. Pittsburgh: University of Pittsburgh Press. xvi, 260p.

Malpezzi, Frances M. "Christian Poetics in Donne's 'Upon the Translation of the Psalmes.'" *Renascence* 33:221–28.

———. "Thy Cross, My Bower: The Greening of the Heart," in *"Too Rich to Clothe the Sunne": Essays on George Herbert*, edited by Claude J. Summers and Ted-Larry Pebworth, 89–100. Pittsburgh: University of Pittsburgh Press. xvi, 260p.

Marcus, Leah Sinanoglou. "George Herbert and the Anglican Plain

Style," in *"Too Rich to Clothe the Sunne": Essays on George Herbert,* edited by Claude J. Summers and Ted-Larry Pebworth, 179–93. Pittsburgh: University of Pittsburgh Press. xvi, 260p.

Mulder, John R. "*The Temple* as Picture," in *"Too Rich to Clothe the Sunne": Essays on George Herbert,* edited by Claude J. Summers and Ted-Larry Pebworth, 3–14. Pittsburgh: University of Pittsburgh Press. xvi, 260p.

Nardo, Anna K. "Play, Literary Criticism, and the Poetry of George Herbert," in *Play and Culture,* edited by Helen B. Schwartsman, 30–38. West Point, N.Y.: Leisure Press.

Nestrick, William V. "'Mine and Thine' in *The Temple*," in *"Too Rich to Clothe the Sunne": Essays on George Herbert,* edited by Claude J. Summers and Ted-Larry Pebworth, 115–27. Pittsburgh: University of Pittsburgh Press. xvi, 260p.

Nuttall, A. D. *Overheard by God: Fiction and Prayer in Herbert, Milton, Dante, and St. John.* London and New York: Methuen. x, 147p.

Osmond, Rosalie E. "George Herbert: Richness in Austerity." *ESC* 6:133–44.

Parrish, Paul A. *Richard Crashaw.* (Twayne's English Author Series, no. 229, ed. Arthur Kinney.) Boston: Twayne Publishers, A Division of G. K. Hall. 189p.

Rollin, Roger B. "Self-Created Artifact: The Speaker and the Reader in *The Temple*," in *"Too Rich to Clothe the Sunne": Essays on George Herbert,* edited by Claude J. Summers and Ted-Larry Pebworth, 147–61. Pittsburgh: University of Pittsburgh Press. xvi, 260p.

Rubey, Daniel. "The Poet and the Christian Community: Herbert's Affliction Poems and the Structure of *The Temple*." *SEL* 20: 105–23.

Severance, Sibyl Lutz. "Numerological Structures in *The Temple*," in *"Too Rich to Clothe the Sunne": Essays on George Herbert,* edited by Claude J. Summers and Ted-Larry Pebworth, 229–49. Pittsburgh: University of Pittsburgh Press. xvi, 260p.

Stanwood, P. G. "Seventeenth-Century English Literature and Contemporary Criticism." *Anglican Theological Review* 62:395–410.

Strier, Richard. "Ironic Humanism in *The Temple*," in *"Too Rich to Clothe the Sunne": Essays on George Herbert,* edited by Claude J. Summers and Ted-Larry Pebworth, 33–52. Pittsburgh: University of Pittsburgh Press. xvi, 260p.

1981

Asals, Heather. *Equivocal Predication: George Herbert's Way to God.* Toronto, Buffalo, London: University of Toronto Press. xii, 145p.

Bond, Ronald B. "John Donne and the Problem of 'Knowing Faith.'" *Mosaic* 14:25–35.

Calhoun, Thomas O. *Henry Vaughan: The Achievement of* Silex Scintillans. Newark: University of Delaware Press; London and Toronto: Associated University Presses. 265p.

Carey, John. *John Donne: Life, Mind and Art.* London: Faber and Faber; New York: Oxford University Press. 303p. (Paperback edition, 1983.)

Kronenfeld, Judy Z. "Herbert's 'A Wreath' and Devotional Aesthetics: Imperfect Efforts Redeemed by Grace." *ELH* 48:290–309.

Malpezzi, Frances M. "The Feast of the Circumcision: The Return to Sacred Time in Herrick's *Noble Numbers.*" *NDEJ* 14:29–40.

Merrill, Thomas F. "Sacred Parody and the Grammar of Devotion." *Criticism* 23:195–210.

O'Connell, Patrick F. "The Successive Arrangements of Donne's 'Holy Sonnets.'" *PQ* 60:323–42.

Rudrum, Alan. *Henry Vaughan.* (Writers of Wales.) [Cardiff]: University of Wales Press on behalf of the Welsh Arts Council. 135p.

Seelig, Sharon Cadman. *The Shadow of Eternity: Belief and Structure in Herbert, Vaughan, and Traherne.* Lexington: University Press of Kentucky. 194p.

Shaw, Robert B. *The Call of God: The Theme of Vocation in the Poetry of Donne and Herbert.* Cambridge, Mass.: Cowley Publications. xiii, 123p.

Slights, Camille Wells. *The Casuistical Tradition in Shakespeare, Donne, Herbert, and Milton.* Princeton: Princeton University Press. xix, 307p.

Sloane, Mary Cole. *The Visual in Metaphysical Poetry.* Atlantic Highlands, N.J.: Humanities Press. 110p.

Stachniewski, John. "John Donne: The Despair of the 'Holy Sonnets.'" *ELH* 48:677–705.

Stanwood, P. G. "Time and Liturgy in Herbert's Poetry." *GHJ* 5, nos. 1 & 2 (1981–1982): 19–30.

Strier, Richard. "George Herbert and the World." *JMRS* 11:211–36.

Wengen-Shute, Rosemary Margaret Van. *George Herbert and the Liturgy of the Church of England.* Oegstgeest: Drukkerij de Kempenaer. 183p.

Woods, Susanne. "The 'Unhewn Stones' of Herbert's Verse." *GHJ* 4, no. 2: 30–46.

Yarrow, Ralph. "Admitting the Infinite: John Donne's Poem 'Batter My Heart.'" *SMlit* 1:210–17.

1982

Bell, Ilona. "Circular Strategies and Structures in Jonson and Herbert," in *Classic and Cavalier: Essays on Jonson and the Sons of Ben*, edited by Claude J. Summers and Ted-Larry Pebworth, 157–70. Pittsburgh: University of Pittsburgh Press.

Bennett, J. A. W. "Donne, Herbert, Herrick," in *Poetry of the Passion: Studies in Twelve Centuries of English Verse*, 145–67. Oxford: Clarendon Press; New York: Oxford University Press.

Boenig, Robert. "George Herbert & Mysticism." *SMy* 5:64–72.

Booty, John E. "Contrition in Anglican Spirituality: Hooker, Donne, and Herbert," in *Anglican Spirituality*, edited by William J. Wolf, 25–48. Wilton, Conn.: Morehouse-Barlow.

Clark, Ira. *Christ Revealed: The History of the Neotypological Lyric in the English Renaissance.* (University of Florida Monographs, Humanities, no. 51.) Gainesville: University Presses of Florida. xiv, 221p.

Cooper, Robert M. *An Essay on the Art of Richard Crashaw.* (Salzburg Studies in English Literature, Elizabethan & Renaissance Studies, edited by James Hogg, no. 102.) Salzburg: Institut für Anglistik und Amerikanistik, Universität Salzburg. iv, 96p.

Day, Malcolm M. *Thomas Traherne.* (Twayne's English Authors Series, ed. Arthur F. Kinney, no. 342.) Boston: Twayne Publishers. 176p.

Dreher, Diane Elizabeth. *The Fourfold Pilgrimage: The Estates of Innocence, Misery, Grace, and Glory in Seventeenth-Century Literature.* Washington, D. C.: University Press of America. x, 165p.

Evans, Gillian R. "John Donne and the Augustinian Paradox of Sin." *RES* 33:1–22.

Harman, Barbara Leah. *Costly Monuments: Representations of the Self in George Herbert's Poetry.* Cambridge, Mass.: Harvard University Press. x, 225p.

Malpezzi, Frances M. "Herbert's 'The Thanksgiving' in Context." *Renascence* 34:185–95.

Manley, Frank. "Toward a Definition of Plain Style in the Poetry of George Herbert," in *Poetic Traditions of the English Renaissance*, edited by Maynard Mack and George deForest Lord, 203–17. New Haven: Yale University Press.

Martz, Louis L. "Meditation as Poetic Strategy." *MP* 80:168–74.

Maurer, Margaret. "The Circular Argument of Donne's 'La Corona.'" *SEL* 22:51–68.

Post, Jonathan F. S. *Henry Vaughan: The Unfolding Vision.* Princeton: Princeton University Press. xxii, 243p.

Robertson, Jean. "Robert Southwell's 'New heaven, new warre.'" *HLQ* 45:82–83.

Rudnytsky, Peter L. "'The Sight of God': Donne's Poetics of Transcendence." *TSLL* 24:185–207.

Sherwood, Terry G. "Tasting and Telling Sweetness in George Herbert's Poetry." *ELR* 12:319–40.

Spinrad, Phoebe S. "Death, Loss, and Marvell's Nymph." *PMLA* 97:50–59.

Stull, William L. "Sacred Sonnets in Three Styles." *SP* 79:78–99.

Takano, Miyo. "'Saint Peters Complaint' in the Genre of Complaint," in *Poetry and Drama in the Age of Shakespeare: Essays in Honour of Professor Shonosuke Ishii's Seventieth Birthday*, edited by Peter Milward and Tetsuo Anzai, 61–71. (RenM 9.) Tokyo: Renaissance Institute, Sophia University, 1982. xviii, 226p.

Tatsumi, Toyohiko. "Southwell's 'Saint Peters Complaint' as Poetry for Martyrdom," in *Poetry and Drama in the Age of Shakespeare: Essays in Honour of Professor Shonosuke Ishii's Seventieth Birthday*, edited by Peter Milward and Tetsuo Anzai, 42–60. (RenM 9.) Tokyo: Renaissance Institute, Sophia University, 1982. xviii, 226p.

Yearwood, Stephenie. "Donne's *Holy Sonnets:* The Theology of Conversion." *TSLL* 24:208–21.

Young, R. V., Jr. *Richard Crashaw and the Spanish Golden Age.* (Yale Studies in English, no. 191.) New Haven: Yale University Press. x, 204p.

1983

Berry, Boyd M. "Childhood and Self in *Silex Scintillans*." Special Issue on Henry Vaughan. *GHJ* 7, nos. 1 & 2 (1983–1984), 73–90.

Chernaik, Warren L. *The Poet's Time: Politics and Religion in the Work of Andrew Marvell*. Cambridge, New York, New Rochelle, Melbourne, and Sydney: Cambridge University Press. x, 249p.

Davis, Walter R. "The Meditative Hymnody of Richard Crashaw." *ELH* 50:107–29.

Dimler, G. Richard. "The Jesuit Emblem Book in 17th Century Protestant England." *Archivum Historicum Societatis Iesu* 53:357–69.

Doherty, Mary Jane. "*Flores Solitudinis:* The 'Two Ways' and Vaughan's Patristic Hagiography." Special Issue on Henry Vaughan. *GHJ* 7, nos. 1 & 2 (1983–1984), 25–50.

Elsky, Martin. "George Herbert's Pattern Poems and the Materiality of Language: A New Approach to Renaissance Hieroglyphics." *ELH* 50:245–60.

———. "John Donne's *La Corona:* Spatiality and Mannerist Painting." *MLS* 13:3–11.

Fischer, Sandra K. "Crashaw, St. Teresa, and the Icon of Mystical Ravishment." *JEP* 4, nos. 3–4: 182–95.

Fischler, Alan. "Herrick's Holy Hedonism." *MLS* 13:12–20.

Halley, Janet E. "Versions of the Self and the Politics of Privacy in *Silex Scintillans*." Special Issue on Henry Vaughan. *GHJ* 7, nos. 1 & 2 (1983–1984), 51–71.

Houston, John Porter. "Devotional Poetry: A Confluence of Styles," in *The Rhetoric of Poetry in the Renaissance and Seventeenth Century*, 160–201. Baton Rouge: Louisiana State University Press.

Johnson, Jeff S. "Images of Christ in Vaughan's 'The Night': An Argument for Unity." Special Issue on Henry Vaughan. *GHJ* 7, nos. 1 & 2 (1983–1984), 99–108.

Kedra-Kardela, Anna. "The Function of Symbols in Henry Vaughan's *Regeneration*." *KN* 30:167–76.

Klause, John. *The Unfortunate Fall: Theodicy and the Moral Imagination of Andrew Marvell*. Hamden, Conn.: Archon Books. x, 208p.

Klawitter, George. "Craft and Purpose in Alabaster's Incarnation Sonnets." *HSL* 15–16 (1983–1984): 60–66.

Kronenfeld, Judy Z. "Probing the Relation between Poetry and Ideology: Herbert's 'The Windows.'" *JDJ* 2, no. 1: 55–80.

Oliveira e Silva, J. de. "'Plainness and Truth': The Secular and Spiritual Sonnets of Henry Constable." *HSL* 15–16 (1983–1984): 33–42.

Ottenhoff, John H. "The Shadow and the Real: Typology and the Religious Sonnet." *HSL* 15–16 (1983–1984): 43–59.

Pearlman, E. "George Herbert's God." *ELR* 13:88–112.

Raspa, Anthony. *The Emotive Image: Jesuit Poetics in the English Renaissance.* Fort Worth: Texas Christian University Press. x, 173p.

Schoenfeldt, Michael C. "Submission and Assertion: The 'Double Motion' of Herbert's 'Dedication.'" *JDJ* 2, no. 2: 39–49.

Sellin, Paul R. *John Donne and "Calvinist" Views of Grace.* Amsterdam: VU Boekhandel/Uitgeverij. 61p.

Severance, Sibyl Lutz. "'To Shine in Union': Measure, Number, and Harmony in Ben Jonson's *'Poems* of Devotion.'" *SP* 80:183–99.

Sinfield, Alan. *Literature in Protestant England 1560–1660.* London and Canberra: Croom Helm; Totowa, N.J.: Barnes and Noble. viii, 160p.

Strier, Richard. *Love Known: Theology and Experience in George Herbert's Poetry.* Chicago: University of Chicago Press. xxi, 277p.

Stull, William L. "Sonnets Courtly and Christian." *HSL* 15–16 (1983–1984): 1–15.

Wilcher, Robert. "'Then keep the ancient way!': A Study of Henry Vaughan's *Silex Scintillans.*" *DUJ* 76:11–24.

Yearwood, Stephenie. "The Rhetoric of Form in *The Temple.*" *SEL* 23:131–44.

1984

Baumgaertner, Jill. "'Harmony'in Donne's 'La Corona' and 'Upon the Translation of the Psalms.'" *JDJ* 3:141–56.

Bell, Ilona. "Revision and Revelation in Herbert's 'Affliction (I).'" *JDJ* 3:73–96.

Benet, Diana. *Secretary of Praise: The Poetic Vocation of George Herbert.* Columbia: University of Missouri Press. 207p.

Blakemore, Steven. "The Name Made Flesh: Crashaw's Celebration of 'The Name above Every Name.'" *CP* 17:63–77.

Booty, John E. "Joseph Hall, *The Arte of Divine Meditation,* and Anglican Spirituality," in *The Roots of the Modern Christian Tradition,* edited by E. Rozanne Elder, with an introduction by Jean LeClercq, 200–228. (The Spirituality of Western Christendom, 2.) Kalamazoo, Mich.: Cistercian Publications.

Dickson, Donald R. "Vaughan's 'The Water-fall' and Protestant Meditation." *EIRC* 10:28–40.

Doerksen, Daniel W. "Recharting the *Via Media* of Spenser and Herbert." *Ren&R* n.s. 8: 215–25.

Duncan, Joseph E. "Donne's 'Hymne to God my God, in my sicknesse' and Iconographic Tradition." *JDJ* 3:157–80.

Elsky, Martin. "The Sacramental Frame of George Herbert's 'The Church' and the Shape of Spiritual Autobiography." *JEGP* 83: 313–29.

Ford, Brewster. "George Herbert and Liturgies of Time and Space." *SoAR* 49:19–29.

Linden, Stanton J. "Alchemy and Eschatology in Seventeenth-Century Poetry." *Ambix* 31:102–24.

Linville, Susan E. "Contrary Faith: Poetic Closure and the Devotional Lyric." *PLL* 20:141–53.

———. "Enjambment and the Dialectics of Line Form in Donne's *Holy Sonnets*." *Style* 18:64–82.

Shaw, Robert B. "George Herbert: The Word of God and the Words of Man," in *Ineffability: Naming the Unnamable from Dante to Beckett*, edited by Peter S. Hawkins and Anne Howland Schotter, 81–93. (AMS Ars Poetica, no. 2.) New York: AMS Press.

Sherwood, Terry G. *Fulfilling the Circle: A Study of John Donne's Thought.* Toronto, Buffalo, London: University of Toronto Press. 231p.

Sledge, Linda Ching. "Typology and the Ineffable: Henry Vaughan and the 'Word in Characters,'" in *Ineffability: Naming the Unnamable from Dante to Beckett*, edited by Peter S. Hawkins and Anne Howland Schotter, 95–108. (AMS Ars Poetica, no. 2.) New York: AMS Press.

Smith, Julia J. "Donne and the Crucifixion." *MLR* 79:513–25.

Summers, Claude J., and Ted-Larry Pebworth. "The Politics of *The Temple*: 'The British Church' and 'The Familie.'" *GHJ* 8, no. 1: 1–15.

Wilcox, Helen. "'Heaven's Lidger Here': Herbert's *Temple* and Seventeenth-Century Devotion," in *Images of Belief in Literature*, edited by David Jasper, 153–68. New York: St. Martin's Press.

Young, R. V., Jr. "Christopher Dawson and Baroque Culture: An Approach to Seventeenth-Century Religious Poetry," in *The Dynamic Character of Christian Culture: Essays on Dawsonian Themes*, edited by Peter J. Cataldo, 127–58. Lanham, Md.: University Press of America.

1985

Bloch, Chana. *Spelling the Word: George Herbert and the Bible.* Berkeley and Los Angeles: University of California Press. 324p.

Cunnar, Eugene R. "Crashaw's *Bulla:* A Baroque and Paradoxical Mirror Image of Religious Poetics." *JMRS* 15:183–210.

DeNeef, A. Leigh, and Diane Gerler. "The Grammar of Herbert's Calling." *RenP:* 51–59.

Goldberg, Jonathan. "Herbert's 'Decay' and the Articulation of History." *SoRA* 18:3–21.

Gottlieb, Sidney. "Herbert's Case of 'Conscience': Public or Private Poem?" *SEL* 25:109–26.

Hannay, Margaret Patterson, ed. *Silent But for the Word: Tudor Women as Patrons, Translators, and Writers of Religious Works.* Kent: The Kent State University Press. 304p.

Hovey, Kenneth Alan. "'Divinitie and Poesie, Met': The Baconian Context of George Herbert's Divinity." *ELN* 22, no. 3: 30–39.

Idol, John L., Jr. "'The Collar': A Case History of Logotherapy." *ReAL* 12, no. 1: 19–28.

Johnson, Bruce A. "Penitential Voices in Herbert's Poetry." *GHJ* 8, no. 2: 1–17.

Jordan, Richard Douglas. "Thomas Traherne and the Art of Meditation." *JHI* 46:381–403.

Kerrigan, William. "Ritual Man: On the Outside of Herbert's Poetry." *Psychiatry* 48, no. 1: 68–82.

Malpezzi, Frances M. "The Withered Garden in Herbert's 'Grace.'" *JDJ* 4:35–47.

Mann, Lindsay A. "Sacred and Profane Love in Donne." *DR* 65 (1985–1986): 534–50.

Martz, Louis L. "English Religious Poetry, From Renaissance to Baroque." *EIRC* 11:1–28.

Mortimer, Anthony. "Words in the Mouth of God: Augustinian Language-Theory and the Poetics of George Herbert," in *On Poetry and Poetics,* edited by Richard Waswo, 31–43. Zurich: Swiss Association of University Teachers of English.

O'Connell, Patrick F. "'Restore Thine Image': Structure and Theme in Donne's 'Goodfriday.'" *JDJ* 4:13–28.

Parry, Graham. *Seventeenth-Century Poetry: The Social Context.* London: Hutchinson. 256p.

Sabine, Maureen. "Crashaw and the Feminine Animus: Patterns of Self-Sacrifice in Two of His Devotional Poems." *JDJ* 4:69–94.

Summers, Claude J. "Herrick's Political Counterplots." *SEL* 25:165–82.

Swaim, Kathleen M. "Herbert's 'Paradise.'" *GHJ* 8, no. 2: 19–31.

Veith, Gene Edward, Jr. *Reformation Spirituality: The Religion of George Herbert.* Lewisburg, Pa.: Bucknell University Press. 289p.

1986

Aycock, Roy E. "George Herbert: Poetry as Definition." *Lang&S* 19:3–10.

Bienz, John. "Images and Ceremonial in *The Temple:* Herbert's Solution to a Reformation Controversy." *SEL* 26:73–95.

Bonnell, William. "The Eucharistic Substance of George Herbert's 'Prayer' (I)." *GHJ* 9, no. 2: 35–47.

Cook, Elizabeth. "Figured Poetry" and "George Herbert," in *Seeing Through Words: The Scope of Late Renaissance Poetry,* 21–47; 48–71. New Haven: Yale University Press.

Diehl, Huston. "Graven Images: Protestant Emblem Books in England." *RenQ* 39:49–66.

———. "Into the Maze of Self: The Protestant Transformation of the Image of the Labyrinth." *JMRS* 16:281–301.

Dubinski, R. R. "Donne's Holy Sonnets and the Seven Penitential Psalms." *Ren&R* n.s. 10:201–16.

Fabry, Frank. "Richard Crashaw and the Art of Allusion: Pastoral in 'A Hymn to . . . Sainte Teresa.'" *ELR* 16:373–82.

Gilman, Ernest B. *Iconoclasm and Poetry in the English Reformation: Down Went Dagon.* Chicago: University of Chicago Press. xi, 227p.

Glaser, Joe. "'Goodfriday, 1613': A Soul's Form." *CollL* 13:168–76.

Goldberg, Jonathan. *Voice Terminal Echo: Postmodernism and English Renaissance Texts.* New York: Methuen. x, 194p.

Guibbory, Achsah. "John Donne: The Idea of Decay" and "Robert Herrick: 'Repullulation' and the Cyclical Order," in *The Map of Time: Seventeenth-Century English Literature and Ideas of Pattern in History,* 69–104, 137–67. Urbana: University of Illinois Press.

Healy, Thomas F. *Richard Crashaw*. (Medieval and Renaissance Authors, vol. 8.) Leiden: E. J. Brill. [x], 161p.

Labriola, Albert C. "The Rock and the Hard Place: Biblical Typology and Herbert's 'The Altar.'" *GHJ* 10, nos. 1–2 (1986–1987): 61–69.

Marcus, Leah Sinanoglou. *The Politics of Mirth: Jonson, Herrick, Milton, Marvell and the Defense of Old Holiday Pastimes*. Chicago: University of Chicago Press. ix, 319p.

Marotti, Arthur F. *John Donne, Coterie Poet*. Madison: University of Wisconsin Press. xviii, 369p.

Martz, Louis L. "Introduction," in *George Herbert and Henry Vaughan*, edited by Louis L. Martz, xv-xxvi. (The Oxford Authors.) Oxford and New York: Oxford University Press.

Muldrow, George M. "The Forty Lines of Andrew Marvell's 'On a Drop of Dew.'" *ELN* 23:23–27.

Nardo, Anna K. "George Herbert Pulling for Prime." *SCRev* 3:28–42. (Revised and reprinted in *The Ludic Self in Seventeenth-Century English Literature* [1991], 79–104.)

———. "John Donne in Between," in *The Eagle and the Dove: Reassessing John Donne*, edited by Claude J. Summers and Ted-Larry Pebworth, 157–65. (Essays in Seventeenth-Century Literature, 1.) Columbia: University of Missouri Press. xv, 220.

O'Connell, Patrick F. "'La Corona': Donne's *Ars Poetica Sacra*," in *The Eagle and the Dove: Reassessing John Donne*, edited by Claude J. Summers and Ted-Larry Pebworth, 119–30. (Essays in Seventeenth-Century Literature, 1.) Columbia: University of Missouri Press. xv, 220.

Ponsford, Michael. "Men After God's Own Heart: The Context of Thomas Traherne's Emulation of David." *SMy* 9, no. 4: 3–11.

Rollin, Roger B. "'Fantastique Ague': The Holy Sonnets and Religious Melancholy," in *The Eagle and the Dove: Reassessing John Donne*, edited by Claude J. Summers and Ted-Larry Pebworth, 131–46. (Essays in Seventeenth-Century Literature, 1.) Columbia: University of Missouri Press. xv, 220.

Roston, Murray. "Herbert and Mannerism." *JDJ* 5:133–67.

Stanwood, P. G., and Heather Ross Asals, eds. *John Donne and the Theology of Language*. Columbia: University of Missouri Press. viii, 376p.

Stewart, Stanley. *George Herbert*. (Twayne's English Authors Series, edited by Arthur Kinney, no. 428.) Boston: Twayne Publishers. [xviii], 182p.

Thorpe, Douglas. "'Delight into Sacrifice': Resting in Herbert's *Temple*." *SEL* 26:59–72.

Todd, Richard. *The Opacity of Signs: Acts of Interpretation in George Herbert's* The Temple. Columbia: University of Missouri Press. xii, 223p.

Watson, Graeme J. "The Temple in 'The Night': Henry Vaughan and the Collapse of the Established Church." *MP* 84:144–61.

Whitlock, Baird W. "The Sacramental Poetry of George Herbert." *SCRev* 3:37–49.

Wilcox, Helen. "'The Sweet Singer of the Temple': The Musicians' Response to Herbert." *GHJ* 10, nos. 1 & 2 (1986–1987): 47–60.

Young, R. V., Jr. "Andrew Marvell and the Devotional Tradition." *Renascence* 38:204–27.

1987

Aycock, Roy E. "George Herbert's Serious Fancy." *ABR* 38:84–94.

Bell, Ilona. "Herbert and Harvey: In the Shadow of the Temple," in *Like Season'd Timber: New Essays on George Herbert*, edited by Edmund Miller and Robert DiYanni, 255–79. (Seventeenth-Century Texts and Studies, 1.) New York: Peter Lang. xvi, 396p.

———. "Herbert's Valdésian Vision." *ELR* 17:303–28.

Chambers, A. B. "'Goodfriday, 1613. Riding Westward': Looking Back." *JDJ* 6:185–201.

Christensen, Philip Harlan. "The Sonnets from Walton's Life: Sonnets of the Sonne," in *Like Season'd Timber: New Essays on George Herbert*, edited by Edmund Miller and Robert DiYanni, 169–80. (Seventeenth-Century Texts and Studies, 1.) New York: Peter Lang. xvi, 396p.

Clark, James Andrew. "'The Coronet': Marvell's 'Curious Frame' of Allusion," in *"Bright Shootes of Everlastingnesse": The Seventeenth-Century Religious Lyric*, edited by Claude J. Summers and Ted-Larry Pebworth, 145–61. (Essays in Seventeenth-Century Literature, 2.) Columbia: University of Missouri Press. xv, 222p.

Cunnar, Eugene R. "Herbert and the Visual Arts: *Ut Pictura Poesis:* An

Opening in 'The Windows,'" in *Like Season'd Timber: New Essays on George Herbert*, edited by Edmund Miller and Robert DiYanni, 101–38. (Seventeenth-Century Texts and Studies, 1.) New York: Peter Lang. xvi, 396p.

Dickson, Donald R. "Between Transubstantiation and Memorialism: Herbert's Eucharistic Celebration." *GHJ* 11, no. 1: 1–14.

———. *The Fountain of Living Waters: The Typology of the Water of Life in Herbert, Vaughan, and Traherne*. Columbia: University of Missouri Press. 218p.

———. "Grace and the 'Spirits' of the Heart in *The Temple*." *JDJ* 6:55–66.

DiYanni, Robert. "Herbert and Hopkins: The Poetics of Devotion," in *Like Season'd Timber: New Essays on George Herbert*, edited by Edmund Miller and Robert DiYanni, 369–88. (Seventeenth-Century Texts and Studies, 1.) New York: Peter Lang. xvi, 396p.

Doerksen, Daniel W. "Things Fundamental or Indifferent: Adiaphorism and Herbert's Church Attitudes." *GHJ* 11, no. 1: 15–22.

Dowling, Paul M. "The *Memoriae Matris Sacrum*: The Muse Displaced: The Architecture of the *Memoriae Matris Sacrum*," in *Like Season'd Timber: New Essays on George Herbert*, edited by Edmund Miller and Robert DiYanni, 181–90. (Seventeenth-Century Texts and Studies, 1.) New York: Peter Lang. xvi, 396p.

Fraser, Russell. "George Herbert's Poetry." *SR* 95:560–85.

Fruchter, Barry. "Andrewes and Herbert: Empty Music: Andrewes in the Elegiac Verse of Herbert and Milton," in *Like Season'd Timber: New Essays on George Herbert*, edited by Edmund Miller and Robert DiYanni, 219–30. (Seventeenth-Century Texts and Studies, 1.) New York: Peter Lang. xvi, 396p.

Gaston, Paul L. "The Excluded Poems: Steps to the Temple," in *Like Season'd Timber: New Essays on George Herbert*, edited by Edmund Miller and Robert DiYanni, 151–68. (Seventeenth-Century Texts and Studies, 1.) New York: Peter Lang. xvi, 396p.

Harnack, Andrew. "Both Protestant and Catholic: George Herbert and 'To All Angels and Saints.'" *GHJ* 11, no. 1: 23–39.

Hester, M. Thomas. "Re-Signing the Text of the Self: Donne's 'As due by many titles,'" in *"Bright Shootes of Everlastingnesse": The Seventeenth-Century Religious Lyric*, edited by Claude J. Summers and Ted-Larry Pebworth, 59–71. (Essays in Seventeenth-Century Literature, 2.) Columbia: University of Missouri Press. xv, 222p.

Huttar, Charles A. "Herbert and Emblem: Herbert and Emblematic Tradition," in *Like Season'd Timber: New Essays on George Herbert,* edited by Edmund Miller and Robert DiYanni, 59–100. (Seventeenth-Century Texts and Studies, 1.) New York: Peter Lang. xvi, 396p.

Idol, John L., Jr., "Herbert and Coleridge: He Grows in My Liking," in *Like Season'd Timber: New Essays on George Herbert,* edited by Edmund Miller and Robert DiYanni, 317–28. (Seventeenth-Century Texts and Studies, 1.) New York: Peter Lang. xvi, 396p.

Jacobs, Linda L. "The Image of Mary Magdalene in Seventeenth-Century Poetry." *POMPA:* 62–78.

Johnson, Jeffrey S. "Recreating the World: Typology in Herbert's 'The Altar.'" *C&L* 37:55–65.

McKeon, Michael. "Politics of Discourses and the Rise of the Aesthetic in Seventeenth-Century England," in *Politics of Discourse: The Literature and History of Seventeenth-Century England,* edited by Kevin Sharpe and Steven N. Zwicker, 35–51. Berkeley and Los Angeles: University of California Press.

McNees, Eleanor. "John Donne and the Anglican Doctrine of the Eucharist." *TSLL* 29:94–114.

Malpezzi, Frances M. "The Weight/Lessness of Sin: Donne's 'Thou Hast Made Me' and the Psychostatic Tradition." *SCRev* 4:71–77.

Mazzaro, Jerome. "Donne and Herbert: Striking Through the Mask: Donne and Herbert at Sonnets," in *Like Season'd Timber: New Essays on George Herbert,* edited by Edmund Miller and Robert DiYanni, 241–53. (Seventeenth-Century Texts and Studies, 1.) New York: Peter Lang. xvi, 396p.

Oberhaus, Dorothy Huff. "Herbert and Emily Dickinson: A Reading of Emily Dickinson," in *Like Season'd Timber: New Essays on George Herbert,* edited by Edmund Miller and Robert DiYanni, 345–68. (Seventeenth-Century Texts and Studies, 1.) New York: Peter Lang. xvi, 396p.

Pahlka, William H. *Saint Augustine's Meter and George Herbert's Will.* Kent: Kent State University Press. xxi, 241p.

Pebworth, Ted-Larry. "The Editor, the Critic, and the Multiple Texts of Donne's 'A Hymne to God the Father.'" *SCRev* 4:16–34.

Petry, Alice Hall. "Herbert and Emerson: Emerson's Debt to Herbert," in *Like Season'd Timber: New Essays on George Herbert,* edited by Edmund Miller and Robert DiYanni, 297–315. (Seventeenth-Century Texts and Studies, 1.) New York: Peter Lang. xvi, 396p.

Pinka, Patricia G. "Timely Timelessness in Two Nativity Poems," in *"Bright Shootes of Everlastingnesse": The Seventeenth-Century Religious Lyric,* edited by Claude J. Summers and Ted-Larry Pebworth, 162–72. (Essays in Seventeenth-Century Literature, 2.) Columbia: University of Missouri Press. xv, 222p.

Pinnington, A. J. "Prayer and Praise in John Donne's *La Corona,*" in *Poetry and Faith in the English Renaissance: Essays in Honour of Professor Toyohiko Tatsumi's Seventieth Birthday,* edited by Peter Milward; introduction by Shonosuke Ishii; and postscript by Suekichi Omich, 133–42. (RenM, 13.) Tokyo: Renaissance Institute, Sophia University.

Radzinowicz, Mary Ann. "'Anima Mea': Psalms and John Donne's Religious Poetry," in *"Bright Shootes of Everlastingnesse": The Seventeenth-Century Religious Lyric,* edited by Claude J. Summers and Ted-Larry Pebworth, 40–58. (Essays in Seventeenth-Century Literature, 2.) Columbia: University of Missouri Press. xv, 222p.

Revard, Stella P. "The Seventeenth-Century Religious Ode and Its Classical Models," in *"Bright Shootes of Everlastingnesse": The Seventeenth-Century Religious Lyric,* edited by Claude J. Summers and Ted-Larry Pebworth, 173–91. (Essays in Seventeenth-Century Literature, 2.) Columbia: University of Missouri Press. xv, 222p.

Roberts, Lorraine. "Crashaw's Epiphany Hymn: Faith out of Darkness," in *"Bright Shootes of Everlastingnesse": The Seventeenth-Century Religious Lyric,* edited by Claude J. Summers and Ted-Larry Pebworth, 134–44. (Essays in Seventeenth-Century Literature, 2.) Columbia: University of Missouri Press. xv, 222p.

Roston, Murray. "The World as Anagram: The Poetry of George Herbert," in *Renaissance Perspectives in Literature and the Visual Arts,* 301–42. Princeton: Princeton University Press.

Schoenfeldt, Michael C. "Standing on Ceremony: The Comedy of Manners in Herbert's 'Love (III),'" in *"Bright Shootes of Everlastingnesse": The Seventeenth-Century Religious Lyric,* edited by Claude J. Summers and Ted-Larry Pebworth, 116–33. (Essays in Seventeenth-Century Literature, 2.) Columbia: University of Missouri Press. xv, 222p.

Sessions, William A. "Abandonment and the English Religious Lyric in the Seventeenth Century," in *"Bright Shootes of Everlastingnesse": The Seventeenth-Century Religious Lyric,* edited by Claude J. Summers and Ted-Larry Pebworth, 1–19. (Essays in Seventeenth-Century Literature, 2.) Columbia: University of Missouri Press. xv, 222p.

Severance, Sibyl Lutz. "Soul, Sphere, and Structure in 'Goodfriday, 1613: Riding Westward.'" *SP* 84:24–43.

Shields, David S. "Herbert and Colonial American Poetry," in *Like Season'd Timber: New Essays on George Herbert*, edited by Edmund Miller and Robert DiYanni, 281–96. (Seventeenth-Century Texts and Studies, 1.) New York: Peter Lang. xvi, 396p.

Shullenberger, William. "*Ars Praedicandi* in George Herbert's Poetry," in *"Bright Shootes of Everlastingnesse": The Seventeenth-Century Religious Lyric*, edited by Claude J. Summers and Ted-Larry Pebworth, 96–115. (Essays in Seventeenth-Century Literature, 2.) Columbia: University of Missouri Press. xv, 222p.

Singleton, Marion White. *God's Courtier: Configuring a Different Grace in George Herbert's* Temple. Cambridge, New York, New Rochelle, Melbourne, Sydney: Cambridge University Press. ix, 256p.

Strier, Richard. "Getting Off the Map: Response to 'George Herbert's Theology: Nearer Rome or Geneva?'" *GHJ* ll, no. 1: 41–47.

Sullivan, David M. "Riders to the West: 'Goodfriday, 1613.'" *JDJ* 6:1–8.

Summers, Claude J. "The Bride of the Apocalypse and the Quest for True Religion: Donne, Herbert, and Spenser," in *"Bright Shootes of Everlastingnesse": The Seventeenth-Century Religious Lyric*, edited by Claude J. Summers and Ted-Larry Pebworth, 72–95. (Essays in Seventeenth-Century Literature, 2.) Columbia: University of Missouri Press. xv, 222p.

Summers, Joseph H. "Herbert and Sidney: Sir Calidore and the Country Parson," in *Like Season'd Timber: New Essays on George Herbert*, edited by Edmund Miller and Robert DiYanni, 207–17. (Seventeenth-Century Texts and Studies, 1.) New York: Peter Lang. xvi, 396p.

Walker, Julia. "The Religious Lyric as Genre." *ELN* 25:39–45.

Whitney, Charles. "Bacon and Herbert: Bacon and Herbert as Moderns," in *Like Season'd Timber: New Essays on George Herbert*, edited by Edmund Miller and Robert DiYanni, 231–39. (Seventeenth-Century Texts and Studies, 1.) New York: Peter Lang. xvi, 396p.

Wilcox, Helen. "Herbert's Musical Contexts: Countrey-Aires to Angels Musick," in *Like Season'd Timber: New Essays on George Herbert*, edited by Edmund Miller and Robert DiYanni, 37–58. (Seventeenth-Century Texts and Studies, 1.) New York: Peter Lang. xvi, 396p.

Wittreich, Joseph. "'In Copious Legend, or Sweet Lyric Song': Typology and the Perils of the Religious Lyric," in *"Bright Shootes of Everlastingnesse": The Seventeenth-Century Religious Lyric*, edited by Claude J. Summers and Ted-Larry Pebworth, 192–215. (Essays in Seventeenth-Century Literature, 2.) Columbia: University of Missouri Press. xv, 222p.

Yoshida, Sachiko. "The Language of Robert Southwell's Poetry," in *Poetry and Faith in the English Renaissance: Essays in Honour of Professor Toyohiko Tatsumi's Seventieth Birthday)*, edited by Peter Milward; foreword by Shonosuke Ishii; postscript by Suekichi Omich, 37–47. (RenM 13.) Tokyo: Renaissance Institute, Sophia University.

Young, R. V., Jr. "Donne's Holy Sonnets and the Theology of Grace," in *"Bright Shootes of Everlastingnesse": The Seventeenth-Century Religious Lyric*, edited by Claude J. Summers and Ted-Larry Pebworth, 20–39. (Essays in Seventeenth-Century Literature, 2.) Columbia: University of Missouri Press. xv, 222p.

1988

Batley, Karen E. "Martyrdom in Sixteenth-Century English Jesuit Verse." *UES* 26:1–6.

Bienz, John. "Herbert's 'Daily Labour': An Eschatological Pattern in 'The Church.'" *GHJ* 12, no. 1: 1–15.

Coiro, Ann Baynes. "The *Hesperides* of Herrick's 'Saints' and 'Heroes,'" in *Robert Herrick's* Hesperides *and the Epigram Book Tradition*, 133–54. Baltimore: Johns Hopkins University Press.

Duncan, Joseph E. "Resurrections in Donne's 'A Hymne to God the Father' and 'Hymne to God my God, in my sicknesse.'" *JDJ* 7:183–95.

Flynn, Dennis. "'Awry and Squint': The Dating of Donne's Holy Sonnets." *JDJ* 7, no. 1: 35–46.

Gottlieb, Sidney. "The Social and Political Backgrounds of George Herbert's Poetry," in *"The Muses Common-Weale": Poetry and Politics in the Seventeenth Century*, edited by Claude J. Summers and Ted-Larry Pebworth, 107–18. (Essays in Seventeenth-Century Literature, 3.) Columbia: University of Missouri Press. viii, 223p.

Guibbory, Achsah. "The Temple of *Hesperides* and Anglican-Puritan

Controversy," in *"The Muses Common-Weale": Poetry and Politics in the Seventeenth Century,* edited by Claude J. Summers and Ted-Larry Pebworth, 135–47. (Essays in Seventeenth-Century Literature, 3.) Columbia: University of Missouri Press. viii, 223p.

Hoey, Michael. "The Interaction of Discourse and Lexis: A Stylistic Analysis of "Vertue" by George Herbert," in *Styles of Discourse,* edited by Nikolas Coupland, 139–62. London: Croom.

Jasper, David. "Two or Three Gathered in His Name: Reflections on the English Pastoral Tradition in Religious Poetry." *C&L* 38:19–32.

Judge, Jeannie Sargent. "From Vine to Wine: Signs and Symbol in 'The Bunch of Grapes.'" *MHLS* 11:12–18.

Luxton, Andrea. "The Rest That Remaineth: A Study of Five Poems by George Herbert." *GHJ* 11, no. 2: 49–62.

Martz, Louis L. "Donne and Herbert: Vehement Grief and Silent Tears." *JDJ* 7:21–34.

Merrill, Thomas F. "George Herbert's 'Significant Stuttering.'" *GHJ* 11, no. 2: 1–18.

Milward, Peter. *A Commentary on the Holy Sonnets of John Donne.* (RenM 14.) Tokyo: Renaissance Institute, Sophia University. 110p.

Olson, John. "Biblical Narratives and Herbert's Dialogue Poems." *GHJ* 12, no. 1: 17–28.

Parrish, Paul A. "The Feminizing of Power: Crashaw's Life and Art," in *"The Muses Common-Weale": Poetry and Politics in the Seventeenth Century,* edited by Claude J. Summers and Ted-Larry Pebworth, 148–62. (Essays in Seventeenth-Century Literature, 3.) Columbia: University of Missouri Press. viii, 223p.

Piret, Malcolm. "Herbert and Proverbs." *CQ* 17:222–24.

Schoenfeldt, Michael C. "'Subject to ev'ry mounters bended knee': Herbert and Authority," in *The Historical Renaissance: New Essays on Tudor and Stuart Literature and Culture,* edited by Heather Dubrow and Richard Strier, 242–69. Chicago: University of Chicago Press.

Skillen, John E. "Revisionism and Renaissance Poets." *CSR* 18, no. 1:81–86.

Veith, Gene Edward, Jr. "The Religious Wars in George Herbert Criticism: Reinterpreting Seventeenth-Century Anglicanism." *GHJ* 11, no. 2: 19–35.

Wall, John N., Jr. *Transformations of the Word: Spenser, Herbert, Vaughan.* Athens: University of Georgia Press. xv, 428p.

1989

Allchin, A. M. "The Sacrifice of Praise and Thanksgiving," in *Profitable Wonders: Aspects of Thomas Traherne,* edited by A. M. Allchin, Anne Ridler, and Julia Smith, 22–37. Oxford: Amate Press. 56p.

Brown, Nancy Pollard. "Paperchase: The Dissemination of Catholic Texts in Elizabethan England." *English Manuscript Studies 1100–1700* 1:120–43.

Brunner, Larry. "'Love at Lower Rate': A Christian Reading of 'To His Coy Mistress.'" *C&L* 38:25–44.

Corthell, Ronald J. "'The Secrecy of Man': Recusant Discourse and the Elizabethan Subject." *ELR* 19:272–90.

Entzminger, Robert L. "Doctrine and Life: George Herbert and the Augustinian Rhetoric of Example." *GHJ* 13, nos. 1–2 (1989–1990): 37–47.

Gottlieb, Sidney. "Herbert's Political Allegory of 'Humilitie.'" *HLQ* 52:469–80.

———. "The Two Endings of George Herbert's 'The Church,'" in *A Fine Tuning: Studies of the Religious Poetry of Herbert and Milton,* edited by Mary A. Maleski and Russell A. Peck, 57–76. (MRTS, 64.) Binghamton: Medieval & Renaissance Texts and Studies. xi, 317p.

Hester, M. Thomas. "Altering the Text of the Self: The Shapes of 'The Altar,'" in *A Fine Tuning: Studies of the Religious Poetry of Herbert and Milton,* edited by Mary A. Maleski and Russell A. Peck, 95–116. (MRTS, 64.) Binghamton: Medieval & Renaissance Texts and Studies. xi, 317p.

Höltgen, Karl Josef. "Henry Vaughan's *Silex Scintillans:* Emblematic Tradition and Meaning." *Emblematica* 4:273–312.

Johnson, Parker. "'Worthy to be here': Protestant Sacramental Devotion and Herbert's 'Love' (III)." *GHJ* 13, nos. 1 & 2 (1989–1990): 49–62

Kronenfeld, Judy. "Post-Saussurean Semantics, Reformation Religious Controversy, and Contemporary Critical Disagreement." *Assays* 5:135–65.

Lynch, Kathleen. *"The Temple:* Three Parts Vied and Multiplied." *SEL* 29:17–26.

McColley, Diane. "The Poem as Hierophon: Musical Configurations in George Herbert's 'The Church,'" in *A Fine Tuning: Studies of the Religious Poetry of Herbert and Milton,* edited by Mary A. Maleski and

Russell A. Peck, 117–43. (MRTS, 64.) Binghamton: Medieval & Renaissance Texts and Studies. xi, 317p.

Martin, Louis. "The Trinitarian Unity of *The Temple:* Herbert's Augustinian Aesthetic." *GHJ* 13, nos. 1 & 2 (1989–1990): 63–77.

Martz, Louis L. "The Generous Ambiguity of Herbert's *Temple*," in *A Fine Tuning: Studies of the Religious Poetry of Herbert and Milton*, edited by Mary A. Maleski and Russell A. Peck, 31–56. (MRTS, 64.) Binghamton: Medieval & Renaissance Texts and Studies. xi, 317p.

Parry, Graham. "Varieties of Religious Experience," in *The Seventeenth Century: The Intellectual and Cultural Context of English Literature, 1603–1700,* 181–211. (Longman Literature in English Series, gen. eds., David Carroll and Michael Wheeler.) London and New York: Longman.

Patrides, C. A. "George Herbert: The Transfiguration of Plainness" and "Richard Crashaw: The Merging of Contrarieties," in *Figures in a Renaissance Context*, edited by Claude J. Summers and Ted-Larry Pebworth, 117–39, 141–60. Ann Arbor: University of Michigan Press.

Pruss, Ingrid. "George Herbert's 'Prayer (I)': From Metaphor to Mystery." *GHJ* 12, no. 2: 17–26.

Ridler, Anne. "The Essential Traherne," in *Profitable Wonders: Aspects of Thomas Traherne*, edited by A. M. Allchin, Anne Ridler, and Julia Smith, 9–21. Oxford: Amate Press. 56p.

Roche, Thomas P., Jr. "Typology, Allegory, and Protestant Poetics." *GHJ* 13, nos. 1–2: 1–17.

Roy, Kalyan Kumar. "Meditative Tradition and Growth of Mysticism." *BSEAA* 28:133–43.

Rudrum, Alan. "Henry Vaughan, the Liberation of the Creatures, and Seventeenth-Century English Calvinism." *SCen* 4:33–54.

Schoenfeldt, Michael C. "'Respective Boldness': Herbert and the Art of Submission," in *A Fine Tuning: Studies of the Religious Poetry of Herbert and Milton*, edited by Mary A. Maleski and Russell A. Peck, 77–94. (MRTS, 64.) Binghamton: Medieval & Renaissance Texts and Studies. xi, 317p.

Sherwood, Terry G. *Herbert's Prayerful Art.* Toronto: University of Toronto Press. ix, 190p.

Shullenberger, William. "The Word of Reform and the Poetics of the Eucharist." *GHJ* 13, nos. 1 & 2 (1989–1990): 19–36.

Smith, Julia. "Traherne from His Unpublished Manuscripts," in *Prof-*

itable Wonders: Aspects of Thomas Traherne, edited by A. M. Allchin, Anne Ridler, and Julia Smith, 38–51. Oxford: Amate Press. 56p.

Strier, Richard. "John Donne Awry and Squint: the 'Holy Sonnets,' 1608–1610." *MP* 86:357–84.

———. "Sanctifying the Aristocracy: 'Devout Humanism' in François de Sales, John Donne, and George Herbert." *Journal of Religion* 69:36–58.

Wood, Chauncey. "An Augustinian Reading of George Herbert's 'The Pulley,'" in *A Fine Tuning: Studies of the Religious Poetry of Herbert and Milton,* edited by Mary A. Maleski and Russell A. Peck, 145–59. (MRTS, 64.) Binghamton: Medieval & Renaissance Texts and Studies. xi, 317p.

Young, Diane. "The Orator's Church and the Poet's Temple." *GHJ* 12, no. 2: 115.

1990

Baker-Smith, Dominic. "'Th' old broad way in applying': John Donne and his 'Litanie,'" in *A Day Estivall: Essays on the Music, Poetry and History of Scotland and England & Poems Previously Unpublished In Honour of Helena Mennie Shire,* edited by Alisoun Gardner-Medwin and Janet Hadley Williams, 47–58. Aberdeen: Aberdeen University Press.

Benet, Diana Treviño. "Crashaw, Teresa, and the Word," in *New Perspectives on the Life and Art of Richard Crashaw,* edited by John R. Roberts, 140–56. Columbia: University of Missouri Press. xi, 234p.

Booty, John. Introduction to *John Donne: Selections from Divine Poems, Sermons, Devotions, and Prayers,* edited and introduction by John Booty, with a preface by P. G. Stanwood, 1–72. (The Classics of Western Spirituality.) New York and Mahwah, N.J.: Paulist Press.

Braden, Gordon. "Unspeakable Love: Petrarch to Herbert," in *Soliciting Interpretation: Literary Theory and Seventeenth-Century English Poetry,* edited by Elizabeth D. Harvey and Katharine Eisaman Maus, 253–72. Chicago: University of Chicago Press.

Chambers, A. B. "Crooked Crosses in Donne and Crashaw," in *New Perspectives on the Life and Art of Richard Crashaw,* edited by John R. Roberts, 157–73. Columbia: University of Missouri Press. xi, 234p.

Clements, Arthur L. *Poetry of Contemplation: John Donne, George Herbert, Henry Vaughan, and the Modern Period.* Albany: State University of New York Press. xvii, 306p.

Cunnar, Eugene R. "Crashaw's 'Sancta Maria Dolorum': Controversy and Coherence," in *New Perspectives on the Life and Art of Richard Crashaw,* edited by John R. Roberts, 99–126. Columbia: University of Missouri Press. xi, 234p.

———. "Illusion and Spiritual Perception in Donne's Poetry," in *Aesthetic Illusion: Theoretical and Historical Approaches,* edited by Frederick Burwick and Walter Pape, 324–36. Berlin: de Gruyter.

Fischlin, Daniel T. "'And Tuned by Thee': Music and Divinity in George Herbert's Poetry." *EIRC* 16:87–99.

Frontain, Raymond-Jean. "Donne's Imperfect Resurrection." *PLL* 26:539–45.

Healy, Thomas F. "Crashaw and the Sense of History," in *New Perspectives on the Life and Art of Richard Crashaw,* edited by John R. Roberts, 49–79. Columbia: University of Missouri Press. xi, 234p.

Hodgkins, Christopher. "'Betwixt This World and That of Grace': George Herbert and the Church in Society." *SP* 87:456–75.

Judge, J. Sargent. "Beyond the Branches: The Nature of George Herbert's Protestantism." *Cithara* 29:3–19.

Lamont, William. "The Religion of Andrew Marvell: Locating the 'Bloody Horse,'" in *The Political Identity of Andrew Marvell,* edited by Conal Condren and A. D. Cousins, 136–56. Hants: Scolar.

Latz, Dorothy L. "The Mystical Poetry of Dame Gertrude More." *MysticsQ* 16:66–82.

Linkin, Harriet Kramer. "Herbert's Reciprocal Writing: Poetry as Sacred Pun," in *Traditions and Innovations: Essays on British Literature of the Middle Ages and the Renaissance,* edited by David G. Allen and Robert A. White, 214–22. Newark: University of Delaware Press.

Lull, Janis. *The Poem in Time: Reading George Herbert's Revisions of* The Church. Newark: University of Delaware Press; London and Toronto: Associated University Presses. 167p.

McCauley, Janie Caves. "On the 'Childhood of the Yeare': Herrick's *Hesperides* New Year's Poems. *GHJ* 14, nos. 1 & 2 (1990–1991): 72–96.

Mazzaro, Jerome. "Recusant Sincerely: Henry Constable at Spiritual Sonnets." *ELWIU* 17:147–59.

Norbrook, David. "The Monarchy of Wit and the Republic of Letters:

Donne's Politics," in *Soliciting Interpretation: Literary Theory and Seventeenth-Century English Poetry*, edited by Elizabeth D. Harvey and Katharine Eisaman Maus, 3–36. Chicago: University of Chicago Press.

Osmond, Rosalie. *Mutual Accusation: Seventeenth-Century Body and Soul Dialogues in Their Literary and Theological Context.* Toronto: University of Toronto Press. xiii, 284p.

Parrish, Paul A. "'O Sweet Contest': Gender and Value in 'The Weeper,'" in *New Perspectives on the Life and Art of Richard Crashaw*, edited by John R. Roberts, 127–39. Columbia: University of Missouri Press. xi, 234p.

Revard, Stella P. "Crashaw and the Diva: The Tradition of the Neo-Latin Hymn to the Goddess," in *New Perspectives on the Life and Art of Richard Crashaw*, edited by John R. Roberts, 80–98. Columbia: University of Missouri Press. xi, 234p.

Roberts, Lorraine M. "Crashaw's Sacred Voice: 'A Commerce of Contrary Powers,'" in *New Perspectives on the Life and Art of Richard Crashaw*, edited by John R. Roberts, 66–79. Columbia: University of Missouri Press. xi, 234p.

Roy, Kalyan Kumar. "Henry Vaughan: A Divine Mystic." *BSEAA* 31:221–33.

Schoenfeldt, Michael C. "'That Ancient Heat': Sexuality and Spirituality in *The Temple*," in *Soliciting Interpretation: Literary Theory and Seventeenth-Century English Poetry*, edited by Elizabeth D. Harvey and Katharine Eisaman Maus, 273–306. Chicago: University of Chicago Press.

Schweers, Gregory. "Bernard of Clairvaux's Influence on English Recusant Letters: The Case of Robert Southwell, S. J." *ABR* 4:157–66.

Shuger, Debora Kuller. *Habits of Thought in the English Renaissance: Religion, Politics, and the Dominant Culture.* Berkeley and Los Angeles: University of California Press. ix, 284p.

Summers, Claude J. "Tears for Herrick's Church." *GHJ* 14, nos. 1 & 2 (1990–91): 51–71.

Tomlinson, T. B. "Donne's Poetry & Belief in 17th-Century England." *CR* 30:25–39.

Wilcox, Helen. "Exploring the Language of Devotion in the English Revolution," in *Literature and the English Civil War*, edited by Thomas Healy and Jonathan Sawday, 75–88. Cambridge, New York, Port Chester, Melbourne, Sydney: Cambridge University Press.

Young, R. V., Jr., "Crashaw and Biblical Poetics," in *New Perspectives on the Life and Art of Richard Crashaw,* edited by John R. Roberts, 30–48. Columbia: University of Missouri Press. xi, 234p.
———. "Ineffable Speech: Carmelite Mysticism and Metaphysical Poetry." *Communio: International Catholic Review* 17:238–60.
Yunis, Susan S. "George Herbert's 'Jordan (I)': Catching the Sense at Two Removes." *ELN* 27:20–26.

NOTES ON THE CONTRIBUTORS

EUGENE R. CUNNAR is Associate Professor of English at New Mexico State University. He received his Ph.D. from the University of Wisconsin–Madison. He has published essays on Crashaw, Donne, Herbert, and bibliography and has recently completed a book-length study, tentatively entitled *Richard Crashaw: The Baroque and Liturgical Poem.* He also has in progress critical studies of Spenser, Donne, and Renaissance art and is currently working on the commentary on Donne's *Songs and Sonets* for the forthcoming variorum edition. He serves as Executive Director of the John Donne Society.

JUDITH DUNDAS is Professor of English at the University of Illinois at Urbana-Champaign. She received her Ph.D. from the University of Wisconsin–Madison. She has published two books, *The Spider and the Bee: The Artistry of Spenser's Faerie Queene* and *Pencils Rhetorique: Renaissance Poets and the Art of Painting*, as well as numerous essays on Spenser, Jonson, Shakespeare, Sidney, Michelangelo, Titian, Chapman, the court masque, wit, emblems, and various aspects of the relationship between literature and the visual arts.

ACHSAH GUIBBORY is Professor of English at the University of Illinois at Urbana-Champaign. She received her Ph.D. from the University of California–Los Angeles. The author of *The Map of Time: Seventeenth-Century English Literature and Ideas of Pattern in History*, she has also published numerous essays on Donne, Jonson, Bacon, Herrick, Browne, Cowley, and Dryden. She is currently working on a book with the descriptive working title *Literature and Religious Conflict in the Period of Charles I and the English Civil War,* as well as on a study of the politics of love in seventeenth-century poetry. She is an editor of the *Journal of English and Germanic Philology.* She received the John Donne Society Award for Distinguished Publication in Donne Studies for her article on Donne's *Elegies* published in *ELH* in 1990.

324 • Notes on the Contributors

CHRISTOPHER HODGKINS is Assistant Professor of English at the University of North Carolina–Greensboro. He received his Ph.D. from the University of Chicago. His essay on Herbert in this volume is part of a larger study, entitled *Authority, Church, and Society in George Herbert: Return to the Middle Way*. He has also published several essays on Herbert.

ANTHONY LOW is Professor of English and Chair of the Department of English at New York University. His books include *Augustine Baker, The Blaze of Noon: A Reading of Samson Agonistes; Love's Architecture: Devotional Modes in Seventeenth-Century English Poetry;* and *The Georgic Revolution*. His essay on Donne in this volume is part of a larger study, entitled *The Reinvention of Love: Poetry, Politics, and Culture from Sidney to Milton* (forthcoming from Cambridge University Press). He recently received the John Donne Society Award for Distinguished Publication in Donne Studies for his article on Donne's secular love poetry, published in *English Literary Renaissance* in 1990.

LOUIS L. MARTZ is retired Sterling Professor of English at Yale University. He is the author of four books on seventeenth-century poetry: *The Poetry of Meditation: A Study in English Religious Poetry of the Seventeenth Century; The Paradise Within: Studies in Vaughan, Traherne, and Milton; The Wit of Love: Donne, Carew, Crashaw, Marvell;* and *Milton: Poet of Exile*, along with various essays on Renaissance and seventeenth-century poetry included in his collections *The Poem of the Mind: Essays on Poetry, English and American* and *From Renaissance to Baroque: Essays on Literature and Art*. He has published *Thomas More: The Search for the Inner Man*, has edited More's *Dialogue of Comfort*, and has served as Chairman of the Editorial Committee for the Yale edition of More's works. He has also written essays on twentieth-century literature and has edited both the *Collected Poems* and the *Selected Poems* of H. D.

STELLA P. REVARD is Professor of English at Southern Illinois University–Edwardsville, where she teaches courses in both English and Greek. She received her Ph.D. from Yale University. She is author of *The War in Heaven: Paradise Lost and the Tradition of Satan's Rebellion*, which received the James Holly Hanford Award of the Milton Society of America. She has published essays on Spenser, Drayton, Jonson,

Donne, Crashaw, Cowley, Marvell, Shelley, Verlaine, Mallarmé, Yeats, Aristophanes, Pindar, Propertius, Vergil, and the ode. She is coeditor of *Acta Conventus Neo-Latini Guelpherbytani*. She is currently working on two books—one on the influence of Pindar on English Renaissance poetry and the other on the influence of classical and neo-Latin literature on poets from Donne to Marvell.

JOHN R. ROBERTS is Professor of English at the University of Missouri–Columbia. He received his Ph.D. from the University of Illinois at Urbana-Champaign. He is author of *A Critical Anthology of English Recusant Devotional Prose, 1558–1603; John Donne: An Annotated Bibliography of Modern Criticism, 1912–1967; John Donne: An Annotated Bibliography of Modern Criticism, 1968–1978; Richard Crashaw: An Annotated Bibliography of Criticism, 1632–1980;* and *George Herbert: An Annotated Bibliography of Modern Criticism, 1905–1984* (revised and expanded edition of *George Herbert: An Annotated Bibliography of Modern Criticism, 1905–1978*). He is editor of three collections of critical essays, *Essential Articles for the Study of John Donne's Poetry, Essential Articles for the Study of George Herbert's Poetry,* and *New Perspectives on the Life and Art of Richard Crashaw*. He has published essays on Donne, Southwell, Crashaw, Herbert, and bibliography. He is general editor of the commentary for the forthcoming Donne variorum edition and is editing (with the assistance of Diana Treviño Benet) the commentary on Donne's *Elegies* for the edition. He is past president of the John Donne Society.

MICHAEL C. SCHOENFELDT is Associate Professor of English and Associate Chair of the Department of English Language and Literature at the University of Michigan–Ann Arbor. He received his Ph.D. from the University of California–Berkeley. He is author of *Prayer and Power: George Herbert and Renaissance Courtship* and has published essays on Spenser, Donne, Herbert, Herrick, Milton, and Marvell. He is currently writing a book-length study, tentatively entitled *The Conduct of Desire in the Renaissance,* which will consider the issues of courtesy and sexuality from Castiglione to Milton. He is also a contributing editor to the forthcoming Donne variorum edition.

P. G. STANWOOD is Professor of English at the University of British Columbia. He received his Ph.D. from the University of Michigan–

Ann Arbor. He has edited John Cosin's *A Collection of Private Devotions;* Henry More's *Democritus Platonissans;* William Law's *A Serious Call to a Devout and Holy Life and The Spirit of Love; John Donne and the Theology of Language* (with Heather Ross Asals); Richard Hooker's *Of the Laws of Ecclesiastical Polity* (Books VI, VII, VIII); Jeremy Taylor's *Holy Living and Holy Dying* (2 vols.). He has written essays on Spenser, Donne, Hooker, Herbert, Jeremy Taylor, Joseph Beaumont, John Cosin, Crashaw, Milton, Christina Rossetti, and T. S. Eliot and has contributed four entries to *The New Cambridge Bibliography of English Literature, 600–1600.* He has also published a collection of his essays, entitled *The Sempiternal Season: Studies in Seventeenth-Century Devotional Writing,* and has edited a forthcoming collection of essays, *Of Poetry and Politics: New Essays on Milton and His World.*

CLAUDE J. SUMMERS is William E. Stirton Professor in the Humanities at the University of Michigan–Dearborn. He received his Ph.D. from the University of Chicago. He is author of *E. M. Forster: A Guide to Research; Gay Fictions: Wilde to Stonewall; E. M. Foster; Christopher Isherwood;* and *Christopher Marlowe and the Politics of Power.* He is editor of *Literary Representations of Homosexuality in Renaissance and Enlightment England* and coeditor (with Ted-Larry Pebworth) of *On the Celebrated and Neglected Poems of Andrew Marvell; Figures in a Renaissance Context* (by C. A. Patrides); *"The Muses Common-Weale": Poetry and Politics in the Seventeenth Century; "Bright Shootes of Everlastingnesse": The Seventeenth-Century Religious Lyric; "The Eagle and the Dove": Reassessing John Donne; Classic and Cavalier: Celebrating Jonson and the Sons of Ben; "Too Rich to Clothe the Sunne": Essays on George Herbert;* and *The Poems of Owen Felltham, 1604?–1668.* He has also coauthored (with Ted-Larry Pebworth) *Ben Jonson* and has published essays on Spenser, Shakespeare, Marlowe, Donne, Herbert, Owen Felltham, Herrick, Vaughan, Milton, Marvell, Byron, Richard Hall, Christopher Isherwood, W. H. Auden, E. M. Forster, and Willa Cather. He is co-organizer (with Ted-Larry Pebworth) of the Biennial Renaissance Conference held at the University of Michigan–Dearborn and is past president of the John Donne Society.

HELEN WILCOX is Professor of English Literature after the Middle Ages and American Literature and Chairman of the Department of

English at the University of Groningen (The Netherlands). She received the D.Phil. from St. Anne's College, University of Oxford. She has edited (with Elspeth Graham, Hilary Hinds, and Elaine Hobby) *Her Own Life: Autobiographical Writings by Seventeenth-Century Englishwomen;* (with Ann Thompson) *Teaching Women: Feminism and English Studies;* (with Keith McWatter, Ann Thompson, and Linda R. Williams) *The Body and the Text: Helene Cixous, Reading and Teaching.* She has published essays and/or chapters of books on Shakespeare, Donne, Herbert, Milton, Rochester, English Civil War writings, autobiography, devotional literature, women's writings, and the relationship between literature and music, as well as numerous notes and reviews. She has edited *George Herbert's Poetry* for the Longman's Annotated English Poets series and is working on a study of the seventeenth-century religious lyric for Longman's Mediaeval and Renaissance Library. She is also writing a volume on Shakespeare's tragicomedies for Routledge's Feminist Readings of Shakespeare series, and editing *Women and Literature 1500–1700* for Cambridge University Press.

R. V. YOUNG, JR., is Professor of English at North Carolina State University at Raleigh. He received his Ph.D. from Yale University. He is author of *Richard Crashaw and the Spanish Golden Age* and has published essays on Donne, Jonson, Crashaw, Marvell, Christopher Dawson, Jacques Derrida, Walker Percy, and Walter Miller. He is completing a book-length study, entitled *Dogma and Devotion in Seventeenth-Century Poetry.* He is coeditor of the *John Donne Journal.*

INDEX TO WORKS CITED

This index includes only primary works quoted in the essays, excluding the Bible. Lengthy titles are abbreviated, and anonymous works are alphabetized by title.

Alabaster, William: "The Portrait of Christ's Death," 7, 111–12; "The Difference 'twixt Compunction and Cold Devotion in Beholding the Passion of our Saviour," 265–66

Andrewes, Lancelot: *Private Devotions*, 106–8; *Sermons*, 206

Androzzi, Fulvio: *Certaine devout considerations of frequenting the Blessed Sacrament*, 250

Augustine of Hippo, St.: *Confessions*, 180, 188; *Homilies on the Gospel of John*, 244–45

Baxter, Richard: *The Saints' Everlasting Rest*, 198

Bembo, Pietro: "Julii Secundi" in *Carmina, Quinque Illustrium Poetarum*, 162

Bernard of Clairvaux, St.: *On the Perfection of Life*, 247–48; *On the Song of Songs III*, 245–46

Bolton, Edmund: *Hypercritica*, 124

Bonaventure, St.: *The Mystical Vine*, 247; *Stimulus Divinii amoris*, 246–47

Book of Common Prayer, 11, 38, 53, 55, 67, 95, 106, 112, 119, 120

Britanniae Natalis (1631), 164

Browne, Thomas: *Religio Medici*, 43

Burton, Henry: *Truth's Triumph over Trent*, 34

Calvin, John: *Institutes of the Christian Religion*, 177

Camden, William: *Remaines concerning Britaine*, 135

Campion, Thomas: *Two Bookes of Ayres*, 14, 18, 25

Capilupi, Ippolito: "Ad Apollinem" in *Capiluporum Carmina*, 150

Carew, Thomas: "An Elegie upon the Death of the Deane of Pauls, Dr. John Donne," 211

Cary, Patrick: "Whilst I beheld the necke o'th'Dove," 16–18

Chapman, George: *The Memorable Masque*, 163; *Ovid's Banquet of Sense*, 129

Clement of Alexandria, St.: *Hymni in Christum*, 145

Collins, An: *Divine songs and Meditation*, 22; "The Discourse," 22; "The Soul's Home," 20

Corbett, Richard: "The Distracted Puritan," 50

Cosin, John: *A Collection of Private Devotions*, 106, 254–55; *Notes and Collections on the Book of Common Prayer*, 41

Crashaw, Richard: "An Apologie for

the fore-going Hymne," 113; "The Flaming Heart," 113; "Hymn for New Year's Day," 153, 154, 156; "Hymn in the Assumption," 113; "Hymn in the Glorious Epiphanie," 153, 154, 156–58; "Hymn in the Holy Nativity," 19, 153, 154, 156; "A Hymn to Sainte Teresa," 113; "Hymn to the Name of Jesus," 155–56; "I am the Doore," 258; "Lectori," 253–54; "Letter to the Countess of Denbigh," 258; "Luke 11. Blessed be the paps which Thou hast sucked," 259–60; "Office of the Holy Crosse," 113; "On our crucified Lord Naked, and bloody," 237; "On the wounds of our crucified Lord," 242–51, 260–62, 264–67; "Reverendo Admodum viro Benjamin Lany . . . ," 356–57; "Sancta Maria Dolorum," 242; *Steps to the Temple*, 21; "Upon the Duke of York his Birth A Panegyricke," 164; "The Weeper," 14, 19, 113, 262–64

Davenport, Robert: "A Dialogue between Pollicy and Piety," 88
Donne, John: "The Anniversarie," 211; "The Crosse," 15; *Devotions upon Emergent Occasions*, 16; *Divine Poems*, 114, 173, 177, 202, 206; "Elegie on the Lady Marckham," 136–37; "The Extasie," 11; *The First Anniversarie: An Anatomie of the World*, 189, 192; "Goodfriday, 1613. Riding Westward," 89, 114–15, 151; *Holy Sonnets*, 80, 81, 85, 105, 112, 168, 169, 172, 189, 204–5, 207, 218, 221; Holy Sonnet ("As due by many titles"), 85, 215; Holy Sonnet ("Batter my heart"), 206, 217–18, 221; Holy Sonnet ("Death be not proud"), 127–28, 131; Holy Sonnet ("Father, part of his double interest"), 206; Holy Sonnet ("I am a little world"), 206, 215–16; Holy Sonnet ("If poysonous mineralls," 82; Holy Sonnet ("O Might those sighes"), 216–17; Holy Sonnet ("O my blacke Soule!"), 206; Holy Sonnet ("Oh, to vex me, contraryes meet"), 81–82, 83, 91, 173, 206; Holy Sonnet ("Since she whome I lovd"), 173, 175, 204–5, 212–13, 218; Holy Sonnet ("Show me deare Christ"), 47, 171–72, 202, 214–15, 218, 221; Holy Sonnet ("Spit in my face"), 82–83; Holy Sonnet ("Thou hast made me"), 83–84, 127; Holy Sonnet ("What if this present"), 171, 205, 215; "A Hymn to Christ, at the Authors last going into Germany," 174–75; 207–11, 213, 218; "A Hymne to God the Father," 151; *La Corona*, 112, 132–33, 134, 195; La Corona 2 ("Annuciation"), 133; La Corona 7 ("Ascension"), 112, 151; La Corona 5 ("Crucifying"), 133; La Corona 1 ("Deigne at my hands"), 133, 171; La Corona 3 ("Nativitie"), 112; La Corona 6 ("Resurrection"), 112; La Corona 4 ("Temple"), 112, 133; *Letters*, 14, 80, 80–81, 81, 83–84, 84, 85, 113–14, 211; "A nocturnall upon S. Lucies day, Being the shortest day," 113–14, 211; *Of the Progres of the Soule: The Second Anniversary*, 189, 192; "The Relique," 211; "Resurrection, imperfect," 151; *Sermons*, 12, 79–80, 100, 127, 136, 142, 172, 201, 202, 205, 206, 207, 220; *Songs and Sonets*, 105, 113, 204, 211–12, 213; "To Mr. Tilman after he had taken orders," 218–20; "Upon the translation of the Psalmes by Sir Philip Sidney, and . . . his Sister," 134–35; "The Will," 86
Duppa, Brian: *The Correspondence of Bishop Brian Duppa and Sir Justinian Isham*, 51

Ferrar, Nicholas: "The Printers to the Reader" (Preface to *The Temple*), 87
Francis de Sales, St.: *Introduction to the Devout Life*, 196; *On the Love of God*, 266–67

Gascoigne, George: *Certain Notes of Instruction*, 135
Genethliacum Illustrissimorum Principam Caroli & Mariae (1613), 164
Goodman, Cardell: *Beawty in Raggs Or Divine Phancies putt into Broken Verse*, 21, 22
Goodwin, Thomas: *An Expositon of the Revelation*, 50
Gregory of Nazianzen, St.: Odes and hymns in *Poetae Graeci Veteres*, 145

Habert, François: "Hymne du Soleil" in *Oeuvres Poétique*, 150
Hales, John: *Golden Remains of the ever Memorable John Hales*, 43
Hall, Joseph: *The Art of Divine Meditation*, 24; *The Revelation Unrevealed*, 51
Harvey, Christopher: *The Synagogue*, 21, 94
Herbert, George: "Affliction (I)," 82, 92, 112, 169, 179–81; "Anagram of the Virgin Marie," 113; "The Answer," 227; "The Bag," 185–87; "The British Church," 47, 93, 98; "The Bunch of Grapes," 112, 132; "Charmes and Knots," 91; "Christmas," 152; *The Church*, 87–89, 195, 226; "Church-monuments," 137–38; *The Church-Porch*, 89, 95, 104, 125, 132, 139, 142, 226; *The Church Militant*, 88–89; "Church-rents and schisms," 93; "The Collar," 97, 116–18, 180; "Colos. iii. 3," 139; "Confession," 139; "Conscience," 131; "Death," 131; "The Dedication," 87, 93, 184; "Deniall," 228; "Dialogue," 92; "Divinitie," 93; "Dulnesse," 92; "Easter," 19, 151–52, 227–28; "Easter-wings," 92; "Employment (I)," 92; "Employment (II)," 92, 126; "Evensong," 138; "The Flower," 12, 60, 181–83; "The Forerunners," 23, 24, 138, 183, 184, 185; "The Glance," 236; "Good Friday," 138; "Gratefulnesse," 97–98; "Grief," 228–29; "The Holdfast," 178–79, 229–30; "Holy Scriptures (II)," 20–21; "Humilitie," 131; "Jesu," 13–14, 15; "Jordan (I)," 14, 15, 25, 228; "Jordan (II)," 228; *Letters*, 225–26; "Love (I)," 130; "Love (II)," 131; "Love (III)," 92, 131, 185, 229, 230, 235; "Man," 139; "Marie Magdalene," 113; "Mattens," 152; "Miserie," 138; "Mortification," 138–39; "Obedience," 93, 94; "Paradise," 126, 226; "The Pearl," 126, 226; "The Posie," 226; "Praise (I)," 92; "Praise (III)," 93; "Prayer (I)," 227; "Prayer (II)," 92; *A Priest to the Temple, or, The Country Parson*, 125, 222–25, 230–36; "The 23d Psalme," 25; "The Pulley," 89; "The Quidditie," 226; "The Quip," 92, 226–27; "Redemption," 96; "The Sacrifice," 132; Sonnet ("Sure, Lord, there is enough in thee"), 22; "The Starre," 91, 96, 150; "Submission," 92; "Sunday," 19; "The Temper (I)," 92; "The Temper (II)," 92; *The Temple*, 20, 22, 86–93, 97, 98, 102, 105, 151, 168, 177, 181, 184, 185, 195, 196, 226, 230; "The Thanksgiving," 92, 132, 229; "To all Angels and Saints," 90–91; "Trinitie Sunday," 115–16, 118; "A true Hymne," 24; "Ungratefulnesse," 139; "Vertue," 138; "The Windows," 132, 234; "A Wreath," 133–34; "The World," 139–40
Herrick, Robert: "All things run well for the Righteous," 57; "Another"

332 • Index

(Art thou not destin'd?), 53; "Another" (Sin is an act so free), 53; "Another" (Sin is the cause of death), 53; "Another" (Wassaile the Trees), 39; "Another" (Who with thy leaves shall wipe), 29; "Another Charme for Stables," 38; "Another New-Yeares Gift, or Song for Circumcision," 39, 98; "Another to the Maids," 39; "The Argument to his book," 19, 21, 22, 29; "Ceremonies for Candlemasse Eve," 39; "Ceremonies for Christmasse," 39; "Ceremony upon Candlemas Eve," 39; "A Christmas Caroll, sung to the King in the Presence at White-Hall," 55, 56, 98; "Christmasse-Eve, Another Ceremonie," 39; "Christs twofold coming," 51; "Clouds," 59; "Corrina's going a Maying," 31, 36; "Doomes-Day," 58–59; "Evensong," 30; "The Faerie Temple: or, Oberons Chappell," 38; "The Funerall Rites of the Rose," 35; "Gods keyes," 59; "Good Friday: Rex Tragicus," 56, 62, 98; "Graces for Children," 52; *Hesperides*, 28, 29, 30, 32, 35, 38, 39, 42, 44, 58, 62; "His charge to Julia at his death," 38; "His Confession," 52; "His Creed," 53; "His coming to the Sepulcher," 62; "His Letanie, to the Holy Spirit," 53; "His Offering, with the rest, at the Sepulcher," 62; "His Prayer to Ben. Johnson," 29, 38, 97; "The Judgement Day," 59; "The Judgment-Day," 59; "Julia's Churching, or Purification," 38; "Julia's Petticoat," 36; "A Lyrick to Mirth," 39; "Mattens, or morning Prayer," 30, 38; "Mora Sponsi, the stay of the Bridegroom," 57; "The mount of the Muses," 31; "Neutrality loathsome," 59; "The New-years Gift, or Circumcisions Song, sung to the King in the Presence at White-Hall," 39, 55, 56; "A New-Yeares gift sent to Sir Simeon Steward," 39; *Noble Numbers*, 28, 30, 48, 49, 52, 53, 55, 56, 59, 62, 64, 68, 73, 74, 97; "Of all the good things whatsoe're we do," 62; "The old Wives Prayer," 38; "On Heaven," 61; "On Jone," 37; "The Parasceve, or Preparation," 53–55, 69; "Patience, or Comforts in Crosses," 57, 68; "Persecutions purifie," 52, 57, 68; "Pray and Prosper," 36; "Prescience," 53; "Predestination," 53; "Purgatory," 38; "Sin," 53; "The Spell," 38; "The Star-Song: A Caroll to the King; sung at White-Hall," 55, 56, 98; "Teares" (God from our eyes), 69; "Teares" (Our present Teares), 58, 69; "Teares" (The teares of Saints), 69; "Thanksgiving," 98; "A Thanksgiving to God, for his House," 98; "This, and the next World," 59; "To Anthea," 38, 44; "To Blossoms," 35; "To Daffodills," 35; "To find God," 99; "To God: an Anthem sung in the Chappell at White-Hall, before the King," 55; "To God" (Come to me God), 59, 60, 68, 71; "To God" (Do with me, God), 58, 61; "To God" (God is all-sufferance), 58, 59; "To God" (The work is done), 98; "To God, in time of plunderings," 57; "To his Book's end," 29; "To his Friend Master J. Jincks," 44; "To his Kinswoman, Mistresse Penelope Wheeler," 29; "To his Honoured Kinsman, Sir Richard Stone," 29; "To his Saviours Sepulcher: his Devotion," 62; "To his Saviour. The New Years gift," 98; "To Julia" (Help me, Julia, for to pray), 38; "To Julia" (Holy waters hither bring), 38; "To Julia" (Offer thy gift), 38; "To Mistresse Katherine Bradshaw, the lovely, that crowned him with Laurel," 39; "To Perenna," 38; "To Perilla," 38; "To read my Booke the Virgin shie," 29; To the reverend shadow of his religious Father," 38; "To Sir George Parrie, Doctor of the Civill Law," 39; "To the same Reader," 29; "The Transfiguration," 36; "Upon Dundrige," 33, 37; "Upon Jone and Jane," 37; "Upon Julia's Clothes," 36; "Upon Julia's Recovery," 35; "Upon Julia's sweat," 37; "Upon Lungs. Epigram," 33; "Upon Peason. Epigram," 32; "Upon Kinnes. Epigram," 37; "Upon Skoles. Epigram," 33; "Upon Sudds a Laudresse," 29; "Upon Zelot," 32; "Wages," 59; "The Welcome to Sack," 39; "What God is," 99; "When he would have his verses read," 29–30; "The white Island: or place of the Blest," 61, 69; "The Widdowes teares: or, Dirge for Dorcas," 48, 53, 55, 57, 98

Heylyn, Peter: *Antidotum Lincolniense*, 41

Hooker, Richard: *Of the Laws of Ecclesiastical Polity*, 106, 135–36

John of Damascus, St.: "Hymn to the Theogonian" in *Poetae Graecae Veterae*, 145

Jonson, Ben: "An Epigram to the Queen, Then Lying In," 164

Knevet, Ralph: *A Gallery of the Temple*, 94

La Ceppède, Jean de: "Deux de cés trous gardez en l'immortalitié" in *Les Théoremes sur le Sacré Mystère de Nostre Rédemption*, 261–62

Lampridio, Benedetto: "De suis temporibus" in *Carmina Illustrium Poetarum Italorum*, 162–63

Laud, William: *The History of the Troubles and Tryall of . . . William Laud*, ed. Henry Wharton, 42; *Relation of the Conference Brtweene . . . Laud . . and Mr. Fisher the Jesuite*, 42

Luis de Granada: *Of Prayer and Meditation*, 249–50

Luther, Martin: *Commentary on Galatians*, 177

Major, Elizabeth: "Eternal God, open my blinded eyes," 15; *Honey on the Rod*, 21

Manual of Prayers newly gathered out of many . . . authores, A (1583), 106

Marullo, Michele: *Carmina*, 149; *Hymni et Epigrammata Marulli*, 149; *Hymni Naturales*, 148–50; *Marulli Constantinopolitani Epigrammata & Hymni*, 149

Marvell, Andrew: "Bermudas," 141; "The Coronet," 9–10, 24, 25–26; "A Dialogue between the Resolved Soul and Created Pleasure," 128, 129–30; "A Dialogue between the Soul and Body," 128–29; "On a Drop of Dew," 25–26, 140–41, 142; "Upon Appleton House," 15

Milton, John: *Areopagitica*, 165; "At a Solemn Music," 118; *The Christian Doctrine*, 34; "Elegia Sexta," 161; "In Quintum Novembris," 166; "Lycidas," 118, 153, 167; *Of Reformation touching Church-Discipline in England*, 34; "On the Morning of Christ's Nativity," 118, 152–54, 157, 159–60, 161–62, 164–67; *Paradise Lost*, 34, 105, 119–23, 167; Sonnet: "To Lady Margaret Ley," 161

Montagu, Richard: *Apello Caesarem*, 42

North, Dudley: *A Forest of Varieties*, 22

The Old Catholic Missal, 245
Oley, Barnabas: "A Prefatory View of the Life and Vertues of the Author" in *Herbert's Remains*, 22

Peacham, Henry: *The Compleat Gentleman*, 125; *The Garden of Eloquence*, 140
Perkins, William: *The Arte of Prophecying*, 225, 231–33, 236
Picklington, Thomas: *Altare Christianum: or, The dead Vicars Plea*, 255–56
Pontano, Giovanni: "Ad Solem" in *Pontani Opera*, 149
Proclus: *Inni*, 144, 145
Prynne, William: *Healthes: Sicknesse. Or, A Compendium and briefe Discourse; proving the Drinking and Pledging of Healthes, to be Sinfull, and utterly Unlawful unto Christians*, 33; *Histriomastix*, 33, 34, 35, 39
"Puritan Charges Against Crashaw and Beaumont": in Harley MS 7019 in the British Library, 259
Puttenham, George: *The Arte of English Poesie*, 126, 127, 132, 133

Raymond of Capua: *The Life of St. Catherine of Siena*, 248–49
Roman Breviary, 262–63, 264
Ronsard, Pierre de: *Les Hymnes de Pierre de Ronsard*, 150

Sarbiewski, Casimire: *Lyricorum, Libri Tres*, 163
Sarum Breviary, 263
Sarum Missal, 245
Savonarola, Girolamo: *De Simplicitate Christianae Vitae*, 195
Secundus, Joannes: "De Sole" in *Opera*, 149–50

Shakespeare, William: *Hamlet*, 139; *Richard III*, 223; *Venus and Adonis*, 129
Sidney, Philip: *An Apology for Poetry: or The Defence of Poesy*, 11, 16, 21, 130–31, 142; *Arcadia*, 125; *Astrophil and Stella*, 141; Sonnet 1: "Loving in truth," 195, 228
Southwell, Robert: "The Assumption of our Lady," 111; "The Author to his loving Cosen," 23; "The burning Babe," 111; "The Epiphanie," 111; "Her Nativity," 111; "Her Spousals," 111; "The Nativitie of Christ," 111; *Marie Magdalens Funerall Teares*, 203–4; "Saint Peters Complaint," 111, 124; "The Virgine Maries conception," 111; "The Virgins salutation," 111
Synesius of Cyrene: *The Essays and Hymnes of Synesius of Cyrene*, 144–45

Tasso, Bernardo: *Rime*, 150
Tasso, Torquato: "Nel giorno della Natività," 160
Taylor, Edward: *Preparatory Meditations*, 199
Taylor, Jeremy: *Holy Living*, 196
Thomas Aquinas, St.: *Summa Theologiae*, 183
Traherne, Thomas: "The Author to the Critical Peruser," 101; "The Estate," 113; "An Hymne upon St. Bartholomews Day," 101; "Love," 103; "The Rapture," 99; "Shadows in the Water," 18, 100; "Solitude," 101; "Thanksgivings for the Body," 103; "Wonder," 113

Vaughan, Henry: "Abels blood," 64, 70, 72, 96; "The Brittish Church," 48, 65; "Buriall," 68; "Chearfulness," 68; "Childe-hood," 96; "The Constellation," 64, 65, 96; "The Dawning," 69; "Day of Judgement," 68; "The day of Judgement," 71–72; "Dressing," 69; "The Feast," 69–70; "Jacobs Pillow, and Pillar," 66; "The Law, and the Gospel," 69; "L'Envoy," 64, 73–74; "The Match," 94; "The Men of War," 72–73; *The Mount of Olives: or, Solitary Devotions*, 63; *Of Temperance and Patience*, 63; "Palm-Sunday," 69; "The Palm-tree," 65, 72; "The Proffer," 64; "Providence," 68–69; "Regeneration," 64–65, 96; "Religion," 65; "The Retreate," 18, 19; "Rules and Lessons," 95; "The Seed growing secretly," 70; *Silex Scintillans*, 21, 48, 49, 63–67, 69, 73–74, 94, 95, 97; Preface to *Silex Scintillans (II)*, 66; St. Mary Magdalen," 72; "Tears," 69; "The Throne," 69; "White Sunday," 64, 72; "The World," 67–68, 96; "The Wreath," 69